D0471354

UNIVERSITY OF WINNIPEG
515 PORTAGE AVENUE
WINNIPEG, MAN.   R3B 2E9

DISCARDED

LIBERALISM
A Guide to Its Past, Present, and Future in American Politics

HOSTILE ALLIES
FDR and Charles de Gaulle

THE GREAT DOCUMENTS OF WESTERN CIVILIZATION

FALL FROM GRACE
The Republican Party and the Puritan Ethic

HUSTLERS AND HEROES
An American Political Panorama

Books by Milton Viorst

LIBERALISM
A Guide to Its Past, Present, and Future in American Politics

HOSTILE ALLIES
FDR and Charles de Gaulle

THE GREAT DOCUMENTS OF WESTERN CIVILIZATION

FALL FROM GRACE
The Republican Party and the Puritan Ethic

HUSTLERS AND HEROES
An American Political Panorama

E
840
.6
.V5

Milton Viorst

HUSTLERS AND HEROES

An American Political Panorama

SIMON AND SCHUSTER   NEW YORK

The author gratefully acknowledges permission to reprint previously published articles to the following:

Esquire for "Jewish Republican in a Presidential Fantasy" © 1966, "Pied Piper of the Hinterland" © 1966, "Small-Town Boy in a Fast Crowd" © 1967, "Chinaman in the Soup" © 1967, "Johnny Reb Goes to Vietnam" © 1968, "Good Night, Sweet Prince" © 1968; *Washingtonian* for "Dirty White Liberal" © 1966, "Hillbilly in the Service of the Lord" © 1967, "Tycoon in the White House" © 1967, "Amiable Thunderer of Populism" © 1968, "Black Mayor, White Mind" © 1968; *The New York Times* for "Wall Street Administers Justice" © 1969, "Intellectual as Insider" © 1969, "Intellectual as Outsider" © 1970, "Frontiersman on the Court" © 1970, "Black Overseer on the Presidential Plantation" © 1970; *Saturday Evening Post* for "Operator of the Big Machine" © 1968.

All rights reserved
including the right of reproduction
in whole or in part in any form
Copyright © 1971 by Milton Viorst
Published by Simon and Schuster
Rockefeller Center, 630 Fifth Avenue
New York, New York 10020

First Printing

SBN 671–20978–7
Library of Congress Catalog Card Number: 70–156163
Designed by Jack Jaget
Manufactured in the United States of America
By H. Wolff Book Mfg. Co., Inc., New York, N.Y.

For Gershon C. Jaffe

CONTENTS

7

INTRODUCTION

This may turn out to be a "non-book," as the critics have tended recently to call the pages that stand between two hard covers and yet, somehow, don't hang together. They are particularly cruel in applying the term to collections of previously published magazine pieces. So I recognize that there are risks to this undertaking. I won't claim, then, that this started as a book. Quite simply, it began in late 1965 as a hard-pressed free lance writer's chance to get an article published in *Esquire*. I didn't care particularly what the article was about. My chief requirement was that it have my by-line on it and lead to further decent writing assignments. To be sure, I had faith in my idea for a profile of Senator Jacob Javits—and it was almost triumph enough to persuade Harold Hayes, *Esquire*'s editor, to assign it to me formally. What I did not anticipate was that it would turn me, more or less, into a professional writer of political profiles and serve as the germ of a full-length bound volume.

After the Javits piece, *Esquire* suggested that I go to work on Everett Dirksen, the late Republican Senator from Illinois. I hesitated, at least for a moment, on the grounds that he was, apart from the President himself, the most written about man in Washington. It seemed to me that he must be literarily supersaturated. But Harold Hayes has a remarkably sure instinct. He insisted that there was, in the theatrics of Everett Dirksen, something that was certainly amusing, probably instructive, and perhaps even poignant. When I began working on the profile, I discovered that Hayes was right. If two points make a straight line, in literature as in geometry, then I was on the way to producing this work.

After Dirksen, I was more or less able to pick my own subjects. Anxious to diversify, I chose as many different political types as I could. I selected a hillbilly evangelist, an Irish city boss, a Southern rifleman, a new urban black, an Eastern intellectual. I found it instructive, even exciting, covering the spectrum of American politics.

Of course, I had some disappointments along the way, too. For some of my ideas I simply couldn't find an interested editor; for others I faced a recalcitrant subject. For example, George Meany, by refusing me an interview, effectively stopped me from doing a piece on the character we have since come to call the "hardhat." David Rockefeller bought me lunch but would not talk either, so I was deprived of a good look at our moneyed aristocracy. Naturally, I regret these omissions, as I do the omissions of, say, a Chicano (Cesar Chavez) or a new militant (Tom Hayden, Bobby Seale). In these days of Women's Liberation, I suppose I must also apologize for the absence of a woman, but I confess that women do not yet seem to me to be an identifiable political force. Basically, I think I obtained a wide enough variety to claim herein a panorama of American political life.

I hope that by putting these profiles together I have presented a useful perspective on the forces which are constantly at work in our system. I also hope that they stick together well enough to earn, at least, the designation "book."

M.V.

Washington, D. C.

HUSTLERS AND HEROES

Jacob K. Javits

JEWISH REPUBLICAN IN A
PRESIDENTIAL FANTASY

I first proposed an article to Esquire *on Senator Jacob Javits back in the early 1960's, when part of my duties as Washington correspondent for the New York* Post *consisted of watching him very closely. Harold Hayes, the editor of* Esquire, *wouldn't buy the idea then, but, when I resubmitted it in 1965, he recognized that its time had come. Javits seemed about to make it big.*

In 1965, the Republican Party was in disarray, having recently emerged from the Goldwater debacle. It was looking around desperately for Presidential prospects. Jack Javits was, at best, a long shot for the nomination in 1968. But the very fact that the Republican Party would consider the leadership of a liberal New York Jew was extraordinary.

Having known Javits for some time, I could conceive of his being an excellent President. I knew most of his staff and I was aware that he had something of an eccentric wife, who was both his agony and his joy. I had heard of his hovering Jewish mother, of a brother. Javits enjoyed talking candidly about himself and, if his sense of self-importance peeped through even in a chat, he

13

nonetheless had a sharp focus on himself. He was, of course, de-
lighted at the prospect of a magazine article based on the premise
that he was a serious Presidential candidate.

I enjoyed wandering around New York with Javits to do the
research—to his elegant Park Avenue apartment, his sleek legal
offices, the "21." We were both pleased when, shortly after the
piece appeared, Time *decided to put him on the cover and the*
press generally began to treat him with new respect. Javits himself
was thrilled with this attention but, in the circles around him, the
piece received mixed reviews. His law partner said of me, "If that's
Jack's friend, who needs enemies?" Mrs. Javits didn't talk to me
for years afterward, and brother Ben wrote a letter to Esquire
challenging my assertion that he wore rumpled suits (it wasn't my
fault, was it, that I interviewed him on a rainy day?). Meanwhile,
Javits surged ahead as a national figure.

Then, as the election of 1968 came closer, Javits began to slip
further and further behind. A liberal New York Jew might have
made it if a Republican defeat were certain, but as the prospect
of victory grew, the more Republicans were determined to nom-
inate someone who was really one of their own. Dick Nixon, who
in 1965 seemed an even longer shot than Jack Javits, suddenly
appeared to be the natural Republican candidate. Today, Javits
no longer thinks of himself as a Presidential possibility. I suspect
his self-image is that of the dashing elder statesman, a role he
fills very well. I am still convinced he'd have made a fine President
—but the Republican Party sees politics much differently from
the way I do.

IDA LITTMAN JAVITS, citizen of the Lower East Side by way
of Palestine and Vienna, never doubted that there was reality in
the American dream. But she wasted no time in wondering
whether her youngest boy, whom they called Jakela at home,
would ever be President of the United States. No matter how hard
things were, God forbid she should have given in to such vanity.

With a husband who lived in the Talmud, but worked as a janitor? With a flat crowded with greenhorn *mishpocha,* who paid board only when the sweatshops were at full employment? With a brothel in the adjoining tenement, rats in the cellar, and the kids arriving home from school with faces bloodied by the Wops from the gang on the next block? President of the United States—yet? A lawyer maybe or, with God's help, even a doctor. But President of the United States—even in America that's only for *goyim.*

But Ida Littman Javits would not have believed either that a plaque would be put up in her honor in Safad, where she was born, simply because she was Jakela's mother. So maybe, if she were alive, she wouldn't be so pessimistic. Jews are very stylish these days. There's got to be a first Jewish President, after all. Suppose the Republicans in 1968, desperate for a candidate, admitted that a bloodless Anglo-Saxon hadn't a chance and decided, by whatever unintelligible process they follow, on a Lower East Side Jew. Haven't they done crazier things before? Then suppose that the Democratic candidate got caught in a scandal or dropped dead the day before the election or sold out Chiang Kai-shek to Mao Tse-tung. Why, then Jacob K. Javits would be President of the United States! And wouldn't Ida Littman Javits be surprised and proud.

Jack—as he's always been called outside the family—is one of the few Jewish politicians to become a recognized figure from coast to coast. And what's so amazing about it is that he's such a Jewish Jew. Javits is not a white-collar New England Jew like Ribicoff, a pioneer Alaskan Jew like Gruening, a Western, conservationist Jew like the late Dick Neuberger, or even a multigeneration German Jew like the late Herbert Lehman. He's not even a rich Jew, though he is, as they say, "well-to-do." Jack Javits is a genuine, one-hundred-percent, all-wool-gabardine, Yiddish-speaking Old Country Jew, the kind who knows how to cut a matzoh ball with the side of the spoon without splashing the soup. Javits is a regular Huckleberry Finn Jew. Who knows if someday schoolboys won't learn about George Washington's hatchet, Abe Lincoln's log cabin and Jack Javits' *cheder?* Jacob

K. Javits is a folk hero, as American as apples, nuts and raisins on Saturday morning at the synagogue.

Javits is now the most powerful Republican in New York, the most politically potent of states. When it was announced recently that he'd had enough of supporting a perennial loser for President, Nelson Rockefeller took the hint and replied that he no longer would be a candidate. Javits is now for all practical purposes the leader of the New York delegation to the Republican National Convention. He'll go to the convention as New York's favorite son. He makes no claim to being the object of a great popular ground swell, but he says, adopting a pose meant to be both jaunty and humble, "Republicans take me very seriously indeed."

At sixty-one, Javits is beyond the ideal age for a Presidential candidate, but he is still young. The gym, the swimming pool and a measured diet keep him at about 175 pounds, distributed as they might be on a wrestler. Javits is far from handsome but—important to a politician—he has presence that commands attention. His face wears the lines of anxiety. His head is almost completely bald. He dresses in well-cut, expensive suits, without looking foppish. Javits long ago shed the inhibiting self-consciousness of the private man and is now regarded as an excellent platform speaker and hand shaker. As a candidate, he would be a formidable competitor.

Javits maintains that if, in 1960, Nixon had picked him instead of Lodge, the outcome of the election probably would have been different. But at the time, he walked in Rockefeller's shadow. Equally significant, he had been linked with the abortive "dump-Nixon" plot in 1956 and concedes that even four years later "maybe I couldn't have stomached Nixon." Today, Javits is on his own, having demonstrated in the 1962 election that, in New York as least, he is a far more appealing candidate than Rockefeller. While winning reelection by almost a million votes, he became the first Republican in modern times to carry the city of New York. Without Javits, there probably would not have been a Lindsay as mayor. Javits appears to have found the secret of getting both the Republican vote and the minority vote. With this key to the cities in his pocket, Javits seems to have a weapon that Nixon lacked in 1960 and which no other Republican possesses. Javits acknowledges that he could use New York's convention votes to bargain for the Vice-Presidential nomination, which may be a more realistic aspiration for him. But his current plan is to feel his way around the political terrain and count himself out of nothing. He'll speak as often as he can, mostly on college campuses, where, he explains, "there aren't many votes, but lots of ferment." Without a blush, Javits announces that his current strategy for achieving higher office is "to project myself into national discussion." After that, he declares, as if he were the plaything of fate, "what's in the cards is."

But Jack Javits has never been the plaything of fate. Kids from the Lower East Side get to the top in politics only by pouncing on fate and beating it into submission. Javits, by himself, may not have been tough enough to do it on his own. He's smart and shrewd, but he lacks the killer instinct. If he didn't have an older brother named Ben, he might today be a successful insurance executive or a cloak-and-suiter. But Ben was utterly relentless in his determination that both of them were going to make it big. Ben gave Jack the drive. Ben gave him the objectives, the ambition, the conviction that he could really be somebody. If Jack is Cinderella, then Ben is the fairy godmother. It was the older brother who wrestled fate to the ground so the kid brother could hustle on by.

When Jack was born in 1904, his mother had no place to put him except in Ben's bed. Ben, who was ten, accepted his brother immediately, not as a burden but as a responsibility. He had already begun to dominate the family. The boys' father, Morris, was gentle and dignified, even as a janitor, but his qualities were not enough for a family that was frantic to quit the slums. Ben filled the void. Taking Jack by the hand, he led him through the exciting, babbling world of the Lower East Side, a world crowded with generosity and misery and hope and determination. Ben introduced the kid to the concert hall and the Yiddish theater, street baseball and boxing, the settlement house and socialism, then on to capitalism. Ben, as a boy, was a fiery idealist, mesmerized by Hillquit and Debs and Eastman and the beautiful goals of the Young People's Socialist League. He was a voracious reader and an intense thinker, tantalized by philosophical as well as pragmatic problems. Whatever Ben knew, he told to Jack. Ben trained Jack to read and ponder, scheme and fight and dream. Until Bar Mitzvah age, Jack remained in Ben's bed. By that time, Ben was ready to get Jack a bed of his own.

One Sunday afternoon, Ben informed the old man that he was moving the family out of the Lower East Side and into Brooklyn. Ben had a good job as a bill collector. He even went to law school at night. Ben told his father that he was welcome to join them but, like it or not, he was taking the family away. Too proud to accept the ultimatum, the old man refused to go. For a few months he lived alone, exchanging visits with the family, pushing his broom daily up and down the tenement steps. Then Morris Javits, never reconciled to his failure to make it as a rabbi, took sick and died. His eldest son was by now established in his own business, collecting bad debts. Every night he attended classes at the Fordham Law School in downtown Manhattan. So that he could devote more time to studying, his brother dutifully rode the trolley in from Brooklyn each evening to bring him supper from home in a brown-paper bag. In 1919, a year after Ben received his law degree, he moved the family out of Brooklyn to the Upper West Side of Manhattan. With Ben as their leader, the Javitses were making remarkable strides.

As Jack grew up, he, too, worked hard. At first he helped his mother sell crockery out of a pushcart. Then he ran errands for a Fifth Avenue candy shop. After he finished high school, he tested pipes at a factory in Elizabeth. Then he went on the road to sell printing products from Philadelphia to Roanoke. For a while, he collected bad debts for his brother and, while Ben sought to drum up legal fees, he took his own turn supporting the family. When he had time, he attended night school at Columbia. But he abandoned the B.A. as a goal and shifted to N.Y.U., to emulate his brother in getting a law degree. Jack put in his year of clerkship, naturally, in Ben's office on Chambers Street, and in 1927 was admitted to the bar. The two brothers immediately established the law firm of Javits and Javits and moved into an office that seemed almost splendid on Lower Broadway.

During the dozen years between the stockmarket crash and Pearl Harbor, Jack Javits and his brother prospered at the practice of law, without attracting much attention in one way or another. Their specialty was corporate bankruptcy and reorganization work. Ben was particularly adept at the research, Jack at the advocacy. While Jack was developing his genius for debate, Ben was exercising his for making money and, lean as the years were, gathered in a modest fortune for the partnership. Having long since lost his Socialist zeal, Ben was now persuaded that the salvation of the world lay in high finance. Jack, at this juncture, was of no definable persuasion, either political or philosophical. He was liberal, but a registered Republican. He was enthusiastic about La-Guardia, but supported Roosevelt in 1940. "I had," he says with some remorse, "no real involvement in such important issues of the day as the Spanish Civil War, as so many people properly did. I didn't go off to fight with the Lincoln Brigade." He read a great deal and, in contrast to his *hamische* brother, played a bit at being a gay blade. In 1936, he married Marjorie Ringling, the circus heiress, but when she divorced him three years later, it was a matter of indifference to him. Javits concedes that as he approached forty, he was bored with the routine of small-time society and a law practice that was getting him nothing but rich. When the war broke out, he saw it as an opportunity to break away and get out into the world.

Javits regards the beginning of the war in Europe as the turning point in his life. It galvanized him into a realization that he wanted to do more than just watch passively as the world went by. He tried several times to enlist but was rejected because of age. After a chance meeting with a general at a dinner party, he volunteered as a dollar-a-year civilian in the Army's Chemical Warfare branch in Washington. By the fall of 1941, he was working full time in Chemical Warfare at a dollar a year. In the spring of 1942, when it became clear that he could no longer perform his functions as a civilian, he was commissioned as a major. Though he was overage, he insisted on taking six weeks of basic training with the teen-age recruits. Then he returned to Washington to reorganize an important segment of the Chemical Warfare branch, an assignment for which he received the Legion of Merit and as a consequence of which he collapsed of exhaustion and remained hospitalized for two months. When he recovered, he went into training for a field command and was sent overseas to plan ordnance requirements for the invasions of both Europe and Japan. Javits' experiences in the war were exactly the tonic he needed to escape the torpor that had overcome him on his professional and social life in New York.

It was in Washington during the war that Javits first fell victim to the political contagion. One of his closest friends during these years was David Niles, the tough young liberal who served as an adviser to Franklin Roosevelt. Javits had nothing of his own to recommend him in the status-conscious capital, but his friendship with Niles was enough to open most political doors for him. It admitted him to a circle of young liberals and intellectuals, most of whom were Jewish and somehow involved in government. When Javits got out of the Army late in 1945, he knew he couldn't go back to practicing law. His new life, he decided, could only be politics.

Ben, by now a Republican of some small prominence, has insisted that it was he who arranged his brother's appointment as chief of research for Judge Jonah Goldstein, the candidate for mayor in 1945 against William O'Dwyer. Others, in the wake of the Javits success story, have also claimed the credit. Javits himself takes a more realistic position. Who wanted to be an unpaid, unloved research director in a losing mayoralty campaign? The job was there. Javits was free and he took it. He performed so loyally that when the Republicans began searching for a candidate for Congress from the Upper West Side, Javits looked like a good possibility. Ben applied some muscle, but once again the key factor was the scarcity of competition. In a district so overwhelmingly Democratic, any Republican with enough money and energy to make a decent fight of it could have had the nomination. Methodically, Javits surveyed the possibilities. The district was largely Jewish and liberal, the Democratic incumbent was Irish and conservative. The American Labor Party, far to the left, also ran a candidate. When Javits concluded that he could win a three-way race, he volunteered to run. The Liberal Party's decision to endorse him—which Ben once again claims to have engineered—may have been decisive. Javits spent his money wisely and copiously. He campaigned like a dynamo. He even hired the Roper poll and tailored his speeches to the results of its canvass. To the surprise of almost everyone but himself, Javits carried the election.

Once in Washington, Javits wasted no time in establishing a reputation for being intelligent, ambitious, unconventional and brash. Contemptuous of the rule that freshmen should keep their mouths shut, he talked on anything and everything that struck his fancy. He has never departed from the practice. In his eight years in the House, Javits managed to alienate himself from most of his colleagues by his presumptuousness and from his party leaders by voting consistently against them. He was one of eleven Republicans who voted to defeat Taft-Hartley. ("When I was growing up," he explained, "the sight I remember most vividly was the stove covered with pots—during the three or four months of the 'season' when my greenhorn relatives worked night and day. The rest of the year they starved. Yet for all their slavery, they were beaten by the machines and, if they got interested in unions, they were beaten over the heads by goons, too. And in the House they wanted me to vote for Taft-Hartley?") He was one of the eight who voted against Mundt-(Richard M.) Nixon, the Communist-registration act. He voted in favor of the Truman Doctrine and the Marshall Plan, against the McCarran Immigration Act and the Tidelands oil giveaway. He voted in favor of FEPC long before civil rights was stylish, and even had the audacity to ignore the predictions of imminent ruin from New York's shipping interests to vote in favor of construction of the St. Lawrence Seaway. While the regular Republicans denounced him from the right as an apostate, the American Labor Party, a force to be reckoned with in his Congressional district, denounced him from the left as a phony liberal and a bourgeois fink. But, thanks as much to his enemies as to his friends, he won each successive election by a bigger majority. By 1954, Javits had become well enough known in New York to go on to something bigger and better.

Because of Marion, Javits wasn't completely happy in the House. He had met her—Marion Ann Borris—when he was working on the Goldstein campaign. Twenty years younger than he, she was pretty, with dark hair and dark eyes, freckles on her face and a fine shape. She was full of life, laughed easily and cultivated a kind of zany eccentricity which men enjoy more than women. Like Jack, Marion was relentlessly ambitious, but the chief agent of her ambitions was by no means the intellect. Marion, too, had started out in the slums. Her way to escape had been the theater, and every nickel she could find she put into drama lessons. Shortly after the war started, she took it into her mind to go to the Coast, where she hoped to be discovered. When she failed as an actress, she took flying lessons and thought of becoming an Army ferry pilot. But then she decided she wasn't cut out for military service and went back home. Not long after his first Congressional election, Javits married her. Marion didn't make it any easier for him to be a Congressman.

Marion took the position from the beginning that Washington was too dull and boring for her. She loved New York and remained passionate about the theater. Being married to a Congressman was all right but she had no intention of being simply a Congressman's wife. Javits quickly learned that if he was going to keep Marion, he would have to adjust to her, since she wouldn't adjust to him. It meant lonely nights in Washington, too much time on airplanes and a life more orientated to society than social problems. A year after their marriage, Joy was born. She was followed two years later by Joshua. Javits found that he liked the family, perhaps better than Congress. The prospect of alienation from Marion and the children—to perform petty congressional chores, to campaign endlessly, to travel, to hold the same office as 434 others—was decisive in persuading Javits to submit to his ambition and play for bigger stakes.

Javits wanted to run for Mayor in 1953 but the city's Republican bosses, who preferred to lose with a candidate they could dominate than win with one they couldn't, refused him the nomination. The following year, the gamble was more precarious. Franklin D. Roosevelt, Jr., possessor of the most popular name in New York and a politician apparently on the rise, was running for state's Attorney General. Republicans scarcely rushed forward to oppose him. Javits, perhaps sensing something that escaped the others, agreed to take Roosevelt on. His chances for winning were not regarded as good. Yet not only did Javits win by a substantial margin but he was the only Republican winner that year in any state-wide contest. A plausible explanation of the collapse of F.D.R., Jr. still remains elusive but, for Javits, beating a Roosevelt was like blowing down the walls of Jericho. It seemed almost anticlimactic when Javits, in a race two years later against another New Deal scion, beat Robert F. Wagner, Jr. and became Senator from the State of New York.

It was in the contest for the Senate that Jack Javits came close to being destroyed forever as a politician. While the American Labor Party continued to denounce him from the left, the McCarthyites were sharpening their claws for him on the right. The claws fell at the very moment that Javits was trying to persuade Tom Dewey and the other bosses of New York Republican politics that he was the man for the Senatorial nomination. The claws belonged to the pudgy hands of one Jay Sourwine, who had been and is once again today the chief bird of prey for the Internal Security Subcommittee of Senator James O. Eastland of Mississippi. Sourwine, campaigning in a Nevada primary for the Democratic Senatorial nomination, plucked some raw accusations from secret files made available by the FBI and from testimony by Bella Dodd, the professional exposer. He charged that Javits had sought Communist support in his early Congressional races and had spoken to some Communists at San Francisco in 1945 while he was attending the UN charter session. Sourwine's accusations broke just in time to circulate wildly through the hotel corridors of an otherwise boring national convention that the Republicans were conducting to renominate Dwight Eisenhower. The feeling in the New York delegation at the time was that Javits was doomed, like a pike dropped into the gefilte fish.

Back in New York, Javits went off with Marion to Fire Island for the weekend to lie on the beach and think. Behind the charges, quite clearly, were Eastland and Republican Senator William Jenner of Indiana. In desperation and, as it turned out, in vain, they were fighting to keep the Senate from slipping out of the right wing's grasp. Among the potential candidates from New York, Javits represented the most substantial threat to the right's domination. Their objective was to drive him out of the contest. Eisenhower, with his usual blurred perception and cream-puff audacity, would say only of Javits that "as of this moment, I think he is a fine American." Dewey and his New York pals, whose enthusiasm for Javits stopped at the exit to the polling places, kept quiet. Javits' best testimonial came from Representative Walter Judd of Minnesota, a Republican of impeccable anti-Communist and reactionary credentials, who went out on a limb to wire that "if any Communist supported you politically it certainly was a bad bargain for them, because . . . no one has been more intelligently and effectively anti-Communist than you." Judd, however, didn't have much of a constituency in New York. Javits decided, during his weekend on Fire Island, that he alone could turn back this mortal threat to his future.

Javits demanded of Eastland the opportunity to testify in open session on the charges, however nebulous, that had been made against him. Eastland, in no hurry to give Javits a forum, put off an answer for more than a month. Finally, a few days before the Republican State Convention in New York, Javits took the stand. His performance, if not brilliant, was adequate to discredit most of the substance and all of the meaning of the innuendo that had been cast against him. Any meetings he may have had with Bella

Dodd, who lived in his Congressional district, were clearly casual encounters. He did not know her nor was he aware that she was a high Communist functionary. He had not sought Communist support, if only because it would have been self-defeating. Whatever cocktails he had sipped with Reds in San Francisco had been sipped inadvertently, and even if it hadn't been inadvertent, so what? Javits emerged from the hearings a vindicated hero. Even Dewey didn't try to stop him now. Javits overwhelmed the state convention and took the nomination effortlessly. Sourwine, by the way, ran last in Nevada in a field of four.

Despite the happy outcome, Javits still regards the episode as the most painful of his political career. It was American politics at its worst and even Javits did not show up at his best. Enough residue of the incident remains so that right-wing nut groups unrelentingly torment him with it. By dialing the telephone, you could have heard during the Goldwater campaign a recorded message which said that "Jacob Javits has had many associations with notorious Communists and . . . received the all-out support of the Communist Party." As recently as last October, for a dollar you could have placed an order by phone for a kit on Javits and the Reds. To this day, Javits refuses to talk about the episode. Obviously, it settled into a weak spot in his tough political hide and bored its way in.

When Javits reached the Senate in January, 1957, his Republican colleagues were scarcely waiting for him with open arms. A team of uninspired conservatives, they knew he would be with them rarely and against them frequently. Javits at once found he had a community of interests with Case of New Jersey, Kuchel of California and a handful of others, but, even if he wanted a haven they were too few to have provided one. After the Democratic sweep of 1958, the relative importance of the nonconforming Republicans increased it little. Kuchel was elected Minority Whip. But Javits, the loner, the individualist, the anti-team man, remained isolated. From the moment he first arrived in the Senate until today, the Republican powers in the Senate have practiced on Javits a policy of quarantine. It is only because Javits has had *chutzpah* enough to challenge them that they have not succeeded in rendering him impotent.

"When Jack got down here," said one of his few Washington friends, "he saw that they were going to close him out of the committee structure. So do you know what he decided? He decided he was going to be on all possible committees."

That, in effect, is what Javits has done. He has fixed his attention not on one or two specialties, like most Senators, but on every conceivable subject that crosses the agenda. He has become the best-informed man in the Senate. His range is prodigious. Over the course of a few days, he may talk about civil rights, Federal assistance to the arts, banking regulations, automation, air pollution, the Brooklyn Navy Yard and the intricacies of the tax codes. His knowledge of legislation has made him invaluable as a negotiator of legislative compromises. Though few laws bear his name—because he is of the party perpetually in the minority—his personal impact is discernible to the tutored eye in dozens of amendments to major measures. Javits drives his staff mad in his quest for the information that makes his method viable. His standard conversational opener, "What's going on?", is never meant as an amenity. Impotent within the formal leadership structure, Javits has made his mark by dominating the give-and-take between Senators. When he has had to, he has shown that he is not averse to using his wiles in the practice of the quiet little mischief which characterizes Senators in their power struggles. But he takes far greater satisfaction in proposing the kind of original idea that won him one recent editorial in Britain's *Punch* entitled "Rare and Upright Jacob," and another in Washington's *Post* called "Javits Breaks Through." As an outsider in a minority party, Javits by all the rules should be a pygmy in the Senate. But because, more than any other Senator, he has learned to use the intellect as an instrument of power, he is one of the giants.

Javits' deep commitment to Senate business keeps him on the floor more than any other member. He loves the arena. He's like an overage letterman who can never get enough of the ball game. There is no scene on the Senate floor more familiar than Javits standing across an aisle, arm extended, finger pointed at the debating adversary, snapping off facts with cool logic in his hard nasal voice, so resplendent with the accent of New York. Javits looks upon himself as the conscience of the Senate, always ready to thwart some dubious maneuver, defend some noble cause. He likes to think of himself as the tribune of the underprivileged, the defender of the city, the champion of enlightenment. Javits is never finer than when he takes on a Southerner in a civil-rights debate. (Southerners find Javits particularly incomprehensible, as well as obnoxious. In an unguarded moment, one Dixiecrat Senator called him a "Jewish merchant pandering to the nigger vote." It does not outrage Javits that they should dislike him; it does that they should question his sincerity.) Such a debate exalts him. It evokes his self-esteem and his sense of virtue, it lights up his brain cells and stimulates his heart, it makes him quiver with righteousness. Jack Kennedy, after his Presidential nomination, felt the sting of Javits' tongue. Lyndon Johnson, as Vice-President, heard Javits call him a "hollow shell" for failing to make an important ruling on a civil rights question. Johnson has never quite forgiven him for it. The experience may have led Javits to increased self-restraint. Still, no Senator goes out of his way to swap invective with him on the Senate floor.

Inevitably, the question arises of why Javits, the prototype of the Northern liberal, became and remains a Republican. Javits is scarcely more convincing than anyone else in answering it. He spends a substantial portion of his book, *Order of Battle*—one of his less noteworthy achievements—on a tedious and unpersuasive explanation. It all started, he says, because his father, between reading the Talmud and sweeping the stairs, was a part-time ward heeler for Tammany. The corruption that he observed, he claims soulfully, turned him cold on the Democratic Party. He then goes on to denounce Woodrow Wilson's postwar economic policies, the Palmer Raids, the flirtation between the Democrats and the Klan, the Jimmy Walker scandal and Franklin D. Roosevelt's first campaign for the Presidency. Javits continues by declaring his fidelity to the early Hoover, George Norris, Fiorello LaGuardia,

Wendell Willkie and Arthur Vandenberg. Modestly, he places himself in the tradition of the great fathers of Republicanism— Hamilton, Clay, Lincoln and Teddy Roosevelt—whom he heartily misrepresents, whom he scarcely resembles and whose paternity seems totally irrelevant to the party today. But if Javits' philosophical arguments sound silly, he gives one clue in *Order of Battle* that has a compelling ring. He writes:

> . . . No matter how independent I was in my own thinking on public issues and how intensely I espoused issues even in the face of considerable Republican grumbling, I was always most careful to maintain the best relations with the Republican organization and Republican Party workers and to do everything that I properly could for them and with them. I did not want my independence of ideas and action to be confused with lack of devotion to the development and improvement of the party structure and the party machinery.

What Javits seemed to be saying was that party membership has no ideological but only organizational meaning. By supporting Eisenhower against Stevenson and Nixon against Kennedy, he seemed to affirm a distinction between party loyalty and political philosophy. But could he then justify abandoning Barry Goldwater as he did in 1964? Goldwater, he argued, was an exception who was outside the "mainstream" (the expression, he claims, was originally his) of Republicanism. If Javits is right in his contention that ideas and action are not to be confused with party structure and machinery, then there is no logical reason whatever for the Republicans not to switch from Barry Goldwater in the last election to Jack Javits in the next.

Whatever the Republicans may think of him in the Senate, Javits can afford his independence, thanks to another powerful source of strength that he has within the Party. That source, surprising as it may seem to those who still equate high finance with reaction, is in Wall Street. Since he started in politics, Javits has had the backing of the Whitneys, the Loebs, the Rockefellers, the Morgan heirs, and many of the others who can tap stones and make millions gush forth. Somehow Javits—unlike, say, Jack Kennedy and the early Humphrey—has persuaded the top money men that, however liberal he may be, he will not tamper with the financial institutions on which their power is founded. Wall Street, in contrast to the Puritan Middle West, takes no offense at the welfare state, as long as it leaves ample room for profits. Javits, while a welfare-stater, has been fastidious about keeping America safe for the monied interests. He watches carefully, for example, that there is a place for the private entrepreneur in all public-housing legislation. He saw to it, as the price of liberal Republican support, that the Medicare bill provided an outlet for private insurance companies. He has consistently pressed for investment credits and other tax benefits for business and industry. He loves grandiose schemes to mobilize capital—at a substantial return—in behalf of such worthy causes as rehabilitating South America or Africa. For years, Javits quietly but effectively looked after the interests of the New York financial community while serving on the Banking and Currency Committee. Even though he abandoned the Committee, he never forgets his dependence on that community. He is deferential—some might say obsequious—to its members. He lunches with them, plays squash with them and likes to consider some of them his friends. "They think I'm a helluva fellow," he explained. "I admire the way they get things done and they respect me because I've got a little power." These financiers throughout Javits' career have remained a loyal, generous and powerful base of support.

Javits, in pursuit of his ambitions, also has the advantage—thanks largely to Ben's early foresight—of a substantial independent income. He admits to personal assets of perhaps $1,000,000, which are well invested, in addition to an annual return from his law firm of some $35,000 to $40,000 after taxes. By living on this outside money, Javits can devote most of the $33,400 of his Senate salary to office expenses. He estimates that he spends some $20,000 to $25,000 a year, over and above the government's expense allotment, for such purposes as travel, entertainment, contributions, private consultants, and maintaining what must certainly be the best staff on Capitol Hill. Racially and religiously, the staff is completely integrated, but this is only partly the result of conscious principle. Superior to principle is the practical consideration that Javits is most comfortable with members of minority groups and particularly, of course, with Jews. He does not discriminate against Anglo-Saxon Protestants but they tend to get lost in the ethnic shuffle. Javits has had WASP assistants who have been both efficient and capable, but he has been heard to complain that they don't understand him—and vice versa. For the most part he chooses from that mélange of minorities—Jews, Negroes, Italians, Greeks—that make up Manhattan. His chief assistant is Dick Aurelio, a shrewd Italian who has a Jewish wife. Javits' feel for minorities was illustrated recently when, between two qualified applicants, he selected the one with a physical handicap because, he said, "He's suffered like us." Javits, with good reason, has supreme confidence in his staff. It is an example of how a private fortune can be used effectively to advance a political career. Javits, though scarcely rich enough to finance a Presidential campaign on his own, can afford the costs of playing politics well in a high-priced league.

With brains, money, dedication and loyal supporters, Javits really ought to get on better in Washington, where political and legislative excellence *are* respected. But he has the bad fortune of neutralizing many of his assets by being a stiff. Javits doesn't understand the sense of camaraderie that pervades the Senate, enabling political enemies to be personal friends. He is too self-absorbed, excessively burdened with feelings of responsibility, overly persuaded that his objectives are the most vital objectives in the Capitol. Javits is as greedy for publicity as most politicians, but he tends to think that his headlines are somehow more honestly earned than those of his colleagues. The bureaucrats, the Congressmen and the newspapermen that a Senator runs into during the course of a day are often put off by a chilliness in Javits, a lack of perspective about himself. On closer examination, Javits is not so much ill-humored as humorless, not so much pompous as proud, not so much distant as detached. From Javits emerges not the condescension of aristocracy but the priggishness of insecurity.

Javits is probably the only Senator who insists on putting a five-cent stamp on his personal mail, when he could send it free. He may be the only Senator who imposes limitations on his personal law practice that exceed the limitations imposed by the normally accepted Congressional code of ethics. It is unlikely that there is another Senator who, when approached by an unsuspecting streetwalker outside a posh hotel a few years ago, would have thrust out his hand, introduced himself politely and, to her total astonishment, asked her to vote for him at the next election.

Javits has no time to waste. He begins his day early and keeps it filled with appointments, all of which invariably run late. If he gets to his office in the morning and finds he has no luncheon date, he snaps out a command that he get one. If he's flying to New York, he dictates to a secretary on the way to the airport, then resumes his dictation to a secretary who meets him when he lands. If, by chance, he arrives early for a plane, he runs to the phone to slip in a final call. He wouldn't think of passing an evening at a movie, just for diversion. Javits is, quite literally, unwilling to have an idle moment, for fear it might reflect on his importance.

Never unmindful that he is a Senator, Javits has the fixed idea that Senatorial dignity equals grand solemnity. He can be charming when he tries, but he rarely bothers. He avoids the political and diplomatic cocktail circuit in which Senators normally travel. He has no close friends in the government. When he dines occasionally with an old friend, it is a friend who dates from his House or his Army days. More often, he'll remain in the office doing paperwork until eight or nine o'clock, then dragoon an unwilling aide into joining him for dinner in a down town restaurant. If all work and no play make Jack a dull boy, it accounts for Jack's being looked upon in Washington as a dreadfully dull boy.

Yet New York has been exposed to a different image of Javits. "I work in Washington," Javits explains. "I live in New York." Because Marion persists in her refusal to displace the household,

Javits is forced to spend his nights in Washington by himself. But as soon as he can spare a moment, he flies back to New York for an experience in real living.

Real living, for Javits, revolves around Marion. He beams when he talks of her, his eyes light up with love, and his voice takes on a vibrant quality. He is pleased that she has found in her independence the means for personal self-expression. He raises no protests over her involvement with the theater, her quest for status on the committees that run charity balls, even her capers at the discothèques in the company of assorted innocuous escorts. Javits admits that he is unhappy at having failed to move her to Washington, but has long since resigned himself to their temporary separations. Normally, he is home from Friday night to Tuesday morning and, often, a night or two during the week. He spends as much time as most fathers with the children—Joy, now seventeen, Joshua, sixteen, and Carla, ten—and manages to have breakfast with them on more mornings than he misses. New York, not Washington, is home for Jack Javits. The reason is that Marion has arranged it that way.

If the ponderous side of Javits comes from brother Ben, the light side is all Marion. Only with Marion can Javits shed the inhibitions that he wears when he is operating as Senator. And even then he finds it hard to forget. "If I ask him a serious question," she reveals, "sometimes he buttons up his jacket before he answers." Javits himself testifies to the problem. "When I get to be a stuffed shirt," he said, "she gives me a kick in the tail. But if I'm youthful at all, it's because of her."

Marion likes the bright lights, so they rarely miss a play. Marion adores dancing, so they frug until closing at Arthur or whatever other place she would like to be seen. Marion is big on Op this year, so their apartment is filled with framed optical illusions. Marion loves to assemble scintillating guests for sparkling dinner parties. She brings in actors and artists and writers and the *in* people of New York's transient high society of acquired money and recognized talent. Or, for a quiet evening at home, she finds diversion in summoning one or two of the couples—intelligent, aggressive, successful, and much younger than the Senator—whom she regards as her closest friends. Javits is poor at entertaining by small talk. Though he's an excellent dancer, he's a little embarrassed being the spectacle on a dance floor. Sometimes he objects to Marion's guest lists, but he says, "If you don't have the jet set, you have something else, like bores or relatives." Personally, Javits would prefer the opera to the theater, the ballet to the frug, Rembrandt to Rauschenberg. But he rarely complains. As he says, "On balance, I'm ahead."

The Javits apartment on upper Park Avenue, a complete turn of the earth from the Lower East Side, is neither big nor ostentatious, but it too is thoroughly Marion. The living room is dominated by her full-length portrait, in profile, which does more than ample justice to her *tush* and is tactful with her little-girl bust. For some peculiar reason, it has an arrow passing through her forehead, which is most distracting. "True art connoisseurs," she declared with a touch of girlish insolence, "don't ask what it means." But then she added, as if to amend any indiscretion, "that Boris [Chaliapin, the artist] told me it meant that when I was pierced I didn't bleed. Isn't that lovely?" Marion has a small antique desk in a corner of the study, where she and her two-day-a-week secretary prepare her correspondence. Javits doesn't have a niche of his own in the apartment. When he wants to work, he sits at the dining-room table. To take a phone call, he goes to his wife's desk, where he gazes at a snapshot of Marion in a bikini. But Javits shows no sign of discomfort because it's *her* apartment. He also thinks of it as *her* city and because she is his, so is New York.

New York, to Javits, is like the family domain to an English nobleman. Take this phone conversation, overheard in the Javits office: "Hello, Alan, I'm glad you called. I've been meaning to talk to you for weeks. . . .

"I'm taking the eight o'clock plane up and going directly to '21.' I've got to see some people there. I plan to spend the whole evening. . . .

"Come in any time after nine o'clock. I'll be delighted to see you. We'll have a chat. You might have to wait a few minutes, if I'm with someone else.

"Yes, Alan, '21.' Any time between nine and, say, one or two A.M."

Life with Marion is the top hat for Javits' vision of himself as a "Mr. New York" who casually holds court in "21." He has come to appreciate having his name in the papers with Zero Mostel as much as with Hubert Humphrey. He has substituted the friendly wave of a Manhattan taxi driver for the grudging approval of a fellow Senator. In New York, he feels it's no violation of his Senatorial dignity when the doorman of a famous restaurant greets him informally as an old customer. He takes pleasure in jockeying his Lincoln Continental with the prestige license plates through the city streets. Javits adores the races and loves going to his club for a swim on a Saturday afternoon, though he knows there are still clubs where he cannot swim because, as a friend discreetly put it, "He can't pass the physical." Javits sees not betrayal but, on the contrary, redemption of his humble origins in his becoming a latter-day Jimmy Walker, without hand in till. In New York, Javits discerns no contradiction in a Senator also being a man-about-town.

Ben has never understood all this high life. He is a Jewish millionaire who would rather go home than go out for supper. A diminutive but more wrinkled version of his brother, Ben is still fierce and active at seventy-one. Toward Jack he displays the mixture of pride and resentment that parents often feel for the child who has gone off to make good. Ben, in his rumpled suits, and Marion, in her Paris copies, naturally don't get along. She shrugs at the mention of his name. He says with melancholy: "There's a marriage situation which is not very conducive to my relationship with Jack." Ben never goes to his brother's house. They lunch occasionally, talk on the phone quite frequently. Jack, torn between a loyalty to both brother and wife, tries to make the best of the situation. Understandably, Marion has come out better in the rivalry.

When Javits was elected Attorney General of New York in

1954, he withdrew, after twenty-seven years, from the Javits and Javits partnership. He could not, without risking a conflict of interest, practice in the state as well as be the state's chief attorney. After he became Senator two years later, he was no longer subject to such an inhibition and Ben assumed he would return. The firm, which by now had its offices in Rockefeller Center, had remained Javits and Javits during his absence. Jack, however, insisted that as a Senator he must not deal with cases involving the Federal government, and though Ben agreed to meet the stipulation, Jack maintained that he could not impose such a financial burden on his brother. With Ben looking on helplessly, Jack formed a partnership with John Trubin, one of his assistants in the Attorney General's office. The firm, with an elegant suite in the Seagram Building, takes no business in which the Federal government is a party. It is a "high-quality" operation that specializes in civil matters, most of which involve substantial sums of money and, consequently, substantial fees. Javits, who bears the title "of counsel," lends his name and prestige and some small advice, without participating in any of the cases himself. To this day, Ben is brokenhearted that his brother has left him. He has a grown son, natty and sleek, as befits the next generation in the dynasty. The son, with political ambitions of his own, has taken up the spare Javits in the company title. But the impression is strong that Ben still thinks of Jack as the most important thing in his life.

"I guess I have a sort of stupid sense of what brothers ought to be like," Ben said, rather sadly. "He's the closest friend I ever had. Until he was twenty-eight, our relationship was the biggest thing in his life. Until he married, there was one pocket for the both of us. I was very idealistic and exacting about what we meant to each other. I consciously did all I could to make him a great man. Of course, I'm disappointed that we've drifted apart. But I must bow to his judgment. . . ."

As much as possible, Ben still holds onto the dream world he created with his younger brother. He takes pride in having been the architect of a great political career. He continues to think of himself as his brother's inspiration and source of ideas. Although

Ben's politics have become more identified with the right, he insists that he and his brother share the same ultimate goals, while perhaps disagreeing from time to time on "tactics." It is important to Ben to feel he is performing a vital, positive function in Jack's life.

Quite by coincidence, as Ben was speaking the phone rang and a secretary's voice announced over a loudspeaker: "Mr. B. The Senator is on the line." Ben looked across the desk with satisfaction, as if all his claims had been redeemed. Nervously he picked up the receiver.

"Hello, dear. How are you? . . . I'm sorry you couldn't make it to the cemetery with me yesterday to see mother's grave. . . . I sent Nixon a position paper on that labor matter. . . . When can we have lunch? . . . What's happened with our friend Everett and that bill? . . . How about that other piece of legislation? . . . Jack? Jack?"

Ben frowned at the receiver. Obviously his brother had hung up on him abruptly. Ben looked across the desk and smiled uncomfortably.

Ben admits he had made no provision in his master plan for Jack Javits to become President of the United States. That would have required even more *chutzpah* than he possessed. But he might have dreamed it on some grim, cold night on the Lower East Side or in Brooklyn, as he lovingly contemplated the future of the boy sleeping at his side. Ben's view, after all, has always been that nothing is too exalted for the younger brother he brought up to be a *mensch*. But even President of the United States? Yes, Ben indicated, nodding his head, even President of the United States.

It's almost as if a rerun is being prepared of a play that opened a few years ago and enjoyed a brief success. This time the backdrop has been modified, the ages of the chief characters have been changed and the players have been called upon to shift their accents from Boston Irish to New York Jewish. There's Jack, the star, still fresh from his immigrant heritage. He's bright, decent, willful and tireless. There's his wife, dark-haired and dark-eyed, with some pretensions to culture and a determination to be self-sufficient. There are the children, handsome and well-mannered. There's the Founding Father, fount of the family ambition. He yearns to lead, but has been thrust aside, as if to conceal his fortune and embarrassing right-wing views. Though the play may never make the bright lights of Pennsylvania Avenue, the writers are busy at work preparing the lines. The cast has been assembled, the angels have readied the money and the producers, cautiously, have begun to look ahead to opening night.

Everett McKinley Dirksen

PIED PIPER OF THE HINTERLAND

It was the morning after my arrival in Pekin, Illinois, that I met with a bunch of Ev Dirksen's old friends at the local newspaper office. These were men he had played ball with, served with in the American Legion, gone out with when he courted his wife. They were nice men, all graying, wearing sport shirts and khaki pants. They seemed content not only that they had spent their lives in the pleasant little town of Pekin but that their old friend Ev, for whom they felt no apparent envy, had gone out into the world to make something of himself.

While we were talking, a much younger man, wearing a black coat and tie and exuding a great intensity, entered the office and was introduced to me as "Ev Dirksen's pastor." I don't even remember his name, but I remember that he took over the conversation immediately. He opened up by saying, "You can't understand Everett Dirksen until you understand something of the Midwestern Calvinism that is so deeply a part of him." It was my cue to move to the edge of the seat. It was exactly what I wanted to hear. I was excited.

UNIVERSITY OF WINNIPEG
LIBRARY
515 PORTAGE AVENUE
WINNIPEG, MAN. R3B 2E9
DISCARDED

The reason I felt that way was that I was then doing the re-search for a book about the influence of the Protestant ethic on the Republican party. The thesis of my book, published in 1968 as Fall From Grace, *was that the Republican Party was an organiza-tion designed, consciously or unconsciously, to maintain the po-litical dominance of old-stock Protestants in American society and that Calvin's Puritan ethic was its political doctrine. What Ev Dirksen's pastor was telling me seemed to confirm all of my theoretical ruminations. It occurred to me at once that the Dirksen profile could very well serve as a trial run for the book.*

I tried the idea out with a draft to Harold Hayes at Esquire. *That was as far as it went. Hayes didn't have anything against Protestants. He was one himself, I suppose. But he wanted a piece on Everett Dirksen as an entertainer. So I rewrote the profile as he wanted it, and I'm sure it made better reading as he proposed it. But if you examine it carefully you'll find that I did slip in some of my weightier observations about the role of Protestant thought in Republican politics, and Hayes didn't mind at all.*

Everett Dirksen, by the way, was a joy to be with during the preparation of the article. It wasn't easy at first to see him. He was just emerging from convalescence, having broken his hip be-fore I went to Pekin. He was, as a consequence, both low in en-ergy and behind in his work. But finally I arranged the interview and, over the course of a few weeks, I met with him several times under the tinkling chandeliers of the Minority Leader's office in the Senate.

Dirksen was a bit more subdued than I had anticipated, doubt-less because of his accident, but he was decent, thoughtful and courteous. I guess I hadn't really wanted to like him quite so much, since I didn't really approve of his politics, but I was drawn to him in spite of myself. Dirksen, as it turned out, also liked the profile, being far too sophisticated to take offense at the various criticisms I made of him. I am not among those who consider Everett Dirksen one of the great men of American political his-tory, but when he died, I felt that the Senate had lost a figure who brought to it not only mirth but warmth, commodities which are forever in short supply there.

POLITICS, like any other sport, demands its heroes. Without them, of whom would the troubadours sing? To whom would the tired common man turn for diversion? Both call out for heroes. Once upon a time, Jack Kennedy answered them, as did two Roosevelts before him. But if real heroes do not exist, the demand is no less rigorous. If they do not exist, the troubadours must create them.

As a hero, Everett McKinley Dirksen is a creation. He is not a great man, though he is a good one. He is not an extraordinary leader, though he is extremely useful. He is not an eminent statesman, though he has made statesmanlike decisions. He is a hero because he is the best of all the available candidates. Not that he is without heroic attributes. Like Willie the Wonder, when he steps before a crowd he generates excitement. He has a capacity to arouse and to absorb. As Minority Leader of the United States Senate, Everett Dirksen holds a rather insubstantial post. But as Oleaginous Ev of Illinois, he is currently the rage of Washington. He is a hero of the political sport.

Admittedly, the competition for the title was not very keen. Lyndon Johnson, whatever may be his capacities, is a non-hero and a bore. Bobby has not quite arrived and Teddy probably never will. Nelson's washed up and Hubert's repressed. Ike, as always, is a disappointment and Barry's gone to pasture. Murphy has missed his cue and Reagan's hasn't come. Fulbright overplays to the boxes, Long to the peanut galleries. Many of the seats in the Senate and House are filled by politicians who are intelligent, lucid and dedicated but few of them are distinguishable in outlook and demeanor from Main Street's prototype businessman. Thus, in a seller's market, the troubadours selected Dirksen as their hero.

For Dirksen the hero's badge has not come easily. He did not start with the casual good looks of a Kennedy, the resources of a Rockefeller, the box-office familiarity of a Murphy or a Reagan, the piercing intellect of a Fulbright, the glib insouciance of a

Long, the Galahadian aura of an Eisenhower, the fervid commitment of a Humphrey or a Goldwater. Ev Dirksen emerged from a desperately poor immigrant family trying to extract a living from the soil of the Illinois prairie. He was big-boned, strong, and loved to work. His intelligence was above average and he had a thirst for reading. He was ambitious and he yearned for some sort of glittering career. As it turned out, the best thing he had going for him was a magnificent set of vocal cords.

Oh, the praise that the troubadours heap on those vocal cords! Each vies with the others to immortalize their prowess. They are "tonsils marinated in honey," writes one. They "blow word rings like smoke," exclaims another. They have earned for their bearer such sobriquets as The Wizard of Ooze, the Chautauqua Hamlet, the Pagliacci of American Politics.

Everett Dirksen's secret is that he, alone among major American politicians, has mastered the technique of translating style into power. What is power? In politics, as in other forms of human endeavor, power is nothing more than the capacity to make one's will prevail. In the United States, its most obvious instrument is public office, which conveys power by consent. The higher the office, of course, the greater the power. But rare is the politician who attains a public office of substantial *inherent* power without first obtaining the *coercive* power of money and organization, instruments of independent force. Everett Dirksen, however, makes his will prevail through neither high office nor money nor organization, but through the *persuasive* power of his style. Such power has an elusive quality, hard to fix in the conventional terms that Washington understands. It is exercised through entertainment and ingratiation. Its symbols are the mask and the oilcan. Dirksen has placed himself on the public marketplace as a comic and won himself a top rating. He has thrust himself, unarmed but for his charm, among the political gladiators and has proved himself a champion. Dirksen's *inherent* power is negligible and his *coercive* power is practically nonexistent. It is astonishing that through the *persuasive* power of an ingenious style Everett Dirksen has become a major force in American politics.

Dirksen, of course, gladly would have swapped his magic for

the automatic power—to say nothing of the glory—of the Presidency. Not surprisingly, the White House has played a prominent place in his dreams. Throughout the 1940's, he tried desperately to persuade Republicans to give him their nomination, if not for the Presidency then for the Vice-Presidency. In another day, his chances would have been better. A Midwestern Republican with big ambitions, humble origins and unexceptional conservative views could reasonably aspire to the Presidency, even though he would have been expected to use its powers sparingly. Dirksen, however, reached maturity after the electoral formula of the long Hayes-McKinley-Hoover era had lost its potency. At seventy, Dirksen's last glimmer of hope for the grand prize has faded. In Washington, where political failure is commonplace, what is unusual about Dirksen is not his frustration but that, given his political hunger, he was not more ruthless in seeking its satisfaction.

It belies Everett Dirksen's ambition that he has behaved throughout his life as if he were indifferent not only to money but to the political wonders it often achieves. To be sure, he, like any candidate, puts the arm on political debtors at campaign time. He admits accepting a thousand or two from "friends" when expenses pile up between campaigns. But, despite allegations, no shred of evidence has ever been produced that he is on the take from any of the industries whose interest he serves in the performance of his Senatorial duties. Not only is he barren of the funds that can swing a close election here, resolve a dispute there, buy some television time somewhere else, he also lives modestly and still makes mortgage payments on the bungalow in Florida to which he may someday retire. Dirksen collects his Senate salary, an annuity from his old law firm in Peoria and an occasional fat speaking fee. But if he's rich, he's managed to conceal it. And if he has money available to augment his power, he's not doing very much about it.

Dirksen has also eschewed the organizational route to gratify his yearnings. Though Republicans are powerful in Illinois, he has never showed much interest in controlling them. After a feeble try for the gubernatorial nomination in 1940, he gave up all notion of running for state office. He leaves his local politicking almost exclusively to his Chicago assistant, a longtime associate named Harold Rainville, whose huge political appetite makes him a freewheeling force in state Republican circles. "I don't get the feeling," said the political editor of one of Chicago's dailies, "that Dirksen is part of the local scene. He's an orator, not an organizer. He has no real influence in Illinois, but not because he can't have it. He just seems to like it that way."

In Washington, one peculiar route to power—independent of money and organization—is seniority. It makes lions out of pussycats, dynamos out of dotards. By 1948, it had promised to make Dirksen—then a veteran of sixteen years in Congress—the most influential Republican in the House. Two years before, the party had won its first House majority since the New Deal. The career prospects for a senior Republican of Dirksen's talents seemed limitless. Then, suddenly, Dirksen surprised Washington by announcing his retirement from politics. The ostensible reason was an eye ailment, which he said threatened to blind him. But in the fall election, he was actively campaigning for the Republican ticket and, by the end of the year, he had announced his intention to run for the Senate. It is, of course, normal for a House member to seek promotion to the Senate. It is less common for him to sacrifice sixteen years of seniority and the likelihood of a fine future for a risky shot at a strong incumbent. In 1950, Dirksen's risk paid off and he started a new political career. But whatever the advantages, it was late at fifty-four to expect seniority to be much help in the quest for power.

Occasionally some figure with neither money nor organization nor seniority achieves substantial power through a quality imprecisely labeled *charisma*. Essential to it appears to be an intensity of conviction, which somehow attracts a large following. Goldwater was such a figure. So was Adlai Stevenson. But Dirksen certainly is not. Dirksen has no intense convictions. He's a Neanderthal conservative by instinct and a twentieth-century pragmatist by expediency. He's a Calvinist who sees politics as a facet of religion but, to balance it, he's a sophisticate who relishes politics for its delights. He exalts individualism and favors the rights of property over the rights of society. But, recognizing that the voting majority of Americans disagree with him, he often defies his own dogmatic certainties and opts painfully for the other side. Dirksen does not find political decisions an easy responsibility. A Chicago paper some years ago figured that he had changed his mind thirty-one times on preparedness, sixty-two times on foreign policy and seventy times on agriculture. He has reversed his position to became a supporter of civil rights and, when he saw he could no longer thwart it, he even voted last year for Medicare. In a panegyric on the subject of foreign aid a few years ago, Dirksen declared, "I remember the day when I used to attack this program. I take it back. Publicly and privately, I take it back." Asked about his political philosophy, Dirksen once said: "I am just an old-fashioned, garden variety of Republican who believes in the Constitution, the Declaration of Independence, in Abraham Lincoln, who accepts the challenges as they arise from time to time and who is not unappreciative of the fact that this is a dynamic economy in which we live and sometimes you have to change your position." Such platitudes, or bits of whimsy, may be Dirksen's apology for his doctrinal dilemma. But they can scarcely be expected to stir the troops with a passion to enlist in his ranks.

Yet, despite his rejection of the trodden paths to power, Everett Dirksen is a force to be reckoned with in the White House, on Capitol Hill and in those stuffy chambers where Republican Party decisions are made. It is Dirksen whose approval President Johnson seeks first in his pursuit of consensus. It is Dirksen to whom Congressional Democrats turn for the word on whether a controversial piece of legislation will pass. It is Dirksen to whom the Republican Party looks—from left, right and center—to heal its self-inflicted wounds. Dirksen's influence is an established fact, even if it is hard to reduce to conventional terms. It is influence that is enveloped in melody, like the Pied Piper's. Dirksen's pipes render words into action, form into substance, style into power.

"I've had an uncommon interest in drama all my life," said a relaxed Dirksen, speaking in the whisper that carries across a room, "I fixed the habit in high school and it persisted. It gave me slightly distorted ambitions. I began to make plans to pursue a theatrical existence, which I confided to my widowed mother. But she had a typical old-country, small-town, puritanistic view of the stage as a wicked domain. She demanded that I assure her right there that I would not essay it as a career. I gave her that assurance but that, of course, did not destroy the urge. I had to appear before people. So I decided on politics."

Young Dirksen interrupted college to sign up for World War I, then returned to his shabby hometown of Pekin to prepare himself for a political career. He was only a baker's helper then but he was an enthusiastic Legionnaire, in those postwar days when the American Legion was the most potent force in Illinois politics. Dirksen's specialty was arranging parties and entertaining at them. Later he cultivated a reputation as a toastmaster and after-dinner speaker. Soon he was volunteering his services to towns nearby, ultimately to groups throughout downstate Illinois. Dirksen would talk to anyone on any subject. One still hears in Pekin how Everett Dirksen dazzled a hardware dealers' convention by a *tour de force* on the history of tools. "It started out that nobody heard of him," said "Peach" Preston, an old Legion buddy who perpetuates Dirksen lore in Pekin, "and ended up that everybody wanted him." A whole crowd of Pekin septuagenarians, including some Democrats, will testify that even forty years ago Everett Dirksen was known for his ability to delight and amuse.

"Those were the trial years," said Dirksen. "I went around studying my techniques. I'd make a sally and see what kind of response it received. Then I'd try another. I particularly watched the audiences. I learned how to appraise an audience—whether it was hostile, friendly or indifferent. The indifferent ones, they're the worst. I learned to make contact with an audience—because if you don't make contact, only a little will be remembered and even less understood. I made a study of people, their attributes and their foibles, what registered with them and what didn't.

"Those were the years when I learned to tell a story. There are very few good storytellers, you know. Most storytellers are too verbose. They're dabblers. They lose their audiences. A good story has a genuine biological effect. If you can get a good sound belly laugh, it starts a blood surge. Your audience might have been tired, its attention was wandering. You come up with a good story and they're back with you. You have to keep stimulating the audience. If it becomes ill at ease, you lose your effectiveness. Many people remember nothing about a speech but the story. I get letters from people asking me to repeat a story they heard me tell years before. It's a great asset to be a storyteller.

"But if I acquired nothing else during those years, it was poise and, let me tell you, poise is transcendent in dealing with an audience. It will dictate the mannerisms, the gestures, the style, the dedication you bring to a speech. The kind of poise I bring to the platform is one of total informality. The stilted and brittle style of another age simply won't do. I'll bet you don't know who Edward Everett was. He's the fellow who delivered the *other* speech at Gettysburg. It was a long speech, written out in great detail. When we think of Gettysburg, we think of Lincoln's few simple but immortal words. Who thinks of Everett? It's the informality that establishes a bond with the audience and allows you to keep it. That, for me, is the real meaning of poise."

Dirksen today is the undisputed master of the informal speech. He disdains a prepared text. He often begins with the ageless trick of holding up the back of an envelope or a laundry ticket and announcing, "I scribbled a few notes on this and out of it will come thousands of words. I wonder what they'll be." From it he draws a guffaw that sets the tone for the rest of the talk. But because he carries only a laundry ticket does not mean that Dirksen goes into a speech unprepared. "Webster said," he notes, "that it took him only a few minutes to prepare for a speech but fifty years to get ready for it. The incubation process is always going on. You never know when a happy thought will strike you." Over the years, of course, Dirksen has acquired more and more material to draw on. "The great handicap of a newcomer," he said, "is that he doesn't have a reservoir of recollection and data committed to memory. I've been dealing with housing bills, for example, since 1934. I don't have to do research on that kind of speech." Dirksen's standard oratory is not characterized by research. On his staff are neither researchers nor speech writers. Dirksen's addresses are a personal thing. They are characterized by reminiscence, literary allusions, Biblical reference. He makes his points by deducing from history rather than from fresh evidence. A Dirksen speech is not elegant when it is read; it is rambling and often repetitious. It has none of the beauty and polish of, say, a Stevenson speech. "My speeches have an immediate purpose," Dirksen maintains. "They are not intended as timeless documents. I have never confronted myself with questions on posterity." Dirksen's objective is to move his audience, whether for votes, for money or just for pleasure. His goal is to generate a reaction on a human-to-human level. Such is the quality of his manner that both friend and foe find themselves reacting with thoroughly uninhibited delight.

Over the years Dirksen has learned to exploit those characteristics which others would treat as liabilities. At seventy, there is nothing boyish left about him. He has none of the dash of the teenage thespian, none of the tone of the high-school athlete, none of the innocence of the young scholar. The hanging jowls give him, in repose, the expression of a faithful basset hound. When he is in action, this excess of flesh becomes the raw material for setting expressions that can be alternately—or even in combination—quizzical, amused, bewildered, astounded, displeased, bored, excited. Dirksen is adroit at shifting the eyebrows over the bright blue eyes or twisting a corner of his copious mouth, as either may suit his purpose. He somehow makes use even of his body which, though six feet or more in height, is soft and round, with loose-hanging arms and legs that magnify its rotundity. Dirksen stands with it at an angle which conveys attention, walks with it in a roll that announces concern, sinks into a chair with it like a sack of potatoes as if to say, "All right, boys, there's the ice. Fill up."

But Dirksen's real triumph is his hair. Though an ignoble gray in color and scraggily thin in texture, it takes on a genuine dignity from the patrician head which is its pedestal. Dirksen's hair is his most evocative stage prop. From the center it grows in undulating curlicues and complex labyrinths to both sides of the head, until it finally takes flight over the ears, like little Cupid wings. Its look is one of fastidious neglect. In contrast to its delicacy are the big, rough, bony, farm-boy hands which Dirksen regularly runs through it as a gesture of distraction. Dirksen's hair, a defiant challenge to contemporary Senate manners, transports its wearer to another age, when Senators were supposed to be flamboyant, to say nothing of eccentric. The hair is to Dirksen what the corncob pipe is to MacArthur, the beard to Castro, the derby to Chaplin.

Dirksen's horn-rimmed glasses are another prop; so is the diamond ring that he wears, usually askew, on his little finger. His clothes became a prop only a few years ago when, having lost on doctor's orders some fifty pounds, he found how useful to his purpose ill-fitting suits could be.

Dirksen, naturally, is resourceful enough to turn to his histrionic ends whatever new opportunities thrust themselves upon him. When he broke his thigh last spring, he had the choice of playing the crochety cripple or the gay convalescent. He didn't hesitate to choose the latter. In recent months, Dirksen has performed happily as the wounded Achilles, with confident laugh and stiff upper lip. Rolling merrily on his wheelchair through the corridors of the Capitol, he acknowledges the cheers of the crowd with a modest wave of the hand or a discreet tip of the cane.

But whatever the props that Dirksen manipulates, they are all but a foil for the Dirksen voice. Ah, the voice! Surely the great Webster could not boast an instrument of such beauty and virtuosity. It can be a solo flute or a symphony orchestra, a call to love or to battle, a weapon to flay or to beguile, but always to fascinate, to captivate, to mesmerize. Its rhythm—slow and deliberate, like a Beethoven second movement—is under the perfect control of its conductor. His timing is as hypnotic as a metronome, his pauses refresh, his phrasing is precise, his nuances tap the widest range of emotions. The natural habitat of the Dirksen voice is the lower depths of the octave but if called upon it can sound any note. Its natural volume is modest but not because it cannot swell, if commanded, to a Wagnerian pitch. Rarely, however, does it need to. The master breathes like a diva and the voice throbs, pulsates, vibrates from deep within his caverns to cover vast audiences, to penetrate huge auditoriums.

"Shortly after Jack Kennedy was nominated," Dirksen relates, "and while he was preparing for the hustings, he came over to me and said, 'You know, Ev, there's one thing that bothers me. I'm afraid I'm going to lose my voice.' I said to him, 'Jack'—he was a fellow Senator and I could talk familiarly with him—'Jack,' I said, 'you *will* lose your voice. You constantly talk off your cords. You must talk out of your diaphragm. If I were you, I'd pick up the best voice teacher in town. Three or four lessons and you'll be taught to let your voice come out of your belly.' And, by golly, that's what Jack did and he never had any trouble after that."

If there is anything that has saved Dirksen, with all his style, from being a plain old windbag, it is a certain perspective on himself. In an atmosphere inhospitable to Midwestern Republicanism, Dirksen's unique capacity to satirize himself comprises an essential part of the heroic image. Dirksen would be a stylistic failure if his entertainment depended on the gag, the clever repartee, a stab of ridicule, the exquisite thrust of wit. Dirksen, in fact, is not witty with words. His phrases are rather banal. His metaphors are familiar and often clichés. His stories are clean and wholesome and he has never been known to tell an off-color joke. Dirksen's humor is endearing because its subject matter is inherently fascinating. The fun that Dirksen makes is of an old-fashioned politician, a claghorn, a caricature, a prototype of the Senator as it has come down through American folklore. The fun he makes is of Dirksen. He is one of the rare souls who sees himself as others see him—which enables him, with his own gentle mockery, to beat others to the critical punch.

Satire dominates Dirksen's oratory. His typical speech begins with what its maker refers to as a "felicitous introduction." It is liberally laced with erudite quotations, most of them astonishingly accurate, from such authorities as Lincoln and Jefferson, Shakespeare and St. Paul, Wordsworth and Burke. It contains long, didactic sentences ("President Monroe said that Congress was really the seat or center of the government, meaning of course that virtually all the powers of government, whether for the Judicial Branch or for the Executive Branch, stem from the action by the Congress"), rendered palatable only by the seductive delivery. It is marked by such pretensions as "essay" for "try," "abode" for "home" and "discommode" for "inconvenience." It is illustrated at regular intervals by pithy stories, usually humorous and loving expositions of human foibles. Most of all, it is characterized by a confidence that permits its maker to say whatever comes to his mind without fear of making himself ridiculous. It is characterized by total poise.

"I remember the man," Dirksen told the Senate, in a speech inveighing against the national debt, "who was on the wrong floor of the hospital in Peoria. He was on the floor where the baby ward was. There were little tykes squalling and bawling. The nurse came out. She had a long, dour countenance. When she got close to him, the fellow said, 'Nurse, what makes all the little brats squall and bawl the way they do?' The nurse, remembering the portion of the national debt for the baby was about $1,971, said, 'Well, Mister, if you were out of work, if you owed $1,971 as your share of the debt and if your pants were wet, you would squall, too!' "

Another time, complaining of the complexities of a particular piece of legislation, Dirksen said, "I think I am like the bureaucrat downtown whom a constituent of mine went to see. When he got through talking, he looked at the button the bureaucrat had on his coat and asked him, 'What do those letters BAIK mean?' The bureaucrat said, 'They stand for "Boy, am I confused." ' The constituent said, 'You do not spell confused with a K.' The bureaucrat said, 'You don't know how confused we are.' "

A few years ago, while in the hospital receiving treatment for one of his periodic ailments, Dirksen composed a speech to complain about the rejection of Republican amendments to a series of tax reforms which President Johnson had proposed to spur the national economy. "We Republicans," he said, "are very literal, and frequently literate, people. When we read perfectly plain English we are invariably led into taking it at face value. If we read that capital investment should be encouraged, consumer purchasing power should be stimulated, that consumers should be protected, or, for example, that higher education should be encouraged, who can censure us—except possibly for our innocence—for believing that any proposals we might make to foster these ends would not receive White House approval, even active support? So perhaps you can understand my bedridden amazement, my pajama-ruffled consternation, yes, my pill-laden astonishment this week to learn that three Republican-sponsored proposals to assist in achieving these laudable goals had been defeated by very narrow margins, victims of that new White House telephonic half-Nelson known as the 'Texas-twist.' "

Probably no Dirksen speech is as famous as the one he periodically delivers, with substantial variations, in behalf of designating the marigold the national flower. It invariably draws a crowd to the Senate floor, although the designation of a national flower is scarcely the kind of issue that evokes deep partisan zeal. The Senators come for the show. What other grown man in America would have the courage, as Dirksen did in 1963, to speak the following lines?

The rather cold and distressing weather which has enveloped the earth has doubtless made people conjecture as to whether spring would ever come. I find great comfort in the lines of Shelley: "If winter comes, can spring be far behind?"

So, unless some supernal force disturbs the procession of the seasons, there will be a spring; and when spring comes, there will be flowers. We shall be delighted with the earlier flowers—the tulips, the daffodils, the redbud and the dogwood blossoms.

A little later will come all the delightful annual flowers, which nature compels us to cultivate every year, but leaves a residue of seed which makes them almost perpetual. They will include the humble but beautiful petunia, the zinnia and the calendula, and also the marigold.

Two or three years ago, I introduced a joint resolution to make the marigold the national flower. That stirred quite a controversy; and, as a result, the corn tassel and the rose and other flowers were advanced as candidates for our national floral emblem.

But I still find myself wedded to the marigold—robust, rugged, bright, stately, single-colored and multicolored, somehow able to resist the onslaught of insects; it takes in its stride extreme changes in temperature, and fights back the scorching sun in summer and the chill of early spring evenings. What a flower the marigold is! I am looking forward to the time when these gay flowers will salute and intrigue our sense of beauty.

So, once more I find myself impelled to introduce a joint resolution to make the American marigold—its botanical name is *Tagetes erecta*—the national flower of our country.

When Dirksen finished, the Senate—normally surfeited with words—still had not had enough. Mike Mansfield, the Majority Leader, rose to move that fifteen more minutes of a busy day be granted "in view of the extraordinarily exhilarating speech the distinguished Minority Leader is making." Dirksen responded:

O, I shall not take fifteen minutes, because it takes only a moment for one to express the sense that is in his heart about the beauty of flowers. I remember what Wordsworth wrote in his poem on the daffodils: "Ten thousand saw I at a glance,/ Tossing their heads in a sprightly dance."

In those two lines Wordsworth captured a sentiment which probably I could not capture if I took not only the fifteen minutes allowed me, but even much more time, in order to extol the grace, the beauty, and the loveliness of that flower. . . . So, in order to make sure that our discriminating public will have a chance to evaluate the importance of the matter . . . I humbly submit the marigold.

In the annual marigold speech, Dirksen is at his carefree best. More often, however, he is not carefree but somber in his humor.

The subjects that most frequently recur in his speeches seem somehow related to death and illness. It is as if Dirksen, like Chaplin, understood that humor, to have real dimension, must be enriched by pathos. More typical than the marigold is the story Dirksen told one day to protest the befogging of an appropriations bill. "I am reminded," he said, "of the man who filled in an application for an insurance policy. One of the questions he had to answer was, 'How old was your father when he died and of what did he die?' Well, his father had been hanged but he did not like to put that in his application. He puzzled over it for quite a while. He finally wrote, 'My father was sixty-five when he died. He came to his end while participating in a public function when the platform gave way.' . . . I like to see language in the bill that the taxpayer can understand." Thus Dirksen obtained his laugh, but not before he had evoked some sympathy for the human condition.

To Dirksen, pathos comes naturally, for beneath his surface lies the grim Calvinism which leaves him uncertain about his own salvation and pessimistic about society's. At the same time, there is working relentlessly within him a notorious hypochondria, which complements his chronic ill health and makes him see tragedy in every ache, drama in every pain. A sense of the flimsiness of human well-being, of the nearness of human misery is always close to Dirksen. Several years ago, he regaled the Senate with a story that twitted for his half-truths the Majority Leader, Lyndon B. Johnson, who was never one of his favorites in Washington. "It is like," Dirksen said, "the man who fell off the twentieth floor of a building. As he passed the sixth floor, a friend of his shouted to him, 'Mike, so far you are all right.' " Dirksen is a man who is acutely aware of life's constant flirtation with death.

It is no coincidence that the smile is not one of Everett Dirksen's stage props. He abjures the device, dear to a Nixon, of exposing the teeth. He is sparing in reacting to his own humor, as John Kennedy used to do. Dirksen plays his satire straight, lugubriously, like the deadpan Chaplin. His solemnity affirms that, while funny, he is far from frivolous. Dirksen is a serious man whose humor is meant to purvey his personal brand of truth. He conveys the Calvinist dogma that man's fate is in God's hands and that government ought not interfere with it. But at the same time, he reflects a gentleness which softens his somber outlook on life and/or the world.

Everett Dirksen, whatever his indifference to social man, deeply dislikes hurting people. He is kind to his wife, to his staff, to the Senate pages, to the family he left so far behind in Pekin. On the platform, he subdues hecklers with kindness. In the Senate, he kills with kindness. It is this fundamental gentleness, he says, which always stood between him and the acquisition of political power through organization and money. "I cringe when I see the way some men talk to their underlings," he said. Dirksen is a tough political partisan who knows that he must inflict punishment to win battles, but his technique—to the distress of the gut fighters on his team—is rarely, if ever, directed at inflicting pain on an opponent. "I make it a practice never to demean a man, no matter what kind of bloke he is," Dirksen explains. He has followed the dictum in campaigns and in dealing with such diverse political associates as Joe McCarthy, Lyndon Johnson and Dwight Eisenhower. Even among those who bitterly disagree with his politics, it is conceded that Everett Dirksen is a decent human being who would rather do a good turn any day than an evil one.

Dirksen himself, who has so often drunk the bitter herbs of defeat, likes to tell how he was magnanimous in victory last year after he almost singlehandedly turned the Senate against Frank Morrissey, Teddy Kennedy's dubious candidate for a Federal judgeship. It was the only glitter the Republicans had acquired in the entire Congressional session. "When Teddy came over to tell me he was going to withdraw the nomination," Dirksen relates, "he had tears in his eyes. I could have made enemies forever of the Kennedys. Then Bobby walked across the chamber and said, 'Could you say a good word about Teddy? He feels terrible.' Well, of course, I could. So I talked about Teddy's courage as a freshman Senator in withdrawing that name. Instead of an enemy, I made a friend." Another politician might have gloated over the episode and exploited it for its maximum partisan advantage. To Dirksen, it is uncertain whether there was more satisfaction in his victory or in his making the friend.

Dirksen expressed the feeling of camaraderie which he exudes toward his Senate colleagues in a remark some years ago on the floor. During a particularly intense barrage of public criticism over the paralyzing nature of the Senate's "club" system, Dirksen said: "I am always delighted to think of the Senate as a club, because it seems to me the Senate functions effectively and functions earnestly if we never quite lose the 'clubby' spirit. We can become very angry and at times, I suppose, so intolerant of one another, but I remember the almost iridescent line written by the great sales manager of Christianity [Dirksen venerates the American businessman as the truest specimen of Calvinist individualism], the Apostle Paul, who said: 'Let your forbearance be known in the sight of men.' Nothing can quite equal that line, because this is an arena in which tolerance and forbearance are so urgently necessary." It is no exaggeration to say that Dirksen, in the practice and the preaching of forbearance, thinks of himself as the Apostle Paul's vicar on Capitol Hill.

Dirksen has his own epigram for interpreting the power he exercises over men. "The oil can is mightier than the sword," he says. He keeps an oil can on his desk, not as a reminder—which he does not need—but as a kind of official seal. Dirksen is not called Oleaginous Ev for nothing. There is no doubt that the oil is an element vital to the Dirksen power machine. With a bare minimum of coercive tools, he exercises his will. He is able to do so because politicians—softened by his ideological flexibility—are willing to respond affirmatively to his pleas, to listen to him and follow him, to be persuaded when he seeks to prevail. Unlike other leaders, Dirksen does not command by invoking fear, legal authority or the prospect of reward. He commands by wielding the oil can. He commands, in obedience to Paul, through forbearance. At his best, he commands through love.

What Dirksen's oil can cannot achieve, his comedy often can— but no one knows better than Dirksen that his comedy, to serve its purpose, must reach a wide audience. For this, he needs the troubadours. Though the Dirksen style, more or less spontaneously, has generated a cult in Washington, it would mean nothing to Dirksen's national stature if the press were not intrigued. Dirksen is generous to the troubadours. He has made their labors easy and pleasant. He is quotable if not original, plentiful if not profound. He seldom refuses an interview. He appears freely for press conferences and, even if he has nothing to say, his manner of saying it makes good copy. Dirksen talks to the troubadours by their first names, with a sincerity normally reserved for intimates. And troubadours, too, respond to the oil. Barely a day passes that they do not gild the already golden image, over radio and TV, in newspapers and magazines.

To a politician, being a hero means nothing more exciting than network time, top billing, lead pieces, big headlines. Who transmits the message of the Republican opposition more widely than Dirksen? What other functioning Republican does the public know so well? Who could buy advertising as good as that which Everett Dirksen, for himself and the party, gets for free? With Dirksen the effective Republican spokesman, whom must the Democrats placate and please? For whom would a Republican candidate, anxious for voter approval, feel more gratitude? Without Dirksen, the Republican Party's access to the voters would be substantially diminished. One often hears the complaint that the Presidential office, by its inherent power, monopolizes the channels of communication. Everett Dirksen is its competitor, by virtue of his style. His success helps make his will prevail.

The Dirksen style, then, is a beautiful machine. It is complex, to be sure, but its pieces fit harmoniously with one another. The theatrics are linked to the ambition, the self-satire to the theatrics, the gentleness to the self-satire, the ambition to the gentleness. It is a curious combination to spell P-O-W-E-R, but its range is enormous.

When Dirksen speaks on Vietnam, Johnson listens and often acts. When he talks on civil rights, the Attorney General and the movement know he's got the votes. When he tells Mike Mansfield that he wants a bill rewritten in such and such a way, chances are that it will be rewritten, if it is to pass at all. Dirksen, of course, is not capable of the impossible in the exercise of power. He is, after all, the leader of only a weak minority, in the Senate and in the country. He cannot overcome the burden of vastly inferior numbers. But he is the only general of Republican troops who consistently brings home victories.

In the long run, perhaps it is within the party itself that Everett Dirksen's influence will prove most significant. As a party man, he's at the disadvantage of having neither money nor organization. But he has a fat portfolio of political debts, accumulated for his party services. Republicans know that Dirksen, at seventy, will not draw from this portfolio to propel himself into higher office. With his motives above mistrust, Oleaginous Ev is free to play the elder statesman who wants nothing more than to crown his political career by saving the party he loves and which, to many, appears destined to oblivion.

"Everett's everybody's friend," said Kentucky's Senator Thruston Morton, a man of the political right. "He's one of the few who think about others in this party. He'll campaign for any Republican. He doesn't care about ideology. He's a Republican and he's the best we've got."

"Ev's got something for everybody," said New York's Senator Jacob Javits, a man of the political left. "He thinks of himself as Big Daddy. In a party like ours, without its own ideology, he can step in where others can't. Let's face it, he's all we Republicans have got in common."

In a party bitterly riven, Dirksen is unquestionably the only member who has the esteem and confidence of both right and left. He is the bridge between factions, the linchpin of the party mechanism, the emissary of conciliation. "You have to have the charm of Barrymore and the wisdom of Solomon to keep this party together," Dirksen said. "I've got to talk some of these people into making sacrifices. I don't suppose there's anyone else who can make them sit down at the table together and try to work something out. I'm not sure I can myself. But I'm trying."

Joseph L. Rauh, Jr.

DIRTY WHITE LIBERAL

When I first came to Washington as a green newspaper reporter in the mid-1950's, I knew the reputation of Joe Rauh as a fighter against McCarthyism, a pioneer in civil rights, the spark of the liberal A.D.A. When I met Joe Rauh, I found a man of deep conviction, uncompromising rhetoric and great energy. As a human being, he was no disappointment to me, either. Joe Rauh became my friend then, and I am proud that he is my friend now. I consider him, perhaps along with Ralph Nader, as one of the few secular saints of our time.

You can imagine my surprise then, to say nothing of my bewilderment, when some of my activist civil rights acquaintances a few years ago suddenly began to use "Joe Rauh" as a dirty word and "white liberal" as a scathing denunciation. Maybe I was behind the times, but I didn't know what they were talking about. I wondered whether there was a strain of evil in Joe that had, over the years, somehow eluded me.

One day shortly afterward, I received a phone call from Mark Baldwin, managing editor of the Washingtonian, *a magazine that had been founded a few years before and was stumbling along in search of an identity. Mark, a very young man, had been hired because he seemed to have a clearer vision than most about what a magazine should be. He invited me to lunch and asked whether there was anything I would be interested in writing for him. All I could think of at the time was my puzzlement over why my friend Rauh had become anathema among people with whom I was thoroughly in sympathy. Normally I would not have thought it right to do a profile of a good friend. Professionally, I can live with my political prejudices, but it's another thing to live with my personal attachments. I was genuinely curious, however, and I wanted to find out what made Joe Rauh, in those eyes, nothing but a "dirty white liberal."*

I'll give you a hint of the plot by announcing that now, four years later, it's a lot easier to understand what was going on then. I think even those who were deeply in the movement sensed only dimly that what was afoot was a major shift in leadership from whites to blacks or, to take it further along, from white liberals to black militants. Joe Rauh, who was as uncertain as anyone about what was happening, has since come to understand it, too. He is no longer a leader in the civil rights battle, although he continues to fight for civil rights legislation on Capitol Hill. He remains as dedicated as ever to liberal causes and, if he is out of sympathy with all violence, he is no less committed to the movement's goals. But he knows that the day is over for a white liberal to stand as the recognizable symbol of the campaign for black emancipation. And happily, in my view, some of those very acquaintances of mine who freely denounced Joe Rauh four or five years ago no longer feel resentment toward him. The last time the subject came up in my presence within movement circles, my acquaintances were saying what a swell guy Joe was because he was so willing to help them, without demanding to be repaid in public gratitude or real authority.

JOE RAUH'S break with the Black Power wing of the civil rights movement happened at the Democratic Convention at Atlantic City in August 1964. It's only in retrospect, however, that it becomes clear that this was the dividing line. Nobody talked about Black Power then. Whatever the ferment was, it didn't yet have a name. There were some stubborn Negroes from Mississippi who seemed unable to recognize a good deal when the President of the United States offered it to them. Joe Rauh, who was their lawyer, thought they ought to take it. So there was a dispute, which became bitter, and Rauh wound up a kind of symbol of one segment of the civil rights movement. Black Power wound up the symbol of the other. And the fight's been getting worse ever since.

Rauh went to Atlantic City wearing several hats, but there was nothing extraordinary—at least for Rauh—in that. He was—and is—a one-man interlocking directorate of liberal organizations. For years, he had been deeply immersed in liberal politics and given his loyalty to a hundred liberal causes. For years, these causes seemed somehow part of a coherent philosophy—though, on closer examination, one might have found that what they had in common was that their champions labored for them in vain. It never occurred to Joe Rauh that there could be a conflict between his various liberal commitments. Some maintain that he arrived in Atlantic City wearing too many hats. But Rauh believed simply that he had come well armed for battle.

In approximate order of importance, Joe Rauh attended the Democratic National Convention of 1964 playing the following roles:

• Head of the District of Columbia delegation and, as such, a member of the Credentials Committee.

• Attorney for the Mississippi Freedom Democratic Party (MFDP), which was making an appeal before the Credentials Committee to unseat and replace the regular lily-white Mississippi delegation.

• Intimate friend (and presumed spokesman) of Hubert H. Humphrey, would-be nominee for the Vice Presidency and, as such, a dependent upon the good grace of Lyndon Johnson.

• General Counsel for the United Auto Workers of Walter Reuther, who sympathized with the claims of MFDP but strongly supported the President.

• Legal counsel for the Leadership Conference of Civil Rights, an umbrella organization encompassing virtually any group with an interest in racial equality.

• Vice Chairman for Civil Rights of Americans for Democratic Action, the liberal organization which, since 1948, had led the fight for civil rights within the Democratic Party.

Each day, Joe Rauh would enter Convention Hall in his delegate's hat to take his seat on the Credentials Committee, switch to his MFDP hat to argue for his client, change to his Humphrey hat to hear the requirements of practical politics, put on his Reuther hat to get the thinking of the White House, don his Leadership Conference hat to talk business with the Wilkinses and the Kings, then slip on his ADA hat to report to the liberal delegates who looked to him for direction on civil rights matters. Joe Rauh's wardrobe of headgear unquestionably made him one of the powerful men at the convention. And nothing pleased Rauh more than to use this power in behalf of a cause in which he believed.

When the convention opened, no one gave Rauh's MFDP a black man's hope in a lynch party. What chance did a band of renegades, many of them with the dirt of the cotton field still on their shoes, have against the duly elected Mississippi delegation— no matter how hard they argued that it was duly elected in local conventions from which Negroes were excluded? But MFDP was not without assets. The year 1964 was a good year for civil rights, when the Deep South was Goldwater country anyway and many Democrats thought it was good riddance if Mississippi walked out. The Mississippi regulars themselves unwittingly helped the cause, blustering over television about their racial obsession and behaving as if they were a burlesque on red-neck white supremacists.

Rauh marshaled his forces astutely, extracting the most from television by having his clients tenderly recount their most searing experiences under the white lash. In the Credentials Committee, he had barely a dozen votes out of 110 and he obviously couldn't win. But he had the exalting memory of another Democratic Convention twelve years before when, at the head of a small band of dissidents, he forced a floor vote and won a strong civil rights plank, to the dismay of Harry Truman and the old-line party leadership. Though the odds were even more heavily against him in 1964, Rauh was ready to bring the civil rights fight to the convention floor again.

Lyndon Johnson wanted no fight to mar his party's unity. He wanted consensus, flawlessly expressed. He knew he faced trouble and he finally had to acknowledge that compromise was his only hope of getting out of it. After four days of bitter argument, Johnson passed down the word that MFDP was not to go home empty-handed. The white Mississippians could retain their seats, he ordered, only if they pledged their loyalty to the party—which was virtually the same as their being unseated, since they had already indicated they would make no pledge to a party committed to civil rights. Johnson agreed, furthermore, to give MFDP two seats at-large and the promise that never again would a lily-white Mississippi delegation be admitted to the Democratic Convention. Unquestionably the Johnson deal meant a moral victory for MFDP, as well as a strategic triumph for Joe Rauh.

Lyndon Johnson, let it be noted, was no friend of Joe Rauh's. The two men had behind them a series of unpleasant encounters that dated back to the early 1950's, when Johnson first attained prominence in the Senate. For Joe Rauh's taste, Johnson was far too tolerant of Joe McCarthy. He was also too Southern. In 1957, after Johnson became Majority Leader, the two men clashed over the Eisenhower civil rights bill, which Johnson acted first to weaken, then to pass. "To give the devil his due," Rauh says now, "he got us the first civil rights bill since Reconstruction, but he also took out its teeth." At the Democratic National Convention in 1960, Joe Rauh waged a fiery, if brief, revolution against Johnson's vice-presidential candidacy. When he learned of Johnson's selection, he arose angrily on the convention floor, grabbed a microphone, and declared before the television cameras: "Wherever you are, John F. Kennedy, I beseech you to reconsider." Rauh never quite forgave Kennedy for what he considered an act of betrayal of the liberals, nor did Johnson ever quite forgive Rauh. After the assassination, Johnson, in his efforts to win the allegiance of the party's liberals, began to court Rauh, who was surprised to find himself the frequent object of warm presidential attention. While Johnson was giving consideration to the vice-presidential ambition of Hubert Humphrey—Rauh's fellow founder of ADA and comrade of countless political battles—Rauh certainly wanted to do nothing to disrupt the new harmony. Beneath the patina of cordiality, however, it was clear Lyndon Johnson and Joe Rauh distrusted and disliked each other as much as ever.

So, when word of the President's compromise plan came down on the fourth day of the wrangling, Rauh was not at all sure that he had obtained the best possible bargain. The power balance had shifted dramatically since the opening sessions. MFDP had clearly won the sympathy of both the country and the convention delegates. Rauh was tempted to negotiate further, but now he was subject to a host of conflicting pressures. Humphrey and Reuther both desperately wanted him to accept the Johnson plan. The response of the convention delegates suggested that, in a floor vote, the compromise would be overwhelmingly approved. Rauh went to Martin Luther King, Roy Wilkins of NAACP, and James Farmer of CORE, and found that they, too, favored acceptance. As for the MFDP leadership, it was sharply divided, with Aaron Henry, the nominal chairman, inclined to follow the lead of the major civil rights leaders. Weighing all the alternatives, Rauh finally decided that he, too, would go along and recommend to the MFDP representatives that they consent to the deal and take their two seats on the convention floor.

But just as Rauh made the choice to put his weight behind the compromise, the militants within MFDP—led by a brilliant and magnetic young Negro named Bob Moses—made their bid. Moses, a few days before, had seemed willing to settle for a moral victory, but now he was calling for full recognition of MFDP's claims. After a long session of speech-making at a Negro church in downtown Atlantic City, the Moses wing emerged dominant over the moderates. Deaf to the pleas of the other civil rights heads, Moses announced that MFDP would accept nothing less than its original demand for all of Mississippi's seats. Then Moses strode before the television cameras aligned outside the church and declared to the country that the Democratic Party was racist to the core and that Joe Rauh and all the other liberals who favored compromise had sold MFDP out. Empty-handed by its own choice, the Mississippi Freedom Democratic Party went home.

"Maybe Moses was right in rejecting the compromise," said Rauh recently, musing on history. "Maybe he needed the issue to go back with to Mississippi if he had any hope of organizing the Negroes in the state. I can see that rejection might have had a perfectly legitimate, long-term political purpose. But this purpose could have been achieved without Moses' accusing me and the liberals of betrayal.

"I finally recommended acceptance because I concluded that it was the best arrangement MFDP could get. King and Wilkins and Farmer agreed. So did many of the members of the MFDP. Sure, I was getting heat from Walter, in behalf of the President, but I wasn't working for him and I wasn't working for Hubert. As MFDP's counsel, I was giving the best advice I could. The outcome was far better than anyone had expected a week before. What I resent is the way that Moses turned on me after it was over.

"I have no way of knowing if there was an ulterior purpose to his actions. But his denunciation was a turning point. After that, the civil rights movement started going in two different directions."

At fifty-five, Joe Rauh finds it rather ironic and just a little bewildering to be a whipping boy within the segment of the civil rights movement that is moving in the other direction. He has devoted a lifetime to the cause of civil rights. In the years after the war, he and his friends founded ADA and, from the forum it provided, he kept civil rights alive as an issue before the American people. As much as any man, he bled during the battle in which control of the Democratic Party was ultimately wrested from Southern hands. In 1957, he was the chief lobbyist for the first of the civil rights bills of this generation and in 1960, he was the head strategist in the vain struggle to amend Rule 22 and end the destructive power of the filibuster. During the Thousand Days he pressed John Kennedy relentlessly to take up the cause of racial equality and he was one of the architects of the Civil Rights Act of 1964, the greatest of the equality measures. For weeks this year, he made the pilgrimage daily to Capitol Hill to argue for the 1966 civil rights bill. Joe Rauh, it can be fairly said, had good reason to believe he had won his medals fairly in the civil rights war.

Throughout this long war, Joe Rauh's only popular power base has been in the District of Columbia. Back in 1947, he and a group of his friends filed a suit to get on the ballot in a primary against the incumbents of the Democratic Central Committee. For years the local machine had kept Washington a rotten borough, responsive only to the command of the party's national leadership. Decadent and lethargic, the machine proved an easy target for the Rauh crowd. On their first try, they won control not only of the Central Committee but also of the delegation to the Democratic National Convention. Since 1948, Joe Rauh has been the undisputed power behind the local Democratic organization, although it is only in recent years that he has become its titular chief. Rauh made the local party an instrument in the fight for Home Rule, school integration, and other civil rights objectives. It was he who extracted from the local organization the mandate to fight for the civil rights plank at the National Convention of 1948 and for MFDP at the convention of 1964. As leader of the city's dominant party, Joe Rauh is, quite literally, the highest elected official in the District of Columbia. He has used his power decently, he believes, in order to make the District a better place for both its whites and Negroes.

"What most people today don't understand," Rauh explained,

"is that twenty years ago this was an absolutely segregated city. You couldn't go to a movie, a hotel, a restaurant which wasn't segregated. I remember one night, when I had just won a case for Phil Randolph, we couldn't even go out to have a drink together to celebrate and Phil, with his great dignity, simply said, 'Goodnight, Joe, we'll make it another time.' This was the most legally segregated Southern bastard of a town in the whole United States.

"The break came in 1947, when a group of liberal organizations started a campaign and the first target was the National Theater. I remember that the local ADA chapter was assigned Friday nights. Every Friday we'd go out and have dinner, then spend the last hour before curtain time walking it off on a picket line in front of the National. I remember getting calls from some of my friends—I guess most of them were liberals—advising me to lay off. That was the beginning of 'white backlash.' We didn't lay off and, after a few months, we busted the National. Then the movies followed, and the restaurants and the hotels, and finally, with some help from Eisenhower, the schools. Now, as a result of pressure I helped apply, we even have a fair housing ordinance here.

"I point all this out because the people who say that nothing has changed really don't know what they're talking about and they hurt my feelings. I don't maintain that the poor Negro in the slums is living any better than he did, but the legal situation is totally different. A massive economic change for poor people has not taken place, but this city is nothing like it was."

Perhaps it is the very facts which Joe Rauh cites—that the law has been tamed, though poverty has not—which persuades many civil rights activists that the day of the Rauhs is done. After two decades of persistent labor in the vineyards of civil rights, Joe Rauh finds himself derided as nothing more than a "white liberal," as if being a white liberal is far from enough. The struggle for racial equality, say Rauh's detractors, must henceforth be fought in those slums that have been untouched by law. The objective of the civil rights worker, they say, is not to mobilize Congressmen or convention delegates or Central Committeemen but poor Negroes from the city's vast expanses of ghetto, so they can exercise the rights and powers that are theirs as Americans and as humans.

"Joe Rauh's been in the game a long time," said Julius Hobson, one of the city's most militant and most sensitive civil rights activists, "and he's concerned himself with what he should concern himself. I think he has a genuine belief in civil rights. I feel that any man who comes out and does work in an area of social welfare is better than a man who stays home. But Joe Rauh's not close enough to the black people to appreciate their problems. He's a political boss and, by definition, he's a compromiser. The civil rights bills that he helped to pass fill up the archives but they don't do anything for the poor Negro.

"The white liberal today ought to stay out of Negro affairs. Negroes don't trust them. I'm not saying that's right. I'm just saying it is. The poor Negro needs self-esteem and self-respect and, as a Negro, I might be able to help him because he doesn't distrust me. The white liberals ought to be working in the white communities—where black men have no influence—to change the attitude of the storekeepers, the apartment house managers, and the others who exploit the Negro. That's a big enough job for the white liberal.

"The trouble with Joe Rauh and his crowd is that they drain off energy from what really has to be done."

Another civil rights militant, a mild-mannered minister who becomes aroused when he talks of Negro needs, was far less charitable about Rauh. He said this:

"Joe's from another century. He's a Rudyard Kipling kind of guy. Like Mayor Daley, he doesn't understand the mood of this generation. There's no doubt in my mind that he'd like to be part of it. I don't question his sincerity. But he grossly misunderstands the deep feelings of Negroes today, their desperate desire to do things for themselves. Joe's an old-fashioned political tyrant. He pushes a button and he wants you to jump."

When confronted by the views of his critics, Joe Rauh stops a minute to reflect, and a look of puzzlement flashes briefly across his face. It is hard for him to contemplate whether there is truth in what they say.

"I can't believe I'm that insensitive to people," he said, "but since I first heard about this hostility to the 'white liberal,' I've been surprised. Now I know the feeling is there. I guess I've been aware for five or six years that the 'Black Power' outlook exists. But I find it hard to grasp. I'm incapable of doing it justice."

It is noteworthy that Rauh's critics from within the civil rights movement question not his convictions but his methods. Rauh himself has no regrets. He has the feeling that he has done decent things. Joe Rauh has an acute sense of social justice, a sympathy for the underdog, and a willingness to brawl to achieve worthy ends. Few political bosses—if a boss he is—can be as highly motivated. Joe Rauh, even in the eyes of his critics, has given himself generously to enriching society. If he is not a man of the people, he has demonstrated, at least, that he is consistently for them.

It is hard to say where Joseph L. Rauh, Jr., acquired these convictions of his. He was born and raised in Cincinnati, son of an immigrant Jew who prospered as a small industrialist. Among Jews, those from Germany are considered the aristocracy. Among Jewish Americans, those who name a son "junior" are regarded as terribly assimilated. Rauh's father, in fact, was even a Republican. But, whatever the family signs may mean, it is certain that Joe Rauh was brought up in a totally secure environment, in which he worried about neither money nor status. On the negative side, it has made Rauh almost smug, too little given to introspection, perhaps excessively sure of himself. But on the other hand, he is without the traces of anxiety that show on the faces of those who are ill-at-ease about their place in society. Joe Rauh is one of those rare men who seem completely comfortable in their own skin. However he acquired his political views and however unpopular they have sometimes been, Rauh has never been assailed by self-doubt or irresolution.

Though he continues to acknowledge his kinship with Judaism and belongs to a synagogue, Joe Rauh is a completely secular man. He sometimes attends religious services but is unmoved by religious feeling. It is significant that Joe Rauh's principal religious affirmation is his membership on the Social Action Commission of Reformed Judaism, which has served as just one more forum from which to fight for civil liberties and civil rights. "Joe's a good humanist," said the Rabbi of his synagogue. "Judaism to him means social justice. Otherwise, he doesn't function as a Jew."

From Cincinnati, Rauh went to Harvard, where he graduated from the College in 1932 and from the Law School three years later. Shortly after he passed the bar, he married Olie Westheimer, a tall attractive blonde who, like him, came from a distinguished German-Jewish family but who, unlike him, tends to shyness and reserve. In the years between graduation and the war, Rauh served as law clerk for Supreme Court Justices Benjamin Cardozo and Felix Frankfurter and as a lawyer for various New Deal agencies. During the war, he was assigned to General MacArthur's staff in the Pacific and, after the liberation of the Philippines, became the unofficial "mayor" of Manila, responsible for restoring the economy and public services of a city that had suffered through four years of enemy occupation. Rauh returned to Washington for another turn at Government service in 1946 but decided, soon afterward, that he'd had enough. Through three Democratic administrations, Rauh has refrained from taking a Government post and, to this day, exercises his power through a variety of relationships he has established as a private lawyer.

From the start, Rauh's law practice has served as an outlet for his political convictions. He became counsel for Philip Randolph's Brotherhood of Sleeping Car Porters and won some important legal victories for Negro labor. During the Red Scare, he defended the targets of loyalty and security investigations, congressional persecution, and public libel. Rauh won landmark decisions in the Watkins and Kutcher cases and considerable fame in the defense of William Remington and Arthur Miller (partly because Marilyn Monroe, who was then Miller's wife, boarded at his house). He became a loud and relentless critic of McCarthy and, though he had joined in founding the ADA for the very purpose of building a non-Communist left, he was inevitably subjected himself to all manner of attacks from the witch-hunters. To this day, Rauh unplugs his phone at night to avoid being awakened by crank callers. During the McCarthy era, Rauh was criticized for not taking up the defense of Communists. To this he replies: "I am, admittedly, deeply anti-Communist, but I will defend the civil liberties of Communists or anyone else. What I will not do is defend anyone who will not be completely honest with me and very few Communists would. Every civil liberties case is a crusade. Why should I undertake it if I don't know the facts?" Some of Joe Rauh's detractors argue that he played civil liberties and civil rights into a profitable law business. The charge, however, overlooks not only that Rauh has always taken many of his cases without fee but also that he has not, as a lawyer, made himself very rich. For him, the fight for civil rights and civil liberties gives meaning to his life. It is his exhilaration, his challenge, his real *raison d'être*.

At fifty-five, Joe Rauh is a contented man. He is big and healthy, with a barrel chest and enormous biceps. His hair is copious, though gray, and his face, if not handsome, is alive with color and imposingly strong. Olie, his wife, is as fair as ever, and he has two admiring sons. Rauh's house is comfortable, though scarcely elegant, and his swimming pool is a source of great pleasure both for him and his friends. He loves bow ties, a martini or two at lunch, and the sports pages. He moves with a bouncy, aggressive step and conveys the bubbling enthusiasm of a college boy. If Joe Rauh never seems in repose, he at least expresses his restlessness with warm, outgoing energy and an easy, infectious laugh. His mind works quickly and his words follow one another in rapid succession. He exudes a sense of certainty, without being dogmatic. Joe Rauh is a man who is satisfied about his past and confident over his future.

If there is a prize about which Joe Rauh is unhappy at not winning, it is Home Rule for the District of Columbia. He has fought for it throughout his twenty years in local politics. For the past three or four, it has seemed almost attainable but tauntingly elusive. "The local ADA chapter and the Democratic Party got it through the Senate five times over the years," says Rauh, the pitch of his voice mounting as it often does with ardor, "but in the

House, Sam Rayburn bitterly opposed it. 'As long as I'm Speaker,' he used to say, 'there won't be Home Rule.' The real action started when Rayburn died in 1962. It reached a climax last year."

It goes without saying that an issue as contentious as Home Rule is bound to generate, among supporters, bitter disputes over strategy. Perhaps more than any other, the Home Rule campaign has laid bare the cleavages within Washington's liberal, civil rights community. It has rendered the contrasts vivid between the groups labeled, for lack of more precise terms, the Joe Rauh crowd and the Black Power crowd. But the differences are not limited even to them.

"Joe Rauh," said one Black Power militant, "looks at the Home Rule fight as just another exercise in political manipulation. He wants to get Home Rule by pulling strings. If he gets it, that's the way he'll want to rule the city. He may not want to be Mayor himself, but he'll get himself some Negro sycophant—and there are plenty of them—to be his front man. I'm not sure Washington will be any better off being run from Joe Rauh's house than it is being run from the House District Committee. When we organize the Negroes in this city and make them conscious of their democratic powers, then we can have real Home Rule."

Rauh looks at the arguments of the Black Power crowd and answers in these terms:

"Everybody's got to go after Home Rule in the way he knows best, and my way is to keep up the pressure where I think it matters, on Capitol Hill.

"I was denounced for refusing to support the Free D.C. Movement's boycott of businessmen not favorable to Home Rule. I couldn't join because it runs contrary to my civil liberties convictions. A man shouldn't be penalized, by boycott or other means, for his political beliefs. But SNCC, which I think runs the Free D.C. Movement, can't claim I fought the boycott. I won't interfere with another organization's efforts for Home Rule.

"A couple of weeks ago, Stokely Carmichael was in town and he was quoted in the newspaper as saying, 'If we don't get the vote, we're going to burn down the city.' Well, I'll admit that the threat of violence, to say nothing of violence itself, achieves certain ends which rational argument can't achieve. It might get some swimming pools and fire hydrants and rat control and housing-code enforcement—which are good. But I can't join the violence. I'm congenitally incapable of it and I won't condone it. It will get concessions but, let me assure you, it won't get Home Rule. Congress certainly won't be threatened into Home Rule. I think Carmichael understands that and I wonder if that's what he wants.

"As for Negro leadership, I wish we had more in Washington. I know that many of the Negroes who now occupy important positions are not all they should be. Many of them are Uncle Toms who couldn't care less about the ghetto. I see some new names in the papers now and then. I honestly don't know many of them. But if Julius Hobson, for instance, ever gets to be Mayor, I assure you he'll stop denouncing me for being a politician because he'll be a politician himself. That's the nature of responsibility. I try to convince Congress that Home Rule will temper the intemperate. I look forward to genuine and responsible Negro leadership."

Even among "white liberals," Joe Rauh has his critics on the Home Rule issue. Most of the accusations can be reduced to a resentment—justified or not—of Rauh's concentrating too much power in his own hands. He has been criticized for failing to set up a national committee for Home Rule, perhaps with former Presidents Truman and Eisenhower as honorary co-chairmen. He has been criticized for failing to make better use of the Democratic Central Committee, to reorganize it, for instance, into a "shadow cabinet" to dramatize Home Rule's potential. He has been criticized for turning the Washington Home Rule Committee into a transparent front for himself and the local Democratic organization. His motive, according to all these critics, is to extend his influence, not only within the city but throughout the affairs of the nation. Some critics have gone so far as to say that Joe Rauh doesn't really want Home Rule, because it will deprive him of his only popular base of support and seriously diminish his standing as a national political figure.

Rauh, while admitting that there may be legitimate differences of judgment between him and his critics, denies vehemently the substance of these charges. He laughs at the contention that he somehow secretly opposes Home Rule and he rejects with irritation the suggestion that he wants to keep the issue alive for his own political purposes. Rauh acknowledges that some may disagree with his reasoning, but he believes he has adopted the best possible strategy for salvaging the fading hopes for Home Rule.

"We came within an eyelash of getting a vote on Home Rule on the House floor last September but I've got to admit we were outmaneuvered. Our nemesis was a fake named Sisk [Rep. B. F. Sisk of California, member of the District of Columbia Committee and the Rules Committee], who pretended he was on our side and played the Southern game all the way. Sisk collaborated with McMillan [Rep. John L. McMillan of South Carolina, chairman of the District Committee and foe of Home Rule] and Smith [Rep. Howard Smith of Virginia, chairman of the Rules Committee, also a Home Rule foe] to rig the parliamentary situation in such a way that the House couldn't get a clear vote on Home Rule. Did you know that Sisk was the only Northern Democrat who voted to gut the 1965 voting rights bill? Did you know he voted on the floor against bringing up the 1966 civil rights bill? He voted against Home Rule in the District Committee, he did not sign the discharge petition, and he voted against it on the House floor. This guy knew what he was doing when he brought up the substitute on the House floor. He's nothing but a doughface and a reactionary, who provided a way out for other doughfaces and reactionaries."

The Sisk plan, which the House approved in place of a Home Rule bill, provides for the election by District voters of a board to draft a local government charter. It would submit its proposal for congressional approval one year later. If Congress disapproved, it was "sudden death." The board would have been without power to revise its work. Home Rule would have been back where it started.

"I've been criticized," Rauh said, "for refusing to accept the

Sisk bill, for holding out for Utopia in the form of some pure Home Rule proposal.

"Well, that's not quite accurate. I was prepared to accept the Sisk bill last fall, right after it was passed. Why not? We're the ones who'd be elected to the charter board and we'd make a stronger District government than any that Congress itself would create.

"But the key to the matter was acceptance of the Sisk bill *immediately*. We'd have had to elect the board by late fall so that the charter could come back before the current Congress adjourned. That was the crucial point. This has been the most liberal Congress since the early New Deal and still, according to our calculations, we have a clear Home Rule majority of only five or six votes. In 1966, the Democrats will not be running against Goldwater again. They are sure to lose those half-dozen seats and more. To have submitted a viable charter to the next Congress would have been sheer suicide.

"Sisk himself knew that and looked forward to killing Home Rule that way. As it happened, we couldn't get the Senate to approve the Sisk plan in time for a fall election. So I decided there was no use supporting it and that we had to go all the way.

"Since then, we've picked ourselves off the floor and we're making another try at it. You know that Senator Morse [Wayne Morse of Oregon, a Home Rule supporter] has attached a Home Rule rider to another bill and we're doing our best to get it to a vote in the House.

"We'll get it if Lyndon Johnson supports us. But you know Johnson. For the moment, he seems to have lost interest in Home Rule. We're doing our best to revive it."

Rauh acknowledges that the responsibility is his alone for the District's rejection of the Sisk bill. He defied the Washington Home Rule Committee, which was once considered his stooge but which favored acceptance of the compromise, and he won the approval of the Democratic Central Committee, which had no use at all for the Sisk plan. It was he who devised the legislative strategy which he hopes will bring a real "up or down" House vote on Home Rule. It is he who is directing the pressure campaign against all those Northern Democrats who voted for the Sisk bill when they should, according to him, have recognized it at once as a Trojan horse.

"Sure I'll be blamed if we don't get Home Rule this time, especially when it came so close," Rauh said. "But then I'd have been blamed if I took the Sisk plan and lost it later on. This is what I believed we have to do."

It is ironic that the man who was castigated at Atlantic City for selling out is now being denounced by the same militants for being too stubborn about Home Rule in Washington. But that's the way it is when you're a symbol. No matter what you do, you're a hero to some, a villain to others. It's hard denying you're a white liberal when, in fact, you're a white liberal. So if the Black Power crowd wants to call Joe Rauh a "dirty white liberal," Rauh reasons that he's got to take it.

"No matter what he says, Rauh wants to be Mayor," says a detractor.

"A Negro's got to be the first Mayor of Washington," answers Rauh. "The Negroes have waited too long for this. They deserve to have the Mayor. They can't be done out of it at this stage, after we've fought so hard.

"Besides, I'm overextended. I'm going to have to give up some of my responsibilities after the Home Rule fight, win or lose. I've got to go practice some law."

Undoubtedly, Joe Rauh lacks some quality of rapport with the masses that the activists have brought to the civil rights movement. It is true that he is a politician's politician, not a people's leader. Though he radiates charisma, it seems to affect an intellectual and political elite, rather than the discontented masses.

Still, disfranchised Washington is a poor testing ground for a politician's persuasive powers over the masses. Joe Rauh has handily captured every election in which he has run as a candidate for party office. Both white liberals and poor Negroes have supported him. If Joe Rauh leaves the impression that he is not a man of the people, it may be that he has never had the opportunity to prove otherwise.

Significantly enough, the consensus—to which even the Negro

militants subscribe—is that if an election for a District govern-ment were held today, Joe Rauh and his running mates would win overwhelmingly. But his detractors say that his power at the street level is waning. Since its crest in 1964, they say, it has receded before the organizing efforts of SNCC, the Coalition of Con-science, UPO, ACT, and the other activist groups that have sent missionaries into the ghettos. Though he is still the most popular political figure in the city, in another year or two, say the mili-tants, Joe Rauh may no longer command the strength necessary to dominate Washington politics.

"I'm not convinced that I'm becoming all that unpopular," Rauh answers. "The militants are undoubtedly right about wide-spread Negro distrust of whites. But I believe there'll be Negroes around for a long time who won't pay particular attention to the color of the candidate who has their best interests in mind. I don't think it's time at all for the white liberals to walk out on this fight."

Robert C. Byrd

HILLBILLY IN THE SERVICE OF
THE LORD

By way of introduction, let me say that I regard Senator Robert Byrd of West Virginia as one of the most insufferable men in Washington. I don't think I started out feeling quite that deeply about him. To be sure, I didn't approve of the way Byrd, as appropriations chairman for the District of Columbia, sought to impose his concepts of virtue and morality on the city's black welfare recipients. I just don't like prigs. But I think, in preparing a profile of him, I was willing to give him a fair shake and to present his point of view honestly.

But Byrd, who had good reason to anticipate being treated critically, just could not believe he would also be dealt with justly. I'm sure he was deeply suspicious of my liberal credentials. As a result, he decided not only to give me no cooperation but to put in my way whatever obstacles he could. I remember meeting late one afternoon with one of his former assistants whose appraisal of Byrd contained both positive and negative elements. The former assistant had to go on to another appointment before I finished the interview, but we arranged to meet again the following morning.

Obviously, Byrd got to him that night. Not only did the man stand me up in the morning, but refused ever to talk to me again.

Determined to write the profile, I had as my only alternative an end run, so one morning I took a plane to West Virginia to find out what I could about Byrd on his own turf. The Senator, fortunately, had not thought to phone ahead to give warning of my arrival. After all, none of the Washington papers had ever sent a reporter to explore Byrd's home ground, though he was— in the curious manner that the capital is ruled—the most powerful figure in the city government. He had no reason to think I would go to West Virginia, either.

I spent most of a week in Byrd's state, first in the capital at Charleston, then down in Byrd's mountain country outside Beckley. I interviewed local newspapermen and political leaders, bankers, grocers, preachers and town sheriffs, all of whom had played a role in Byrd's career. They were friendly people, and they spoke freely. Few really liked Byrd, but all recognized him as a powerfully appealing politician. My own favorite recollection of West Virginia was the brisk fall weather and the brilliant colors of the landscape as I made my way from town to town. But I also remember the appalling sight of abandoned strip mines and ghost mining camps, where the presence of an occasional bony child made me wonder how any humans could ever have lived in them and how Bob Byrd's conscience could have tolerated them.

When I returned to Washington, I did my duty in notifying Senator Byrd officially that my profile of him was in preparation. At one point, Laughlin Phillips, publisher of the Washingtonian, *even sent Byrd a telegram to make it clear that I was anxious to hear his side of the story. Byrd didn't budge.*

Perhaps he figured that his position in West Virginia was so secure that no matter what we did in Washington, we couldn't hurt him. If this was his thinking, he was right. I had no delusions that anything I said would affect Byrd's margins at re-election time. Byrd did not so much represent the interests of West Virginians— the miners and the mountain poor, for instance—as their kind of primitive, naïve perceptions of the world. Obviously, he was doing something that the people of West Virginia thought was right and, as many scandals as had touched him, nothing I wrote would change that feeling. I was a little disappointed that Byrd had no trouble, shortly after the profile appeared, in getting elected to the Senate Democratic leadership and, later, in defeating Teddy Kennedy for Senate Whip, but I was not surprised that he conducted himself, after the article appeared, no differently from before. By most conventional measures, Robert Byrd is an immensely successful politician. I still think of him, however, as one of the real bad apples of Washington.

Let me count this day, Lord, . . . as the beginning of a crusade for complete morality and the domination of the Christian church through all the land. . . . We shall yet make these United States a moral nation."

*—*ELMER GANTRY, *by Sinclair Lewis*

IT WAS IN 1943 that Bob Byrd quit the Klan, stopped drinking, joined the church, and began thinking about politics.

For any man as humble as Bob Byrd, it was audacious to contemplate a political career. He was, after all, nothing but a butcher in an impoverished West Virginia mining town. But Bob Byrd was ambitious and he *was* audacious.

As much as any young man brought up in the coal country, Bob Byrd had the attributes for making a break. His mind was quick and he was unafraid of hard work. Though he was basically timid, he could be extremely personable whenever he wanted. Though slight in stature, his energy was inexhaustible and his determination was severe. It should have come as no surprise that Robert C. Byrd became United States Senator from West Virginia. Byrd would call it proof that the Lord helps those who help themselves.

Sitting in a high-backed leather easy chair before a long upholstered table, Senator Byrd is elegant in a dark-blue suit, silver cuff links, and a white pocket handkerchief. His face is curiously young, almost effeminate. His long hair is meticulously combed. Byrd's eyelids droop as he leans back to listen to a District of Columbia school official, who squirms uncomfortably in a hard-backed chair directly across the table. The rococo hearing room is hot and crowded. Overhead, a thousand glittering prisms, brushing against one another on an ancient chandelier, transmit a gentle tinkling sound. Chairman Byrd, in complete control of the meeting, purses his lips and lifts his small, almost delicate hand to his chin. He puts a finger into his mouth and, for long seconds, munches on a fingernail. The setting is the conference room of the Appropriations Committee, but, whatever its opulence might suggest, Bob Byrd still is not far from the barren hills of the West Virginia coal country.

The Senator is chairman of the District of Columbia subcommittee, a virtual autocrat over the city's budget. In a voice that is almost caressingly soft, he says:

"What about the obscene writing in rest rooms? Do you find much of this?"

The official, perspiring a little, admits reluctantly that boys sometimes scratch obscenities on the rest room walls, but he insists that custodians rub them off at once.

"What else is done to control it, other than just cleaning it up?" the Senator commands sternly.

The official replies that lectures are conducted in assemblies and section rooms, in an effort to develop good school spirit and good morals. He insists that disciplinary measures are taken when offenders are discovered.

Then, sensing a snicker in the hearing room, the Senator interrupts to say:

"It seems to me that these questions are important, not that the Senate subcommittee can do anything about obscene writings on the rest room walls, but at the same time, I do think it is good to call attention to that and let you people in the school system know that the members of Congress are interested."

It is not at all clear that the members of Congress are interested. In fact, evidence seems to indicate quite the contrary. But Senator Byrd is interested. "I would like to feel," he says, "that we are trying to keep a sense of balance about the whole thing and that we are certainly trying to inculcate into the plastic minds of our young people a strong and unfaltering, unshakable, faith in the Divinity which shapes our ends."

Back among the folks in West Virginia, there's sympathy for Robert Byrd's heavenly objectives. Theirs is the country known as the Bible Belt, where only last year they reaffirmed in a referendum their opposition to liquor-by-the-drink. These folks don't care much, one way or the other, about the District of Columbia budget. But they think it makes good sense that Bob Byrd is stamping out immorality, dishonesty, and illegitimacy among the poor. There are lots of churchgoers in West Virginia—Baptists and Methodists, mostly—and when they learn that Bob Byrd is trying to bring virtue to Washington, they nod their heads approvingly.

"Bob Byrd," said the Reverend Shirley Donnelly, the pastor of Byrd's church at Crab Orchard, "is a Christian gentleman. He wants to clamp down on those people punching out kids through whoredom. To me, that's religious conviction. I'm glad that Bob Byrd brings religion to politics."

These Baptists and Methodists, these members of a dozen fundamentalist sects that thrive in the West Virginia hills, *these* are Bob Byrd's people. He knows them well and he understands them. He eats at their tables and sits beside them in their parlors. He gives witness at their baptisms and their funerals. He prays in their churches. He has shared their hardships and their poverty. He has suffered with them and, now that he has made good, they are proud of him. These are the people who love Bob Byrd and give him strength.

The man who is now West Virginia's junior Senator was born Robert Sale in North Wilkesboro, North Carolina, on January 15, 1918. His parentage is obscure, but his mother, it is known, died before he was a year old. His father apparently abandoned the children, the youngest of whom was adopted by a family named Byrd from the coal country of West Virginia. It was with this family that the boy was raised.

Byrd's foster father is remembered as a decent fellow but something of a ne'er-do-well. Unable to hold a steady job, he wandered from one coal camp to another, dragging his wife and children behind him. Never more than a day laborer, he performed odd chores around the "tipples," the grimy mouths of the coal mines. As soon as Bob was old enough, he contributed to the family's meager income by delivering lunches to the mines, by collecting garbage to feed hogs kept by the miners' wives, by any other work he could find. It was a hard, miserable life, devoid of amenities and lacking in any satisfaction except that of knowing, many years later, that if you made it, you had made it from the very bottom.

If there was any place young Byrd called home, it was the grubby valley town of Stotesbury, where he attended Mark Twain High School. It was there that he learned to play the violin and, at thirteen, he joined a string orchestra which traveled around the South and won sixth place in a music contest. At sixteen, Byrd graduated as valedictorian of his class. A year later, he married a miner's daughter named Erma James, who was a few months older than he. He took a job screening coal and settled down, as near as anyone could tell, to a life which left men eternally covered with black dust and which broke many of them before they reached their prime.

Byrd, however, didn't remain in the mines for long. He found a job in a grocery store in Crab Orchard, just over the mountain from Stotesbury, and he learned to be a butcher. "Posey" Rhodes, an Erskine Caldwell-type character who has since turned that grocery store into a string of supermarkets, recalls today that "Robert Byrd was a politician even then. He was a real good salesman, friendly as can be, and the ladies loved him." During the war, Byrd interrupted his butchering to go off to Baltimore to work in the shipyards. When he returned, he opened his own shop in Sophia, down the road from Crab Orchard. He, Mrs. Byrd, and their two young daughters lived above the store. Behind the counter, Byrd made a lot of friends and, shortly after the war was over, he made his first bid for political office.

Bob Byrd had no particular ideology, nor did he show any deep indignation over conditions in the coal fields. He did not go into politics to crusade for economic or social justice. Byrd had no zeal for rebellion, scarcely any for reform. His objective, quite simply, was to get himself into the legislature. Politics was his channel of escape from poverty. It was the way to get ahead.

"I remember Bob Byrd back in those days," said a former newspaper reporter from Beckley, the principal city of the region. "I remember we talked while Byrd cut meat for a customer. I remember thinking that he was pretty articulate, which was incongruous for a butcher. Bob Byrd was the most ambitious fellow I ever met."

As a campaigner, Byrd worked alone. He had no help from either the United Mine Workers or the coal companies, to one or the other of which most politicians in the hill country were beholden. What he lacked in money and support, he made up for with his own intensity and drive. He had a slogan that was meaningless but so catchy that to this day it's remembered in the mountains. It went:

> *Byrd by name,*
> *Byrd by nature,*
> *Let's send Byrd*
> *To the Legislature.*

Carrying leaflets with his slogan printed on them, Byrd visited every home in the legislative district. Whenever he could find a crowd, he brought his fiddle and played a hillbilly tune. After a long campaign, he won the election by a substantial majority.

"As soon as Bob was elected," said the former reporter from Beckley, "he came into the paper and said he wanted to write a daily or weekly article on the legislature. We, of course, wouldn't let him. But he wrote letters to the paper every week and he cultivated all the reporters assiduously."

For Bob Byrd, the West Virginia House of Delegates, which meets for a month every two years and pays almost nothing, was scarcely more than a stepping-stone. While Mrs. Byrd tended the butcher shop, he worked relentlessly at politicking, visiting his constituents, perfecting the oratorical arts, playing his fiddle for whoever would listen. Even today, Byrd is known as Fiddlin' Bob back in the hills. While crises worsened in the coal fields, Byrd was out shaking hands. Bob Byrd's appeal was personal and, if he was popular, it was because he remained with the people and they liked him.

Byrd's most effective politicking, appropriately enough for the Bible Belt, was conducted inside the church. From the time he joined the Baptist congregation at Crab Orchard, he was an active worker. He taught Sunday school to boys and, in 1946, the year he first ran for office, he took his entire class on a five-day trip to Washington. But, dissatisfied with boys, he persuaded the pastor to let him form an adult class. Out of the hills Sunday mornings poured hundreds of men and women to hear Bob Byrd talk. Soon the enrollment surpassed six hundred and Byrd had outgrown the church. The Beckley radio station took the cue and began to broadcast Byrd's words throughout the entire mountain region. Before the undertaking was a year old, the Crab Orchard Baptist Church could justifiably claim that the "Robert C. Byrd Bible Class" was the largest in West Virginia, if not in the whole United States. In a biographical sketch he once prepared for the newspapers, Byrd noted that he had been a "legislator upon whom church people could count for support in all things which are right, morally and spiritually." It was in the church, more than anywhere else, that Bob Byrd found his constituency.

In 1950, after two terms in the West Virginia legislature, Byrd ran for the State Senate and won. Two years later, the local Congressman, E. D. Hedrich, decided to run for governor and left his seat vacant. Byrd, though he had much matured, was still basically a hillbilly butcher. He was only thirty-two, but he decided to go after the prize.

In the primary, Byrd faced N. H. Ragland, a popular politician from Beckley, and others, and appeared to be holding a narrow lead until Ragland suddenly made the startling revelation that Robert C. Byrd had once been a member of the Ku Klux Klan. In West Virginia, the Klan was never as popular as it was farther south. Some regarded Byrd as doomed. But Byrd parried the thrust by going on the radio and, in the manner Richard M. Nixon later made famous, delivered a statement rich in rationalization and repentance. After acknowledging Klan membership from "mid-1942 to early 1943," Byrd said:

"Being only twenty-four at the time, I joined the order because it offered excitement and because it was strongly opposed to Communism. After about a year, I became disinterested, quit paying my dues, and dropped my membership in the organization. *During the nine years that have followed, I have never been interested in the Klan* but, on the other hand, I have directed my energies toward the upholding of my community, my church, and my fellow citizens of every race, creed, and color.

"I suppose that in every man's life there can be found a 'skeleton in the closet.' . . . The past cannot be erased. The people will judge my case upon their knowledge of my honorable service to them during the six years I have held public office and upon my reputation, which has been carefully and painstakingly built during the years since my affiliation with the church."

Byrd's declaration was widely hailed for its forthrightness and candor and it was a complete success. On election day, he overwhelmed his stunned opponent and became the Democratic candidate for Congress.

But the matter was not finished. Byrd had declared that he had been a casual member of the Klan and that, in the nine years since quitting, he had never again become interested in it. But just before the fall general election, the Republicans made public a bit of evidence that told a significantly different story. It was a letter written in Byrd's handwriting. It was dated April 8, 1946, and it was addressed to none other than Samuel Green of Atlanta, the Imperial Wizard of the Klan himself. The letter read:

"I am a former kleagle of the Ku Klux Klan in Raleigh County and the adjoining counties of the State. . . . The Klan is needed today as never before and I am anxious to see its rebirth here in West Virginia. . . . It is necessary that the order be promoted immediately and in every State in the Union. Will you please inform me as to the possibilities of re-building the Klan in the Realm of W. Va. . . . I hope that you will find it convenient to answer my letter in regards to future possibilities."

West Virginia seemed to take Byrd's letter far more seriously than the original disclosure of membership. After all, it revealed that Byrd had been a Klan kleagle (organizer), not just an everyday member, and that he had lied about his subsequent interest in the organization. Governor Okey Patteson rushed home from a hunting trip to deal with the crisis. He summoned Byrd to his office in the state house and called upon him to resign. Byrd looked Patteson in the eye and said, "I'm sorry, Governor, but I'll run." Powerless to force Byrd out of the race, the Governor officially withdrew his endorsement. Most of the newspapers followed his lead. Faced with political annihilation, Byrd once again reacted with boldness, declaring that his opponents were "power-mad." Their raising of the Klan issue, he said, was nothing but a diversion by unethical politicians from the "real dangers" of Communism, organized crime, the decay of moral values, and the degeneration of religious life. The Republicans, he said, were "void of moral principle."

The tactic worked. In the November election, Byrd once again won by a great margin. In January 1953, he was sworn in at Washington as a Congressman from West Virginia.

In his years in Congress, Byrd achieved no great distinction. He voted on the liberal side of most domestic economic measures, but in other areas he was generally conservative. As befitted a Klan alumnus, he betrayed a touch of xenophobia by voting against the exchange of atomic information, against the issuance of special visas for political refugees, against extension of reciprocal trade. Oddly, perhaps, he voted in favor of the modest civil rights bills which Eisenhower offered in 1956 and 1957. On the whole, however, his record was such that he attracted little attention, either favorable or unfavorable, but Bob Byrd was hard at work. At night he was going to George Washington and American Universities. By day and on Sundays, he practiced relentlessly the art of politics.

He went back to West Virginia almost every weekend to mingle with the folks and play the fiddle, offering his services to whoever might need them. Nor did he confine his politicking to his own congressional district. Thanks to the church, he had available to him pulpits all over the state and scarcely a Sunday passed that Byrd did not preach or give a lesson before some religious congregation. Thus, as the years passed, Byrd not only consolidated his popularity among his own constituents but became known to voters throughout West Virginia.

He had trouble only once during his campaigns for reelection to the House and he managed to overcome it in a way that had by now become familiar to him. An opponent had the temerity to say publicly what had long been whispered throughout the hill country, that Bob Byrd had been a draft-dodger during World War II. Byrd lashed back with fury. "This is a subject," he declared, "that has been raised in all my previous campaigns by those who envy and hate me. It is a matter of general knowledge that for every man who shoulders a gun in the defense of his country, six or eight other men are needed to build ships, planes, tanks, and guns with which to supply him and support him. I contributed to my country's war effort by helping to build the ships and my deferment was granted by the draft board upon the basis of its own judgment as to whether or not my work was vital to the cause." Whatever the truth of the charge, the explanation obviously satisfied the voters of the district, because they reelected Byrd by a record majority.

It was natural for Byrd to seek promotion from the House to the Senate in 1958. By a quirk, both seats from West Virginia had become vacant and Byrd chose to go for the full six-year term, rather than settle for the remainder of a term left by the previous Senator's death. Byrd had been expected to win the nomination, since his opponent in the primary was barely known. That he received more than eighty percent of the votes cast was stunning. In the mining counties of the south, Byrd's majorities were truly astonishing—96.43 percent in Boone, 97.20 in Logan, 92.24 in McDowell, 93.78 in Wyoming. In no county did he receive less than a majority. The general election was a national sweep for the Democrats—and in West Virginia it was a landslide. Having run for the short term, Jennings Randolph was seated at once and became—to Byrd's everlasting irritation—the senior Senator. But that did not detract from Byrd's triumph. He was just shy of his fortieth birthday when he took his seat as the junior Senator from West Virginia.

It took Byrd no time at all to recognize where the power lay in the Senate. He made friends at once with Senator Lyndon Johnson, the Majority Leader, and made it clear to Senator Richard B. Russell of Georgia that he was sympathetic to the goals of the Southern bloc. With Johnson and Russell on his side, Byrd received appointment to the Appropriations and the Banking and Currency committees. As soon as the next vacancy occurred, Byrd was allowed to swap in Banking and Currency for Armed Services and, though he stood far down on the Senate seniority list, he was now a member of two of the most powerful committees. As a Senator, Byrd still talked little, showed small concern for the more profound problems of the nation, demonstrated scarcely any legislative initiative, and won no particular esteem from his colleagues. But he occupied key posts in the Senate power hierarchy and he was well placed to serve the state of West Virginia.

Byrd has been aggressive in seeking federal largesse for West Virginia—and aggressive in publicizing his efforts. Byrd's pushy way with press releases has angered and alienated his colleagues from West Virginia, but, at home, it has kept his name in the papers. The net result has been to convince the average West Virginian that Bob Byrd is a highly effective Senator.

"Lots of politicians make speeches," said one respected newspaper editor who is not otherwise awed by Byrd, "but his projects are a going concern. I think Byrd's gotten more things for West

Virginia than anyone who ever served in the United States Senate."

It is a reputation Bob Byrd cultivates by driving himself relentlessly, despite enduring the pains of an ulcer and kidney stones. He has never been known to tell a joke. With his staff, his quest for perfection turns him into a mean, often petty tyrant. His home life is simple, even tasteless. As for his social life, it is virtually nonexistent. Today he is scarcely less frugal than he was two decades ago in Sophia. He still does not take a drink. In the performance of his duties, he is conscientious to the point of drudgery.

What matters to him most is staying close to his people. He answers letters instantly and even writes thank you notes to thank you notes. He's been known to talk at one end of West Virginia in the evening, then drive all night to address a breakfast in the morning at the other end. To this day, Byrd seldom stays in hotels. He prefers to accept the hospitality of some voter who will give him a bed and the rapt attention of his admiring kin. On the rare occasions that Byrd finds he must eat out, he never chooses elegance but invariably selects a roadside "dog wagon," where he finds the food familiar (his favorite dish is fried pork chops, which he washes down with milk for his ulcer) and the clientele congenial. In such a place, he usually pays for his meal by personal check, by which he is immediately recognized, then offers sticks of chewing gum and gabs a bit with the customers. But, like other mountain folks, Byrd remains timid with strangers and suspicious of those he feels may be condescending toward him.

Byrd never put on a better show than he did last Memorial Day weekend at the Judson Baptist Church in Belle (population 4,600), West Virginia. For weeks, the bulletin board had been advertising that a "Christian gentleman" named Robert C. Byrd would appear before the congregation. "We thank God," said the notice, "for men in government who are committed to Jesus Christ." For his friends in Belle, Senator Byrd spoke with magnificent evangelistic fervor. When, like the rural preachers of old, he clapped his hands to signal an emotional climax, the congregation went into spasms of joy.

"*I believe,*" Byrd intoned to them, "*in a personal God.* [clap]

Let me say that to the young men and women. . . . We now go around the world in eighty minutes and are talking about landing on the moon and distant planets. . . . The more man accomplishes, the more likely he is to forget there's a God. . . . But remember, man didn't create atoms, he merely discovered them. . . . God created man in His own image. [clap] *I believe that, and I believe He did it from the dust of the earth. I believe in a personal God* [clap]—*one who hears my prayers* [clap]—*and one who punishes the wicked* [clap]. *. . . I believe in Jesus Christ, that He was born not of an ordinary woman but of a virgin . . . that He was crucified and then rose again. If I am wrong, then there is no purpose in life. I believe in the Bible as the inspired word of an omnipotent living God* [clap] *. . . I believe men will be changed by reading one chapter of St. Matthew. . . . I believe in prayer. . . ."*

No one in West Virginia doubts that Bob Byrd is a man consumed by the urge to advance the cause of Christian morality. Byrd himself is convinced that he knows God's will. So in 1961, when he became head of the District of Columbia appropriations subcommittee after just two years in the Senate, it was only natural he should have put his new power in the service of his beliefs. Endowed thereby with almost absolute power over the city budget, Byrd became the stern Baptist God's self-appointed agent in charge of the morals of the Washington poor.

Some Senators, in the course of their careers, make their reputations as authorities on the armed services, on taxation, on foreign relations, on housing, on science and technology, on medical care. Senator Robert C. Byrd has made his reputation as an authority on the mating habits of Washington's underprivileged. In contrast to the Senators whose names are linked to such causes as civil liberties, national defense, social security, Robert C. Byrd's name is linked irrevocably to the "man-in-the-house" rule. If there is a posterity, Bob Byrd will be enshrined in it not for his great vision or grand goals but for decreasing the incidence of love-making among Washington mothers on welfare and for denying public assistance to children of the unemployed.

Byrd, it must be said, did not invent the "man-in-the-house" rule. It dates back to 1955, when the District decreed that no mother could receive welfare payments for herself and her children if an able-bodied man was about to pay for their support. Byrd, convinced that the rule was a major obstacle to immorality, simply insisted that it be enforced. By increasing the number of investigators in the welfare department, he turned up hundreds of cases of ineligibility and succeeded in cutting back the public assistance budget significantly. To the objection of some that welfare investigators were snoopers, Byrd answered that recipients had a constitutional right to privacy, but not if they wanted to get their welfare checks. "What is wrong," he asked, "with looking at the rooms and in the closets with permission of the client?" His preoccupation with the sins of his wards has given him an obsessive interest in their sexual habits, their venereal disease rate, their illegitimacies, into all of which he inquires exhaustively at the annual hearings. (His questions elicit such testimony from investigators as the following: "We have patiently waited for two hours for a woman to get dressed. That time she had the man well hidden, but he was found. He was in a closet hanging on the rod with women's clothes all around him. If I may, I would like to relate another experience we had in relation to finding men in the home. This man was found hanging under a bed. He had his shoes off and he was hanging on the bedsprings with his toes and his hands.") So determined has Byrd been to maintain the "man-in-the-house" rule that he has steadfastly refused to let the District —in contrast to West Virginia—participate in a special federal program of aid for jobless parents. Because of Byrd, say his critics, hundreds of Washington children go to bed hungry every night.

"I believe it is a good rule," Byrd said on the Senate floor, in defending his dedication to "man-in-the-house." "I believe that an able-bodied man who enjoys a continuing relationship of husband and father in the home should bear the responsibility of supporting the mother and the children. . . . This is not asking too much. Society should not be expected to bear the responsibility.

The man should bear the responsibility. All that the woman has to do is tell the man to get out and stay out. . . . So if she is the kind of mother she ought to be, she will think of the children first, and she will see to it that there is not a continuing husband-wife relationship between her and some paramour. . . ."

When asked why the sins of the parents should be visited on their hungry children, Byrd has replied:

"We all get hungry. I have been here all day and I have drunk three glasses of milk and eaten half a bag of peanuts. I am hungry. And children get hungry. I got hungry when I was a child. But hungry children are one thing; starving children are quite another. I have not seen evidence of starving children in the District of Columbia."

Byrd unquestionably sees himself, in his defense of Christian morality, as a kind of latter-day Horatius, holding the bridge against the invading hordes of infidels, mostly black.

"Illegitimacy is, more and more, becoming a frightening factor in this whole equation. How the nation can continue to close its eyes to this disturbing fact is beyond comprehension. Something is going to have to be done about it, or the burden of crime, riots, and the dole will ultimately become unbearable. . . ."

Bob Byrd, after all, has only to look to himself to see a magnificent product of personal discipline. Byrd cannot excuse individual self-indulgence. A Darwinist in fundamentalist clothing, he sneers at all but the fittest. He is his own example to himself and to others. Bob Byrd takes himself as the standard for judging the weak and the irresolute.

"No amount of Government paternalism can take the place of drive and ambition, when it comes to developing the substantial and upright citizen. Hard work, perseverance, and self-accomplishment breed independence and strength, and courage and resourcefulness in the man or woman. Somehow the glory of honest toil is going to have to be restored if this nation is going to survive all of the dangers that confront it. . . . A nation on the dole can never hope to maintain the moral fiber, the spiritual strength, and the rugged resourcefulness to keep her people free.

"Easy money, easy living, laziness, shiftlessness—all these go hand in hand with irresponsibility, a disordered society, and ultimate decay."

Inevitably, the question arises of how much Byrd is motivated in his behavior by purely racial considerations. No one is more conscious than he that the overwhelming majority of welfare recipients in the District are Negro. When he speaks of crime and riots, unemployment and illegitimacy, laziness and irresponsibility, he speaks not of whites but of Negroes. "The high birth rate among low-income Negro families simply cannot be overlooked," Byrd has said. But does the source of these words lie in pure racism?

Byrd gave some philosophical attention to the question of racial equality during the long and bitter debate over the civil rights bill in 1964. Byrd opposed the bill with all his force:

"Men are not created equal today, and they were not created equal in 1776, when the Declaration of Independence was written. Men and races of men differ in appearance, ways, physical power, mental capacity, creativity, and vision. One man is born blind. Another is born lame. Geniuses are not made; they are born. Between two individuals, as between two races, there are broad differences. Equality is not a characteristic in nature, nor is it a characteristic among human beings. . . .

"This bill can never give status to any man or to any race. Men must earn status. Men must earn the respect of their fellows. . . .

"As citizens of this nation, our people are men and women who are unequal. Some of us are among the 'haves,' and some of us are among the 'have-nots.' Some of us succeed, and some of us fail. So it has always been, and so it will ever be."

Byrd's serene acceptance of the differences between peoples unquestionably carries the implication of racial superiority and inferiority. As the Klan membership suggests, Byrd believes in the supremacy of white Anglo-Saxon Protestants in American society. These feelings made him a bitter foe of John Kennedy in the famous West Virginia primary of 1960. They later made him oppose the attempt to modify the "national-origins" immigration quota system, on the ground that the changes would admit Asians and Africans and other "persons with cultures, customs, and concepts of government altogether at variance with those of the basic American stock." They have caused him to break with Lyndon Johnson and the political leaders of West Virginia over civil rights legislation. Recently, Byrd has become the chief advocate in the Senate of greater use of police power to curb both demonstrations and crime. Byrd clearly sees the police as a barrier against the Negro's social encroachments.

"We all have our prejudices," Byrd once said to an NAACP delegation which had come from Charleston to entreat his support for a civil rights bill. "It is a frailty of the human race. I try to think I don't. . . . And I'm not as prejudiced as I once was." He has opposed home rule for the District of Columbia because, he said, "I don't feel the federal city should be under the dominance of the NAACP, SNCC, CORE, ACT, and similar groups."

Yet, whatever the depth of his Negrophobia, there are other, often contrary, influences at work in his mind. Robert Byrd was the first Senator to appoint a Negro to the Capitol Police. He has always had at least one Negro secretary on his staff. In every case, he has said he would not refuse a job to a "deserving" Negro. Byrd has shown a willingness to suppress his prejudices to reward Negroes whom he regards as conscientious and hard-working.

In contrast to Byrd's harsh treatment of Negroes who are on welfare, it must be remembered that Senator Robert C. Byrd has consistently been the District's best friend in the annual hassle over school appropriations, the chief beneficiaries of which are Negroes. And lest one not give him his due, this year Byrd even consented to an increase in welfare payments, to compensate for rising costs of living.

"I think that Byrd," said a West Virginia Democrat, "has become, in a sense, a victim of his own beginnings. He's outraged by chiseling. He's furious at people who he thinks have illegitimate children to get extra money out of welfare. He admires people who work their way up, the way he did. He has contempt for any group that fails to take advantage of opportunity. Byrd's so goddamn proud of himself that he can't abide anybody who hasn't made it the way he did."

Reluctantly, Bob Byrd recognizes that there is a quality of mercy missing from his perspective on the Negro problem. His colleagues on the Senate floor—particularly Senators Morse and Ribicoff—have frequently reminded him that he is dealing not with abstract principles of morality but with human misery, mostly the misery of children. Byrd is unmoved by their arguments. He gives no sign of having heard the countless pleas for understanding made in our time by writers, sociologists, clergymen, Presidents. Byrd chooses not to look at the tragedy of the American Negro from the perspective of three centuries of enslavement and oppression. He takes his standards not from the humane conceptions of contemporary American social thought. Instead, he takes them from the severe strictures of Old Testament theology and from the imperious commands of a harsh fundamentalist God.

Byrd is not indifferent to the criticism he receives for his devotion to inequality in general and to the "man-in-the-house" rule in particular. He has, time and again, denied on the floor of the Senate that he is the hard-headed, cold-hearted skinflint which many depict him as being. He is virtually the only Senator who will challenge on the floor derogatory articles written about him in the newspapers. He won't even talk to writers whom he suspects of being unsympathetic to him. Often his pleas have the piteous ring of the man who thinks of himself as unappreciated and misunderstood. But for all his sensitivity to criticism, he has never given the slightest sign that he would change his conceptions of acceptable behavior by the poor.

A year or so ago, the Reverend Walter Fauntroy, a Negro representing a group of churches and civil rights organizations known as the Coalition of Conscience, appeared at one of Byrd's public hearings on the District budget. "We demand," Fauntroy said, "that funds be made available to and procedures established by the Department of Public Welfare which will provide immediate, on-the-spot assistance to those homeless and hungry victims of our welfare crisis." And he warned that "because our consciences have been aroused, we have resolved to do all that we can to arouse the consciences of the people of the nation generally and *the State of West Virginia particularly.*" In a tone that sounded menacing, Fauntroy concluded: "This we promise you."

Byrd took up the challenge.

"With the utmost respect to you," he said almost mockingly, "you may demonstrate to your heart's content. You may demonstrate by marching, picketing, or any other method that you care to utilize. There are some people who will knuckle under to your demonstrations. But I never will.

"I consider the statement that you intend to 'arouse the consciences of the people of the nation generally and of the State of West Virginia particularly' an insolent statement.

"I do not now, nor will I ever consider your self-appointed coalition to be a guide to my conscience, nor do I think that the people of West Virginia will ever consider themselves bound by it. My conscience will be directed by what I, in my heart, think is right and by what I, in my own mind, judge to be the facts. That has been the position I have attempted to take in the past and that is the decision that I will take in the future.

"You have promised me this, so my answer is, 'Lay on, Macduff, and damn'd be him that first cries, "Hold, enough." ' "

The Reverend Fauntroy, for all practical purposes, has uttered, "Hold, enough." With the prospects for home rule dead for the foreseeable future, the District remains more than ever subject to the individual conscience of Senator Robert C. Byrd. As for the collective, electoral conscience of the people of West Virginia, "they already consider him," said one expert observer, "the next best thing to Jesus Christ. There's more chance of hell freezing over than that Bob Byrd will ever be defeated for the Senate."

Robert E. Kintner

TYCOON IN THE WHITE HOUSE

*I first became interested in Robert Kintner through my friend
Jim Boyd, the man who exposed the shenanigans of Senator
Thomas Dodd. Jim, as you may remember, duplicated hundreds
of documents from Senator Dodd's files, showing how deeply
Dodd was involved in what might generously be called conflicts
of interest. One of the documents concerned Robert Kintner,
then president of NBC. I wasn't so surprised that the head of a
major broadcasting network would violate the highest standards
of personal ethics for corporate gain. But I did think it was a
matter of some concern in Kintner's case, since he had recently
become the chief assistant to President Johnson.*

*It was no easy matter doing a profile of Kintner. Political fig-
ures are, for the most part, willing to take a chance with a writer,
since they need the publicity. Business tycoons are not. Maybe
business egos are as big as political egos, but a business executive
doesn't really have to have his name before the public to thrive.
Furthermore, the milieu of the politician is more hospitable to a
writer, since politicians are accustomed to talking freely about*

their colleagues, but executives of big corporations are related to one another through a tight hierarchy—and they're terrified at getting caught in an indiscretion. Kintner had left NBC under circumstances that were, to say the least, mysterious, and the network's top brass put out orders that no one should talk about him. So almost no one did.

Here and there I found organizational leaks. Then some old friends agreed to talk, along with some journalists from the industry press. I had the documents from Boyd and the testimony from some of Kintner's earlier brushes with authority. Finally, after two or three refusals, Kintner himself agreed to see me on a "background" basis. All in all, I pieced together a profile which, I thought, said quite a lot about Kintner and perhaps even more about the television business.

Esquire accepted the piece as soon as I turned it in and scheduled it for immediate publication. But then the company lawyers read it and decided it was too dangerous to print. Later, the piece went to the Washingtonian, whose lawyers combed it meticulously and after requesting that I modify a phrase here and there for safety's sake, gave their approval. In June of 1967, the profile was duly published, and not so much as a whisper of a libel complaint ensued from any quarter.

What did happen, however, was that two weeks or so after the piece appeared, Kintner abruptly resigned from the White House staff. I haven't the faintest idea whether the profile had anything to do with it. I know that Kintner, at our meeting a few weeks before, made clear that he intended to stay until the end of Johnson's term. When I learned of the resignation, I had mixed feelings. This was a man who, I felt, had served the American public cavalierly in the name of corporate enterprise. But he was a brilliant man, with real organizational genius and tremendous knowledge. So far as I know, since he left the White House he has remained in total retirement. It's a small tragedy that a talent like that had gone to waste.

P RESIDENT JOHNSON was standing on the lawn in front of the ranch house one day recently, telling reporters how great everything was, when he turned abruptly to a chubby man with a squashed but not unpleasant face who was seated near him and said: "Now, if you fellows have any questions for Bob Kintner, I'm sure he'll be glad to answer them."

Robert E. Kintner didn't look glad at all. His squashed face reddened a bit with embarrassment and, behind heavy lenses, he lowered his eyelids, obviously hoping that the fellows would not respond to the offer. In his year or so at the White House, he hadn't uttered a word for the public record and it was clear that he did not regard this as the moment to start. The reporters knew that Lyndon was playing one of his friendly jokes. It was his way —not necessarily intended to be mean—of giving a common touch to his august office. Kintner, as one of the President's boys, played loyally along, but he was relieved when the reporters, predictably, could think of nothing to ask. Since they didn't know what he did at the White House, there was scarcely anything they could question him about. So the President dismissed his audience and, before any one of the reporters could collar him privately, Bob Kintner disappeared inside.

This was Bob Kintner's way. He was a man who loved power but never seemed to give a damn about public recognition. He would work in the shadow of bigger men—if *he* could make the decisions. As president of NBC, Bob Kintner could figure that Pope Paul was more important than Procter and Gamble and, without even asking, shoot a cool few million of General Sarnoff's money. It was Bob Kintner who, until a year ago, determined how forty or fifty million Americans spent several hours of every day of their lives. His was the staggering power to say what would be drummed into their minds. Yet his name hardly ever appeared in the newspaper and so few knew who he was that he didn't even bother to unlist his number in the phone book. Occasionally, of course, some enterprising person, usually drunk, would phone in the middle of the night to prattle about "Bonanza" or Brinkley, but to Kintner, an insomniac anyway, this was a small penalty. Now, in the shadow of the biggest man in the world, he may be on his way to achieving preeminence in the White House, but he's shown himself exceedingly disinclined to have anyone know about it.

In explanation, some say that Bob Kintner is shy; but in a board room, before a dozen executives nervously fingering their silver cuff links, he has demonstrated a terrifying fury. Some say his homeliness gives him an inferiority complex that manifests itself in a desire for anonymity; but if he has an inferiority complex, it did not stop him from choosing a most perilous environment for a career or from landing a most beautiful, rich, and talented wife. Some say Bob Kintner is simply modest and enjoys letting others, whether superior or subordinate, take credit for him; but few men, in the higher interests of the corporation or their own self-preservation, have more effectively shared their blame with others. For twenty years, Bob Kintner reigned as a baron of American business. In being faithful to its ethic, he achieved remarkable success.

Lyndon Johnson was impressed by this success, and Johnson was in need of someone reliable to keep an eye on a multitude of Presidential interests. Then, very suddenly, Kintner became available, and if he was stepping down as one of the half-dozen most powerful men in America, however curious the circumstances, so much the better. Lyndon knew that Kintner was good, very good. He admired Kintner's remarkable achievements in business. And Lyndon, after all, has always had trouble getting and keeping good people on his staff. If Kintner had problems, so has he, Lyndon Johnson—and the President figured he was lucky getting someone of Bob Kintner's competence in the White House. To Johnson, he's an excellent assistant who stays self-effacingly in the background and operates effectively to enhance Presidential grandeur. Now that Bill Moyers is gone, there's nothing standing between Bob Kintner and big power at the top of the White House hierarchy. When Moyers resigned, the President commented to a friend from Congress, "Thank goodness I have Kintner around."

Since he joined the staff last April, Bob Kintner's status has been significantly different from that of the other retainers of Lyndon Johnson. His fundamental strength is that he is Johnson's contemporary and equal, with a great career behind him rather than an uncertain one ahead. To Kintner, unlike the others, the President is invariably polite. Recently Kintner took over Jack Valenti's old role of first man in the Presidential bedchamber each morning. He briefs Johnson on the major news and gives him the daily schedule. But he gets none of the guff that Valenti had to take and he doesn't perform Valenti's chores as *valet de chambre*. The other staff members recognize Kintner's special access to the President and, though mystified by it, they try to make the best of it. When Eric Goldman, luminary in a world Johnson disdains, sought to resign with dignity as resident White House intellectual, he went to Kintner for advice on how to go about it—since Johnson takes poorly to unsanctioned resignations. Kintner drafted him a letter that he said would evoke a kindly Presidential answer. It was scarcely Kintner's fault that Goldman then blabbed to the press, which got him instead some Presidential buckshot in the rump. Kintner himself would never have been so indiscreet. He sees to it that his presence in the White House is girdled with dignity.

To the President, Kintner is a colleague, a welcome relief from the intimidated young Texans who scurry about him all day long. It may even be that he is unique at the White House in a freedom from fear. Since Moyers left, he is the only Presidential advisor who dares stand up to the boss and say no. Kintner may be a flunky like the others, in that his function is to minister to the peculiar needs and eccentric habits of Lyndon B. Johnson. But the President has left him his self-respect, which is recognized as a rare commodity in the White House entourage.

Lyndon B. Johnson and Robert E. Kintner first met some thirty years ago, when they were both young men getting a start in Washington. Kintner, fresh out of Swarthmore, was a junior reporter for the New York *Herald Tribune,* concentrating on business and economics; Johnson, fresh out of Southwest Texas State Teachers College, was the administrative assistant of a Texas Congressman, concentrating on getting elected on his own. They were about the same age and shared a strong passion for FDR and the New Deal. Their wives, themselves vigorous personalities, were fond of each other and together the two couples frequently made the rounds on the party circuit. After the Kintners left for New York and while the two men were climbing to the pinnacle of their respective professions, the two couples—united by a common interest in Democratic politics and the broadcasting business—remained rather close. Until a few years ago, one might have said that when they met it was as equals, if one measures family status by the influence of the husband over American life. If anything, Bob Kintner, as president of a network, was more important than Lyndon Johnson, the Vice-President. Since Johnson's promotion, of course, the contest is over, but the President remembers Kintner as an old friend who made it big in a very tough world.

In 1937, having established a reputation as one of the best reporters in Washington, Bob Kintner quit the *Trib* to join Joseph Alsop in writing a syndicated newspaper column. Soon Kintner and Alsop were selling their product to one hundred seventy papers and, on the side, doing articles under a lucrative contract for the *Saturday Evening Post.* By 1940, they had written two books, one of which was a major best seller. Thirty-two when the war came, Bob Kintner was tops in remuneration and esteem among the country's political writers. On his return from the Army, he had his pick of the best jobs in journalism. But Kintner decided he wanted none of them. Long before, as a cub covering the Securities and Exchange Commission, he saw that the *real money* was in business. Knowing he could always fall back on writing, it was the big dough that he decided to go after.

Bob Kintner got into broadcasting through Edward J. Noble, who took the fortune he had made by putting the hole into Life Savers and bought the Blue Network—on sale by an anti-trust decree—from the National Broadcasting Company. Noble changed the network's name to American Broadcasting Company and Kintner, conventionally enough for an ex-newspaperman, became his public relations director. Within no time, however, Kintner was promoted to chief of news and special events. By the end of 1946, he had been elected executive vice president. In 1949, less than five years after he started in business, Kintner was chosen president of ABC. By now he was forty years old, making $100,000 a year, and knew as much about the new medium of television as any man in America.

Troubled that his network not only lost money but stood a poor third in broadcasting competition, Kintner set out to overtake NBC and CBS. Taking his relative inferiority as a mandate to experiment, even to gamble, Kintner made his moves audaciously. He decided, first, to give new zest to entertainment programming. To exploit the potential of film, he established television's first alliance with Hollywood and gave, thereby, new breadth to action and adventure. It was Bob Kintner, more than any other man, who turned nighttime television into a mindless experience, full of crime, cowboys, and comedies. To be sure, it was not Kintner but Oliver Treyz, his successor, who made ABC the undisputed leader of wasteland programming, and it was not Kintner but Jim Aubrey at CBS whose programming was known for its "broads, bosoms, and fun." But, coincidentally or not, it was Kintner who brought both Treyz and Aubrey to ABC and taught them what they knew. Years later, Kintner was quoted as saying that "if I were still at ABC, I wouldn't have carried the pattern that far." But, significantly, he never denied that it was he who devised the pattern and imposed it, by television's Gresham's law, upon the entire industry.

But if Kintner was turning ABC mindless with one hand, he was making it respectable with the other. Never quite having forgotten the satisfactions of journalism, he did his best to enrich ABC's feeble efforts in news and public affairs. Severely handicapped by lack of funds, he built a news department that was competent, if far below the level of the rival networks. With more success and with much greater significance to television's development, he initiated the practice of giving live exposure to newsmaking events. Kintner made the decision to broadcast the Army-McCarthy hearings direct from its Senate conference room and, justifiably, he remains proud of his role in hastening the downfall of the late Wisconsin Senator. Telecasts such as these were cheap for ABC, since it had few sponsors to preempt in the daytime hours, but they brought new prestige to the industry. They were the first glimpse into television's potential for disseminating great events as they happen—and into television's inherent conflict between the duty to keep the nation informed and the stockholders rewarded.

As president of a hungry network, Kintner was preoccupied with far more than programming, however. To sell air time he paraded up and down Madison Avenue, in constant courtship of possible sponsors and their ad agencies. "The job of a network president," he once explained, "is top salesman. That's because every sale is between one million and three million dollars." By signing up U.S. Steel, General Mills, Chrysler, and other corporations, he invalidated the going theory that ABC could survive only on the crumbs of the other two networks. One month he sold almost twenty million dollars of time. By the mid-1950's, ABC was for the first time showing a profit and was actually growing faster than its competitors. Dozens of new stations now sought ABC affiliation. As for audiences, ABC's most popular programs had already displaced the leadership of NBC and CBS. Kintner, conceded to be one of the shrewdest operators in the business, set his sights on moving ABC into the front rank.

But in his avidity for success, Kintner met his downfall. To put ABC into the big time, he needed—for top talent and the best equipment—resources far greater than the Life Saver fortune. So in 1953, he and Noble merged ABC with Leonard Goldenson's Paramount Theaters. In so doing, they lost voting control over the network's destiny. Almost immediately, Kintner and Goldenson began struggling for power, Kintner becoming outraged as Goldenson men slipped gradually into important offices, Goldenson becoming outraged at Kintner's tenacious retention of the key positions. The inevitable showdown took place late in 1956, when ABC's finances were in the best condition in its history. Valiantly Noble tried to save his protégé but Goldenson prevailed. Acknowledging Kintner's remarkable achievements in building ABC, Goldenson declared that these very achievements required a reorganization of the corporate management. More to the point, he charged that Kintner had been an autocrat. Reluctantly, Kintner resigned, but his honor was intact and his disappointment was offset by the six figures in the contract settlement.

Barely out of the door, Kintner received a luncheon invitation from General David Sarnoff, grand old man of the communications industry and board chairman of the Radio Corporation of America, parent company of NBC. Two weeks later, Kintner— having declined an offer from CBS, along with attractive proposals from other major businesses—was elected an executive vice president at NBC. Robert Sarnoff, son of the General and the NBC president, announced that Kintner would report directly to him on color television. "I didn't know a damn thing about color," Kintner admitted, almost boastfully, at the time. But it didn't matter. He obviously had his eye on something bigger. NBC was itself just recovering from a major executive shake-up and its top echelons were still in flux. Whether by pre-arrangement or not is unclear, but hardly more than a year later General Sarnoff announced that his son Bobby had been promoted to the chairmanship of the board of NBC and that Robert E. Kintner would replace him as president. To say that Kintner had landed on his feet, after his abrupt dismissal from ABC, would be a gross understatement. He went from the leadership of a second-rank operation to the presidency of one of the world's great broadcasting systems.

Bob Kintner was by now no longer a boy wonder, but a man who was mature in appearance, no less than in style and philosophy. Gone was the long hair, combed casually back, and the lithe body of his thirties. Kintner now wore a crew cut, well brushed, and his physique had taken on the proportions of a teddy bear.

His nose had become bulbous, his mouth had thickened, and his eyes, through which he always saw poorly, had narrowed until they were nothing more than slits. An old Army injury that had rendered him deaf in one ear forced Kintner to lean forward to capture normal conversation. His voice, unless carefully modulated, became rasping, and his speech was marred by a slight lisp. Yet, despite the physical distractions, Kintner's face could, when he chose, convey a look of delightful whimsy, even of great pleasure. His insouciant bow ties and his impeccable tailoring contributed a certain distinction to his demeanor. Despite a reputation for being the homeliest man in television, Bob Kintner could, if he wanted to, use his presence to set a roomful of people immediately at ease.

On the whole, Bob Kintner wanted people to like him and he put a lot of effort into it. Like de Gaulle's uniforms, his office was calculatedly unpretentious. He was normally polite, even deferential, to his subordinates. He was magnificent at boosting egos by a thoughtful word or casual gesture. He sent flowers when executives were ill, memos of praise when performers did well. If he had criticism, he usually dispatched it through channels, so the object rarely knew from whom it originated. Kintner's subordinates knew he could be merciless with their failures, but if they did their work competently, he would stay out of their affairs. For himself, he was inexhaustible in his dedication to the job. He put in twice the hours of normal men and was uncanny in knowing everything that transpired in his domain. But he labored quietly, without flamboyance, never flaunting his authority or treading on others to gratify his own psychic needs. For these things, Kintner's people admired him and, if they didn't love him, usually held him in some affection.

At NBC, Bob Kintner was free to indulge his programming fancies. He had the full confidence of the Sarnoffs, who appreciated his indifference to public adulation, his willingness to leave the spotlight to them. Perhaps more important, they were impressed by the remarkable record he was making in earnings. They gave Kintner, to run the network, complete authority and as much money as he wanted. Kintner, by making the network over in his own image, soon surpassed every rival in the control he exercised over America's leisure time. Quite apart from his salary of $150,000 a year, he possessed power that would have given satisfaction to any man.

Kintner's passion at NBC was the news department. On his arrival, he had Huntley and Brinkley but nothing like the long tradition of competence which Ed Murrow, Sevareid, Smith, and others had imparted to CBS. Spending at the rate of sixty million dollars a year, Kintner set out to build the NBC news organization. He hired the best men he could find and paid them well. He sent them where the stories were and he called for thorough coverage. He organized the news staffs of NBC's subsidiary stations to serve as ready reinforcements. He trained his men to react quickly to be first on the air, but he also gave them more time than ever before to treat the news in depth, both on scheduled and special programs. From the office which the newsmen called the "bunker," Kintner watched the news shows incessantly and bombarded his editors with suggestions for improvement. Single-handedly, Kintner turned NBC into one of the world's foremost news organizations. He never hesitated to replace a scheduled program with an important news report, whatever the cost. It was Kintner who, on hearing that President Kennedy had been shot, immediately ordered twenty-four-hour news presentation and the complete suspension of commercials. In awe, the other networks had to follow. Through its influence on the competition, NBC under Kintner improved significantly the level of television news generally.

One may wonder why Bob Kintner, whose thick spectacles seldom strayed from the corporate balance sheets, was so obsessed by the news. It was not, after all, a profitable item, although by adroit packaging he made Huntley and Brinkley into the biggest single money-maker in television, and by advertising deals on news specials he managed to keep the deficits to a minimum. One prominent NBC commentator speculates that Kintner poured money into the news department in atonement for the junk that was put on the air the rest of the time. Others, conceding a less religious inspiration, contend that Kintner understood that first-class news, by enhancing the network's prestige, would pay for itself indirectly in the purchase of time by big corporations in search of status.

Still a third group maintains that Kintner's insistence on excellence in the news was intended to divert the attention of official Washington from the mediocrity—to put it generously—of the entertainment hours. Television, unlike the press, enjoys no constitutional immunities. Radio and TV are transmitted over airways which belong to the public—and the Federal government, at least in theory, accepts the obligation for seeing that broadcasting is conducted in the public interest. Thus far, Washington has let the networks and the stations behave just about as they please. No quality standards are enforced. No limitations are placed either on commercialization or profits. Stations are not even charged a licensing fee. At any time, of course, Congress could start getting tough. The Federal Communications Commission, on its own, could impose stringent regulations over the industry. The government could begin to act as if the airways were a national resource, to be exploited for the public weal. These threats loom large in the thinking of any good broadcaster. And Kintner had ample grounds for apprehension that NBC might provoke trouble with its evening entertainment schedule.

Kintner defends his programming decisions with the claim that he gave the people what they wanted. Television, he argues, is a mass medium, serving not the critics or a handful of intellectuals but the tens of millions who have nothing better to do when they come home from work every evening than to grab a beer and collapse in front of the tube. Though he bids for credit for developing the concept of the "mixed evening" of comedy, mysteries, and westerns, he expresses no pride in his achievements on the entertainment side of television. He says he would have preferred to present opera and ballet and live theater, if only people had agreed to watch them, and he points out persistently the few quality productions for which he was responsible. Bob Kintner complains that he had to accept the reality of the preferences of the television crowd. But by golly, he declares, he was not going to be bullied by the critics, and as president of NBC he would serve up whatever the people asked for.

Kintner confronted the first real crisis in his programming practices in the late fifties, when the nation suddenly discovered that it had been hoodwinked by the big-money quiz shows. Kintner went to Washington in 1959 to tell a Congressional committee that NBC's top echelon had no idea whatever that the quiz shows were a fraud. With an impassive face, he testified that he had heard nothing of the charges of dishonesty when they were first made publicly by a disgruntled contestant in 1957 and that he accepted at face value the denials of his producers when the charges were repeated a year later. He further testified to his ignorance of articles in *Time* and *Look* as early as 1957 which suggested strongly that network quiz shows were rigged. While committee members listened incredulously, Kintner insisted for three and a half hours upon NBC's total innocence. "I personally cannot believe," one Congressman finally told him, "that you, with all of your experience, could serve in the television and radio work for this length of time and not know what was going on." "Mr. Congressman," Kintner replied serenely, "I testified under oath I did not know and I do not know." Kintner was able, as if to purge himself and the network, to reel off a list of employees who had been fired in the interests of NBC's virtue. But, by denying everything, he had closed the door to further snooping. He had kept the hallowed name of the Sarnoffs free of taint and, by sacrificing a few NBC officials, he had apparently kept intact the integrity of the network itself. Kintner had performed with the dexterity of NBC's top stars. He emerged from the crisis a hero at the network and in the industry generally.

He didn't come off unscathed in the next encounter, however, with Senator Thomas Dodd of Connecticut crusading against sex and violence in network programming. The chosen fall guy this time was an NBC vice president named David Levy, whom Kintner had sent to testify because, he informed the committee, the entertainment schedule was Levy's domain. Having been coached carefully, Levy succeeded at first in diverting Dodd's people with some innocuous generalities. Then the roof caved in, with testimony from a variety of independent producers and advertising executives that the Kintner-Levy policy required that all entertainment shows contain a healthy dose of sex and violence. NBC's response was to profess shock, blame Levy for any network departures from high standards, relieve him of his programming responsibilities, and offer him, quietly, a fat sinecure. But Levy, to NBC's astonishment, refused to take the rap. Unwilling to have his reputation sullied, he decided to fight back.

With Levy's help, Dodd's staff undertook a major study of the decision-making process at NBC as it affected the quality of programming. Staff members concluded that without a doubt it was Robert Kintner, not Levy, who decided what programs would run and what they would contain. It ascertained that in the first four years of Kintner's tenure as NBC president, shows containing sex and violence increased from a total of one-half hour of prime time per week to twelve full hours. It found further that in the television industry there was a well-known "Kintner edict" which set the tone for entertainment programs. Staff members charged further that Kintner, against the recommendations of his subordinates, shifted around his questionable entertainment schedule to make the more questionable shows accessible to a younger audience. In a long series of memos, the staff urged Dodd to confront Kintner with its findings, if only so that NBC would, under the harsh light of publicity, mend its erring ways.

But Senator Dodd had other ideas. He never allowed his committee staff to make public the results of the investigation. He never allowed David Levy to defend himself against NBC's public allegations. He never confronted NBC's executives with conflicts in their testimony. At the staff's insistence, he finally called Bob Kintner to be a witness—then refused to allow any serious interrogation on the staff's findings and limited the asking of questions to himself. Kintner's appearance was meaningless. In concluding it, Dodd said to Kintner: "I take it from what you say, you agree there is a need for change and improvement and that you will do what you can to see that such change and improvement takes place." Reassuringly, if not grammatically, Kinter answered: "Yes, I am."

For Kintner, it was a close call. This time, he needed a little help from Bobby Sarnoff, who testified at a closed hearing that David Levy was unprincipled and incompetent and that Bob Kintner's only mistake had been to hire him in the first place. But, all things considered, NBC came out of the hearings very well indeed, and far better, it might be noted, than the other networks. One might wonder why Kintner went to such pains to avoid having to own up to programming decisions which were, if controversial, certainly quite legitimate. Whatever the answer, NBC, obviously, was fantastically worried about its public image. In the ensuing years, Dodd appeared—with unusual frequency for a freshman Senator—on NBC's prestigious "Meet the Press" and other NBC news programs. Mrs. Kintner herself is listed as a patron at a Dodd testimonial. As for Kintner, he came through the episode bloodied but unbowed, his position at NBC apparently more secure than ever.

Over the course of the next few years, NBC looked like the most stable component of a highly volatile industry. At the other networks, top executives—including ABC's Treyz and CBS's Aubrey—were swept out, only to be replaced by others who, in their turn, where also swept out. But Kintner stayed, and under his direction NBC's sales volume and net profits soared, while entertainment ratings remained high and news operations attained a pinnacle of prestige. As far as anyone knew, the two Bobs—Kintner and Sarnoff—functioned harmoniously under the benign eye of the aging General. NBC seemed to be without serious problems.

That, perhaps, was not the case with Bob Kintner personally. Though he was holding it better, he was drinking much more. Those who met with him, whether in the office at 30 Rockefeller Plaza or in some room in Acapulco or Washington, reported that he sipped continuously at a tumbler of vodka on the rocks, though it rarely seemed to impair his concentration. Friends reported that he could be as charming as ever, but that he slipped more often now into fits of gloom, during which he could be downright rude. Tom Wolfe, the chronicler of fashionable society, noted that the president of NBC traveled in a smart set "in which Chester is Chester Beatty who owns the diamond mines, and Nicole is Nicole Alphand, wife of the [former] French ambassador, and Bill is William Kintner. . . ." (It's *Bob,* Tom, *Robert* Kintner.) But most of the time, Kintner just stayed home and watched television—three sets going simultaneously in every room of the whole Fifth Avenue apartment. Whatever else he was, Bob Kintner was a work horse and if he knocked off for some sleep between the end of Johnny Carson and the beginning of "Today," it was because these were the light hours for the network. And, even then, he tossed about with insomnia. It was well known in the broadcasting industry that Kinter was working too hard, much too hard.

Then, all of a sudden, Bob Kintner was fired. Nobody saw it coming and almost nobody knows why it came—but at the end of 1965, the information quietly leaked out that Kintner was finished and the only one that didn't report it, until very much later, was NBC News.

The circumstances, to say the least, were strange to outsiders. The annual report had just disclosed that NBC had broken all its previous earnings records. General Sarnoff had announced that Bob Kintner—in recognition of his great leadership—had been promoted to chairman of the board and would, at the same time, retain his powers as president. His income was to rise to $250,000 a year. Jack Gould of *The New York Times,* who is supposed to know everything about television, flushed Kintner momentarily out of his anonymity and wrote a long profile extolling his brilliance. Some maintain that the Sarnoffs were so incensed at the *Times'* panegyric that they decided to fire Kintner on the spot. But the story is, at best, an exaggeration, for the General, it is known, had for some time been nursing grievances against his network chief. One of them was Kintner's sometimes embarrassing drinking problem. Finally, something happened that made up his mind—and Kintner was out.

Broadcasting Magazine, the trade journal which considers itself the oracle of the industry, gave a broad hint at the trouble. Sol Taishoff, its impresario, is an old friend of Kintner's and maintains that it was he who arranged Kintner's momentous lunch date with Ed Noble some twenty years before. Taishoff, with a mysterious look on his face, says that he knows why Kintner was fired but cannot possibly tell. According to the magazine, involved were "a combination of factors, all of them related to a hard-driving temperament and grueling work habits under the endless pressures that beat on executives at that level." Few doubted what was meant by this long-winded euphemism. Kintner, according to the best information available, just couldn't take the heat any longer and cracked.

The story of Kintner's departure is guarded by NBC as if it were the secret blueprint of the network's future—and the mirror of its past. NBC executives refuse absolutely to discuss their lost leader. In response to a request for an interview with the new chiefs, Syd Eiges, vice-president for public relations and a former Kintner whipping boy, said: "We held an executive meeting to discuss your request. We decided that Kintner's a figure out of our past. We just don't have anything to say about him." What the Bolsheviks did with the historical Trotsky, NBC seems determined to do with Robert E. Kintner. They treat him now as if he never existed.

Kintner himself pretends that his departure from NBC was the most casual thing in the world. He simply got tired of it, he says, and thought he'd try something new. But then, he gives the same explanation for his separation from ABC, of which the circumstances were clear. In taking leave of NBC, he had the consolation of a contract settlement of some $50,000 a year for ten years. The amount substantially exceeded the ABC settlement, though it was less than one might have anticipated for a quarter-of-a-million-a-year executive. Kintner, since closing the door, hasn't said a word in defense of himself or in criticism of NBC. He discreetly maintains that he and his old employers are still the best of friends.

There's a story around New York that General Sarnoff was swimming with Marion Javits, pretty wife of the Senator, in the pool of his mansion in downtown Manhattan when a servant rushed in with the news that Bob Kintner had just been appointed an assistant to President Johnson. General Sarnoff, the story goes, was barely saved from going down for the third time. Actually, the story is inaccurate. General Sarnoff, who had just turned seventy-five, doesn't swim any longer, but he enjoys having friends at his pool, and it was Marion, chatting between dips, who brought up the subject of Kintner's new job at the White House. The General, who is normally unruffled, turned apoplectic at the thought. He had been quite prepared for Kintner to take an important new position—at an ad agency or a big corporation that buys from NBC, at a production studio that sells to NBC, maybe even at CBS. But at the White House? That he never figured. Who knows what power Kintner might have at the side of the President? RCA does more than 200 million dollars a year in business with the Defense Department alone. Kintner might even make life unbearable for the corporation. Unquestionably, Bob Kintner's new post has inspired awe among General Sarnoff and the executives who work for him. Unquestionably, it persuades them to be even more careful than they otherwise might be to preserve Robert E. Kintner's good name. Why who knows, Kintner might even wind up as chairman of the FCC!

For the moment, however, Bob Kintner is nothing more than a member of the President's staff, with ill-defined responsibilities and uncertain powers. He operates out of a cubbyhole in the basement of the West Wing. His status symbols are very modest —a secretary, a row of filing cabinets, and a half-dozen abstract paintings on loan from the Smithsonian. His silver cuff links now display the Presidential seal. But for all this, when Bob Kintner says that he is happy, he sounds as if he means it.

"I've made more money than I could ever have hoped to make," said Kintner recently, musing to a youthful Presidential aide. "I've done more than I could ever have expected to do. I've done it on my own, without any help from a father or anyone else. Now I'm fifty-seven and I've got no ambitions. All I want to do is to serve the President."

Kintner has obviously adjusted painlessly to Washington. "It was really like coming home," said his wife. The car the Kintners drive carried the New York license plate TV-4 long after they gave up the apartment on Park Avenue to take a Georgetown house between Teddy Kennedy and Allen Dulles. They still rarely go to parties—but when they do, it's no longer with the jet set or with corporate millionaires but with politicians and working newspapermen. Kintner continues to work long hours—but he doesn't watch as much television. And Bob Kintner, it's been said, has stopped drinking completely.

"I know about Bob Kintner's drinking problem," President Johnson has been heard to remark among friends, "but he's the one who told me about it. And he said to me: 'Mr. President, if I ever go off on a bat again, I want you to consider that my resignation.' Well, Bob Kintner's been doing a great job for me and I'm not thinking about his resignation."

When Kintner joined the White House staff, the President announced that he would handle "organizational and administrative problems [and] coordination of Great Society programs." Johnson himself, strong as he may be as a politician, is exceedingly weak as an administrator. It is clear that he looked to Kintner, with his twenty-year record as a brilliant executive, for assistance in running the governmental apparatus with which he is charged.

Kintner has been named Secretary of the Cabinet and has begun to reshape that body, which had fallen into disuse under Kennedy, into a genuine Presidential advisory council. He has untangled the lines of communication between the President and the executive departments and agencies. He has, to Johnson's immense satisfaction, turned the White House itself into a smoothly working operation.

To be sure, Kintner advises the President on his television appearances; he is credited with the recent innovations in the press-conference format. He tries to improve the President's unhappy relations with the press. He may also be moving into areas of policy, since it would be unusual for someone with the understanding and judgment in foreign and domestic affairs that Kintner demonstrated as a young journalist to be excluded arbitrarily from making his views felt.

But it is administration that is Kintner's specialty. It is here, acting for the President, that he will acquire more and more power. With dozens of new programs enacted in recent years, Johnson must mobilize a vast amount of administrative machinery. Kintner can show him how to do it. No courtier, Bob Kintner knows how to organize and to get results. He may yet emerge as the strong man behind Lyndon Johnson—his Harry Hopkins, Sherman Adams, Colonel House. He may never again possess the independent manipulative power he had at NBC. But that does not mean he will not again make decisions that influence the lives of millions.

Bobby Baker

SMALL-TOWN BOY IN A FAST CROWD

Like most middle-aged Washington newspapermen, I knew Bobby Baker before he became notorious. "Check it out with Bobby" was one of the commonplace expressions of those who spent their days around the Senate press gallery. I never thought of Bobby particularly as a nice guy. He was aloof, perhaps a little condescending, as if he were saving his real self for the insiders of the press corps, of whom I was not one. But he was invariably courteous, always well-informed, and unfailingly helpful. I never thought it was part of his job to invite me in for bourbon and branch water, too.

So I was sorry when Bobby ran into trouble. I had always known, of course, that he was a skillful operator. It never occurred to me that he was also a manipulator, a hustler and a conniver. After the first revelations of what became known as "the Baker scandal," all sorts of stories began to gush out about Bobby's Senate role. It turned out not only that he was busy making love and money, to which I had no real objection, but that he was also scuttling liberal legislation, to which I did. Still, I held

117

on to my vision of Bobby as a Senate staffer who had dealt with me conscientiously and fairly.

When Harold Hayes at Esquire *asked me to write a Baker profile, I would have liked to refuse. First, I was not anxious to master the intricacies of Bobby's incredibly complex financial affairs. Second, I simply did not like raking up the coals of scandal. I don't mean to sound virtuous or fastidious. But what I like about journalism is revelation and interpretation; what I hate is intrusion. I consider it legitimate to probe the psychology of a political figure; I regard his sex life his own business. I felt it was impossible to write about Bobby without exposing scandal—and my feelings toward Bobby were not mean. Hayes, however, served up the story to me as a challenge, and I didn't have the will to refuse.*

In a way, doing the profile was easy, because almost everyone in town—among the newspapermen and politicians, at least— had his own Bobby Baker story. But Bobby himself was another matter. At the time, Bobby was under indictment, and I am sure that his lawyer, Edward Bennett Williams, had told him to lie low. This was hard for Bobby. He liked to talk to newspapermen. I also think that, having lived for so long in the shadow of Senate prima donnas, he actually enjoyed getting all this publicity on his own. Whenever I phoned Bobby's house, he always greeted me amicably, even jovially, but week after week he gave me excuses why he couldn't meet me for a talk. Finally we arranged to lunch one day at Paul Young's, and, rather to my surprise, he showed up. Furthermore, he was incredibly open and voluble. He actually told me more than I expected but he did not, of course, tell me as much as I'd have liked. So we agreed to meet again.

I never did see Bobby again. The closest I came was an invitation to his palatial house, but he wasn't there when I arrived. I met his children, all polite and charming, and a variety of deferential house servants. With a bit of guile, I persuaded the Filipino houseboy to take me on a tour of the premises. The house was a revelation, what with the autographed photos of Lyndon Johnson and the big, round, purple bed. But Bobby, alas, never appeared. So I went home to write and, for some reason, the profile seemed to flow effortlessly out of the typewriter. As I think back, Bobby himself seems more like that torrent of words than like a real flesh-and-blood person.

It's sad to think of Bobby in jail, because he's not evil. He is, rather, a small-town kid who got caught up with a fast crowd, the Senate, and went astray. When I think of some of those he left behind on Capitol Hill, I can't help thinking the law got the wrong man.

IN WASHINGTON, where Earl Warren strolls home unnoticed up Connecticut Avenue, where Hubert Humphrey has trouble catching a taxi in the rain, where Dean Rusk gets ignored by the Statler's doorman, Bobby Baker still stops traffic.

In the fanciest restaurant downtown, Bobby enters and is at once surrounded by proprietor, maître d', headwaiter, chief busboy, sommelier and hatcheck girl, all inquiring after his well-being. As he weaves through the aisles to his table, he waves like a champ to admirers who smile and call out to him. When he is seated, waiters rush up to light his cigarette, bring him his favorite brand of Scotch, assure him that the specialty will be brought to him the way he likes it. As he dines, passersby greet him effusively. After he finishes, he leaves behind the warm glow that a generous tip from a beloved customer evokes. In Washington, obviously, Bobby Baker is somebody.

At first glance, Bobby doesn't look like a candidate for the title of somebody. His face is totally undistinguished. It is neither handsome nor homely; neither cruel nor kindly; neither strong nor weak; neither intelligent nor stupid. It is nothing. It is insipid, like packaged white bread. His eyes, to be sure, have a certain sparkle. When he speaks, the signs of vigor begin to appear. But the cheeks are flabby, the nose shapeless, the hair wispy. The slightly stooped posture is more reminiscent of a filling-station operator than a Washington somebody. Even in his prime,

Bobby's face had the look of warm cream cheese. Today, after years of torment, one can only conclude that, like Dorian Gray, he has somehow passed on the traces of his experiences to some other soul. It's too bad; the lines of anxiety would serve his face well. But Bobby's formless features do prove that a man can be more than his face, and that appearances deceive. For behind his bland countenance, Bobby does have what it takes to move in a competitive world.

Bobby Baker is somebody, oddly, where almost nobody without power is anybody—and Bobby no longer has power. He retains, nonetheless, the qualities that brought him power, and they continue to make him exciting. Right now, Bobby commands a perverse admiration for the very reason that he had defied power, been sassy to it, made it look pompous and silly. And unlike Adam Clayton Powell and Senator Dodd, he has demonstrated the capacity to become a heretic without getting everybody angry at him. Bobby's a rascal, but somehow he's more fun than his straight men, the accusers. In a city where politics is prosaic, piety is puzzling and power is perishable, Bobby Baker is more dazzling now than he ever was. He had everything that this city honored and he lost it. But in losing it, he showed to all of Washington what only the Senate had known: Bobby Baker has élan. Powell goes off to Bimini and Dodd locks himself up in his office. But Baker walks alone down Pennsylvania Avenue as if he still owns it. He holds stubbornly to the audacity that made him distinctive and the denizens of a humdrum world appreciate him for it.

"I don't think I'll go to jail," he said, with a quality in his drawl that alternated between insouciance and conviction. For a Southerner, Baker speaks at a very quick pace. "But even if I do, it won't be the end of my life. It might be two, three, four years, but that's not forever.

"I'll still be able to read. I'll direct. I'll run things. I'm not going to be dead."

Baker wanders easily over the complex events that led to his trial and conviction for larceny and income-tax evasion. He claims his innocence without betraying an excess of defensiveness, not ponderously like a Sacco or a Sobell, but lightly like a kid who honestly believes that the teacher will find it was some other kid who wrote the dirty words on the blackboard. As usual, he shows no anger.

"I don't hate anybody," he said. "I feel sorry for haters. Haters always lose.

"I feel sorry for the members of that jury, even if they convicted me. They were all just little government workers, putting in their time, filling out their forms, waiting for their pensions. There's none of 'em ever made more than $7,000 a year in his whole life, maybe $10,000 at the most. They just couldn't understand how anybody who worked for the government, like me, could get his hands on so much money. They figured it had to be crooked. It just never occurred to them that it could be honest."

For a while, the story was going around town that Baker was broke, that he couldn't even pay the fees of his high-priced lawyer, Edward Bennett Williams. But right after his trial, he took off with his wife for a three-week vacation in Florida. His five children—comfortably cared for by a trusted factotum, a Negro maid and a Filipino houseboy—give no sign of preparing to move from the big house in Spring Valley, near where Lyndon Johnson and Richard Nixon used to live, that Bobby bought some years ago for $129,000 and which he boasts—to remind you of his business acumen—is now worth $200,000. The second car still stands in front, the knee-high plush still carpets the floor from wall to wall (except for the bare spots covered by antique orientals) and the Paris-in-the-rain and schooner-at-full-sail original oils still hang in every room. Over the fireplace in the library, the shelves of which are filled by a complete, morocco-bound set of *Reader's Digest* book condensations, is mounted the head of an animal. At its throat is a brass plate which reads: "Robert Baker killed this buck at 317 paces on West Ranch, Blanco County, Texas." Guess whose ranch is in Blanco County, Texas, on the banks of the Pedernales. In Washington, no one can say that Bobby Baker shows signs of being a beaten man.

Bobby Baker has always had the showman's touch. Dick Aurelio, Senator Javits' right-hand man, tells the story that when he first came to Washington, seven or eight years ago, he asked his new boss about some bill before the Senate. "Go down and talk to Bobby Baker. He'll tell you everything about it," Javits told him. Aurelio had never heard of Baker and so informed the Senator. "Just go to the floor and find the guy scurrying around who is dressed like a riverboat gambler," Javits instructed him. From that description, Aurelio says, he had absolutely no trouble locating Baker, who dropped whatever he was doing to answer with care and patience every question that came to mind. Behind the flair, Aurelio soon learned, was an intelligence of considerable dimension.

The people around the Senate who were poorly disposed toward Baker were clearly a minority. The aides of Senator Jack Kennedy, knowing that Baker was Lyndon's man, nonetheless respected him, even if they didn't completely trust him. Newspapermen knew that they could rely on Baker to return their phone calls and talk to them straight. In 1961, when Baker received, of all things, an honorary degree from American University, Senator Dirksen said of him: "Of all the persons I could name, I could name no other who so richly deserves this honor." Yet there is some truth in the observation of the tweedy aide of an aristocratic Eastern solon. "I always felt he was kind of pitiful. He took as his models Lyndon and Gorgeous George [the dapper, handsome Senator George Smathers of Florida]. He always wore those dark-blue suits with white-on-white shirts, the way they did. When they bought matching ties, so did he. He was obviously a small-town boy with no mind of his own." But most of Washington readily excused Baker his lack of sophistication and dwelled instead on his courtesy, his knowledge and his ability to get things done.

Far from regarding himself with compassion, Bobby Baker considered himself the luckiest young man in the world. So what if he came from Pickens, South Carolina, where his father was a mailman and the population was less than two thousand? He had left Pickens in 1942, when he was fourteen, and if that wasn't enough good luck for anyone, he went directly to the Senate, where he became a page for the great men of his time. While other kids were being exposed to teachers, Bobby took his lessons from politicians. Though he obtained a smattering of learning in page school, he was getting his real education on the Senate floor. The ways of the world, as Bobby grasped them, were the ways of the Senate, and virtue was its practices. The Senate, to Bobby Baker, was his church and family, his ticket to glory, the womb of his life. It never occurred to him that, whatever the Senate did for him, he might still be a hayseed.

Early in the game, Bobby put his excellent mind to the mastery of the Senate's complex ways. In it he stored a remarkable amount of information, not only on the Senate's intricate rules and parliamentary procedures but also on the character and moti- vation of its members, their mores and folkways, their relation- ships to one another and the tactics and strategies they pursued. This information became the most important—though not the only—instrument in Bobby Baker's carefully conceived campaign for personal advancement. He used it with virtuosity, with un- varying courtesy and, when necessary, with a brashness that showed he merited attention. Bobby Baker could not redeem his ambition by becoming a Senator but he could, if he was cunning, become a power in the Senate. Few suspected, when the Demo- crats made him Majority secretary in 1955, how much of a power he would become.

In the hands of Baker's predecessors, the post of Majority sec- retary had been insignificant, as it might have been in Bobby's, had not Lyndon B. Johnson, the Senator from Texas, become the Majority Leader at the same time. The Majority Leadership had never been much before, either. Majority Leaders had come and gone—four since 1950—without any of them making a measur- able impact within the Washington power structure. Few foresaw that Johnson would transform the office into one of enormous influence, perhaps the second most powerful in the country. He did it because he was, like Baker, a great student of the Senate. Not only did he know what made the Senate function but he rec- ognized, better than any man before him, how to make it function according to his will. Lyndon was lucky that his assistant's ambitions corresponded to his own. Bobby Baker became Lyndon Johnson's indispensable man.

Many things attracted Lyndon Johnson and Bobby Baker to each other. They were both Southerners and they felt at home in each other's company. They were outgoing and gregarious, big talkers and hearty backslappers. They liked nothing better than to end the day over a bottle of Scotch, sharing hospitality with kindred spirits, scheming and joking and gossiping and gloating. Both were indefatigable workers. Both cared far more for political battle than for political ideology. Both loved to achieve their objectives by themselves, manipulating the levers of power. Johnson was, of course, much older; Baker, conscious of the differences in age and rank, deferred to them. But in Baker, Johnson had an assistant whom he respected enormously, to whose judgments he paid careful attention and from whom he did not insist, as he did from others on his payroll, on a debasing obsequiousness. Johnson took it straight from Bobby and he liked it. The two became more than political associates. Lyndon and Bobby liked to think of their relationship as between father and son.

Under Johnson's firm hand, Baker orchestrated the Senate. He ranged far and wide, in the corridors and cloakrooms, testing ideas here, measuring responses there. The information he acquired he gave to Johnson. Baker scheduled legislation, not in the clubby way in which it had been done previously, but with an eye to Johnson's profiting from some Senator's absence or some outside event. He studied every bill carefully, to see how Johnson could take advantage of some inconspicuous provision that might aid this or that Senator's favorite interest. He had a marvelous capacity to predict how a vote was likely to go, and to advise Johnson on the correct pressure to apply to turn the margin his way. Bobby worked both sides of the aisle, Democratic and Republican, though he had official responsibilities only to the Democrats. He was alienated only from a handful of liberals, who found his maneuvering distasteful and of whom he was contemptuous for being doctrinaire. Bobby was neither liberal nor conservative; he was pragmatic. He had no emotional predisposition for or against any Senate bill. His only concern was whether it served the interests of Lyndon Johnson. The team of Johnson and Baker was certainly the most dominating that existed in the Senate's history.

But Bobby's interests were not merely legislative—at least not in the narrow sense. He also took it upon himself to minister to other needs of his Senatorial minions. He could, for instance, be counted on to come up with a copious supply of first-rate liquor during a tiring night session. He was the driving force behind the little hideaway near the Senate Office Building called the Quorum Club, where Senators could discreetly join with lobbyists and other Capitol Hill operators for a quiet drink or two. Later, he became a kind of entrepreneur and bagman for large campaign contributions. Bobby never regarded it as outside the bounds of his responsibilities to accommodate a Senator on anything. If he had any obvious failing, it was that he simply couldn't say no.

Bobby's private life, like his work, was rich in its variety. He had a wife, Dorothy, who worked as a secretary for the Senate Internal Security Subcommittee. He married her when he was twenty and, without her ever giving up the job, she gave birth in due course to five children. Baker was good to his family, but he also liked parties and he became known as the leader of the kickiest crowd on Capitol Hill. Anyone might show up at one of Bobby's parties, from Senator Smathers to a $75-a-week secretary; the only requirement was a love of merriment and a willingness to forgo judgment on anyone else's behavior. Bobby himself was invariably the life of the party. After a hard day at the Senate, when anyone else would be glad to get home to bed, Bobby would be starting the evening's fun with the Mexican hat dance. The frolic might go on till dawn. Bobby's secretary was Carole Tyler, a Tennessee beauty with whom he was often seen in public. Carole's place in Southwest Washington, an upper-middle-class redevelopment area of closely packed high-rises and town houses, became the center where Bobby's friends, male and female, often met. How Bobby spent his off-duty hours was more or less common knowledge on the Hill, but those were the days when Bobby was on top, when there seemed nothing unusual about his diversions and when no one thought that, as Senate practices go, there was anything there to get excited about.

While Bobby was playing politics with Lyndon and arranging parties with Gorgeous George, he was learning about a whole new facet of life from Senator Robert Kerr of Oklahoma. Kerr was a self-made millionaire who freely and publicly expressed the conviction that any man in the Senate who didn't use his position to make money was a sucker. In a body where few of the members are averse to earning a fast buck, Kerr was the chief of the wheelers-and-dealers. For some reason, he took a shine to Bobby and found him an apt and receptive pupil. He helped Bobby get started as a businessman, both with advice and with cash. Bobby learned to play the stock market, then spread out into other ventures. His biggest undertaking in the late Fifties was the Carousel Motel, which he built on a patch of desolate beach near Ocean City, Maryland, a few hours from Washington. Its opening in 1962, which Lyndon and Lady Bird and dozens of other Washington celebrities attended, was a major social event, covered in detail by the status-conscious women's pages of the local papers. It is doubtful that anyone suspected that in the fun at the Carousel lay the seeds of Bobby's downfall. For Bobby, after all, was among the most respected young men in official Washington. He was the protégé of Johnson, Smathers and Kerr. Without a single voter behind him, he had shown he could keep up with the fastest pacers on Capitol Hill. As the Presidential election of 1960 approached, Bobby's potential for growth appeared unlimited.

Bobby Baker, like many other Senate Democrats, did everything he could to get the nomination in 1960 for Lyndon Johnson, the Majority Leader. But his influence lay in a body which—to Johnson's particular dismay—had very little to do with picking the Presidential nominee. What distinguished Baker from the rest of Lyndon's entourage, however, was that he, almost alone, argued that Johnson, failing to get the top spot, should agree to run with Kennedy as the Vice-Presidential nominee. Johnson's other friends, aware of the power of which the Majority Leader disposed, felt this was nonsense. Why Bobby persisted in this argument is by no means clear. After all, his whole orientation was toward the Senate. He knew the Vice-Presidency was an impotent office. He had no great fondness for Jack Kennedy. Yet perhaps he understood better than Lyndon that, from the parochial power base of Texas, the prospects of his becoming President were remote. Baker regarded a Kennedy-Johnson ticket as unbeatable and he thought, perhaps, that only through the Vice-Presidency did Johnson have a hope of getting to the White House. But whatever the reasons, Bobby Baker, exercising his powers of persuasion long before anyone else in the entourage, was undoubtedly an important influence in Johnson's ultimate acceptance of second place on the Kennedy ticket.

"I wanted to resign from the Senate after the 1960 election," Baker said recently. "I had a big offer of a vice-presidency in a major corporation. But Mike Mansfield told me he wouldn't accept the Majority Leadership without me. Bob Kerr called me in to talk me out of going. Even Kennedy put pressure on me to stay."

What Baker said was confirmed by people close to Kennedy.

"I was flattered. I'll admit it. Things were going well and I had no financial problems. Then it turned out that I was trapped in the job in the Senate. It was the worst mistake I ever made not leaving the Senate with Lyndon Johnson."

Bobby, as the world now knows, stayed on, taking more and more responsibility from the weak and ineffectual Mansfield, doubling up as the entrepreneur of an incredible network of financial speculation. Amazingly, no one noted a decline in the quality of Baker's Senate work as he juggled deals in Florida, Las Vegas, California, Haiti, the Dominican Republic and, of course, in Washington itself. Meanwhile, the momentum of his social life continued to increase.

"I did make investments," Baker said, "I did have a lot of energy. I don't think anybody will ever refute that I did my job. . . . If I was able to do my job in an hour a day better than anyone else could do it in twelve I don't see why I ought to be criticized for having other interests as long as they didn't conflict with my job."

Baker's complicated world came tumbling down in the fall of 1963 as a consequence of a civil suit brought against him. Of the man who brought the suit, Baker says indignantly: "I did that guy the biggest favor in his life. I got him a big contract. He was giving me a couple of hundred bucks a month. That's all. Then the company canceled the contract and he blamed me. I didn't have a thing to do with it." From the glimmer provided by the suit there gradually unfolded the panorama of Baker's financial empire. At best, it looked like a conflict of interest with his Senate duties; at worst, it was a serious criminal matter. Baker resigned as Majority secretary and a Senate investigation of his affairs ensued. Baker, as a political figure, was finished.

"I sleep good every night," Baker said recently, "because I have a clear conscience. I never knowingly did anything that was illegal. . . . If it was illegal to be in the motel business, or to be in the vending business, then I did commit an illegal act. But I think that if it's illegal for me to be in it, there ought to be some rules to let you know what they are . . . notwithstanding all that's been written about me, those who know me believe in me . . . my conscience does not bother me."

But whatever Baker's conscience said, Lyndon Johnson had no choice but to abandon the young man he once called "one of my most trusted, most loyal and most competent friends." No one knew better than Baker himself that such were the rules of the political game. If anyone had regrets, it was probably Johnson, for after November 22, he would unquestionably have brought Bobby Baker to the White House, where he would have made excellent use of Baker's many skills. Perhaps this had been Baker's hope when he urged Johnson to run for the Vice-Presidency three years before. Now Johnson could only wash his hands of Bobby Baker.

Baker shows no bitterness toward Lyndon for not springing to his defense. "I can't just write a person off who was formerly very close to me who has not communicated with me since my troubles," he said. "I understand their position very well. My friends have had no choice but to think of me as a bad dream or something."

But Baker is being protective of Johnson, who *has* communicated with his former aide, at least once, "since my troubles." Over the bar in his oak-paneled library, Baker displays a color photograph of President Lyndon B. Johnson delivering one of his first speeches to Congress. It is undated, but Johnson did not become President until well after Baker's troubles began. The handwritten inscription, in a scrawl that is now familiar, reads: "To Dottie & Bobby Baker. With love. Lyndon B. Johnson." In his way, Lyndon can be loyal, too.

When the Senate investigating committee let Lyndon's friend Bobby Baker go with nothing more severe than a reproach, the Republicans were sure they had a powerful issue to bring to the voters in the election campaign. Barry Goldwater denounced Bobby Baker's morals and, by inference, Johnson's. He called the committee action a "whitewash." But Baker, true to form, just laughed it off. "Barry Goldwater doesn't feel that way," he quipped. "It's all a part of politics. My relationship with Goldwater has always been very friendly. . . . I have a lot of Republicans who are my friends. Many of them call me up and explain this is an election year. I understand. . . . After the election Goldwater will grab and hug me." Interestingly, the American people seemed more persuaded by Baker's tolerant cynicism than by Goldwater's somber indignation. The Bobby Baker case, the best publicity the Republicans had, never really caught on as a campaign issue.

In many other ways too, Bobby showed his élan. His reputation as giver of merry parties had hurt him. Then sex's arrow struck again, when a neighbor of Carole Tyler's, a newspaper reporter, discovered, in scanning the list of eligible voters in the residential co-op, that Bobby Baker was actually the owner of Carole's house, now widely known for its lavender carpet (the same, by the way, with which the Baker bedroom in Spring Valley and the lobby of the Carousel are decorated). In explanation, Bobby has since declared: "She and her roommate were paying $250 a month for an apartment. I fussed at her. I said you're getting up old enough where you ought to be building up a little equity in a place. So they went and they found a place that they wanted. And because they didn't have the net worth to get it, I agreed to put a financial statement in whereby they could get it and build up some equity. Is that criminal or illegal or un-American to try to help two young ladies build up equity?" But the public was scarcely interested in looking at Carole's house as a token of philanthropy. It became a tourist attraction and dozens of gawkers passed it in their cars. But Bobby was undeterred. He continued to give parties there regularly. If he encountered an old Senate acquaintance, many of whom lived in the neighborhood, he didn't turn up his coat collar but, on the contrary, said in his usual friendly way, "Hello, how are you? Nice to see you again." On weekends he even washed Carole's car in the parking lot. If Bobby was, in reality, embarrassed by his publicity, he managed to conceal it very well.

A slight acquaintance of Baker's tells a story of walking down K Street one day with an old college friend who had just moved to Washington and was having a terrible time borrowing money to make a down payment on a house. Inadvertently, he bumped into Bobby, with Carole on his arm and a prominent lobbyist at his side. It was at the time when the Senate investigation was on Page One of every paper. "How you doin'," Bobby said. "We're just going for some lunch. How about joining us?" The two men, having no other plans and rather titillated at the prospect of lunching with this now notorious figure, accepted the invitation. During the course of the conversation, the problem of the loan was casually mentioned. Bobby volunteered, "If you don't mind, I might be able to help you." He whipped out one of his calling cards and wrote on it the name of the vice-president of one of Washington's old, established, conservative banks. When the lunch was over, Bobby, naturally, picked up the check and the two groups went their separate ways. The would-be borrower, not taking the prospect very seriously but willing to grasp at any straw, went to the bank and found the vice-president in question. "Bobby's an old friend of mine," the banker said. "I wouldn't say that publicly, but I'll take his word on just about anything." The loan was promptly approved. Baker received nothing for it—except, perhaps, the satisfaction that he was still pretty good at doing favors for people.

Public revelation in no way seemed to restrict Bobby's activities. He still spent a substantial part of his life in airplanes, going hither and yon to consummate this deal or that. His old mentor, Bob Kerr, had died sometime before, cutting him off from his most reliable source of financing. Baker says that Kerr's untimely departure cost him at least $10,000,000 in prospective enterprises which had to be canceled. Still, Baker was far from poor. However rickety his empire might have been, he could still claim to be several times a millionaire. In Kerr's absence, he had to resort to less orthodox methods of financing. But at no point was he either sufficiently deterred by the risks or intimidated by the investigators to cut back or consolidate his holdings.

"Some people are born with the desire to conquer the world," Baker once explained. "I personally like to build things, I like to create jobs, I like the intrigue of the stock market. I like the intrigue of the real-estate market. This is the way my mind thinks."

Still, with all his varied interests, the Carousel remains Bobby Baker's first love. Here, too, Baker has refused to be put off by his notoriety and has, instead, turned it to his advantage. Big billboards along the highways to the Maryland shore proclaim the merits of Bobby Baker's Carousel. The curiosity seekers flock in from Washington and Baltimore, even from Philadelphia and New York, for the pleasure of identifying with the man who shook up the American government. Baker charges them plenty for the pleasure. A week at the Carousel is no budget vacation. Bobby has turned a pretty penny in the Carousel out of the Baker case.

But the Carousel is genuine testimony to Baker's good business head. He built it on a plot of land that he picked up cheap near an old Maryland shore town where the normal middle-class Washingtonian wouldn't have been caught dead. He invested a small fortune giving the place class—at least class as he understood it. Like Bobby himself, the Carousel was garish. Its decor, like that of his house in Washington, has been described as "motel provincial." But among the clapboard boardinghouses that were its only neighbors it was absolutely spectacular. It had decent food, a bar and entertainment. For a time, Bobby had his troubles getting customers, but he hung on, confident that his judgment would be redeemed. Now the Carousel is a great success. The land on which it was built is worth a fortune—and Bobby has more that he hasn't touched yet. During his hard times, he had to sell some of it, but for the rest he has big plans concerning swimming pools and condominium apartments and a shopping arcade and tennis courts, all priced "so working people can afford them." A decade ago, Bobby Baker obviously saw something no one else did and he's cashing in on his clairvoyance.

Bobby takes great pride in the Carousel and gives it a vast amount of his personal attention. Not only does he supervise its operation, by checking the bills and the payroll and the weekly receipts, he's also down there most of the summer, running around in sneakers and a pair of jeans, looking after operations and maintenance. He nails shingles and mows lawns and paints rooms and chops wood for the fireplace. He drives a truck and cleans dirty dishes from the table. He picks up candy wrappers from the lobby floor and throws them in the trash. As diversion from his bookkeeping, Baker loves what he does at the Carousel —and so do the paying guests.

Furthermore, he looks on it as a wonderful place for the family. His wife, Dorothy, serves on weekends as the Carousel's chief receptionist and hostess. His two oldest sons, Bobby, Jr., sixteen, and Jimmy, fifteen, work as bellhops, dishwashers and beachboys. He delights in driving his daughters, Dorothy, thirteen, and Lynda (as in Lynda Bird), seven, in a flashy beach buggy. And of course he loves to romp on the beach with his youngest son, five-year-old Lyndon John Baker. For Bobby, the Carousel is the family's second home.

"My wife is great," Bobby says, "and she's made me a great family. She's amazing, the way she can manage both her career and the kids. She's Catholic. If it were up to her, we'd have fifty kids. I think my children are just wonderful. I get a tremendous kick out of seeing my two oldest boys working hard, then going out on double dates together. But my wife is the superior one. She understands me better than I understand myself. She knows that ninety-five percent of the stuff written about my so-called escapades is nonsense. But she knows I'm normal. That's my problem. As for the other five percent, she regards that as part of the normality."

Carole Tyler used to be a normal visitor to the Carousel. Her figure was familiar on the beach and in the bar. Then, in May, 1965, she was killed. Carole was joyriding in a Waco biplane, when the pilot made a flip, failed to pull out in time and plunged into the Atlantic directly in front of the motel. Bobby was there when they brought her body ashore. He knew that the assembled crowd, mostly townspeople in threadbare clothes, expected him to say something appropriate. But there wasn't much you could say about Carole, beyond noting that she was a very pretty girl from a small town in Tennessee who found zest in Washington and lived her life with more gusto than it required. Her friends agreed later that she had chosen a kicky way to go. "All I can say," Baker uttered finally to the bystanders, "is that she was a very great lady." Baker was more accurate than that in taking head counts in the Senate. Whatever Carole was, that wasn't it. But Bobby had style and he wasn't going to let Carole, who was dear to him, leave the world without some of it as adornment.

"I don't think I've ever been more happy mentally in my life," Bobby Baker said in a recent interview. These might be interpreted as strange words, indeed, for a man who faces prison in his future. But then, seen from the perspective of Pickens, South Carolina, Bobby Baker is a great success story. He's been the intimate of the country's most important men—and he would be loath to concede that the bad habits of some of them rubbed off on him. When the Baker case broke, it was said that Bobby, unless let alone, would blow the Senate apart with his revelations.

Bobby has not only kept his mouth tightly shut—undoubtedly, to the gratitude of many—but has even had the good grace to deny that he was aware of any evil. Baker has not betrayed his Senate heritage.

"I live a typical American life," he said, nonchalantly. "I'm a simple fellow. I like to eat well and have a drink. But I don't need a hundred-foot yacht or a private plane. I've got my health and I don't look back." Pressed a little on whether he would do it all over again, Bobby replies, "Oh, I'm sure that—listen, all of us would do things a little differently." But Bobby Baker has no regrets—at least none that he lets show through. When asked about the prospects for vindication, Bobby expresses a buoyant optimism. The odds are excellent, he says, that he'll stay a free man. "After all," he declares with élan, "I've got the truth going for me."

Tsien Hsue-shen

CHINAMAN IN THE SOUP

Properly speaking, this piece on Tsien Hsue-shen is not a pro-
file at all but an American saga. It is, as I see it, the story of a
man betrayed by the country he had grown to love and the poetry
of his revenge. The idea for the article came to me on the day
after the Red Chinese fired their first nuclear-tipped missile, when
Tsien, the presumed technical genius behind it, was The New
York Times' *"Man in the News." The natural irony in the story*
was too much to resist. Here was a Chinese who was building mis-
siles for us until he was literally forced, during the McCarthy era,
to return home to build missiles for them. This was a story that I
felt I had to do.

   I cleared the idea with Esquire *and persuaded the Immigration*
Service to go back into its files to get out the transcript of Tsien's
deportation hearings for me. Then I made a phone call to Caltech,
where Tsien had taught and done his research, and I boarded a
plane for Los Angeles.

   Caltech is an inbred place, and many of the people who are
now on the faculty were there as students decades ago. So I had

no trouble finding old friends and colleagues of Tsien's, many of them people who had suffered through his trials with him and still loved him dearly. Most of them had stood faithfully behind Tsien, in spite of the personal risks of McCarthyism.

But the Tsien profile, more than any I had ever done, also turned into a detective story, as I tried to follow the thread of the events which led to the deportation proceedings, then unravel the incredibly complex proceedings themselves. I remember spending hours poring through files in the office of Grant Cooper, Tsien's lawyer, who later acquired renown as the attorney for Sirhan Sirhan. I found one broken man in Santa Monica who had served a prison sentence for attending the same cell meetings which Tsien allegedly attended. I talked to former cops on the Los Angeles "Red Squad" and to the immigration officer who prose- cuted Tsien's case. When I returned to Washington, I saw the men who made the decisions which determined Tsien's fate, and I even ran down a former Caltech student who had testified secretly against Tsien in return for immunity from FBI prosecution of his own case. Finally, I examined the State Department's monitor of the Chinese press to find out what happened to Tsien on his re- turn to China. When I was finished, what it added up to was a fascinating but very shabby episode in American history.

I know, of course, that there is still a body of thought which holds that Tsien had always been an evil genius, waiting for the chance to sell out America to the Red Chinese. I don't believe that notion for a minute. I think that, left alone, Tsien would have led a long and productive life as an American, though not without much of the nostalgia an immigrant often feels for his homeland. I can't confirm that view, of course. And I've never met Tsien to ask him. But I've always thought that perhaps some day I will meet him—or maybe he'll write me a letter from Red China to say he wished it had all turned out differently.

DOCTOR TSIEN'S not the type to be vindictive. That, at least, is what his friends have said—his friends at Caltech, in the Air Force, at M.I.T., even at Aerojet, where he used to help build ballistic missiles to defend the United States. But when Robert S. McNamara, the Secretary of Defense, announced recently that the Red Chinese would, by the end of this year, have a nuclear-armed rocket they could lob into Honolulu or, for that matter, Los Angeles—where Tsien spent some seventeen years of his life—none of those friends would have been surprised if Tsien experienced a certain satisfaction. Sitting in his laboratory in Peking, Tsien, they figured, could be excused if he saw poetic justice in the sweat that glistened on the Secretary's brow.

Tsien Hsue-shen is what some would call the evil genius behind Red China's missiles—though those who knew him remember him as a quiet, courteous fellow who wouldn't hurt a fly in the won ton soup. His claim to distinction is that for a quarter of a century he has been acknowledged as one of the world's most original minds in the science of aeronautics. A theoretician rather than a builder, he sits down with paper and pencil and, from fantastic resources of mathematics and physics and engineering, he comes up with prodigious plans for the propulsion, guidance and design of virtually anything that flies. As an architect of lethal rockets, few men rival him. More than anyone else, Tsien is responsible for China's creating the missiles that one day may be tumbling down on our heads.

But it was a long trip back to Peking, and not a pleasant one. During World War II, Tsien helped transform American rocketry —which lagged severely behind that of the Germans—from utter primitiveness to relative sophistication. Having lent an essential hand to construction of the first successful missiles, he put on a uniform and followed Allied armies into Germany to study the formidable aerial weapons devised by Hitler's engineers. On his return, he became a key man in planning the long-term transition of the Air Force from propeller service to the jet engine and, finally, to unmanned craft soaring through space. The worth of Tsien's services was acknowledged again and again by official commendations. Tsien was a bright star in the galaxy of scientists who were helping to make the United States into the world's foremost military power.

Tsien Hsue-shen, born in Shanghai of middle-class parents, came to this country in the fall of 1935, when he was twenty-six years old. He had made an excellent record in his university studies but, because of China's technological deficiencies, he could go no farther in his chosen field, mechanical engineering. When he won a scholarship from the Boxer Rebellion indemnity fund, a small American atonement for the days when China was a province of Western civilization, he decided to leave his homeland to do graduate work at the Massachusetts Institute of Technology. There he shifted to aeronautical engineering and in a year received a master's degree. Then he moved to the California Institute of Technology in Los Angeles' lush suburb of Pasadena. In the ensuing years, he began to think of home not so much as China but as Caltech.

Academically, Caltech's chief attraction was Dr. Theodore von Kármán, a transplanted Hungarian who was, without question, the world's outstanding authority in aeronautics. During the three years in which Tsien worked for his doctorate, von Kármán became more and more impressed by the young Chinese. Tsien became his most favored student, then his protégé, then his disciple. A bachelor, nearing sixty at the time, von Kármán lived with his elderly maiden sister; he took to Tsien as father to son. Finally, Tsien became acknowledged as von Kármán's scientific peer. The two men, mentor and pupil, now worked together as one. Von Kármán, by his genius, earned the title "father of the supersonic age," and in the science of aerodynamics he stands in singular eminence. But just below him ranks Tsien Hsue-shen. When von Kármán was making his revolutionary discoveries in almost every phase of aeronautics, Tsien served as his indispensable adviser and collaborator. Tsien was the heir apparent to von Kármán's aspirations and responsibilities. Since the old man's death, he has been unsurpassed in his field but, as if by irony, he has gone on to attain the pinnacle of his career not by pursuing von Kármán's ends but, in effect, by seeking to thwart them.

The germ of the metamorphosis was introduced in Tsien's days as a graduate student at Caltech. In contrast to most other Orientals on the campus, Tsien mixed quite easily with Americans. To be sure, he was proudly, almost defiantly, Chinese. If he was embarrassed by China's backward technology, he nonetheless gloried in the grandeur and sweep of its ancient culture, and he behaved as if he were custodian of the honor of Chinese civilization. But he was not a racist and he preferred Americans with whom he had common interests to Chinese with whom he did not.

Frank Malina quickly became Tsien's friend at Caltech. They both were students of aeronautics, Malina a few years more advanced. Malina, with von Kármán's encouragement, pursued an interest which was then regarded as highly eccentric. He was a buff for rockets and before long he transmitted his enthusiasm to Tsien. With fascination, Tsien followed the makeshift experimentation in which Malina engaged. But that was not all the two had in common. Both loved serious music. In Shanghai, Tsien had regularly attended symphonic concerts, and at M.I.T. he rarely missed an opportunity to hear the Boston Symphony. Since coming to Caltech, Tsien had attended faithfully the performances of the Los Angeles Philharmonic. Malina was his steady companion. The interests the two men shared, aeronautical and musical, made them very good friends indeed.

Among Malina's other friends were some graduate students at Caltech, all in science or engineering, who played musical instruments together in an amateur string quartet. He introduced Tsien to them. Tsien, who had never before encountered chamber music, liked what they played and collected albums of their favorite pieces. Sometimes he visited these friends even without Malina. Before long, Tsien found himself a part of this stimulating group of young people, drawn together by a common affection for science and music.

As it turned out, they also had a passion for politics and this, too, intrigued Tsien. He was deeply troubled by what was happening to China, crumbling as it was beneath the attacks of the Japanese. He found that his new friends were sympathetic to China's agonies, as they were to Ethiopia's and Republican Spain's. They told him that only the Soviet Union cared about stopping Fascist conquest and indeed that appeared to be true at the time. At their suggestion, Tsien read some Marxist philosophy and subscribed to a Communist newspaper. He enjoyed talking over with them his observations, as he took comfort in sharing with them his indignation. Though he knew little about politics, he had a Chinese scholar's fascination for moral philosophy and moral abstractions. Today his views are remembered—as best they can be, after almost thirty years—as having been "progressive," theoretical and somewhat naïve. Tsien later described these evenings as "bull sessions," which he considered pleasant enough as diversion from his work but hardly very significant in the overall scheme of his life.

Tsien's circle of friends met irregularly, both for music and discourse, throughout the last months of 1938 and most of 1939. Then its members started going off, either to war or to scientific jobs associated with the war. Malina himself began a serious research project on military rockets and, because it was secret, he could no longer discuss his work with Tsien, who, as an alien, was ineligible for clearance to classified material. The two friends drifted apart. By mid-1940, wartime austerity prevailed at Caltech and the old crowd, too busy with war work for frivolity, unceremoniously broke up—presumably never to be heard of again.

Tsien continued to teach and study until 1943, when the government thought better of its restrictions and approved him for military research. He went to work immediately with Malina on the rocket project and, by the end of the year, the two of them, under von Kármán's supervision, completed the designs for America's first military missiles. Then with von Kármán's guidance Tsien spread out into related fields. He did important work in jet propulsion, in which the United States was also behind the Germans. He became a consultant to Aerojet, the company formed by von Kármán and several other Caltech scientists to manufacture the new rockets. Near the end of the war, he took on the task of exploring nuclear energy as a possible power source for aircraft. To meet his commitments, he commuted between the Pentagon and Malina's jet-propulsion lab in Pasadena. On V-E Day, Tsien was in Germany. When the war was over, the Air Forces commended him for his "invaluable contribution" to victory. Tsien's work was regarded as important to the country's military victory and even more important to its military future.

But as a theoretical scientist, Tsien's place was at a university and, after the war, he accepted an offer to become, at thirty-seven, the youngest full professor on the faculty at M.I.T. Being in Massachusetts, however, did not cut him off from California. He and von Kármán remained on as Air Force advisers and traveled frequently together to military installations throughout the country. Later, Tsien joined von Kármán on some NATO projects. In 1949, when aircraft manufacturers began to realize that a deficiency in theoretical knowledge about jet propulsion was seriously hampering practical advances, the Guggenheim Foundation established two major research centers, at Princeton and Caltech; Tsien was offered the directorship of either one. He chose to return to Caltech, with a substantial salary and the title of Goddard Professor of Jet Propulsion. The arrangements proposed to him were ideal and the prospects appeared unlimited.

While he was still at M.I.T., Tsien had made a visit back to China to see his family. Some of his friends predicted that he wouldn't return and, indeed, there was some reason to believe that he would become president of his alma mater, Chiao-Tung University in Shanghai. But the appointment didn't work out and, after three months, he did return, with a pretty wife named Yin who, though selected for him by his family, happened to suit him superbly. Yin, daughter of a diplomat, had been raised in the West, was a student of music and an accomplished singer, and spoke English fluently. She adjusted, perhaps more easily than

Tsien himself, to college life in Cambridge, then to the gaudy sub-tropics of Pasadena.

Tsien and Yin, as far as one could tell, were a happy couple. Insulated at Caltech from the anti-Oriental prejudices of the region, they were warmly received wherever they chose to go. They lived in a spacious, unpretentious old house, in which they were presently joined by two children—both, naturally, American citizens by birth. In his role as father, Tsien soon found himself attending meetings of the P.T.A. and repairing broken toys for the nursery school, but he seemed to enjoy his responsibilities. The Tsiens entertained a great deal in their big house. Many of Tsien's old colleagues remember fondly the evenings in which Tsien himself, with great flourish, cooked a Chinese dinner at the table, while Yin, who had spent all day on the preparations, sat self-effacingly at his side. But Yin was not intimidated by her husband. She alone made jokes about his tendency to be stuffy. Unlike him, she even took a drink now and then and if she became a bit giddy, she paid no attention to his grimaces of disapproval. "I don't know what happened after we left," said one old friend; "perhaps he gave her hell. But we always had fun there and felt relaxed with them. I'd say the marriage was very successful." The Tsiens, apart from being Chinese, seemed indistinguishable from hundreds of families living in an academic environment.

In his professional relations, Tsien was held less in affection and more in esteem. Perhaps because he was a Chinese among Westerners, he was unduly competitive. He made excessive demands not only on himself but on the Chinese students who worked under him. He was profoundly intolerant of mediocrity. Tsien often broke the rules of academic etiquette by his open contempt of inferior work; more than one colleague was left limp by some witheringly candid comment. But the corollary was that Tsien was known as a man totally ungiven to cant: There was nothing of the inscrutable Oriental about him. He was, if anything, too free with his judgments. His colleagues considered him rather arrogant but they agreed it was not so much a character failing as a by-product of his own honesty, self-discipline and rigorous intellectual perfectionism.

Given this unfettered but conscientious spirit, Tsien was made for the kind of arrangement he had at Caltech. He served no boss but his own sense of responsibility. He could do what he chose, teach what he wanted, pursue the research that interested him. He had an ample staff of his own selection and generous funds with which to finance his favorite projects. He had his pick of the best graduate students in his field and he could train them as he saw fit. Once, dissatisfied with a course, he sat down and wrote a completely new textbook, so difficult, it was said, that only the brightest students could understand what it was all about. But as if his work at Caltech were not enough, Tsien continued to serve as a consultant to Aerojet and an adviser, with von Kármán, on national defense and security problems. In December 1949 Tsien received widespread attention—including a picture story in *Time* —for some designs he had made, almost as a whim, for a coast-to-coast rocket airliner. Under Tsien, Caltech's jet-propulsion center became the focus of the world's most advanced research in aeronautics.

It is clear that by now Tsien, with Yin's consent, had made up his mind to remain permanently in the United States. He was probably no less devoted to China than before and it was only with difficulty that he rebuffed the pleas of his ill and aging father to return. But by now he had spent most of his adult life in the United States and his children knew no other home. Perhaps more important, he knew that in China he could never work with as much satisfaction as he did at Caltech. His specialty, after all, demanded a highly technological society for its full exercise. In China he could, at best, perform only on a much lower scientific level. So, in mid-1949, Tsien executed the rite demanded of aliens who wish to remain indefinitely in this country; he went to Canada, acquired a permanent resident's visa and reentered with it. Shortly afterward, he made application to become a citizen of the United States.

But this was the very period when a strange malaise was beginning to infect the country. In quick order, a series of crises bred growing nervousness and distress. In September 1949 the Russians ended the American nuclear monopoly by exploding their first atomic bomb. In November, Alger Hiss went on trial to contend with the assertion that he had been, while a State Department official, a Communist spy. In December, Chiang Kai-shek fled before Mao Tse-tung's victorious armies to the island of Formosa. In February 1950 the British announced that Dr. Klaus Fuchs, one of their top scientists, had passed on to the Russians some of the West's most important atomic secrets. That same month, Senator Joseph McCarthy of Wisconsin told the Women's Republican Club of Wheeling that he held in his hands the names of two hundred five Communists in the State Department. The country began to see betrayal everywhere; anxiety verged on panic.

Inevitably, Caltech felt the effects of the mood. Federal agents suddenly discovered that the discussion group in which Tsien had participated with his friends more than a decade before had actually been Professional Unit 122, the Pasadena section of the Communist Party. Malina, on temporary leave of absence, simply resigned as director of the jet-propulsion lab and took up permanent residence in Paris (where, it might be noted, he has since become a very successful modernist painter). Some of Tsien's other friends of former days fared less well. One was indicted for denying Party membership and shipped off to jail. Others lost their jobs at universities. Some left science altogether, usually to go into business, where they never again made use of their talents. At no point was it alleged that the cell members, as Communists, did anything more serious than talk. But in these days, talk was more than enough. Tsien learned of inpending trouble when FBI agents began poking around the campus, asking questions about him. In June 1950 he was notified that his security clearance had been revoked and that he was no longer welcome to perform services for the Government of the United States.

Tsien was shocked. More damaged than his career, which could thrive nicely without classified work, was his pride. He felt he had given every bit of his energy to the United States and in return had been dismissed in incredibly shabby fashion. He took no consolation from being treated no worse than many others, including some of his own friends. "I am apparently an unwelcome guest in this country," he told one of his colleagues. Out of his indignation emerged the reflection that he had, quite possibly, made a mistake in deciding to become an American. It was at this point, according to all evidence, that he began to contemplate returning to China.

In the previous months, Tsien had received letters from his father with increasing frequency. He needed another operation, the old man wrote. Tsien's sister required guidance. Tsien's friends pointed out to him that the new Communist government might be at the source of the intensified pressure. Tsien agreed, but answered that he nonetheless had filial responsibilities—even if he had, until then, chosen to ignore them. Tsien asked Caltech for a year's leave of absence. He then booked passage on an airplane to Hong Kong for himself and his family. He had his personal belongings packed in crates and delivered to U.S. Customs. Tsien told some of his friends that he would try to get his father out of Red China into Hong Kong; he acknowledged to others that this plan had small prospect of success and that he probably would go to Shanghai and take a temporary job as a teacher. While looking after the affairs of his family, he said, he would think matters over and reach a decision on the future.

Dr. Lee DuBridge, the President of Caltech, did not try to persuade Tsien to cancel his plans, much as he wanted to keep him as one of the faculty luminaries. But he believed, like almost everyone else at Caltech, that Tsien's chastisement was a horrible error, which would be corrected as soon as the proper authorities were brought to their senses. He regarded Tsien as too proud to deceive, too straightforward to masquerade. He could no more conceive of Tsien's lying about Communist Party membership than about the properties of a jet engine. DuBridge wanted Tsien to understand that if he did go to China, he would, at the very least, be welcome to return at any time to resume his career at Caltech. Recognizing, however, that Tsien would not contemplate coming back as long as his reputation lay under a cloud, DuBridge wanted to make one last effort to set matters straight. A few days before the scheduled departure, DuBridge convinced

Tsien that he ought to fly to Washington to try for the restoration of his clearance.

In Washington, Tsien's first stop was Dan Kimball's office in the Pentagon. Kimball, while he was head of Aerojet, had become a friend and admirer of Tsien's. Now he was President Truman's Assistant Secretary of the Navy. Kimball, a Democrat and a liberal, looked upon the surging McCarthyite wave as a national folly. He was absolutely convinced that Tsien was not a Communist. He remembers that Tsien broke into tears in his office when he described the humiliation to which he had been subjected. Kimball referred Tsien to an excellent Washington lawyer and tried, to no avail, to use his own influence to reestablish Tsien's good standing. But what shocked Kimball most of all during the visit was Tsien's declaration that he was returning to Red China. In the clash of loyalties between friend and country, Kimball didn't hesitate over priority. As soon as Tsien left his office, he called the Justice Department and announced that this man, with all the knowledge he possessed, must not be allowed to leave the United States.

At midnight on August 23, 1950, Tsien's plane, arriving from Washington at the Los Angeles Airport, was met by an agent of the Immigration and Naturalization Service. As Tsien stepped away from the aircraft, the agent handed him a paper saying that he was forbidden by law to depart the country. Tsien took the paper without protest and returned home to Pasadena. He and Yin talked the matter over and, after a day or two of uncertainty, decided that she and the children would stay with him. Tsien had no idea how long the restraining order would remain in effect. He canceled the plane reservations to China and, as if nothing had happened, went back to work at Caltech. Meanwhile, FBI agents maintained surveillance over his house and shadowed all his movements.

Down at the Customs office, in the meantime, other agents were examining Tsien's baggage, which had been deposited in anticipation of imminent departure. What they found reduced them to consternation. Tsien's crates contained some eighteen hundred pounds of papers, which they immediately concluded must be highly secret. Customs officials called in the press and announced that the material included "documents, code books, signal books, sketches, photographs, negatives, blueprints, plans, notes and other forms of technical information." From the announcement one was almost forced to conclude that this wily Chinese had all the while been an espionage agent for Mao. But on closer examination, the government discovered that the baggage actually contained, as Tsien had consistently claimed, not security information at all but textbooks, class notes and reprints of articles from scientific journals, many of which Tsien himself had written. It was material which anyone who contemplated teaching a course in his specialty might have been expected to take with him. Weeks before, Tsien had, in fact, gone scrupulously through his files and returned to the government all the classified material that was in his possession. In all the eighteen hundred pounds, not a single secret document was found.

Bit by bit, in the ensuing months, the government released Tsien's luggage to him, without ever publicly admitting the spuriousness of its accusations. But, for the moment, the authorities were scared and they determined that Tsien was too dangerous to remain at large.

On September 7, two weeks after the fateful Washington trip, Tsien was arrested by the FBI. The charge made against him was that he had, in concealing membership in the Communist Party, entered the country illegally when he returned from China in 1947. The Attorney General had actually issued the warrant on August 25, right after Kimball's phone call. Why it was not executed immediately is not clear. The warrant—oddly, for a man whom the authorities wanted desperately to keep in the country—demanded Tsien's deportation from the United States.

DuBridge and Kimball, separately, undertook immediately to have Tsien released from jail. It wasn't easy. DuBridge flew first to Washington to persuade the Attorney General that Tsien was a man of honor, who would not skip if he gave his word to stay. Both DuBridge and Kimball produced letters from Tsien in which he pledged to remain in the country. Finally, bail was set at the unusually high figure of $15,000. DuBridge, and Kimball, succeeded in raising the money by tapping a wealthy friend of Tsien's in the Caltech community. But despite the word of DuBridge and of Kimball and despite the $15,000 bond, the court still was not satisfied. It set the condition that Tsien could not travel beyond the boundaries of Los Angeles County, which implied a kind of house arrest. Tsien had no choice but to accede. After more than two weeks behind bars, he was set free. DuBridge restored him at once to the Caltech faculty and Tsien, silently containing his shame and anger, went back to work.

The Immigration Service—to the surprise of all—wasted no time in going ahead with deportation proceedings. Even today, it is unclear what the government hoped to accomplish by pursuing the case. Most legal experts believe that the order keeping Tsien in the United States was properly drawn on a valid statute. It could, presumably, have stood indefinitely. As an alternative, a criminal charge of perjury—claiming Tsien had lied under oath about Party membership—would, if successful, have at least had the virtue of keeping him harmlessly in jail. But some bureaucrat apparently recognized that the government would have trouble making such a charge stick in court and, anxious to get some sort of legal judgment against Tsien, settled on deportation proceedings. No evidence exists to suggest that the case was reviewed on a policy-making level. On the contrary, the decisions seem all to have been made by Los Angeles Immigration officials, whose everyday work consisted mainly of chasing wetbacks across the Mexican border. Albert Del Guercio, the agent assigned to the case, says today that he personally ordered the proceedings, to strengthen the government's hold on Tsien. Within two months after Tsien's release on bail, the Immigration Service began hearings for the expressed purpose of sending him back to China. And Tsien, who wanted to return to China, had to fight the proceedings, for the purpose of preserving his honor and his freedom of action.

The hearings were, at best, a travesty. Caltech arranged for

Grant Cooper, one of Los Angeles' outstanding trial lawyers, to act as Tsien's counsel. Cooper protested vigorously but in vain, at every step in the long confrontation. He was informed that the rules protecting the respondent in a deportation proceeding were far less rigorous than those protecting the rights of a defendant in a criminal case. Cooper conceded the accuracy of the contention. But he did not admit that the rules permitted introduction into the record of every sort of hearsay, gossip, rumor, guess, innuendo and political opinion.

The Immigration Service paraded in, one after another, the members of Tsien's discussion group of a dozen years before. Most said they had known that it was, in reality, a chapter of the Communist Party. Each testified that he recalled vaguely Tsien's occasional presence at the meetings—a fact never in dispute. All acknowledged that guests, especially foreigners, were frequently invited, that these guests had not necessarily known the meetings were Communist. Not one witness could say with any certainty that Tsien had been a chapter member. A former treasurer testified that he did not recall ever collecting dues from Tsien. To wrap up its case, the Immigration Service produced what it widely advertised to the press as a "surprise witness." This witness had himself recently been indicted for perjury, after refusing to testify against his former friends. He admits now that the FBI hinted at generous treatment if he changed his mind and talked. He did talk, but the most damaging statement he could make about Tsien was: "All I can say is that I *believe* he was a member." The witness was in due course acquitted of the perjury charge. Tsien didn't do nearly as well.

The Immigration Service also took testimony from two members of the Los Angeles Police Department's "Red Squad." One of them had infiltrated the Party long before and had come up with documents which purported to be membership lists. Tsien's name appeared in one series. But, on further scrutiny, none were Communist Party documents at all. They were lists in the handwriting of the cops, which the cops claimed had been copied from other lists. Cooper pointed out that the lists, which were not otherwise identified, could easily have been of *prospective* members, prepared by persons who took Tsien's presence at meetings to mean candidacy rather than membership. At no time did the Immigration Service or the "Red Squad" produce any Communist record in Tsien's handwriting, any evidence that he had paid dues or held a card, or even a listing of membership on an official file or piece of letterhead stationery.

Tsien himself, over the course of the hearings, was grilled extensively. He conceded readily that he had attended gatherings which appeared in retrospect to have been Communist Party meetings. He pointed out that they had consisted of nothing more sinful than talk and he argued that, in their informality, the meetings had no sign of any ulterior objective. In any case, he said, he had never joined the Communist Party and he insisted that in denying membership he had not committed perjury.

But it was not enough for the Immigration Service to stick to the accusation against Tsien. Over Cooper's vigorous protests, Agent Del Guercio spent hours questioning Tsien on political matters. Del Guercio explained that he could tell whether Tsien was inclined to Communism by analyzing his political opinions.

"Mr. Tsien," Del Guerico asked, "do you believe the United States should recognize Red China?" Tsien answered that he had insufficient information to make a judgment.

"Do you feel that you owe allegiance to the Nationalist Government of China?" Tsien said he was not very enthusiastic about the Nationalists because "we have yet to see" if they are doing any good for China. His allegiance, he said, was to the Chinese people.

"Do you owe your allegiance to Communist China?" Tsien answered categorically that he did not.

"In the event of a conflict between this country and Red China, would you fight against Red China for the United States?" Tsien thought a long time before he came up with an answer. He said finally: "My essential allegiance is to the people of China and if the war between the United States and Communist China is for the good of the people of China, which I think it is very likely to be, so then I will fight on the side of the United States. No question about that."

But however bizarre its character, the hearing had the outcome which, for all practical purposes, was foreordained. The Immigration Service simply sustained itself on the charges it had itself brought. Tsien was ordered deported. But the paradox intervened, in that the execution was suspended by the prior order which prohibited his departure. Cooper, who contended that he had no judicial recourse as long as the first order canceled the second, planned to appeal the case to the courts as soon as the deportation decision became effective. He said he was confident of winning. But meanwhile, Tsien was in limbo, free on bail but confined to the county, not at liberty to go but not welcome to stay.

Tsien's status remained in this nether world as months passed into years. Tsien withdrew deeper and deeper into study and research, working so intensively that his colleagues marveled at his dedication. Among a few old friends, he was still warm and outgoing. They had worked for him, risked their good names for him, even helped to pay his painfully heavy legal fees. Tsien, for all his anguish, did not fail to recognize their loyalty and take comfort from it.

Occasionally, they spent a happy evening together, usually when von Kármán came to town. The old man now devoted most of his time to NATO and lived all but a few months of each year in Paris. When he came to Pasadena, it was for some whirlwind consultation at Aerojet or Caltech. On these occasions, Tsien saw to it that he was regally entertained. Tsien and Yin sometimes held a party for von Kármán at their house. Other times, Tsien arranged a big Chinese feast at a restaurant in Los Angeles' Chinatown. Throughout Tsien's troubles, von Kármán, like the group at Caltech, remained faithful to his former pupil. As near as their friends could tell, the two men stayed as close as ever. If von Kármán went on in his work without Tsien—as committed as he was to the security of the West—the student bore his master no obvious grudge.

But there was no mistaking now Tsien's attitude toward the United States generally. As time passed, he grew increasingly bitter. No one doubted, after the imprisonment and the hearings and the protracted confinement, that Tsien yearned for the day when he could leave America for good, and, among his friends almost no one blamed him.

But in official circles, there seemed to be only a vague understanding of what his departure would mean and an incomprehensible indifference to doing anything about it. Kimball, who in 1951 rose to Secretary of the Navy, has said that Truman never considered the matter. DuBridge, who in the next Administration became the President's chief scientific adviser, says that Eisenhower had probably never heard of Tsien. Del Guercio thought of Tsien—and proudly does, in retirement today—as a trophy on his wall. The case, facing downstream in a bureaucratic channel, seemed to be swept along on its own, as if no official with real power could intervene to change its course.

The matter reached its quiet culmination in 1955, a year during which the State Department discreetly negotiated with Peking the exchange of Chinese students and scholars detained in this country for American missionaries, educators and businessmen still held in China. It was also the year in which some American flyers were shot down over China and interned. Whatever secrets Tsien once had stored in his mind were by now believed outdated. Though this outdating in no way impaired his creative genius, of course, it presumably rendered him less dangerous. Almost certainly, Tsien was made part of an unpublicized swap for Americans in China.

On August 4, 1955, Tsien was unceremoniously notified by the Immigration Service that the restraining order on him had been lifted and that he was free to leave. Tsien didn't even bother to ask whether the deportation order was still in effect, and the government didn't volunteer the information. But now he cared no more about sustaining his honor among Americans. He was no longer interested in being free to return to the United States. Tsien wanted to get out. That's all he cared about. On September 17, after making the rounds of his friends at Caltech to say a melancholy goodbye, he, Yin and the two children sailed for the Orient.

Grant Cooper was not so indifferent to the procedures associated with Tsien's release. As the Immigration Service knew, Cooper was pledged to appealing the deportation order to the courts, whenever it might become applicable. When it did, Tsien would undoubtedly have blocked the plan—but what mattered to Cooper was that the Immigration Service never notified him, as attorney of record, of the change in Tsien's status. Cooper learned of Tsien's departure from the newspaper and was furious. He rejected the Immigration Service's contention it had "inadvertently" failed to keep him informed.

"To say that I was shocked," he wrote in a letter of protest, ". . . is to put it mildly. If I, as an attorney in any proceeding, were to deal with a client on the opposing side without notice to or consent of the counsel for the opposing side, I would be subject to severe discipline and probably even disbarment—and I do not feel that an agency of the government is in any different position." The Immigration Service duly noted the protest and filed it. Del Guercio and his colleagues were far too pleased with their triumph—however suicidal the implications—to worry about the vain gripe of a deportee's lawyer.

It took no special perception to predict the significance of what Tsien would be doing on his return to China. "We knew he wasn't going back there to grow apples," DuBridge said. Kimball, at Aerojet once again, finds it hard to contain his frustration. "It was the stupidest thing this country ever did," he says. "He was no more a Communist than I was—and we forced him to go."

Certainly the Red Chinese were not naïve about what they were getting. On his arrival in Canton, his first stop on the China mainland, Tsien was greeted enthusiastically by public officials and a delegation of top scientists. At Peking, he was officially welcomed home by the government, wined and dined by the university and deluged with honors by the Academy of Sciences. The Academy, the government's chief scientific arm, offered him the post of chief of research in applied mechanics. In accepting,

Tsien resumed at once the work on propulsion and rocketry which he was doing at Caltech. Now he had, in addition, responsibility for supervising research in these fields throughout the country.

Somewhat surprisingly Tsien did not prove reticent about talking of his American experiences. He gave several interviews for Red Chinese papers, in which he recounted past events with remarkable objectivity and expressed his own emotions with extraordinary restraint. "I will never forget those fair-minded, decent Americans who helped and supported me during my five years of detention in the United States," he said of his Caltech friends. "They, like all ordinary peace-loving Americans, are quite different from the U.S. Government. The actions of the U.S. Government are not their actions. The Chinese people have no ill-feelings toward the American people. We desire to be friends and coexist peacefully." But more astonishing to read in the Peking press was Tsien's denial that he had ever been a Communist or had attempted to smuggle scientific documents out of the United States. One would have believed that self-interest demanded his boasting of having been a Red agent all along, or at least a Red sympathizer.

Before long, however, reports coming out of Red China indicated that Tsien was getting into the ideological swing. In January 1957 in accepting a major scientific award, he declared that American efforts to keep him from returning home had been a vain effort to undermine the "national defense of the fatherland." Instead of fretting during all those years, he said, he had used his time acquiring knowledge that would be important to China. National defense, he said, had been his dominant thought, until "the diplomatic victory won by China, when I managed to return finally to the embrace of the fatherland." Later that year, Tsien showed a new fondness for political doctrine and declared: "America has an enormous scientific and technical foundation, but it has not brought any great benefits to the people. Which, after all, should we choose, capitalist or socialist leadership? Of course, we can only choose socialist leadership." More recently, Tsien was recorded as saying: "Chairman Mao has taught us how to overcome idealistic and metaphysical errors, how to proceed from reality, how to analyze problems in a comprehensive manner and how to grasp the essence of things. . . . As long as we are able to act in accordance with Chairman Mao's directives, victory will surely belong to us."

Step by step with his ideological development, Tsien advanced politically. Almost from the beginning, he engaged—like most Chinese scientists—in active politics. In 1956, he won several honorific public offices. In 1958, in recognition of his support of Mao in one of the recurring sectarian battles, he was awarded membership in the Communist Party. Later that year, he was elected a deputy from the province of Kwangtung to the National People's Congress, China's nominal legislature, and he was re-elected in 1964. Meanwhile, he was expanding his influence within the national scientific hierarchy by acquiring more and more offices in technical societies. Within the past few years, Tsien's public statements indicate that China has been looking to him increasingly for guidance on technological development generally. Still, it is clear that Tsien continues to pursue his own scientific research and there is a suggestion, at least, that politics are for him nothing more than a device—as it apparently is for other Chinese scientists—for buttressing his freedom to achieve his scientific ends.

One of Tsien's old friends at Caltech, musing recently, said: "I sometimes wonder how he's able to get along over there. When he was here, he simply would not compromise. I don't think that's a characteristic that can be changed." Then, reflecting: "But he was always obsessed about doing things for China. I suppose this ideology is necessary to his job. I believe he feels what he's doing is in China's best interests."

Over at Aerojet the consensus is less well-disposed toward Tsien. "I think he's an immoral bastard," said one high official, who knew him well. "I believe we had no right to do what we did to him. He was no Communist when he was here. But that doesn't mean he has the right to sell out. He's lost all my sympathy for turning on us the way he has."

Tsien himself has not helped his old friends to clarify their opinions about him. They haven't received a word from him in years. At first, some of his former colleagues at the jet-propulsion center received Christmas cards, decorated with red stars. In recent years, the only news—apart from an occasional press dispatch originating in China—has come from a sister of Yin's, living in Brussels. No one has ever seen Tsien at a scientific meeting outside China.

This, perhaps, explains why so much effort is still put into interpreting the meaning of two communications from Tsien which have arrived in the years since his departure. The first came on von Kármán's seventy-fifth birthday in 1956, an occasion of great celebration. Tsien was asked for a letter for von Kármán's scrapbook. In precise script he answered:

On this occasion of your seventy-fifth Birthday, Dr. von Kármán, what would be the proper words for a greeting? Shall I speak about our happy days together in Pasadena, in your house in Pasadena? No, that would not be proper, for I am not just your friend but, more important, your student. Shall I speak about your great contributions to science and engineering, and wish you will do more in the forthcoming years? No, that would be only a restatement of a world-known fact and a repetition of very common birthday greeting. I wish to say more, to say something which may have a deeper meaning— because you are my respected teacher.

I presume that at the heart of every sincere scientist the thing that counts is an everlasting contribution to the human society. On this point, Dr. von Kármán, you may not feel as proud as you might feel about your contributions to science and technology. Is it not true that so many of the fruits of your work were used and are being used to manufacture the weapons of destruction, and so seldom were they used for the good of the people? But you really need not think so. For, since I returned to my homeland, I have discovered that there is an entirely different world away from that world of U.S.A., where now lives 900 million people, more than a third of the world population, and where science and technology are actually being used to help for the construction of a happy life. Here everybody works for the common dedicated aim, for they know only by working together can they reach their goal in the shortest possible time. In this world, your work(s), Dr. von Kármán, are treasured, and you are respected as one who through his contributions to science and technology is helping us to achieve a life of comfort, leisure and beauty. May this statement then be my greeting to you on the occasion of your seventy-fifth Birthday.

No one was quite sure what Tsien was trying to say in the letter. Von Kármán himself was offended by it. He was not so much put off by the political diatribe as by the lack of warmth. He felt that Tsien, whatever the pressures, could somehow have transmitted something of the spirit of their old relationship. But some of von Kármán's friends, who were also friends of Tsien, did not agree that any callousness was intended. They pointed to Tsien's positive phrases. They contended that for a letter written under a totalitarian government, where mail is undoubtedly read by a censor, it was considerate and friendly. They maintained that Tsien, behind a thin veil of propaganda that may have been required of him, was actually trying to say something both kindly and respectful to von Kármán.

Seven years passed before another occasion arose for word from Tsien: von Kármán's death, just before his eighty-second birthday. As soon as he heard the news, Tsien wired this message: "I learn with deep regret the passing of Doctor von Kármán, but I believe he, as a brilliant scientist, will live in the hearts of all of us. We can further comfort us by knowing that his scientific contributions will be acknowledged by all countries irrespective of social systems." Once again, Tsien could not resist a bit of ideology—but this time everyone agreed that he had been civil and decent and had said the right things. It hardly mattered, however, since no one heard from Tsien again. With von Kármán's death, Tsien and his friends parted, apparently forever.

Still, at Caltech, Tsien's memory is a real presence. His books sit on the shelves, with his personal inscriptions on the flyleafs. His memos remain in the filing cabinets. His course outlines are still consulted. His brilliant scientific *tours de force* continue to thrill his old collaborators. The evenings with Tsien and Yin, over bowls of rice and cups of tea, do not cease to evoke nostalgia. Most of Tsien's friends, to this day, wish him well in China. They believe that, if things had gone differently, he'd be with them now. They regard his reaction to the events that befell him as human, if not laudable. They wish he were working here now. For, quite apart from the warm friendship they feel for him, they do not fancy having a missile dropped on them—nor would they take comfort if it happened to be from Tsien.

Dean Rusk

JOHNNY REB GOES TO VIETNAM

It had long seemed strange to me that nothing of significance was written about Secretary of State Dean Rusk, the most prominent exponent of our war policy in Vietnam. Rusk had been an obscure figure in the State Department under President Truman, but there was ample indication of his importance in the formation of our postwar China policy and our involvement in Korea. I was also sure that there was much in the upbringing of this Southern boy that would shed light on the intellectual processes behind American diplomatic policy. I made this argument before Harold Hayes over lunch at the Four Seasons in New York; Hayes, in his characteristically laconic way, nodded his assent.

Having done my homework with the printed matter, I set out for Atlanta, where Rusk was born and raised. Over the course of the next week, I traveled from Atlanta to Knoxville to Chapel Hill, seeing the usual collection of school chums, teachers, relatives and the rest. When I reached Rusk's older brother Roger, I was amazed that no writer had ever taken the trouble to talk to him before. Roger seemed to be waiting to tell everything he knew about his celebrated younger brother, whom he genuinely adored but who he felt had strayed from the family's Southern conservative traditions. Roger Rusk was a college professor, a cultured and sophisticated man; yet he seemed a character out of Faulkner or, to be more generous, perhaps W. J. Cash. Before long, I came to the conclusion that, deep down, Dean Rusk was one of those characters, too.

After my trip South, I went to New York, where I had a series of conversations with Rusk's contemporaries from his earlier Pentagon and State Department days. All these men had found secure niches within the establishment—Wall Street, the foundations, the communications industry. They felt a certain camaraderie with Rusk, but I saw that they all believed he had betrayed them by his fervent advocacy of the Vietnam war. It became clear to me, in the course of all these talks, that the establishment, of which the law firms and banking houses of Wall Street are the hub, genuinely believed that American foreign policy was its personal domain. Rusk, former president of the Rockefeller Foundation, had been one of the establishment's members and had received its stamp of approval to become Secretary of State. But after Johnson became President, I believe, he turned against his establishment friends and reverted to his Southern Populist origins, with its constituent elements of xenophobia, militarism and Calvinist zeal.

After my other interviews were finished, I had two meetings with Rusk himself, each lasting almost two hours. While we sipped scotch together, he spoke rather freely, both about himself and American foreign policy. The impression with which I came away was that the real Dean Rusk, lips clenched tightly together, was not very different from the public Dean Rusk, only a little less reticent, or, to put it differently, a little less diplomatic. I must confess that I didn't like either Rusk very much.

According to the reports which came back to me from the State Department, Rusk was troubled by my profile. He was far too discreet to complain to me, either personally or through an emissary. But he did tell a mutual acquaintance that he felt I was

*unfair in attributing so much to his Southern military background,
which he was sure he had overcome. I still disagree. I thought it
was particularly ironic—even sad—that the University of Georgia
later came close to denying Rusk a faculty position because some
of the trustees thought he had become too heavily infected by
Northern liberalism. Rusk and I spoke again several years later,
after his return to private life. I was seeking to elicit from him
some information for an article I was writing about the processes
of American diplomacy. He was coldly courteous, and would have
no conversation with me at all.*

To HEAR Dean Rusk explain it, we'd be in the same fix in
Vietnam today no matter who was Secretary of State—or, for
that matter, who was President. Foreign policy, he argues, comes
out of the "big enduring things" about the country and doesn't
respond to the whimsy of one individual or another, even if he
happens to be nominally in charge.

Rusk says that sure, he reexamines foreign policy all the time.
"But the people who preceded me were not fools," he declares, so
foreign policy hasn't changed much since Dean Acheson decided
to "contain" the Communists some twenty years ago. Just about
the only difference between Secretaries of State in all these years,
Rusk says, is that John Foster Dulles had a particular addiction
to summoning God to make his case.

Not only does Rusk insist that personality has little to do with
foreign policy, he also maintains that it shouldn't. One of his
major objectives, he says, is to "depersonalize" his office. He
speaks with a hint of condescension of Acheson's flamboyance.
His own aim is to keep himself off the front page, he says, and to
turn foreign policy into a humdrum routine. He's pleased that
journalists, despairing of understanding him, refer constantly to
him as "inscrutable" and "Sphinx-like." Rusk won't quite concede that the logical conclusion of his conception is the conduct
of foreign policy by computer. But he does say that the kind of

man he is has virtually no relation to the way the United States runs its affairs in Vietnam or any other part of the world.

Of course, there's not a soul in Washington who believes that. Senator Fulbright and Senator Morse don't believe it. James Reston and Walter Lippmann don't believe it. Robert S. McNamara and Arthur Goldberg *certainly* don't believe it. They have all tried and failed to change the course of the Vietnam war. Their defeat could be considered evidence of the personality of the Secretary of State.

To be sure, Rusk is no Svengali, exercising some mesmeric influence over the President of the United States. But from the beginning, Rusk has taken a hard line on Vietnam and he has found in Lyndon Johnson an apt pupil. No one doubts that Rusk, with his advocacy of relentless prosecution of the war, has emerged as the preponderant force in the Presidential councils. Should the President ever decide to change his course, Dean Rusk, symbol of the current policy, would have to go first. He can make all the disclaimers he likes about his personal responsibility, but Washington now regards the undertaking in Vietnam as Dean Rusk's war.

Though Rusk sees no anomaly in his being chief hawk in the aerie, there are some who regard the role he has cut out for himself as quite inappropriate for a Secretary of State. Every Cabinet officer, say these critics, has his constituency. The Secretary of Agriculture is supposed to look out for the interests of the farmer, the Secretary of Labor for the interests of the workingman. The Secretary of Defense has the responsibility for presenting arguments concerning the use of force, while the Secretary of State, say these critics, must present the case for diplomacy in international relations. Unless every member of the Cabinet, along with the lesser advisers, sticks up for his own constituency, they say, the President will be without the diversity of opinion he needs to make his decisions. Not so, says Dean Rusk. Government, he insists, just doesn't work that way.

Rusk rejects the adversary system—as practiced during the Kennedy Administration, for example—as essential to the Presidential councils. On the contrary, he considers one of his finest achievements to be the termination of rivalry between the Departments of State and Defense. "There is no longer any confrontation," he said, "but, if anything, an agonizing over each other's problems." Under Rusk and during McNamara's tenure, subordinates were always encouraged to keep in touch with their opposite numbers at all levels of the hierarchy, while hundreds of military and foreign-service officers have taken advanced training at each other's facilities. "We seldom have had to carry any disputes between the two departments to the President to settle," Rusk said proudly. With a Secretary of State predisposed to military force, some feel this all-for-one/one-for-all outlook has been a serious misfortune for the country. But for Lyndon Johnson, who likes consensus even in his Cabinet, it's been proof of Dean Rusk's great sagacity.

This sagacity that the President recognizes is composed, in copious measure, of the personal bond that exists between them. Both Johnson and Rusk started out as poor Southern boys anxious to make their way. Many of Johnson's kin, in fact, migrated to Texas from Rusk's country in Georgia. Both are Scotch-Irish in their origins, with heavy doses of Southern white Protestantism in their heritage. They are of the same generation, old enough to feel the aftermath of the Civil War in which all their grandfathers fought for the Confederacy, but young enough to be modern. Obviously they feel far more at ease with each other than either felt when they worked under President Kennedy.

"How comfortable it was for Lyndon Johnson to find Dean Rusk when he became President," said a close friend of the President. "He inherited a Kennedy world in the Kennedy Administration and he found a kindred spirit in the middle of it.

"Southerners in Washington are a little like Jews. They feel like a minority in a hostile world. They feel a loyalty toward each other and try to protect each other. Here were two Southern boys with the same outlook. Lyndon was delighted to have him there."

Associates report that when they're on a trip together, they chatter like schoolboys, lapsing into the exaggerated language of the South, happy as clams. If it is an overstatement to call Vietnam a Southerners' war, it is surely fair to say that Dean Rusk's dedication to this war, along with Lyndon Johnson's, emerges largely from the ideals and aspirations that have been handed down to him from his forebears in the South.

Dean Rusk was born in 1909 in Cherokee County, Georgia, on a remnant of the land that stories say his great-grandfather had taken from the Indians in the time of Andrew Jackson. He was the third and youngest son among five children. His brother Roger, just three years older, remembers how backward Cherokee County was when the Rusks were children. "When I went to Williamsburg many years later," Roger reminisced, "I saw the culture of the eighteenth century. I was amazed to see that it was identical with the culture of my grandfather in the beginning of the twentieth century." Only indirectly, however, did this rural culture make an impact on Dean. In the summer of 1912, heavy floods made it impossible for the Rusks to get out the crop. "The land didn't want us," said Roger. In 1913 the family picked up and moved to Atlanta, some thirty miles away. It was in Atlanta that Dean Rusk was raised.

Though the Rusks were poor, it is not true that they were "poor whites," in the sense that the term (sometimes rendered as "white trash") is classically used in the South. Robert Rusk, Dean's father, had somehow managed to put himself through Davidson, a small Presbyterian college but one of the South's best, before going on to the Louisville Seminary to become an ordained Presbyterian minister. Dean's mother had attended normal school and did some teaching before she married. In the Rusk household, there was, in contrast to the "poor white" attitude generally, a considerable respect for learning, if not for erudition. Parks, Dean's oldest brother, was too busy in the cotton fields throughout most of his boyhood to get much schooling, yet he went on to a respectable career in journalism. The two younger brothers both had the importance of education drilled into them, and Dean determined early to follow his father to Davidson. Robert Rusk, because he lost his voice, was unable to pursue his career in the ministry and spent much of the rest of his life as a mailman, but neither he nor his wife was persuaded by poverty to abandon the ambitions they had for their sons.

Dean Rusk readily acknowledges the influence that his father's Protestant religion had on him. He has said that when he was young, most of his home life was built around the church. He was faithful in his attendance at Sunday school and midweek prayer meetings. After church on Sunday, the funnies forbidden, he and his family spent the day reading the Bible and memorizing the psalms and the catechisms. Throughout his school years, he was active in the Christian Endeavor, an organization of young people devoted to encouraging Protestant spirituality. Rusk says that, as a matter of fact, until his second or third year in high school, he planned to make a career in the Presbyterian ministry.

Roger Rusk, now a physics professor at the University of Tennessee, maintains that it is impossible to understand his brother without grasping the meaning of Southern Protestantism—a set of tenets which all the best authorities agree is fundamental to the culture of the South. Basic to it is a rigid Calvinism, with the commitment to Original Sin and the essential evil of most men, with the obverse that the Saved will eschew frivolity and lead lives of abnegation and sacrifice. Southern Protestant Christianity was hewn among the rigors of the frontier, where there was little place for subtlety, intellectuality or dissent. Closely bound up with danger, it exalted force, tolerated violence and generated the deep feelings which have evolved from sectionalism into patriotism. Inevitably, Southern Protestantism was identified with the white race, the Scotch-Irish in particular. This is the doctrine, says Roger Rusk, on which Dean was raised and which built civilization on this continent.

"Love of God, love of country," Roger said, "they were exactly the same and they were as natural to us as living and breathing. Even though it's stylish now to downgrade the WASP's, this belief was common to all the families who got here first. Part of the teaching of our homes and of our church was complete devotion to the country.

"We were also taught a sense of service, to be self-effacing. We were taught to abandon personal ambition for the sake of others. I myself have sacrificed my life to the service of the people I've loved here. [He nonetheless drives a new car, owns a handsome home, dresses in elegant tweeds.] Dean has made his sacrifices to humanity. I teach science out of Christian motivation; Dean strives for world peace.

"What people also don't understand about Dean is how deep are his military inclinations. It's part of our Anglo-Saxon heritage. The South always had a military disposition. It's part of our stock.

"During World War I, Dean and I cut out pictures of soldiers from the newspapers and pasted them on cardboard. We had thousands. We dug trenches twenty and thirty feet long across our backyard and built fortifications. We followed all the battle plans. There wasn't a rich kid in town who had as many soldiers as we did. [Roger also says that when they were children, he and Dean used to test which one could outstare the other. That's the origin, he says, of the Secretary's famous expression after the Cuban missile crisis: "We were eyeball to eyeball and the other fellow blinked."]

"I have no apology for saying it, but we never considered war immoral. War is one of the consequences of sin. As long as men are sinful, we'll have war. War is an error to be endured."

Roger Rusk, who admits to a stern conservatism, disapproves of many of the changes that have transformed the South during his lifetime. He is particularly nostalgic about the schools. He said: "The public schools used to be of a Southern Christian Protestant orientation. This was our culture and the schools strengthened it. The Catholics and Jews who lived in the South accepted it. Now the church is not supported by the schools. The schools have become pagan. But when Dean and I were brought up, the home and the church were partners with the schools in teaching values."

Having learned to read from Roger at home, Dean Rusk skipped right into the second grade when he enrolled at the local grammar school. By chance, it was an experimental school, to which the city had assigned its best teachers in an effort to upgrade its programs. Later, Dean went to Boys High, where he received a solid grounding in the "classical" subjects, including Latin and even Greek. His Greek professor remembers him as one of a handful of students, over a long career, who "seemed to be born mature." Old friends say Dean was a neat, well-scrubbed lad, playful enough but, in school, already something of a drudge. They agree, however, that he was by far the smartest kid in the class. It was in high school that Dean Rusk got the notion from a Presbyterian missionary, a former Oxonian himself, to aspire to a Rhodes scholarship. Though he had the benefit of what was probably the finest public education available in the South, it was young Rusk's own industry and intelligence that laid the scholastic foundation for his luminous future.

After taking two years off to earn some money for college by working in a law office, Dean Rusk went on to Davidson as he had planned. He settled down to a full program of studies, found a part-time job in a bank and was elected president of the freshman class. He joined a fraternity, played varsity tennis and center on the basketball team, and acquired a steady girl friend. He attended chapel daily, undertook missionary work for the YMCA, passed his two compulsory years of Bible and never missed church on Sunday. Having already lost most of his hair, he was given by his friends the nickname "Old Folks," which also reflected his solemn countenance and serious view of life. Nonetheless, he was popular and, according to the best recollection, a thoroughly good fellow. In his senior year, he and some chums took a trip to New York for a lark, the first time he had left the South. In 1931, he was graduated from Davidson, with a Phi Beta Kappa key and a Rhodes scholarship.

When he applied for the Rhodes scholarship, the examining board asked Rusk, in view of his proclaimed interest in world peace, to explain his obvious predilection for military values. He had taken four years of ROTC at Boys High and had risen to the command of all the ROTC units in Atlanta. At Davidson, he took four more years of ROTC, attained the student rank of colonel and graduated with a reserve commission. Later Rusk explained: "Well, of course, in the South most of us as we were growing up just took it for granted that if there was to be trouble, if the nation was at war, that we would be in it. I had eight years of ROTC, both in high school and college. The tradition of the Civil War was still with us very strongly. Both my grandfathers had been in it. We assumed that there was a military duty to perform if one is required on the part of all citizens, so we took that for granted as a perfectly natural part of being an American." Rusk said he handled what the board of examiners considered the paradox in this way: "I did at that time point out that the American eagle on the great seal has the arrows in one claw and the olive branch in the other and the two have to go together." Thus Dean Rusk has, from that day to this, looked upon armed force and world peace as simply two sides of the same coin.

The times were grim when Rusk sailed for England, but at Oxford, where he read politics and philosophy, he was insulated from the Depression's miseries. In his second year abroad, Rusk went to a German university for a semester, just as Hitler's regime was beginning to flower. Clearly, his experiences in these years did not fire Rusk with any reformer's zeal. By the time he returned to America in 1934, Southern contemporaries like Lyndon Johnson and Abe Fortas had already staked out careers in the New Deal, while diplomatic contemporaries like Charles E. Bohlen and O. Edmund Clubb were questioning American policy toward Russia and China. Rusk, however, was content to go off to Mills College in California, where he taught political science, married Virginia Foisie, one of the students, and rose to the rank of dean of the faculty. In six years as an academic, he wrote nothing of record and acquired no reputation as a scholar. He did, however, attend law classes at the University of California and he faithfully acquitted his obligations as an officer in the Army Reserve. In 1940, a full year before Pearl Harbor, Dean Rusk was called into the military service.

Assigned to Army headquarters in Washington, Rusk, as a former Rhodes scholar, was given responsibilities in British Empire affairs. But after the United States entered the war, he was sent to the China-Burma-India theater, where he helped plan operations on the staff of General Stilwell. Though he was stationed chiefly in New Delhi, he had an opportunity to travel rather widely throughout Asia. It was Rusk's first exposure to the Orient and it was an intensive one. He spent three years in the C.B.I. and rose to the rank of colonel. Near the end of the war, General George C. Marshall, the Chief of Staff, asked that a group of outstanding young officers be brought back to the United States to do postwar planning. Thus, shortly before V-E Day, Rusk returned to Washington, to work in the heady atmosphere generated by the furious preparations being made for peace. He was in a group headed by Colonel C. H. Bonesteel III (now a general and Commander of the U.S. Army in Korea), who had been Rusk's best friend when they were both Rhodes scholars a decade earlier.

Over the course of the next few years, Rusk crossed back and forth between the Pentagon and the State Department in various staff capacities. He went first to State after his discharge in February 1946, then back to the Pentagon a few months later as special assistant to the Secretary of War. It was at this point that he was offered a regular commission in the Army and, as he said, "had more or less agreed to take it," when Marshall was appointed Secretary of State. Anxious to have men around him familiar with his military ways, Marshall invited Rusk back to State and he accepted. Specializing in United Nations affairs, he gradually worked his way up the ladder until he became an Assistant Secretary. Since the United Nations, at least in those days, was thought of largely in terms of the peace-keeping forces envisaged in its charter, Dean Rusk had no trouble dedicating his energies to it. He could conceive of it much as the American eagle, with an olive branch in one claw and arrows in the other.

The bright young men who worked around Rusk in those days, almost all of whom have gone on to considerable achievement elsewhere, remember him as exceptionally competent and dedicated, modest and affable, serious but not grim. Almost unanimously, they described him as fresh, intellectually flexible, rich in ideas, and without arrogance.

His great strength, they agree, was in lucid articulation of a problem, in which, as one put it, "he knew the value of a fact." Even those who object to his current conduct of the State Department—and that applies to almost every one of them—concede that they saw in him none of the smugness and dogmatism of which he is now accused. At least one of his former colleagues dissents, however, insisting that Rusk's open-mindedness reflected not wisdom but uncertainty and that Rusk was an intellectual second-rater. Another former colleague said that, in retrospect, he recognizes that Rusk was unduly submissive to authority, unwilling to fight for any idea to which his superiors did not immediately subscribe. A third argues that this submissiveness was in reality an intense loyalty to his superiors, "the military side of Dean Rusk," a staff officer's acceptance of the responsibility of his chief for the final decisions. However interpreted, this last quality, combined with his genuine talents, singled out Rusk among his peers and made him a functionary prized at the highest level of the government. One former diplomat remembers a party back in the late forties in which a group of colleagues toasted Dean Rusk as "a future Secretary of State of the United States."

Rusk began to come into his own in January 1949 when Dean Acheson became Secretary of State. Obviously, he concurred with Acheson's new "get-tough" policy toward the Communists and the elevation of the Cold War to the first rank of diplomatic priority. On March 12, Rusk announced the United States was abandoning its frigid attitude toward Nationalist Spain, on the grounds that an anti-Franco policy was no longer "realistic." A week later, he joined in the advocacy of the North Atlantic Pact. "We haven't been able," he explained, "to get through the worldwide security system that we hoped to work out through the United Nations." Shortly afterward, Rusk was promoted to Deputy Under Secretary, the third-ranking post in the Department, with general administrative and policy responsibilities. It was clear that Acheson had the highest regard for him.

But Rusk remained in his new job only a few months. By the end of 1949, the Communists had taken over the Chinese mainland and Dean Acheson, who earlier had ordered an end to American support of Chiang Kai-shek, became the target of a high-powered anti-Red crusade. In the beginning of 1950, the post of Assistant Secretary for the Far East became vacant. As Acheson tells the story, Rusk "came to me and said, 'I am applying for demotion. I'd like to go back to being Assistant Secretary, and I'd like to take over this job.' And I said, 'You get the Congressional Medal of Honor and the Purple Heart all at once for this. Do you really want to do it?' And he said, 'I fit it.' " Exactly why Rusk felt he "fit it" is not clear. He points out now that he had taught a little Far Eastern history at Mills and, of course, had spent the war on China's periphery. But even he cannot say with certainty why he volunteered for what was known to be the hottest job in the Department. What is clear is that he felt very deeply about the "loss" of China. George Kennan has said that Rusk was one of the members of the Department who experienced genuine "moral indignation" over Mao's conquest. Rusk has himself said privately it was unfortunate that the United States demobilized too quickly after World War II to have an army ready for deployment in China. From Acheson's point of view, Rusk was an ideal lightning rod "and so we of course kissed him on both cheeks and gave him the job." From Rusk's, it was apparently an opportunity to make personally sure that the United States would stop Communist China dead in its tracks.

One evening in June, 1950, Rusk was dining with Joseph Alsop, Felix Frankfurter and Secretary of the Army Frank Pace when he received word that the North Koreans had crossed the 38th parallel to invade South Korea. Pace returned to the Pentagon. Rusk phoned Acheson, who contacted Truman in Independence. The next morning, Rusk met with the President, Acheson, and other responsible officials at Blair House, the temporary White House, and recommended that the United States intervene under the auspices of the United Nations. Rusk's hope of making the UN into a genuine security agency was at last to be redeemed. "But it was a very close thing," Rusk said, for the Communists were advancing quickly. Truman dispatched American forces to halt the invasion and the Korean War was on.

So far as anyone could tell, Rusk supported the President loyally during his dispute with MacArthur in April 1951 over the extension of the war into China. But in May, Rusk delivered a fire-eating speech in New York that seemed curiously to take MacArthur's line against any compromise with Peking. Rusk denounced Red China as a "Slavic Manchukuo . . . not entitled to speak for China in the community of nations." He said that the Red regime was "not the government of China" and that the Nationalist group in Formosa "more authentically represents the views of the great body of the people of China." The speech, surprising as it was, created a furor. The cold warriors were exultant, the liberals outraged. *U.S. News & World Report* headlined its story: "Dean Rusk's Coup on China Policy . . . . State Department Has A New Stalwart. . . . And America Has Firmer Goals." The New York *Post* complained that perhaps "Truman fired MacArthur and then adopted his policies." Acheson seemed bewildered by the whole thing. He disclaimed responsibility for the purple language of the speech, but disavowed neither Rusk nor the more rigorous policies he proclaimed. Reports ranged from Acheson's scolding of Rusk to his embracing him. The precise significance of the speech still remains something of a mystery, but it does suggest that Rusk's feelings about China went beyond even the intransigent policies of Dean Acheson and the Truman Administration. Recently Acheson said that "Mr. Rusk had been a loyal and able and courageous colleague of mine in the State Department," which hardly indicated that the two had had a falling out.

Thus Rusk's career, despite the sensitive post he held, moved along flawlessly. Rusk proved invulnerable to McCarthy's rampage. Bohlen had stumbled because he had gone to Yalta with Roosevelt, Clubb because he had found faults in Chiang Kaishek, but Rusk stayed clean. "He was insulated from the McCarthy trouble," said one old colleague. "He had come in from the Pentagon, which meant he had a safe beginning. He retained a close association with the Defense Department. He was on the right side in Korea. He never pushed any audacious proposals or offended anyone. Rusk was always very secure." Despite McCarthy's siege of the Department, Rusk continued to find favor with people in high places.

One of the friends Rusk made was John Foster Dulles, who happened at the time to be Chairman of the Board of the Rockefeller Foundation. A prominent Wall Street lawyer, expert in foreign affairs and a Republican, Dulles had been confident in 1948 of becoming Thomas E. Dewey's Secretary of State. After Dewey's defeat, Truman appointed Dulles an adviser to the State Department to impart a quality of bipartisanship to his foreign policy. When Dulles, in 1951, was given responsibility for negotiating the Japanese Peace Treaty, he had among his advisers Dean Rusk and John D. Rockefeller III who had known each other at the Pentagon at the end of the war. The three men got along famously. Some months later the presidency of the Rockefeller Foundation became vacant, and Dulles and Rockefeller agreed that their friend Rusk, with his combined academic and diplomatic credentials, would be ideal for the job. For his part, Rusk had three growing children and he felt that to bring them up he needed more money than he earned at State. When the Rockefeller job, with its substantial salary (around $50,000 a year) and prestige, was offered to him in 1952, Rusk resigned from the State Department to take it.

Dean Rusk, it should be noted, distinguished himself at Rockefeller by reorienting the foundation and its funds, previously dedicated to domestic concerns almost alone, to the needs of the underdeveloped countries. "We should be fully aware of the historical significance of what is happening in those areas which lie outside the English-speaking democracies, Western Europe, and the Iron Curtain," he wrote in a Memorandum to the Trustees in 1955. "Ideas and aspirations which were generated in the course of democratic, national and economic revolutions in the West are now producing explosive demands for far-reaching changes in other parts of the world. . . . The underdeveloped countries of today are borrowing ideas and aspirations and have examples of more 'advanced' countries before their eyes; but they lack capital, trained leadership, an educated people, political stability, and an understanding of how change is to be digested and used by their own cultures." Under Rusk's leadership, the Rockefeller Foundation undertook remarkable experimental projects in education, resource development, population control and leadership training in many of the backward regions. Rusk's work endowed him with the reputation of someone who appreciates the problems of those countries that threaten one day, by poverty and people, to swallow up their rich industrial neighbors.

Throughout his eight years at the Rockefeller Foundation, Rusk continued to endear himself to the powerful members of the business and financial community in New York. His leadership was considered innovative and efficient. He found time to lecture occasionally on international affairs and serve on the Council on Foreign Relations, an esteemed body of rich, public-spirited citizens. He also was in constant touch with Dulles, now Eisenhower's Secretary of State, advising him on this policy and that. Meanwhile, he lived quietly with his family in Scarsdale, the *right* upper-class suburb, where he dabbled in community affairs and local Democratic politics. Though he was always the first to insist that he was, deep down, still just a simple Southern boy, Rusk acquired a veneer of Eastern sophistication from his New York life. If not a member of the "Establishment" family, he certainly became a first cousin. Highly respected and financially secure, Rusk undoubtedly wanted nothing more than to spend the rest of his days at Rockefeller, but the position he had attained, by chance, gave him just the right qualifications for the dazzling new career that awaited him in Washington.

Well-prepared as he was for the office, John F. Kennedy was elected President in 1960 without knowing whom he wanted as Secretary of State. He had a list of candidates, to which Dean Acheson had added the name of Dean Rusk, but it seemed to stand near the bottom. One by one, however, those who stood higher on the list were eliminated for various reasons. Adlai Stevenson's own personal following was too strong; Chester Bowles was too identified with the liberal left; Senator J. William Fulbright had voted against civil rights; Douglas Dillon was a Republican; David Bruce and Averell Harriman were too old; McGeorge Bundy was too young; Robert Lovett was in poor health. Before long Dean Rusk alone—the first choice only of Acheson —was left on the list.

Kennedy did not even know Rusk, but he was attracted by his credentials. There was no disputing that the man was well-informed, efficient and familiar with the workings of the State Department. All reports agree that he was self-effacing, not likely to challenge Kennedy's primacy in the making of policy. Most important of all, he had the recommendation of men whose support Kennedy now solicited. As President-elect by the narrowest of margins, Kennedy felt himself in an unstable position. He wanted to change old Eisenhower policies, but he could not risk being branded as brash, to say nothing of radical. He needed the "Establishment" behind him and to win them over he wanted the Republican Dillon for Secretary of the Treasury. He had offered a choice of cabinet posts to Robert Lovett, former Under Secretary of State and Secretary of Defense, New York investment banker and board member of countless corporations and foundations, including Rockefeller. When Lovett said he was too ill to take any post, Kennedy asked him for his recommendation for Secretary of State. Lovett proposed, among a group of five, the name of Dean Rusk, who had served him in various subordinate capacities since the war. Kennedy was impressed by the endorsement of Lovett, since it meant that Rusk had the approval of precisely the powers he was anxious to reassure.

It is unclear how much Kennedy knew about Rusk's thinking in 1960. Arthur Schlesinger said that "the Kennedy staff read all his speeches and articles they could find and discovered nothing which would cause trouble." Richard Goodwin, who did much of this reading for Kennedy, recalls coming across no material that raised questions about Rusk's fitness. Members of the Kennedy circle insist that the President-elect was unaware of Rusk's "hardline" attitude toward the Communist world and toward China in particular. But there were allusions in the press to Rusk's record at State a decade before and his statements on China were all in the file. Kennedy's detractors argue that the President-elect, while anxious to preserve a façade of liberalism in foreign policy, actually wanted a "hard-liner" as Secretary of State. The most that can be said for sure is that Kennedy thought he was getting a technician, someone adroit in the ways of diplomacy, who would carry out his policy objectives with skill and loyalty.

What Kennedy did know about Rusk's thinking was that a few months earlier he had declared himself in favor of the kind of aggressive diplomacy which Kennedy thought he wanted. Those were the days when Kennedy was still fresh from his debates with Nixon, during which he had argued that the United States, having lost international prestige under Eisenhower, had to reassert its leadership. In *Foreign Affairs,* prestigious organ of the Council on Foreign Relations, Rusk had written:

> The United States, in this second half of the twentieth century, is not a raft tossed by the winds and waves of historical forces over which it has little control. Its dynamic power, physical and ideological, generates historical forces; what it does or does not do makes a great deal of difference to the history of man in this epoch. . . . When the emphasis in discussion falls too heavily for my taste upon the limitations on policy, I recall from early childhood the admonition of the circuit preacher: "Pray as if it were up to God; work as if it were up to you."

This is the frame of mind that in the early days, when he thought "vigor" would solve anything, John Kennedy liked. After a single conversation, Kennedy became satisfied that Rusk would make a suitable Secretary of State.

From the beginning, however, it is clear that Kennedy was dissatisfied with Rusk. The new Secretary brought neither administrative efficiency nor intellectual rejuvenation to the State Department. He was notably deficient in providing Kennedy with fresh ideas. Perhaps most disappointing of all, he was painfully reticent in foreign-policy discussion, so that Kennedy felt that the State

Department was without an advocate. To be sure, Rusk was excellent at laying out all the facets of the problem, no matter how complex, and Kennedy was grateful for his faithfulness, as well as his pleasant disposition. But he was scarcely satisfied with Rusk's irresolution and he often said that in State, he was pressing up against a "bowl of jelly." Rusk has been credited with having had the wisdom to see the weakness of the Bay of Pigs operation, only he failed to convey his reservations to Kennedy while there was still time to stop it. Throughout the three years of his term, Kennedy was not so much angry at Rusk as frustrated at his passivity.

Many have attempted to explain Rusk's attitude toward his work. The less generous have said that he kept quiet to make sure how the wind was blowing and stay safely on the President's side. Others say that he has a supernumerary's mentality, a faithful subordinate incapable of acting on his own. Still others maintain that he was uncomfortable with the young, irreverent, sometimes unconventional people who surrounded Kennedy. Some postulate that he was profoundly in disagreement with Kennedy on the Cold War, but preferred silence to resigning his office. It is possible, of course, that some aspects of all these explanations help to account for Rusk's reserve. One intimate associate of Kennedy added this observation:

"Basically, I think the problem was that Rusk was a lot less bright than the other people at the table, beginning with Kennedy himself and including Bundy, Sorensen, McNamara and almost all the rest. I'm convinced he was afraid because he thought that all these people were smarter than he. And I'm sure he was right. He might have been very smart at Davidson, but that's another league, and I know he was a Rhodes scholar. But he had an utterly conventional mind. He never had anything interesting to say, nothing to add, nothing that might affect the course of a conversation. I remember once we talked of weapons systems and he didn't seem to get the point. We talked of the balance of payments and he didn't understand the complications. All he ever seemed to say was that we had to stand firm against the Communists and show determination. That's the level on which he gave advice."

After he became Secretary of State, Rusk seemed to lose interest in anything but standing firm against the Communists. He showed indifference to the administration of the Department, though he was once known as a fine administrator. He gave little attention to long-term policy planning, though under Marshall he was instrumental in setting up the Department's current planning machinery. Perhaps most disappointing, Rusk paid small heed to the problems of the underdeveloped world, for which he had shown so much understanding at the Rockefeller Foundation. Here was Rusk's opportunity to make history, to redirect the energies of the United States and, perhaps, the entire Western world to the threat of overpopulation and engulfing poverty. Yet, according to a member of Kennedy's original task force on foreign aid, Rusk was so preoccupied with other matters that he seemed bored by the issue. Kennedy, of course, established the Alliance for Progress, but Rusk's contribution to it was inconsequential. Though there is no suggestion that Rusk was remiss in his duties as Secretary of State, it is clear that in his preoccupation with Communism he had a single-minded view of his responsibilities.

What is not true is that Rusk was out of tune with Kennedy's liberalism in domestic matters. Though not intimately concerned with them, Rusk was certainly sympathetic to Kennedy's objectives at home, including civil rights. On racial matters, Rusk's upbringing had been conventionally Southern. As one of his classmates at Davidson put it: "It never occurred to us in those days to question our society's treatment of Negroes, neither Dean nor any of the rest of us." But something happened to Dean Rusk when he went out into the world, and if any Southerner ever tried hard to overcome racial biases, it was he. Ralph Bunche remembers that it was Rusk who insisted successfully on the integration of recreational facilities when they were both young officers in Washington in the early days of the war. It was this liberal attitude to which Roger Rusk referred when he noted sadly that "Dean, more than I, has sought to transcend Southern values." If it is evidence of his achievement, his eldest son, David, works for the Urban League, while his daughter, Peggy, recently married a

Negro. Rusk explains his liberal outlook as the product of Southern Populism, modified by three years in the C.B.I., "where I was
surrounded by a sea of Indian and Burmese faces." Few of Kennedy's people, whatever their criticisms of Rusk as Secretary,
challenged the sincerity of his liberal convictions.

If Rusk excelled anywhere, according to the standards of the
Kennedy Administration, it was in serving as a link between the
White House and the Southern proconsuls who run the key committees on Capitol Hill, particularly in the Senate. However poor
he may have been in policy formulation, he was considered superb in policy articulation, whenever he appeared before Congress. Rusk, in his quiet Southern way, knew how to talk to Russell of Georgia and Stennis of Mississippi, the powers on the
Armed Services Committee, and it was not until after the Santo
Domingo invasion in 1965 that he ran afoul of Arkansas' Fulbright, chairman of the Foreign Relations Committee. Though
Rusk himself was not sold on the test-ban treaty, he defended it
brilliantly and overcame much early skepticism to win its ratifica-
tion. Though he had major doubts about the virtues of liberalizing
immigration, he argued loyally for Kennedy's proposals to repeal
the old Anglo-Saxon preferences. It is said that his most glittering
performance was his testimony on behalf of the civil rights bill
before the Judiciary Committee of Mississippi's Senator Eastland.
The Southern Senators never ceased making trouble for the Kennedy Administration, but Rusk surely helped to allay some of the
worst effects of their wrath.

The debate, somewhat academic in nature, continues to this
day as to whether Kennedy planned to get rid of Rusk. The very
blandness that made him unpopular within the Cabinet had pre-
served him from criticism within the country. But his immunity
meant that the burden of controversial decisions was shifted to
Kennedy himself. Rusk, furthermore, seemed to be deferring
more and more to the views of the Defense Department in the
conduct of diplomacy. With certainty, it can be said that he had
lost Kennedy's confidence. There is some indication that Rusk
contemplated resignation, and there is persuasive testimony that

Kennedy was preparing for his graceful departure after the 1964 election.

Kennedy's death, of course, changed everything, including the course of American foreign policy. Within a few months, the Vietnamese war replaced *détente* as the dominant concern of the government. Rusk now insists that the basic decision had already been taken by Kennedy when he chose to increase American military personnel beyond the figure authorized by the Geneva agreements of 1954. "He made that decision with full understanding of its implications," Rusk said. "He was pursuing this policy when he died." Notwithstanding Rusk's assertion, when Kennedy died the United States had no more than 16,000 troops in Vietnam and the battles were being fought between Vietnamese. Though it may please the Secretary to see all foreign policy as continuum and his own role as mere stewardship, in fact there are today a half-million Americans fighting in Vietnam and it has become an American war.

Rusk says further that for Cuba, Kennedy's policies remain in effect. "We regard this regime as temporary," he declared, as if he were mocking the words he used about Communist China in 1951. Rusk spoke disapprovingly only of the policy pursued in Laos, where Kennedy, to avert a war, negotiated with the Communists to establish a neutralist government. "He died thinking of Laos as a bitter disappointment," Rusk said. "We got an agreement but no performance." Other Kennedy associates disagree, asserting that Rusk distorts history. Volatile as the situation continues to be, they point out, there has been no war in Laos and the Communists have not taken control. This, they say, was precisely Kennedy's objective. Rusk's contrasting evaluation of Cuba and Laos means that he considers Kennedy's conciliatory policies subject to his review and vulnerable to his powers as Secretary of State. On the other hand, he seems to regard the eyeball-to-eyeball posture, wherever he has found it, as one of these "big enduring things" that doesn't respond to whimsy but somehow proceeds legitimately from American diplomacy's natural, time-honored heritage.

"Lyndon Johnson," said a friend of the President, "showed a great deal of respect for Rusk's judgment from the very beginning. Being from the South was, of course, a natural recommendation, but Lyndon Johnson was impressed further by Rusk's achievements—Phi Beta Kappa, Rhodes scholarship, Rockefeller Foundation and all the rest. Johnson's got no respect for what he calls a 'stay-home boy' who never leaves the South, but for a Southern boy to go where Rusk went is, to him, really something.

"Besides, the President saw Rusk as the outcast of the Kennedy Cabinet. He knew a kindred spirit when he saw one. Both had been kicked around by the Arthur Schlesingers and the Dick Goodwins of the world. The President saw Rusk as wounded and he came to his support. Rusk never forgot that. Rusk immediately acquired a feeling of belonging he never had with Kennedy."

Once Johnson assumed the Presidency, Rusk conducted himself as if freed at last of the constraints on thought and action that had perplexed him. He speaks up now at Cabinet meetings and receives attention. He engages in disputes and regularly wins them. Many are the colleagues whose cadavers he has left behind him. Schlesinger and Goodwin, the diplomatic dilettantes who had always irritated him, went early, incompatible with the new regime. Bundy, once his presumed successor, has departed with many of his staff. Roger Hilsman, his intelligence chief, went years ago. George Ball, author of a shelf of thoughtful memos in opposition to the Vietnam war, felt too impotent as Under Secretary to stay on. And now McNamara, too, is gone.

"There are certain kinds of men who wear out with Johnson," said the President's friend. "Rusk can endure. McNamara didn't have the staying power. There is no room for subtlety with Lyndon Johnson. You've got to be all the way and McNamara had intellectual doubts. With Rusk, there is no hedging. His devotion to Johnson is total."

When McNamara's departure was announced, Rusk mumbled something to the press about losing a brother, but it was as if Jacob were speaking of Esau. Rusk had come to look upon McNamara as a heretic, generating uncertainties about the war. In the past he had showed he could use a stiletto in governmental infighting—in his quiet vendetta, for instance, against his old friend Bowles during the Kennedy days. But on the whole, Rusk has eschewed Machiavellian conduct; it has not been necessary. With Lyndon Johnson as patriarch, Jacob had only to be patient to be sure that the family birthright would be his.

As the pressure over Vietnam has increased, Rusk has shown himself commensurately cool, composed and confident. "It's ironic," said one former Kennedy hand, "that Rusk is proving himself most successful in the role of cornered rat." It troubles even his admirers that he has become so sure of himself, that he is increasingly doctrinaire, that his sereneness has become indistinguishable from complacency.

Still, Rusk conducts his office like a driven man. He avoids the cocktail- and dinner-party circuit, though he can be socially charming. He sees no movie or plays. He rarely relaxes with friends. He has given up golf and even bridge, except during long trips in the air. He is jealous of his private life but he allows himself very little of it. Most of his working hours he spends at his desk inquiring into details that even he admits are trivial. Rusk is a loner, a man without outside interests.

Perhaps more serious, he makes small effort to expose himself to fresh thought. He reads no books. He stays away from the more solemn periodicals. Though he occasionally hears out a professor or an old diplomatic acquaintance over a Scotch-on-the-rocks at the end of the day, he never lets on that he is submitting his own views to reexamination. In recent public statements, he has made fun of intellectuals and dismissed them as ill-equipped to criticize.

Still profoundly a Southern Calvinist, Rusk is instinctively convinced of the ubiquitousness of sin and of his own duty to extirpate it. His view of mankind is not complicated: there are good guys and bad guys and he's for the good ones. In a television interview on the nature of his office, Rusk once said, "One of the consequences of the fact that the world is round is that at any given moment, two-thirds of the world is awake and *up to some-*

thing." An unreconstructed Calvinist would think of mankind in such mischievous terms, suspicious and on guard, conscious of his own role in the process of salvation. Like his brother Roger, Rusk sincerely sees his work in terms of self-sacrifice. "I never wanted to be Secretary of State," he said in the same interview, "up until the moment that I *had to* be and then I *had to* do my duty." Even now, Rusk refuses to contemplate his office as a pinnacle of worldly ambition, a station of respect, fame and power. To him it is a calling, like the ministry, to which he has the solemn obligation to respond.

"It is not enough to 'contain' communism and to try to negotiate specific agreements to reduce the danger of a great war," Rusk said in a speech some months after Johnson became President. "The conflict between the Communists and the free world is as fundamental as any conflict can be. Their proclaimed objectives and our conception of a decent world order just do not and cannot fit together." In his heyday, John Foster Dulles would not have been more unqualified about the hopelessness of reconciliation, nor more satisfied about it.

In private conversation, Rusk pursues the same line. He rejects any parallels between the ambitions of Czarist Russia and the Soviet Union today. The Czars, he says, simply pressed outward on their own borders. Communist Russia's end, he insists, is world revolution.

"They have an insatiable appetite for their objectives. There is no limit to their goals. The USSR has not abandoned world revolution. It may be prudent about its means, because the world's getting to be a dangerous place in which to live. But whatever the change in tactics, their leaders are still committed to world revolution. That's their creed."

Rusk willingly entertained the hypothesis that America's dynamic concern for making the world safe for democracy is a doctrine that appears threatening to the Communist world. He answered: "Maybe it is, but in matters of that sort, I'm on our side. That's understandable. I'm the Secretary of State of the United States."

Does that mean, Mr. Secretary, that we cannot aspire to a real end to the Cold War, that this rivalry will last indefinitely or until one side or the other is destroyed?

Rusk responded quickly, as if he had often thought about the question and knew the answer well. He said, "There will be an element of political competition between us and the Communist world for a long time. In the course of it, we've got to keep from blowing up ourselves and the rest of the world. The job of diplomacy, my job as Secretary, is to buff off as many of the jagged edges as possible. I am deeply and passionately dedicated to peace and I am gratified that in the seven years that I have been Secretary of State there has been no nuclear war. But in this competition, we don't give away any countries."

Because we don't give away any countries in the competition with the Communist world, we are now in Vietnam.

Lyndon Johnson has accepted Dean Rusk's order of priorities. He has conceded that our presence there is more important than world opinion, more important than the crisis in the ghettos, more important than the Middle East, more important than the balance of payments, more important than the European alliance, more important than—politics. He has even made the decision that it is worth his risking defeat at the polls, to say nothing of a place in history, to win a Vietnamese victory.

Rusk, of course, is aware that he has become a symbol of intransigence and a target of vilification for those who disapprove of the war. But, more in sadness than in anger, he rejects the validity of the antiwar protests.

"I wouldn't mind the demonstrations of the young people so much," he said. "They can be forgiven. They didn't know about Hitler and Mussolini and Tojo. Many of the young people now in college were in grade school when I became Secretary of State and didn't really experience even Berlin and the Cuban missile crisis.

"It's the older people who lived through all this and are now getting careless and indifferent about preserving peace who disturb me. These people say that old Ho Chi Minh is just a nationalist—but North Vietnam is in Laos and Cambodia and Thailand. In the thirties, they said Manchuria was too far away to matter and I found myself at war in Burma. Now they say you cannot believe all the rhetoric that comes out of Peking, which is what they said about Hitler—and six million people were exterminated before anyone believed it. These aren't new ideas. We heard them before and we didn't get peace. Give an aggressor a little and he wants more and more. I am not saying Ho is the same as Hitler, but it's what they have in common that concerns me. Two burglars may be quite different from each other but what is important to the police is that they have burglary in common. We have to stop what these nations have in common—aggression.

"People understood this in 1945 when the UN Charter was written, when the fundamental principle was established that acts of aggression must be suppressed. We had learned that lesson in World War II. I know, as few people do, that there will be nothing left after World War III and no lessons to draw. Of course I am troubled when I see all the people who have forgotten the lessons of the last fifty years."

A close associate once asked Dean Rusk whether it had ever occurred to him that he might be making a mistake in Vietnam. "Well, if I am," he snapped back, "it's a beaut." But apparently, it had never really occurred to him. For Dean Rusk doesn't stay up nights worrying if he's made a mistake. As sure as there's a God in Heaven, he knows he has not.

Richard J. Daley

OPERATOR OF THE BIG MACHINE

This portrait of Mayor Richard Daley and his city appeared as the cover story of the Saturday Evening Post *the week the 1968 Democratic National Convention exploded in Chicago. As you might guess, I took a lot of guff from my friends in the wake of the ensuing fiasco, since the piece is not fundamentally anti-Daley. But I have no apologies, even about the favorable comments I made on the Mayor and his powerful political machine.*

But let me, for the sake of perspective, summarize what I think the profile says. It pictures Dick Daley as an essentially decent man with a simple, primitive sense of morality, whom time has outraced but who runs as hard as he can to keep its lead from growing. Dick Daley knew of the dangers that loomed for Chicago at the Democratic Convention. The primitive in him sternly disapproved of street demonstrations, while the runner in him recognized that he had to compromise with a new concept of political expression. While I was in Chicago in the late spring of 1968, Daley agonized over the stand he should take. The rigid moralist told him to repress the bastards; the malleable opportunist in him said he should ride with the pressure by making concessions. I confess that, recognizing his dilemma, I thought he would come

186

out, however offensive it was to his character, on the side of flexibility. I was wrong. As events turned out, so was he.

But I stand my ground in the contention that Richard Daley is an anachronism rather than a scoundrel. The day of the Irish political machine is over. It is gone in New York, Philadelphia, Pittsburgh, Boston. It will not last much longer in Chicago, either. But in its day, it served a useful purpose as the political arm of the urban underdog. The machine saw to it that the city's services, on the whole, were adequately performed. In its rather unsophisticated way, it saw to enough redistribution of income so that no one starved. By gradually yielding bits of its power, it fended off overt strife between contending ethnic minorities. Even in the best of cities, the decline of the machine has been replaced not by some new and more democratic form of political organization but, unfortunately, by a disarray in service, an ugly welfare system and open racial hostility. The times were different, of course, when the urban political machine reigned unchallenged. But I am not at all sure that with its vanishing, the cities are better governed. Though the atmosphere of urban reform is clean and zesty, I suspect there is a relationship between the decay of the central city and the institutional disintegration of the Irish political organization.

I spent a few weeks in Chicago in 1968 and have gone back there to write stories on several occasions since then. To me, Chicago is a source of excitement and despair. It is a contrast of energy and lethargy, of beauty and squalor, of smugness and bitterness. But what has happened to Chicago is not Richard Daley's fault, for it has happened in almost every other American city. Somehow, the voters of Chicago—black and white—seem to recognize this, for in 1971 they re-elected him to his fifth term as mayor. Raymond Aron, the French political philosopher, once told me that urban ruin in America emerges from the indifference felt for permanent places of habitation by a society that is still essentially nomadic. It also emerges from racism, Calvinism, industrialism and Jeffersonianism. What I am saying is not that Dick Daley is or should be one of our national culture heroes.

*But I do believe he will be remembered for something better than
his blunders on the Chicago streets in August 1968.*

IT IS HARD enough for Mayor Dick Daley—the most powerful politician west of Washington—to get Chicago through just
an *ordinary* summer. His domain is restless and surly, deeply
divided and highly unstable. And this is no ordinary summer.
Later this month the Democratic National Convention is scheduled to come to town, and unless Daley puts on a virtuoso display of skill and authority, all hell is certain to break loose.

Place twenty thousand exuberant Democrats in an overheated
metropolis, and the potential for trouble inevitably is great. Add
the usual number of kooks who are tempted by a carnival atmosphere and political turbulence, and the hazards multiply. But the
politicians and their hangers-on are only a small part of the tur-
moil.

The antiwar protest movement promises to bring tens of thousands of demonstrators—mostly young students—into the city.
According to present plans, the crowds will build to a climax at
the time of the nomination, when they will surround the meeting
site with a "sea of people."

The Mississippi Freedom Democratic Party is calling upon
SNCC and CORE chapters around the country to get thousands of
ghetto dwellers to Chicago to dramatize the grievances of America's black people. Their presence could trigger the discontent of
Chicago's own slum residents, who only last April staged an orgy
of rioting.

The supporters of Senator Eugene McCarthy threaten to walk
out of the convention if, in their view, the nominating process is
not open and fair. Their secession could touch off mass action by
ghetto blacks and antiwar whites.

Mayor Daley's problems are made worse by the location of the
convention site. The Chicago Amphitheater is in a crowded section of the city, the stockyards at its back and a series of narrow

streets at its front. It is twenty minutes away, in the best of traffic, from the major downtown hotels. Even if the celebrities are brought to the convention by helicopter, an organized effort at blocking the streets—or a demonstration that gets out of hand—could bring politics to a standstill.

But Richard Daley knew the dangers when he bid to bring the convention to Chicago. President Johnson wanted the Democrats to meet in a major northern city. Any one of several would have been fine, but Daley was determined to show that Chicago, whatever its troubles, was still a great metropolis. In January 1967 fire had destroyed McCormick Place, the huge convention hall celebrated for its giant trade fairs. As Daley saw it, cavorting Democrats, meeting at the newly renovated amphitheater, would tell the nation that Chicago remained an attraction for businessmen and investors, vacationers and tourists. Solemnly, Daley pledged his word that there would be no embarrassing disturbances in Chicago.

Throughout the early summer, Chicago was distracted by the possibility that a phone strike would force the Democrats to go elsewhere, but the Daley administration pressed quietly ahead with its plans to keep the peace when the delegates arrived. The city's 11,000 policemen were given riot training and will be mobilized in full force during the entire week. They will be backed by 10,000 federal troops, stationed just outside the city. The fire department was brought to a peak of strength. The National Guard is standing by. Daley has called on the FBI and leading experts in civil disorders to help devise the strategy. The battle plans are elaborate and tough.

But Dick Daley is a politician, not a soldier. He would rather solve his problems by agreement than by force. It is because of his political skills, not his armed might, that Dick Daley is a powerful figure, and because of his power the odds favor Chicago's keeping the streets open.

"So far, the city has been very cooperative about our plans for protests," said Rennie Davis in mid-July. Davis, the young coordinator of the National Mobilization Committee to End the War in Vietnam, is in charge of arrangements to house and feed up to 50,000 demonstrators, publish a daily convention newspaper, organize mass meetings and seminars, and keep the communication lines open to the city administration and the police. "They've used Mace and clubs on us in the past," Davis said, "but a decision has apparently been made to reach an understanding with us this time. We'll follow the rules, if they give us the permits. If they continue to play straight with us, we won't be storming the amphitheater."

Dick Daley's willingness to reach an accommodation with a rival power bloc is central to his basic technique for maintaining control. Chicago is a sprawling and heterogeneous city, composed of forces that often clash with one another. Its equilibrium, Daley knows, depends upon how wisely he balances these forces. If Daley has little sympathy for these extra-political methods of the antiwar or civil rights activists, he respects the constituencies for which they speak. As he deals with them, Daley is willing to be benevolent, if not permissive. His goal is clear: He has no intention of letting anyone upset the national convention, or, more important, his city of Chicago.

Two summers ago the Rev. Martin Luther King, Jr., decided to challenge Richard Daley's power. For weeks he marched the streets of white neighborhoods, demanding that Daley do something about Chicago's segregation. Daley was careful not to confront King directly. He parried King's attack with swimming pools and fire hydrants, job and recreation programs, health and welfare funds. Working skillfully with his judges, his police and his political machine, he kept King from winning the allegiance of the black community. But even in victory he helped King to salvage his pride by establishing a council to seek a policy for ending segregation. The device placated the Negro community—without alienating hostile whites. When the summer ended, King went home and Chicago returned to its uneasy peace. Daley had again shown who was boss.

In Chicago there are few who challenge the world of Richard J. Daley—sixty-six years old, lifetime Democrat, mayor since 1955

—and even fewer who succeed. But his power extends far beyond the city limits. Because he dominates the Democratic Party in Illinois, his power radiates into the legislature and the governor's mansion in Springfield, and into the polling places in every downstate town. It extends to other major cities of the country, where Chicago's experience and innovations in urban administration serve as guidelines. It reaches into the Capitol in Washington, where Daley's nine congressmen write the legislation he wants.

A display of Daley's power occurred when some anti-poverty groups in Chicago threatened to acquire political strength with funds furnished over the mayor's head by the Office of Economic Opportunity in Washington. Daley persuaded President Johnson to change the funding rules, then used his delegation in Congress to ram through legislation passing all anti-poverty funds through the city administration.

Lyndon Johnson has left instructions at the White House switchboard that he is always at home to Dick Daley. Some politicians maintain that it was Daley's reproaches that persuaded the President to shift his course in Vietnam, and, perhaps, even influenced his decision to withdraw as a candidate.

Dick Daley, seated nervously in his unostentatious city-hall office, dismisses the stories of his power, as he would a beloved Gaelic fable. With a graceless wave of the hand, he declares, "It's just an invention of you great writers and journalists." And then, slowly relaxing, he emits a round laugh from the belly, unsophisticated and unfabricated. To explain further, he lowers his deep, unmelodious voice, disclosing a vestige of a brogue. "I suppose when a man is a successful politician and mayor, people watch him because they figure he knows what's up. They have a certain respect for his judgment—and I concede that I haven't been reluctant to give advice. But my word's no better than anyone else's."

Such disclaimers are too modest. Eugene McCarthy's supporters have sought to generate a massive letter-writing campaign in Illinois, dedicated exclusively to impressing Mayor Daley with the popularity of their candidate. Vice-President Humphrey's backers have called on the mayor over and over again in quest of his support. At stake are not simply Illinois' 118 delegates to the national convention, which Daley controls, but hundreds of other votes that will be swayed by Daley's judgment. For the moment the mayor is keeping his own counsel. He will decide for the candidate who he thinks will most help the lackluster Democratic ticket in Illinois, Sam Shapiro for governor and William Clark for senator. But whoever he chooses will undoubtedly be the Democratic presidential candidate for 1968.

Late last year, when Bobby Kennedy was agonizing over whether or not to challenge Johnson for the Presidency, he sought the word of Mayor Daley, as had his brother Jack eight years before. Jack had made a very favorable impression on the mayor. After the election, Jack liked to say it was Dick Daley's support that had made him President. Besides the support, Daley's machine had delivered—over Republican cries of fraud—the key precincts that carried the vital state of Illinois.

When Bobby came to call, as the story is told in Chicago, Daley was courteous, even affable, but gave no hint of sympathy for his visitor's aspirations. Finally, with much deference, Bobby asked if the mayor had any advice to give him. Warmly, without sarcasm, Daley replied, "Get a haircut." The suggestion was not offered idly. To Daley, long hair, like street demonstrations, suggests defiance of the system within which he rules. Daley understands opposition and tolerates dissent, but nonconformity puzzles and affronts him. Bobby got a haircut.

Richard J. Daley's strength—and perhaps his weakness—lies in his reverence for conformity. He was raised on the morality of the devout and hardworking Irishmen who settled Chicago. Whenever he can, he showers thanks on his late parents, whom he publicly refers to as "my Mom and Dad." He still lives in the Irish enclave of Bridgeport, just a few blocks from where he was born. Save for the cop who stands in front, his frame house, its windows covered with lace curtains, is indistinguishable from the others on the street. Five of his seven children, all grown, live with him; the other two are married. The parish priest is one of his closest friends, and early Mass is a daily habit. The mayor has never had

reason to question the values of his upbringing. Now he is attempting to translate them into the public policy of Chicago.

Many Chicagoans will quarrel with some of his programs, or
insist that Daley is not equal to the city's challenge, or argue that
he is out of touch with the times. "He gives us no spiritual leadership," says Warren Bacon, a perceptive liberal on the school
board. "He runs the city without idealism." But hardly anyone in
Chicago—black or white, conservative or militant, Christian or
Jew, dedicated Republican or anti-organization Democrat—
claims that Daley's motives are sinister in any way. "Daley loves
this city like you love your wife and kids," says a Republican
state appointee. "He considers Chicago *his* city. The sidewalks
are *his* living room. The parks are *his* backyard. He just doesn't
want anyone to screw it up." No one accuses Daley of using his
office to enrich himself, or even to aggrandize himself politically
or psychologically. His staunchest adversaries have not called him
a cynic or a hypocrite. Unquestionably there is about Dick Daley
a kind of old-fashioned purity, a lace-curtain conformity that
borders on priggishness but that nonetheless evokes respect and
even affection.

George Dunne, a Democratic politician who has long labored
in Daley's shadow and is considered to be a potential successor,
recalls the advice the mayor gives to aspiring politicians: " 'Prepare your talks carefully, and don't go over five minutes. Don't
tell off-color stories. If you've had something to drink, stay
home.' " The mayor's favorite expression, he says, is " 'We know
right from wrong.' " Whenever Daley learns that some follower
has been improperly tempted by the perquisites of office, he sum-
mons him and sternly advises: " 'Young fellow, don't get
hungry.' " Daley's temper has a low boiling point, Dunne says,
but he usually phones whoever has been the object of his wrath
and apologizes. " 'Nothing personal,' the mayor tells them," says
Dunne.

A veteran Chicago newspaperman is convinced that Daley
maintains an underground morality network to keep his people in
line. "One of his administrators told me he was sitting in a bar

one night, drinking too much, when he received a phone call. On the other end came a curt voice, 'This is Mayor Daley. Your wife is rather upset. I think you'd better get home.' 'I don't know how he knew where I was but, of course, I went home right away.' "

On first meeting, Daley seems to have little charisma, supposedly the *sine qua non* of the modern politician. In an electronic age the advantage belongs to the Lindsays, although Daley conducts a televised press conference almost every day. New York's Mayor Lindsay, in fact, stands as a kind of personal challenge to the Daley entourage, just as New York itself stands as a general challenge to Chicago. On any pretext a Daley supernumerary will furnish irrefutable evidence of the superiority of his man. So Lindsay walks the streets of the ghetto, what's he accomplished? We've planted 212,445 trees. So he makes a lot out of Fun City, but what's it mean? We've constructed sixty-seven parking lots and eleven public garages.

But defensive as they are in Chicago about the Lindsay image, there is unquestionably a curious magic about the Daley presence. Dick Daley has a paunch and hangdog jowls. He rarely gets through a sentence without stumbling, mistakes "flaunt" for "flout" and makes such monumental bloopers as "we will climb to greater platitudes together." But, somehow, nobody makes fun of him. His style comes through not as inept but as unpretentious. The image that emerges, whether on the public platform or the television screen, is not that of a bumbling machine politician but of a sweet old grandfather. For all his obvious handicaps, Dick Daley charms the young swingers on the Near North Side, the Poles in back of the stockyards, and even the blacks of Woodlawn and Lawndale and the professors at the University of Chicago. When last reelected in 1967, Richard Daley carried every one of Chicago's fifty motley wards.

If the reason for Dick Daley's personal appeal remains elusive, the mechanism of his power is easy to understand. He learned his métier well. Step by step, he rose from the bottom of the Democratic ladder, taking basic training in party affairs and the administration of city, county and state. Two decades ago he was Governor Adlai Stevenson's state treasurer, and, according to the mayor's partisans, really ran Illinois. Stevenson's friends dismiss this claim, but acknowledge that the governor gave Daley the support that made him the power he is today.

In Chicago, Daley is Kosygin and Brezhnev rolled into one, chief not only of the government but of the political party that controls it. He is simultaneously the mayor, directing the city's vast administrative apparatus, and the chairman of the Cook County Democratic Organization, which has direct access to agents on virtually every street in the city and the suburbs. In other cities the machine runs the mayor; in Chicago the mayor runs the machine. John Lindsay, a renegade Republican with a Democratic city council, cannot match Daley's command of either the administrative or the political hierarchy. Richard Daley's power is not absolute but, within his realm, it is probably as close to being absolute as the elective process permits. The question for Chicago is whether such power is good or whether, as Lord Acton suggested, it corrupts.

As mayor, Daley controls something like half of the forty thousand jobs on the Chicago payroll. These twenty thousand jobs are held, overwhelmingly, by loyal Democrats, who make financial contributions to the party and perform important services for it. These men are also party functionaries at the level of ward, precinct and block. They see to it that the vote comes out on Election Day and that the voters behave as is expected of them. Between elections, party officials respond to complaints about unswept streets, poor service at the public-health clinic, hazardous equipment on the neighborhood playground. They hand out the building permits and inspect the tenement houses. They find out whether some unemployed head-of-household needs a job repairing streets or collecting trash. They make sure relief checks arrive on time. When there's potential trouble, they pass the word around to cool it. In short, the agents of the Daley organization serve as a liaison between an impersonal city administration and a normally inarticulate population. This is the classic function of the "machine" in American urban politics.

What is not classic is that Daley rigorously insists that the machine serve not only its own interests but those of Chicago. A job is not a ticket to the public trough; Daley demands that the city get an honest day's work from everyone on the payroll. A job is not a license to steal, and although no one denies that there inevitably is graft at all levels, Daley has cracked down immediately at every hint of scandal. A job is not an annuity; this year Daley retired eighty-six-year-old Congressman Barratt O'Hara, as he retires others who are no longer useful. Would-be reformers have charged that the Daley patronage system costs the city as much as forty million dollars a year, but the assertion is hard to prove. Daley wants the machine to stay lean and energetic, if only because history shows that machines that grow fat and corrupt cannot survive. Chicago, in fact, is probably the only city in the country in which the term "machine" does not provoke derision or contempt. Although Daley himself avoids the term, it evokes a certain warmth in Chicago, and perhaps even a touch of affection.

Daley's concept of governing the city is illustrated by the way he forms his personal cabinet. By convention, the top bureaucrats in a machine are hacks who have reached the peak by virtue of their loyalty and seniority. Daley, however, has surrounded himself with men who are in their thirties and forties, who have no background in politics, and who are usually trained as engineers. Ray Simon, named corporation counsel at thirty-three, is an exception, not in being unqualified but in being the son of an old political crony. Lew Hill, forty-two, the commissioner of development and planning, is a Texan who graduated from the Illinois Institute of Technology and made his way to the top of the city's administration. Milton Pikarsky, forty-four, the commissioner of public works, is a New Yorker who began as a consultant on the construction of O'Hare Airport, one of Daley's major achievements. At almost any time of day the anteroom to the mayor's office is crowded with young men, Manila folders tucked under their arms, waiting to get a decision on this project or that. "I think he likes young people around him because they keep feeding him fresh ideas," says Simon. "But you can't fool the mayor. No matter what you give him, if it's superficial, he spots it." Even Daley's critics concede that Chicago is well served by its administrative apparatus, and that the machine has not become an obstacle to good government.

Tirelessly working his two levers of power—municipal administration and party organization—Richard Daley tries to offer everybody enough to keep Chicago a peaceful and happy place. He is beholden to no single group, ethnic, financial or social, but looks upon them all as being part of the Chicago family, over which he exercises paternal supervision. "He even considers it his duty to support the symphony and the opera," said one of his closest aides, "and let me assure you he does not come easily to being a patron of the arts." A while ago Daley was sold on the idea that it would be great for Chicago to put a fifty-foot Picasso sculpture in the Civic Center Plaza. Daley knew there'd be controversy. The abstraction was attacked on every ground from Picasso's politics to his sexual behavior. The *Tribune* called it a "predatory grasshopper," and an alderman proposed replacing it with a statue of Ernie Banks of the Cubs. But Daley was determined to give Chicago some style, and he did. Obviously Daley is more comfortable with some of his constituencies than with others. But his objective is to enclose them all in his benevolent Hibernian embrace.

When Daley was first nominated in 1955, the downtown business community—bankers and railroad men, department-store magnates and builders whose fortunes determine Chicago's destiny—shrank away in dread, convinced that the notorious days of "Boss" Ed Kelly were about to return. Backed by three of the city's four daily papers, they opposed him in a solid phalanx. But their view of him changed as he reorganized the police department, modernized the fire department, reformed the sanitation department, enlarged the health department, installed new lights on the city streets and vastly extended the network of highways and mass transit. And with all his changes, he kept the municipal debt at the lowest level of any major city in the country. Now the businessmen make up the mayor's most enthusiastic constituency.

In response to Daley's sound administration, the downtown financiers set off a massive construction boom, raising dazzling office and apartment buildings throughout the Loop and in the area immediately to the north. This intense activity, attracting the rich, the young and the vigorous back downtown, has made Chicago one of the most exciting cities in America. The business leaders now work closely with the Daley apparatus—at least they do until seriously inconvenienced. Railroad men, for instance, sit on Daley's boards, dispensing free advice, but firmly refuse to surrender the priceless Loop property they have held since robber-baron days, although it is a blemish to the eye and a barrier to development southward. Daley presses them only so hard. Having brought them into his Chicago family, he is loath to drive them out. Their money and support, after all, are fundamental to his designs for the city.

Daley's genius for embrace has, at various times, made him "Man of the Year" of such diverse groups as the Lithuanian American Association, the Cook County Council of the AFL-CIO and the Junior Association of Commerce and Industry. According to Aloysius Mazewski, president of the Polish National Alliance and a former Republican committeeman, Chicago's Poles love Daley because he stands for law and order and promotes fellows like Danny Rostenkowski and Tom Kluczynski in his political organization. Daley, it seems, has even neutralized the Mafia. Chicagoans say the administration seems to tolerate petty gambling and semi-legitimate businesses but fights strong-arm racketeering and other forms of terror. Daley, it is agreed, has no sympathy for the syndicate but, lacking the resources to destroy it, appears to have settled for its good behavior.

Perhaps, then, Chicago would be a place of serenity—but for the relentless, poisonous, baffling problem of race, the city's most profound source of unrest and the bane of Dick Daley's existence. Since 1940 migration from the rural South has increased Chicago's Negro population from less than a tenth to almost a third. For a while the city administration treated the movement with the same official indifference it had shown to every previous wave of migration. Then, as pressure increased on the old neighborhoods, and the white middle-class began the race to the suburbs, the city built high-rise public housing—mile after mile of it—to keep poor Negroes off the streets and out of sight. Finally Chicago came to realize that the situation had leaped out of control, that it had generated new slums, undermined a school system and bred a generation largely unfit to meet the demands of urban society.

Dick Daley responded to the growing crisis in the manner that was orthodox to him. As the Democratic machine had earlier absorbed the Irish, Italians, Poles, Slavs and Jews, he sought to absorb the blacks. From within the organization, Congressman William Dawson emerged as the Negro boss, serving first as Daley's patron, then as his agent in the black community. Dawson developed a black machine at the ward, precinct and block level, always lagging in numbers and power behind Negro voting strength, but probably not significantly behind other ethnic groups at comparable stages of urbanization. For years Daley believed the technique was working, for at each election he carried the Negro wards with the biggest majorities in the city.

But the cleavage between white and black was growing, and if Daley understood its significance, he chose to do nothing about it. The celebrated Back of the Yards Council, organized during the Depression to rescue a neighborhood behind the stockyards from poverty, evolved into an instrument for constructing barricades against a black invasion. Al Mazewski, the head of the Polish National Alliance, denies any racial animosity, but acknowledges that his Poles have been inhospitable to Negroes. Their motive, he says, is the preservation of the homes they have worked so hard to buy. Meanwhile, Chicago's urban-renewal program, designed to lure middle-class whites back from the suburbs, intensified the segregation of the races by displacing poor blacks, who were forced deeper into their ghettos. At the same time, suburban real-estate practices kept middle-class Negroes boiling in the slums.

The situation had become so bad by 1965 that the United States Department of Education filed to withhold federal school funds on the grounds that Chicago violated anti-segregation statutes. Then Daley showed his power by having Johnson reverse the case. To be sure, similar housing patterns were emerging in all major cities. But Martin Luther King was probably not exaggerating in 1966 when he called Chicago the most segregated city in America.

The eruption of the black revolution some half-dozen years ago left Dick Daley—like many other white Americans—in a state of bewilderment. Whatever prejudices he might have brought with him from Bridgeport, Daley wanted to do the right thing. Privately he bemoaned the fact that the Negro kids growing up in public housing didn't have a Mom and Dad like his, nor an environment that provided rigid discipline and guidance. Daley began programs of rat control, building-code enforcement, job training, comprehensive medical care, housing rehabilitation. But, handicapped by insufficient funds, as in other cities, the programs were too little—and perhaps too late. To Daley's chagrin, the slums have failed to respond. Daley concedes that the city must do more, and he points to new and ambitious plans. But, as a practical matter, the city can move only so fast and, what is worse, it has run dead into the resistance of much of white Chicago, which is more determined than ever to surrender no privileges to accommodate the black migration.

"I've worked for Dick Daley since he's been mayor," says one veteran aide, "and I've never seen anything like it. I can take the blacks. It's the whites who scare me. Talk about violence: It's white men who call me up in the middle of the night and threaten to bomb my house. During the fight over school busing, it was a white mob that surrounded city hall, screaming obscenities." Daley knew in 1966 that if he tried to meet King's desegregation demands—by putting public housing in an all-white neighborhood, for instance—he faced real civil war.

Now the pressures are intensifying from the other side as the Negro leadership becomes more militant and more daring. Daley fumes with outrage, but he cannot stop angry blacks from accusing him of "white racism" and denouncing him for living in Bridgeport, which is still all-white. Anti-machine upstarts have already unseated three aldermen in the city council and have generated a new combativeness among many of the blacks within the organization. In the last primary a Negro militant put up a strong fight against one of Daley's veteran congressmen on the volatile Southwest Side.

But this is the kind of power struggle—conducted within the system—that Daley understands and can manage. As a politician he can forget grudges; the renegades of yesterday become the regulars of today. In one congressional primary Daley supported Abner Mikva, an aggressive liberal who had long fought the machine. "The militants are pressing us as they should," says the mayor in a rare reflective moment. "We've had militants before, of course, Jews and Irish and others. As long as they conduct their fight within a framework of law, they serve a useful purpose." If Daley could only deal with racial unrest through the democratic process, he would almost certainly succeed in getting it under control.

The mayor gave a superb demonstration of his political finesse this spring when he was faced with a crisis over filling five vacancies on the school board. He had sought to avert the burden of just such a crisis by promising, long before, to abide by the recommendations of a citizens' commission that he appointed. But when the commission recommended five liberals, Daley decided to break his promise and intervene. An increase in school taxes was coming up in a referendum, and Daley did not want the backlash vote to kill it. He overruled the commission by nominating two conservatives, one of whom was the incumbent president. Then Daley named Mrs. Carey Preston, secretary of the Chicago Urban League. Finally he added two more liberals who were on the commission list and submitted them all to the city council for confirmation as a package. Both sides were outraged—and at the same time delighted by the appointments of their own symbols. A month later the tax referendum was approved by a margin of less than three percent.

Daley, however, cannot use political manipulation to control the black militants who take to the streets to express their grievances. The mayor is infuriated that public order in the ghetto has eluded his control and that, periodically, his city explodes with riots. Daley is sincere in believing he has done everything he can to alleviate the hardships of the slums. He also believes his police have developed the most effective techniques for stopping disorder cold, before it spreads into mass uprising. Time and again in recent years Chicago police have rounded up everyone in sight at the first sign of unrest, leaving the American Civil Liberties Union to protest the high bail set by the city's judges, and the charges that were subsequently dropped. It was with the certainty that he had the threat of disorder under control that Daley bid for the Democratic National Convention. It was in a tantrum of rage that Daley announced, after the extensive burning and looting of last April, that his police were now under orders to "shoot to kill" in any riot. He had hardly made the statement when he knew it was a mistake. He was denounced all over the country and, a few days later, he backed partly away. But only partly—for the statement had brought joy to too many whites in Chicago to be rescinded completely.

The mayor is similarly angered by the young white militants of the "new left," who began arriving in Chicago some years ago to organize the poor, found themselves unwelcome in the black ghettos and turned their energy to campaigning against the Vietnam war.

"We understand something about Daley, I think, that the rest of Chicago does not," says Rennie Davis, the soft-spoken coordinator of the antiwar protests. Davis knows that Daley does not hesitate to use force. Davis's stories of police raids in the middle of the night are confirmed in essence by outside sources. Countless eyewitnesses to a peace march on April 27 testify to brutal tactics by the police, who warned, "This is half of what you'll get in August." It was only after the widespread outcry that followed the April 27th episode that Daley decided to shift to a more tolerant policy.

Many Chicagoans say that the evidence is growing that Daley, at sixty-six, has become too rigid and may not be able to keep

Chicago under control much longer. They take the "shoot to kill" order as a sign that the relentless pressure of racial instability is having its effect. They see signs of weakening, from local election victories by Republicans on one hand and by anti-machine Democrats on the other. They take the nomination of the party regulars, Shapiro and Clark, instead of more glamorous figures, such as Adlai Stevenson III and Sargent Shriver, as an indication that the organization is at last becoming self-indulgent, like the fabled machines that have become extinct.

But even among those who maintain that Daley's power is waning, there is a feeling that no Chicago mayor will ever again be as strong—and among those who applaud the signs of decline, there is the admission that no mayor may ever again be as effective. For Dick Daley is unique. There is apprehension in Chicago, among his friends and enemies alike, that *après lui, le déluge.*

Paul Rand Dixon

AMIABLE THUNDERER OF POPULISM

When Paul Rand Dixon was appointed chairman of the Federal Trade Commission back in 1961, the liberals in Washington were exultant. Dixon, by his association with Senator Estes Kefauver, had acquired a reputation as a fearless crusader against the social depredations of the business world. It seemed exciting that he would bring his convictions downtown to the FTC. We believed that the hard-pressed consumer was finally going to get a spokesman of his own.

But the months rolled by and very little happened. Sometimes in Washington, of course, it takes a while to crank up a bureaucracy, so we tried to be patient. But gradually, the murmurs of discontent became audible. I heard more than one of my liberal friends say that Paul Rand Dixon—along with a few others in the Kennedy administration—had sold out, turned coat, become the captive of industry. As the months turned into years, it became apparent that the FTC was indeed not an agency that was going to make the businessman shape up.

For myself, I was willing enough to accept the conventional liberal view that Dixon had, explicitly or tacitly, entered into some sort of collusive arrangement with commerce, designed to thwart the will of the people. Then I received a proposal to write a profile of Paul Rand Dixon and the FTC. I had never before made a serious study of that kind of bureaucratic organization, and the task seemed monumental. But it seemed like an interesting opportunity to find out what had gone wrong, in this instance, in the implementation of the liberal faith.

The FTC people were certainly cooperative. I had no trouble getting documents or seeing people. Dixon himself was readily accessible, as were the other commissioners. I detected no absence of candor, no pattern of deceit. In fact, some of the self-criticism within the agency was extremely intelligent. What I did find more than anything else were mousy gray men with high bureaucratic ranks sitting behind the desks of drab offices. They all seemed concerned, sincere and well informed—but not, I'm afraid, very energetic or competent. Finally, I recognized that the trouble with the FTC was really quite prosaic. It wasn't collusion or venality, as I came to understand it, but simple physical and intellectual lethargy.

But I'm getting ahead of the story. I'll just confess that I had to abandon the devil theory, which held that the FTC was the incarnation of liberalism betrayed. The new one I acquired was more human. I think it was a useful lesson to learn that much in politics emerges from the pedestrian weaknesses of men, not from their ideology or even their greed.

For ALMOST eight years, an affable Tennessean named Paul Rand Dixon has been Chairman of the Federal Trade Commission. He's not one of the powerful people in Washington, but he's among the more popular. Everybody calls him Rand, remembers instances of kindnesses he's performed, and offers testimony on his capacity for good cheer. Paul Rand Dixon's chairmanship of the FTC evokes expressions of affection, not of admiration. It's considered something of a pity that the agency he directs is such a disappointment.

Yet is not fair to say that Dixon has been ineffective. Under his leadership, the FTC has scored some important victories in the public interest. It has extended its scope of activity and made some significant innovations. Certainly the agency has not declined during his chairmanship. After eight years in office, Dixon's record is not so much poor as elusive, his reputation not so much inglorious as equivocal. The trouble is that no one in Washington is quite sure what the FTC should be and, if it were, what it might achieve. There is no common agreement on how Paul Rand Dixon could do better—simply the uneasy feeling that the FTC isn't doing all it should.

Dixon alone can't be blamed for this feeling, since it seems to apply, to greater or lesser degree, to all of the seven major agencies known as the independent regulatory commissions. The first of these agencies, the Interstate Commerce Commission, was established in 1887. The most recent, the Civil Aeronautics Board, came along in 1938. In between were founded the FTC and the Federal Power Commission in Woodrow Wilson's day, and the Federal Communications Commission, the Securities and Exchange Commission, and the National Labor Relations Board during the early New Deal. There is about these agencies a common inadequacy which has led them, with some justification, to be called the "headless fourth branch of Government."

For the Constitutional purists, the independent regulatory agencies represent a troublesome violation of the doctrine of separation of powers. They were set up to make rules in certain fields that Congress itself has neither the time nor the skill to make; thus their functions are legislative. They were given responsibility for enforcing these rules, which is an executive role. Finally, they were also authorized to penalize infractions of these rules, which assigned them judicial powers. Chiefly because they had these judicial duties, but partly because their functions were so diverse, Congress made these agencies, in theory at least, independent of all three branches. Presumably their legislative mandate gave them the guidance they needed to serve the nation's policy. In practice, this mandate was so vague that they were set adrift, uncertain of their role as instrumentalities of the Federal Government.

Congress has, periodically, reexamined the regulatory agencies, but its interest has normally been less in how they operate than in whose interest. The courts have sustained the propriety of Congressional intercession, whether Congress overrules the Federal Power Commission on gas rates or the Federal Communications Commission on television programming. But Congress has been extremely weak about establishing policy guidelines for the regulatory agencies to follow. In the void, sometimes the agencies have made their own policy, hoping not to offend Congress; or sometimes they have made none at all, conducting their administrative tasks rather aimlessly. In 1961, a task force under the late James M. Landis recommended to President Kennedy that an office be established in the White House to oversee the operations of the regulatory agencies. But from Congress came the charge of "czar" and Kennedy never pursued the idea. Thus the agencies continue their more or less useful course from pillar to post.

Of all the regulatory agencies, perhaps Paul Rand Dixon's Federal Trade Commission is the most directionless. While the other commissions have particular industries to regulate, the FTC's mandate applies to all commerce. When it was established in 1914, it was envisaged as a powerful and far-reaching instrument of public policy. In its original statute, it was instructed to forbid nothing less and nothing more specific than "unfair methods of competition in commerce, and unfair or deceptive acts or practices in commerce." In addition, it was given direct antitrust responsibilities under the Clayton Act. Wilson saw the FTC as a body of technical experts with unobstructed range of inquiry, far more qualified than Congress to specify, or the courts to judge, what was commercially "unfair." Armed chiefly with administrative rather than punitive powers, it was authorized to issue "cease-and-desist" orders whenever it detected an intolerable practice.

As Wilson envisaged it, the FTC would be able to move quickly and deftly, unburdened by the requirements of criminal procedure, wherever the system of free enterprise was not working as it should.

But from the beginning, misfortune overtook the FTC, preventing the theories of the Wilson era from being submitted to a test. Hardly had the agency been organized than World War I came along, and the FTC was told to stop everything and devise ways of increasing industrial production. Then, in the 1920's, it fell into disuse, apart from one or two commendable investigations, because Republican administrations were opposed to meddling in the affairs of business. When Franklin Roosevelt became President in 1933, he found that the FTC had become a dumping ground for political patronage. One of his first acts was to dismiss Commissioner William E. Humphrey, a particular thorn; but the Supreme Court, in a classic decision, ruled that a President was without power to discharge a member of a regulatory commission —with its quasi-judicial duties—for reasons of public policy. Roosevelt promptly denounced these agencies for lack of Constitutional sanction or democratic purpose. Then, persuaded that the FTC could never be transformed, he made the next best use of it: He restored it as a dumping ground for patronage. Throughout the New deal years, the Federal Trade Commission was known as the personal fief of one of the big men on Capitol Hill, Senator Kenneth McKellar of Tennessee.

Everybody knew in those days that McKellar's man at the FTC was Ewin L. Davis, a former Tennessee Congressman, state judge, and product of "Boss" Ed Crump's Memphis machine. Davis wasn't exactly pro-business, as the Republican leadership of a decade before. In fact, like many Tennesseans, he had a touch of the old Populist in him, with an abiding aversion to the trusts. Davis ran the FTC not in the interests of private property but in the interests of Tennessee. It was to Judge Davis, for example, that Boss Crump sent young Fletcher Cohn, whose mother was a Crump functionary, and whose luck seemed to have run out in Tennessee politics. There's a story around the FTC that while

Davis was contemplating just what job to give to Cohn, a delegation from the staff came to see him and said: "But, Jedge, don't
you know that . . . why, er, Fletcher Cohn, he's Jewish." No
Jew, it appears, had ever before held a staff job in the FTC. But
Davis, in the grand tradition of Jefferson and Paine, would not be
diverted from doing justice. As the story goes, he rose to his full
height and, with much dignity, emitted one of the immortal
affirmations of American liberty: "But he come from Tennessee,
don' he?" Davis hired Fletcher Cohn as an FTC lawyer, as he did
young Paul Rand Dixon, former star quarterback at the University of Tennessee. Fletcher Cohn is still at the FTC, in one of the
top positions. So is Paul Rand Dixon, in the highest position of
them all.

Rand Dixon, thus, is a product of the FTC. It was his first job
after law school at the University of Florida, and the only law
office he has ever known. Dixon stayed with the FTC through
depression and war, through Democratic and Republican administrations. Save for a tour in the Navy during World War II, he
left the FTC only briefly, to serve as Tennessee Senator Estes
Kefauver's chief counsel and staff director during the sensational
investigations a decade ago into the malpractices of American
business. The senior staff people at FTC today are, for the most
part, his old associates like Fletcher Cohn—often his close personal friends. The peculiar rules and procedures of the FTC are
those with which Dixon is comfortable. For thirty years, Rand
Dixon has wandered the gray corridors of the FTC building on
Pennsylvania Avenue, ready with a friendly Southern greeting for
whomever he passed. Today, at fifty-four, Rand Dixon is the em-
bodiment of the FTC, serious in the face and paunchy in the
belly, reflecting the strengths and weaknesses of the agency to
which he has given a lifetime of service.

"To understand Rand," said one old friend, "you've got to realize that he comes from a part of the country in which hatred of
monopolies was a way of life. I'm talking about the South, convinced as it has been that northern business has bled it dry since
the Civil War. Wall Street and monopoly, they represented synon-

ymous terms, and both stood for exploitation of the economically weak. That's what Southern Populism was all about. That's what was behind Estes Kefauver, the greatest Populist the South ever sent to Washington. Kefauver regarded business concentration as a threat to American freedom, a threat in fact to American society itself. That's what Rand Dixon believes in, too."

Under the wing of Tennessee's Kefauver, Paul Rand Dixon acquired a reputation around Washington as a man who feared no adversary from the business world. When Kefauver frightened the great magnates of steel, autos, and drugs, Dixon shared in the glory. After the 1960 election, Kefauver notified the President-elect that he wanted only one favor, the appointment of Paul Rand Dixon to the chairmanship of the FTC. John Kennedy hesitated. He had resolved, on the basis of the Landis recommendations, to instill new vigor into the regulatory agencies. He was not sure that Dixon, a product of the very system he wanted to reform, was the right man. But Kefauver, who he knew could be troublesome if thwarted, persisted and Kennedy finally gave in. In 1961, then, Paul Rand Dixon returned to the Federal Trade Commission. From President Kennedy he carried instructions to shape up the agency into a tough, lean guardian of the public interest. From his old friends at FTC headquarters he received a warm and appreciative welcome home.

The staff that greeted Dixon on his return had changed somewhat since Judge Davis's day, but there were a remarkable number of holdovers. More important, the patterns had remained unchanged. In almost all cases, the top people at FTC were still patronage appointments, known openly for being the "boy" of somebody on Capitol Hill. Joe Shea (Secretary of the commission) was said to be "like a son" to House Speaker McCormack. John Brookfield (Chief, Division of Food and Drug Advertising) belonged to Representative Howard Smith, chairman of the Rules Committee. Bill Jibb (Director, Office of Information) came at the vigorous recommendation of Senator George Smathers of Florida. Cecil Miles (Director, Bureau of Restraint of Trade) was regarded as the boy of Representative Wilbur Mills, chairman of the Ways and Means Committee. Not surprisingly, Fletcher Cohn maintains that "I never heard anyone on the staff say anything against Rand. He's a great guy, a real straight shooter." As far as anyone could tell, Dixon did not fire or demote a single old-timer at the FTC in his campaign to reform the agency.

"Nobody ever worked hard at that place and nobody works hard now. That's most of its trouble," said a lawyer who once held one of the highest offices in the FTC. "When I first went to work there, Sigurd Anderson—then a Commissioner—said to me, 'Son, you'll find that the FTC is the greatest job in the world. You're well paid and nobody asks much of you. The junior men do the research and write the opinions. The President leaves us alone, and we're on the best of terms with Congress. And there aren't many afternoons when you can't get in some golf.'

"Well, I found that Anderson's description proved very accurate. This agency has a long history of lethargy and Rand Dixon didn't make any real effort to change it. I think he would like to, but he doesn't know how. You never find a soul in the FTC building after five o'clock in the afternoon. Nobody ever comes in on Saturday. The lawyers and administrators think of themselves as clerks, and you can't run a good agency on clerks."

Paul Rand Dixon's chief failure, then, seems to lie not in indifference to the public interest, softness on business, or political conservatism. Rather, it seems to be that he's been with the Federal Trade Commission for too long. Dixon is so accustomed to doing what he's always done that he finds it difficult to conceive of doing anything very different.

It is true that Dixon did, for example, set up a Special Projects Division so he could bypass the regular bureaucracy and assign important matters to a particularly well-qualified team of experts. He did hire Willard F. Mueller, a first-rate economist, perhaps the finest in the Government, to direct the commission's studies of economic trends. He has attempted to recruit the best graduates of the law schools into the FTC. Is it his fault if the Special Projects Division is often mired in trivia, that Mueller decided to resign, that the best young lawyers quit after a year or so under the FTC's gang of old-timers? It would not be fair to attribute to Dixon a blind attachment to the status quo. He recognizes FTC's considerable potential for influence in American economic life. He simply lacks the clarity of conception necessary to give the FTC broad new objectives, as well as the tenacity of spirit needed to build a staff equal to achieving them.

The effect, then, is that the FTC goes about its day-to-day tasks without a feeling of mission, uncertain even when it succeeds what it has achieved. In contrast to Woodrow Wilson's sanguine expectations, its machinery has proven neither simple nor effective. Stubborn businessmen know that they can tie up a cease-and-desist order in the courts almost interminably. It is a matter of pride with Fletcher Cohn that for sixteen years he handled the litigation that finally took the "Liver" out of Carter's Pills. Yet the FTC, for all its aimlessness, remains the only agency in Government with a vast jurisdiction over the nation's economic life and the powers, real or potential, to exercise influence over it.

Dating back to its founding, the FTC retains the duty to defend the economy against monopolistic practices, a particular duty it shares with the Justice Department's Antitrust Division. Most observers agree that neither agency has distinguished itself in the effort, although both have occasionally won important anti-merger fights. Dixon himself points out that fifty-eight percent of the dollar sales in the nation are currently in the hands of the two hundred largest corporations. He also points to disquieting trends towards "conglomerate" mergers, the bringing together of diverse businesses into a single firm. FTC analysts point out that to change current patterns, they would have to take on such giants of the American economy as General Motors or IT&T. To do so, however, would require a major policy decision, which the agency is not prepared to take on its own. The tendency, then, is to let matters take their own course, with no one assuming the responsibility for a major departure from conventional activity.

Even more difficult for FTC to grasp than a coherent antitrust policy have been its obligations in the field of unfair competitive practices. The mandate is so loose and the possibilities so wide that no consistent program of enforcement has ever been pursued. Sporadic campaigns have been undertaken against fraudulent advertising. Cases have been brought here and there against deceptive merchandising methods. An occasional order has been issued to get some dangerous product off the market. But, certainly, no convincing argument can be made that these haphazard efforts, given the cumbersome machinery of the FTC, have had either a penetrating or a widespread impact on the economy. During the New Deal, Congress added to the FTC's duties the enforcement of the Robinson-Patman Act, a complex and controversial law aimed at protecting small business by forbidding price discrimination by suppliers. Experts, to this day, disagree on whether the law hurts the consuming public generally; they also question whether, in its pricing provisions, it serves the interest of small business itself. Whatever it does, however, the law drains away the FTC's manpower and resources, to become one more obstacle to development of a sensible and coherent policy to serve the national interest.

The issue of the role most appropriate to the FTC within the framework of the American economy is a constant source of discord among the agency's five Commissioners. Though Dixon, by law, is the FTC's chief administrative officer, on matters of policy he is but one voice among the five. All around Washington the commission is known for its bitter quarrels and sharp voting divisions. Less clearly understood is that the Commissioners rarely divide in conventional political fashion, right versus left, conservative versus liberal, in a manner that is comprehensible to most Washington observers. The Commissioners, all Kennedy or Johnson appointees, generally see eye-to-eye on social objectives. Their dissatisfaction with one another proceeds, instead, from the effort of each to plot out some course for the agency. Over this issue, they wrangle interminably.

Chief of Dixon's antagonists is Philip Elman, whom Robert Kennedy, then Attorney General, took out of the Justice Department, purportedly to serve as the President's watchdog over

Dixon and the FTC. Elman, it is said, misses the bite of his old job as a Federal prosecutor and resents the passive, quasi-judicial role he plays as a Federal Trade Commissioner. A sharp-tongued New Yorker, he has been known to be haughty, opinionated, unpredictable and rude. But he is readily conceded to be a brilliant member of the commission, perhaps the most brilliant in the commission's history. In short, Philip Elman is the antithesis of the genial, easy-going, undemanding Southerner, Paul Rand Dixon. It is significant that the FTC staff complained angrily when Elman broke tradition and chose his personal assistants from outside the agency. Dixon would never have done that. Occasionally, the two men have worked together, each relying reluctantly on the strengths of the other. Most of the time, however, they rub each other abrasively. Elman's antagonisms emerge, in narrow terms, in eloquent dissents from commission decisions and, in wider ones, in a well-developed and profoundly different conception from Dixon's on what the FTC ought to be.

Elman contends that the FTC under Dixon has been the victim of a kind of "Gresham's law of administrative process," in which "preoccupation with the trivial and atypical leaves little room for, and tends to drive out, concern for the substantial and significant. Immersion in a multitude of trivia may give one the feeling of being busy and doing much; but it is only an illusion." Elman challenges the conception that the FTC can meet its responsibilities by constantly issuing complaints and orders and, indeed, even Dixon concedes that the agency has been obsessed by a "numbers game," in which it has tended to equate achievement with the number of cases, compared with the previous year, under adjudication. Elman argues that the Justice Department should handle prosecutions, in both the antitrust and deceptive practices field, and that a case-by-case attack to maintain competition within the American economy is a waste of FTC's effort.

What Elman envisages is a return by the commission to the role Woodrow Wilson assigned to it more than a half-century ago. The agency should, he argues, "conduct general economic studies and investigations, spot problem areas, and probe for trends, identify practices which, if unchecked, might lead to full-blown monopolies or bring about changes in industry structure or market organization that would adversely affect competition." The FTC, Elman maintains, must rely more on "industry-wide remedies for industry-wide evils." It would depend for its influence on the inherent persuasiveness of its proposals and on the publicity they would generate. In other words, Elman would have the FTC recede from the daily battle with merchants, producers, and advertisers to a more lofty perch, where it is able to supervise, in rather detached fashion, the overall operation of the American economy.

To a considerable degree the commission has adopted Elman's theories. Since 1961, it has developed a wide program to establish and apply rules throughout entire industries, without undue resort to orders and complaints. No longer must a businessman learn of a violation when he receives an official notice of action being brought against him. Over the last few years, the FTC has adopted dozens of guides on fair industry practices, based on previous decisions of its own or of the courts, sometimes on official consultations with industry members. From these guides, a businessman should presumably be able to tell whether some practice he is contemplating is fair or unfair. If he is uncertain, FTC lawyers will give him an advisory judgment, which is understood to be binding on the FTC. These new procedures have undoubtedly reduced the quantity of litigation in which the FTC engages. Whether they have raised the ethical level of commercial practice is yet another matter.

Lawyers debate whether the FTC's new reticence toward adjudication points the way toward a sounder economy or whether it actually lowers the barriers against deception and fraud. They argue that law enforcement still requires coercion, either real or implied, and that businessmen will take advantage of any vacuum. They say that the new procedures simply shift the challenge from defense against FTC complaints to evasion of FTC guides. One private lawyer with an FTC practice said the word is out among businessmen that if an industry practice is ruled illegal, one need only wait a few months, then try it again. Lawyers seem to feel that the FTC remains plagued by a staff that brings lethargy to the new rules, however wise they may be, and thereby nullifies their impact. Though the test of Wilson's theories is still tentative, they do not, as the agency currently applies them, appear to offer the answer to the economy's needs.

Commissioner Mary Gardiner Jones, indifferent to Elman's call for a Wilsonian restoration, wants the FTC to break new ground by helping the ghetto poor to get the most for their shopping dollar. Miss Jones, distinguished among the Commissioners not only by her sex but by her Northeast finishing school accent, came out of the Republican political organization of New York's Mayor John Lindsay. Her appointment met the requirement that the FTC be bipartisan. Though she had made her name as an antitrust lawyer, since her appointment in 1964 Mary Jones has given most of her attention to the plight of the impoverished consumer. "We ought to go after the practices that are most harmful to those least able to help themselves," says Miss Jones. "The FTC has a real potential to respond affirmatively to the demands of consumers in general and to the urgent needs of the poverty-stricken consumer in particular for effective protection against chicanery in the marketplace." Mary Jones, the only woman Commissioner in the agency's history, has established herself on the FTC as a resourceful and tenacious battler for the consumer viewpoint.

The opposition which Mary Jones encounters on the FTC does not emerge from any hostility to the consumer on the part of the Commissioners, but from a prior concern for the small businessman who is so often the consumer's adversary. Commissioner Everette MacIntyre is known as the FTC's most indefatigable defender of small business. Like Dixon, he is a Southern Populist who began working at the Commission during New Deal days. In 1954, he became chief counsel to Congressman Wright Patman of Texas, a Populist himself and co-author of the Robinson-Patman Act. After the 1960 election, Patman lost to Kefauver in the effort to make his man the FTC chairman, but MacIntyre was promised and received the next commission vacancy. MacIntyre, as might be expected, is a true believer in the Robinson-Patman Act, with all its intricacies and nuances, and would devote even more of the agency's resources to its enforcement.

His view is that the FTC's first responsibility is to the maintenance of competition in the marketplace. It often clashes with Mary Jones's view that the FTC's job is to maintain a marketplace free of deception. When the two goals are in conflict the two argue bitterly, though not without acknowledging some validity in the other's concern. At the moment, the future seems to lie with Mary Jones's consumers, but MacIntyre's small businessmen haven't given up yet.

"What these fights seem to prove," says Miss Jones, "is that the commission can't seem to decide where it's going. Sometimes I think we don't even know how our machinery operates. We react —to complaints made to us in the mail, to pet projects undertaken by the staff, to pressures from Congress or Cabinet members, to our own history and momentum."

Perhaps the severest criticism that can be directed against Paul Rand Dixon is that, consciously and unconsciously, he is the chief apostle of this planlessness. More than any member of the commission, Dixon reacts to outside pressure. (James M. Nicholson, the fifth Commissioner, was too recently appointed by President Johnson to have staked out a course within the agency.) He reacts to the White House, the press, the FTC staff, business lobbyists, even disgruntled citizens. Mostly he reacts to Congress, which supervises the FTC's performance and controls its budget. Out of this habit of reacting—in positive or negative fashion—comes policy.

The best example of the reaction method of policy-making can be observed in the FTC's growing interest in consumer problems, an interest intensified but by no means initiated by Mary Jones's advocacy. President Kennedy first focused attention on the matter during the campaign of 1960. When he appointed Mrs. Esther Peterson as his consumer spokesman, he seemed to be rebuking the FTC for its failures in this field. Dixon resented the innuendo but he got the point. Mrs. Peterson reports that he was unhappy about moving into the new area, but that under White House pressure he surrendered with grace. Since then, the FTC has cited with pride its consumer orientation.

Probably even more important than the White House in determining this policy has been the impact of the consumer movement on Capitol Hill. Senator Warren Magnuson of Washington and Representative Benjamin S. Rosenthal of New York are among the many who have needled Dixon about FTC expansion into consumer activities. Thanks largely to Magnuson, the FTC has undertaken investigations into insurance, home improvements, automobile warranties, frozen foods, and credit practices. In response to hearings by Rosenthal, the FTC had the government stop the resale on the open market of products that it did not consider fit for its own use. Dixon has had reservations about the allocation of time and manpower in such a fashion, but he has accepted the Congressional mandate with little complaint. In submitting to Congressional pressure, Dixon declares fidelity to his concept of public responsibility.

"We were created by Congress to do their job," he declaims with a wave of his big hand. "The Constitution assigns them the duty of regulating interstate and foreign commerce. So they are our master. They set the rules and we obey them. This is a people's government and they are the representatives of the people. That's the way it is and that's the way it ought to be."

Dixon knows how to give Congress what it wants. During the heated cigarette-labeling dispute of 1964, he vigorously maintained that he favored harsh requirements but bowed meekly when Congress overruled him in favor of the tobacco industry. Sensing continued Congressional sympathy for the cigarette interests, he recently dissented from a recommendation by the commission majority that cigarette advertising be banned from television.

Similarly, he dissented bitterly, though vainly, to a proposal that the commission attack discrimination in housing by investigating deceptive newspaper advertising. Candidly, Dixon explained that Congress would disapprove of intrusion by the FTC into the civil rights field.

Dixon also prides himself on tailoring money requests to Congress's whims, rather than to his own requirements. To the cheers of budget-cutters Dixon has seen to it that the FTC has had no increase in three years in its modest $15 million appropriation.

Perhaps Dixon is unduly deferential to Congressmen, but he probably is right in maintaining that Congress is responsible for establishing the public policy by which the FTC operates. Most experts agree, for instance, that the FTC had all the authority it needed to undertake a "truth-in-packaging" campaign long ago, but it was the duty of Congress, not of an agency removed from the recourse of the electorate, to make such a decision. It may be unfortunate that Congressmen meddle too much in FTC affairs in order to obtain patronage or favors; it is perhaps more unfortunate that Congress concerns itself too little with the FTC's role in the American economy. However commendable it may be that Congress has turned over administration of certain policies to independent regulatory agencies, Congress cannot be excused for abdicating the responsibility to supply real—not vague and illusory—policy guidance. Of the seven major regulatory agencies, some feel this abdication more than others. But the Federal Trade Commission, with an almost infinite jurisdiction, probably feels it the most.

Yet Dixon does not complain. Sensitively attuned to the desires of Congress, he makes no attempt to usurp authority that has not willingly been conveyed to him. Newton Minow tried just that when he was Chairman of the Federal Communications Commission at the start of the Kennedy Administration. His tenure was both brief and unfruitful. Not surprisingly, Minow now advocates the dismantling of the entire system of independent regulatory agencies. But Congress is apparently satisfied with it as it is. If Congress fails to use the agencies more vigorously, the explanation probably is that it does not choose to. The evidence suggests strongly that Congress doesn't want the direction of an agency to be more provocative than that offered by Paul Rand Dixon.

How well Dixon has succeeded in pleasing Congress can be measured by the overwhelming support he mobilized last year, from both Republicans and Democrats, for reappointment to his chair. Though his patron, Senator Kefauver, was dead, not a word was to be heard from Capitol Hill about rival candidates for the job—a remarkable achievement, indeed.

Dixon is now beginning his second seven-year term, having already served far longer than any chairman in the FTC's history. In looking back, it is hard to detect any deep influence he has had. Nor is the prospect great for his exercising deep influence in the future. Throughout its lifetime, the Federal Trade Commission has been a disappointment. The unhappy moral one must draw from the story of Paul Rand Dixon is that it probably will remain so, not so much because Dixon is an inept fellow, but because those with the power to do something about the agency really like it as ineffectual as it is.

Robert F. Kennedy

GOOD NIGHT, SWEET PRINCE

The saga of the Kennedy family is an American tragedy which every one of us, in greater or lesser measure, feels personally. I loved Jack, who was President when I first acquired my credentials to cover the White House. I hardly knew him well, but one day he invited me to lunch with a delegation of foreign diplomats. I remember my embarrassment at drinking my champagne with dessert, completely unaware that I was supposed to save it for the toasts. My only excuse is that I was not accustomed to the company of Presidents. In Jack Kennedy's case, I'd have liked to be —but I never felt that way about either of his successors. Not long after that luncheon, I took my tiny son Anthony to see Jack Kennedy's funeral cortege, knowing he wouldn't remember it but wanting desperately for him to be able to say that he had, in a way, paid his homage. I found it extraordinary that the democratic process somehow picked out Jack Kennedy for the Presidency— and unforgivable that we killed him.

I never felt quite as deeply about Bobby. I remember him as Attorney General, strolling casually into the Justice Department's

221

press room, his sleeves rolled up and his tie loosened, to chat with some of the reporters during a break in the day's activities. I treasure a handwritten note he sent me about a piece I did in The Nation on nuclear disarmament. But I also remember, much less fondly, that he simply didn't show up one day for a television show I had been asked to moderate, announcing later that he had been working on a speech. So we had to cancel the show. This same lack of consideration for others, I think, showed up on a much larger scale when he chose the day after Eugene McCarthy's victory in New Hampshire to announce his Presidential candidacy.

Yet I could never dismiss Bobby, and neither could most other Americans. There was something haunting about him, which I noticed after Jack died much more than before. At times he seemed almost ethereal. So often he behaved like the most commonplace, vulgar politician, but even when he did he seemed to be enveloped in some special atmosphere, which distinguished him not only from ordinary politicians but even from his late brother. Bobby was different. He was mysterious.

Esquire had long been fascinated by the Kennedy family—or sensed that readers were so fascinated by the Kennedys that the magazine could run piece after piece on them. I, frankly, had long since become tired of this Kennedy obsession and had stopped reading the articles. But when Harold Hayes phoned to ask whether I would do a study of Bobby's "charisma," I decided to accept. This, I figured, would not be another bit of chitchat about the personage of Robert Kennedy, rendered even more distasteful by the fact that he was now dead. It would, if it succeeded, be the serious explanation of a phenomenon—the phenomenon of Robert Kennedy's magic.

It was an interesting piece to do, because what I was looking for were not so much facts as perceptions. The facts were there. I wanted an explanation of that extra measure of love or hate that, in Bobby's case, seemed invariably to accompany them. It was an unusual piece to write, because it was by its very nature so elusive. It was, in any event, the closest I ever came to understanding this man who might have been President.

IN MEDIEVAL times, people would probably have said he was possessed by demons—maybe good demons, maybe bad—and even today many people think of Bobby Kennedy as if there had been within him some supernatural presence.

Bobby Kennedy was not a politician like others. Depending on your viewpoint, he was Savonarola, the Pied Piper, David, Tiberius Gracchus, Cromwell, Joan of Arc. He was a mystic in an age of technology, a myth in a period of banality. He was the hero of an Irish folk fable, the villain of a Shakespearean drama. Bobby Kennedy was passion, when it was in to be cool; he was ardor, when all his peers were skeptics; he was candor, when the going style was hokum. Like the medieval witches, he had the power to beguile, no less than the faculty to frighten. Whatever he was, Robert Kennedy wasn't commonplace, he wasn't familiar, and, being unique, he evoked the most zealous love and hatred of any public figure in recent memory.

In an earlier time, it was the fate of the bewitched to be burned at the stake. In our own day, they're disposed of less ceremoniously, by little men who lie awake at night and tremble over impending doom. Only in retrospect is it clear that Robert Kennedy's death—like his life—was fashioned out of transcendental matter. Bobby's trip through history was brief, but it was so fierce that scarcely a soul seemed to go untouched by it.

Mary McGrory is one of those who have thought much about Bobby Kennedy's special capacity for lifting the pitch of human feeling. She is one of those—and there were many—who felt in copious draughts both love and hatred for Bobby. A writer for the *Evening Star,* Mary is Washington's favorite columnist, deeply admired for her intelligence and perception, her high imagery and, most of all, her intuition and her whimsy. She adored the Kennedys, first Jack, then his younger brother, and being Irish herself, felt a bond with them that readers sometimes mistook for desire. Maybe "hate" is too strong a word for the sentiment that

Mary held toward Bobby at the end, for beneath her solid news-
paperwoman's crust is a femininity that seems to preclude fanaticism. But Mary, as so many of her columns conveyed, felt deeply
aggrieved about Bobby, for he had led her to the mountaintop
and then had dropped her down.

"I first met Bobby in 1952, when he was working on his brother's Senate campaign in Boston," Mary said. "I liked him from
the start. He was very tough but very straightforward, sitting there
in his shirt sleeves in campaign headquarters. He treated me in a
tough, respectful way that I took to immediately.

"When he talked to you, he communicated. You *had* to respond to the sort of force he transmitted. His emotions were so
near the surface. He had a good mind, but he was a feeling rather
than a thinking person. He was fantastically intuitive. He was
Irish, remember—brooding, intense, laughing, seeing every issue
in terms of good and bad. I remember Robert Lowell once said to
me at a party: 'He is unassimilated, isn't he?'

"Bobby wasn't as attractive as Jack. I think Jack was the most
attractive man who ever lived. But Bobby, in his way, was more
appealing. He was warmer, more vulnerable, his feelings were
closer to the surface. He cared a lot about what people thought of
him. You could tell there was a kind of melancholy about him.

"There was so much urgency and authenticity in Bobby's feelings about Vietnam and the cities. He could have convinced anyone of his sincerity. So many people were counting on him, waiting for him, and, when it really mattered, he disappointed them."

Mary explained, almost confessionally, that New Hampshire
was the transforming experience for her. There she discovered
another Irishman, named McCarthy. There, too, she said, she discovered the new generation in America and her relationship with
Bobby was changed forever.

"Bobby had aroused these wonderful young kids to an excruci-
ating point, then said, 'Sorry, I'm for Lyndon.' I got mad because
he didn't go into the race, then I became furious because he did—
the day after Gene McCarthy won the primary. I honestly
couldn't believe it. He didn't even let Gene and the young people

all around him have a few moments to savor their victory. They were bitter and wounded by what Bobby did, and so was I. They were sick. I remember one young kid who said to me, 'He didn't even give us twenty-four hours so we could raise the money to pay our bills.'

"But Bobby didn't seem to understand what he had done. He didn't think he was breaking any rules. He felt that by entering all the primaries, he was letting the people talk. He believed that if he made it, it would absolve him. But he was wrong. I don't think he would have been forgiven.

"One of my good friends, a real Bobby fancier, said to me after New Hampshire, 'Somehow I have the feeling that I'm just not going to get over this.' As for myself, I hoped, when the campaign was finished, that Bobby and I would pick up where we'd left off. We wouldn't have laughed about it. The whole thing hurt too much. Maybe we'd have exchanged a few grimaces and left it at that. But I'm not sure."

For most people, the emotion that Bobby Kennedy evoked was not as raw, not as personal, not as poignant as Mary McGrory's. Certainly, most could not express it with Mary's lively Irish fervor. But, however sophisticated or primitive, the emotion was there, all out of proportion to the real or imagined reasons at its source. People were fascinated by Bobby, positively or negatively, but they were not persuasive in explaining why. Most of them simply reacted to Bobby Kennedy without understanding the mystery of their feelings. Perhaps a demon *was* at work, exacerbating small hurts, enlarging little gratitudes into full-scale passions. People were free with their opinions about Bobby, while hopelessly inadequate in the evaluations of them. On another plane, it was almost as if Robert Kennedy were an aesthetic experience, whom you liked or you didn't, in the fashion of an Antonioni movie or a Picasso sculpture. Much as you analyze either one, it still comes down to a question of taste. This departure from the cause-and-effect process was, perhaps, the most curious aspect of the Kennedy phenomenon.

Speaking of the top leaders of the labor movement, Don Ellinger said, "They just didn't like him and that was all there was to it." Ellinger, political director of the Machinists Union, used to work for Bobby during the time he was Attorney General. Ellinger remained a strong Kennedy partisan, in a generally hostile environment. "I used to ask them why they felt so strongly about Bobby and they couldn't really say," Ellinger declared. "Oh, there were the standard reasons—the persecution of Hoffa and the wiretapping. But these are guys who hated Hoffa and didn't give a damn about wiretapping. There was much more to it than what they stated. There was something irrational about it all."

Hobart Rowen, financial editor of the *Washington Post,* had the same experience in dealing with the potentates of business. "They hated him instinctively," Rowen said. "They hated Jack, too, but they hated Bobby more. I never understood why, because basically Bobby's fiscal ideas—as much as he ever expressed them—were conservative. Both he and Jack stood for policies that were good for business. But businessmen hated them both.

"We took a Presidential preference poll last spring and one hundred sixty top business executives in the country answered. Bobby got three votes. When I'd talk to these fellows at meetings, they'd say, 'He just isn't safe for the country,' or 'He's demonstrated only a sketchy knowledge of economics.' But Presidents are notorious for knowing little about economics and these businessmen had no evidence to back up their statements. They'd talk about Bobby's ruthlessness in the steel crisis in 1962, but Bobby's role in that episode was not great. I remember that one big man on Wall Street said to me, 'Bobby's power-hungry, overly ambitious and oversexed.' I suppose that last reference was to the size of Bobby's family. I can't imagine what else he meant. As deeply as they felt about him, they could never articulate their feelings. They had to resort to mumbo jumbo. They were playing a hunch that Bobby was bad."

A conservative like Victor Lasky has little trouble articulating his grievances against Bobby Kennedy. Lasky, a contributor to William F. Buckley's *National Review,* became a professional Kennedy critic with the appearance of *J. F. K.: The Man and the Myth,* a book which made him famous. He has since written *Rob-*

ert Kennedy: The Myth and the Man, which does a comparable hatchet job on Bobby. Lasky is a professional, yet, for all his professional detachment, he cannot talk about Bobby, even today, without getting angry. His feelings run so high, he says, that sometimes he must remind himself that Bobby is no longer alive. Lasky thinks of Bobby not as the subject of his biography, but as a mortal foe.

"That son of a bitch got away with everything," said Lasky, the fury tightly reined in his voice. "He was the biggest wiretapper in American history. He was an anti-Semite in his day. He was a dedicated McCarthyite. He was one of the biggest supporters of the Vietnam misadventure. If Nixon did what Bobby did, Nixon would be crucified. There was always a double standard where Bobby was concerned.

"If he was such an idealist, why did he have to go after a liberal Republican like Ken Keating when he wanted to run for the Senate in 1964? He lived in Virginia. Why didn't he go after Harry Byrd or one of those other Southern reactionaries?

"When he got to the Senate, he set out in search of issues to make the move to the White House. He found Vietnam. He said he had made a mistake when he supported the war originally. My feeling is he changed position for purely opportunistic reasons. He never thought of civil rights until 1960. His only interest in the labor movement was the racketeers. All his speeches were ghostwritten. I don't think he mellowed, as some say. He was just a schemer.

"What I don't understand is why the liberals, who never forgave Dick Nixon for anything, closed their minds about Bobby."

But liberals, too, were outraged by Bobby, sometimes more than the conservatives, the racists, the Republicans. Like others, they had more than opinions about Bobby; they had emotions, which had little to do with ideology and which far surpassed the grievances they held. Politically, those who often seemed most furious with Bobby—those who seemed most affected by the Kennedy demons—were the very Democrats one might have supposed to be his natural allies.

Joe Resnick couldn't stand Bobby. Resnick, a Democratic

Congressman from upstate New York, was relentless in his dedication to liberal doctrine—at least until Vietnam made a mess of it. He was one of those who, after Jack's assassination, encouraged Bobby to come into New York to run for the Senate. But hardly had Bobby announced and begun to campaign than Resnick experienced misgivings. Bobby wasn't like the average politician. When he came into the district to speak, Resnick found him aloof, even cold. Resnick was put off by Bobby's indifference to the amenities of political conduct. He said talking to Bobby was like talking to himself.

"I remember shortly after the election he called a luncheon meeting of all the Democratic Congressmen in the New York delegation. We thought he wanted to discuss the great issues. He came very late, just as many of us were about to leave. What did he talk about? He said *he* wanted to make the announcement of all the Federal contracts that were handed out in New York. Naturally, none of us liked that a bit. And as the months passed by, we found we got a better break from Javits' office than from Kennedy.

"I guess I broke openly with him in April 1966 after he came into my district to speak at a nonpolitical dinner and proceeded to level a major attack on President Johnson. It was a total violation of political etiquette. He had no right to make a speech like that, in my district, without clearing it first with me. He knew better and didn't give a damn. It was inexcusable. I think Bobby was a demagogue. I never trusted him after that and we became political enemies."

Resnick sensed an anti-Kennedy swell in New York and, as the months passed, attacked Bobby with increasing frequency. Late in 1967 Resnick announced his candidacy for the Senate and, although his ostensible opponent was Jacob Javits, the target of his campaign was Bobby. For months, he appeared to be the favorite to win the Democratic primary. He insists that sentiment against Bobby was still growing among New York voters when, two weeks before the election, Bobby was shot. On election day, Resnick came in last in an extremely close, three-way race, but he remains convinced he would have won but for a late surge of sympathy for Kennedy. Though Resnick's campaign was based on a calculated anti-Bobby strategy, Resnick himself persists in his private hostility to Kennedy, a hostility unusual in the game of politics—except insofar as it seems to touch Robert Kennedy.

Sarah Kovner was another of those who shared that hostility. A pretty girl in her early thirties, she has been a political pro since the days when the reformers in New York began the long fight to unseat Carmine DeSapio. Sarah first met Bobby in 1960, during his brother Jack's Presidential campaign. This year, she was to be found at McCarthy headquarters.

"One evening, shortly after Jack's nomination, Bobby called a meeting of New York reform leaders," Sarah said. "There were about twelve of us there. He walked in, sat down and asked us, one by one, 'Who are you?' and 'Why are you here?' That was reasonable enough, but I couldn't stand the way he refused to look at us. He just kept staring at our shoes, as if we really weren't there at all. Then, without asking for our advice or opinions, he made his statement: 'Look,' he said, 'I'm not interested in the differences between you and DeSapio. As far as I'm concerned, the blood can flow in the streets between New York factions until the next primary. I don't care. I just want to elect my brother President.'

"Well, I suppose he was being admirably candid, but he didn't endear himself to us. Bobby didn't give a damn about anything except his own immediate objective. He had to have undivided loyalty. He seemed to need sycophancy. He wasn't interested in any causes and he played ball with every cruddy politician in New York to reach his ends. Bobby was not a good guy."

In 1964, Sarah Kovner worked to keep Bobby out of New York and voted for his opponent, Kenneth Keating, in the Senate race. In 1968, she became one of the leaders of the McCarthy-for-President movement in New York.

Mayor Sam Yorty of Los Angeles was another of those Democrats—more or less liberal—who hated Bobby. He, too, had good reasons to nourish disproportionate feelings. In August 1966

Bobby embarrassed him in a Senate hearing on urban problems by alleging that little was being done for the poor Negroes and whites of Los Angeles. Yorty fought back by charging that Bobby was grandstanding in an effort to advance his own chances for the Presidency. In the succeeding months, Yorty, like Resnick, became a professional Bobby-baiter, presumably on the conviction that it was good California politics.

"Bobby Kennedy was the product of the public-relations men," Yorty reminisced. "He had ability, of course, but they made him, just as they would a movie star. He was the Rudolph Valentino of our day.

"Bobby incensed me because he was a demagogue. I remember when he came to Los Angeles and, for the first time, linked the war in Vietnam with the civil rights movement. That was a great victory for the Communists, one of their greatest in decades. I don't think Bobby was so smart. He just was willing to manipulate emotion.

"I liked Jack Kennedy. I knew him when we served together in Congress. But he had too much money, too, and knew how to use it for political purposes. I guess I just don't like wealth, particularly inherited wealth. In Jack's case, it was as if the Eastern establishment were moving in to buy out the West. That makes me nervous. It's unhealthy when only a rich man can run for office, especially for the Presidency. Bobby, I think, was worse than Jack. Bobby Kennedy, with the vast amount of money he used to buy analysts and organizers and speech writers, was a real threat to democracy."

Jack Newfield, political writer for *The Village Voice* in New York, has a theory on why so many liberals were outraged by Bobby. Newfield is a young man of the left who moved from profound hostility toward Bobby Kennedy to unmitigated admiration. Bobby apparently reciprocated the esteem, for he often turned to Newfield for information, especially on the thinking of the New Left. Through Newfield, Bobby acquired a channel to these young radicals, whose fresh ideas seemed to intrigue him. Gradually, Newfield became Bobby's apologist, a role which cost him much of his credibility as a detached political observer. But such was Newfield's dedication that he didn't seem to care. Newfield had great hopes for Bobby and he was most contemptuous not of enemies on the right but of those on the left whose perceptions, he believed, had failed them.

"Bobby showed the liberals their own inadequacies," Newfield explained, in a seedy restaurant in Greenwich Village. "He began as a conservative and jumped over a whole generation of liberal thinking—Cold War, welfare, labor unions. He jumped from Joe McCarthy to a kind of post-Stevensonian liberalism and the old-timers just couldn't stand it.

"Bobby made his break with the Cold War on the Vietnam issue and left so many of the conventional liberals behind. He had no emotional commitment to the civil rights revolution and downgraded integration as a social priority. Bobby was for black power. He was for job creation and recognized how bad the old welfare system was. He made the liberals feel as if they were standing still, as if they were not up to the demands of the times—which, in fact, they are not.

"Look who was for Bobby: Michael Harrington, Cesar Chavez, Julian Bond, the radical activists of our time. The liberals were against him, the reform Democrats, the Jewish middle class, the ADA, the labor leadership, the purveyors of ideas that Bobby discredited. They saw Bobby as a troublemaker, a Katzenjammer kid. That wasn't their style.

"Don't misunderstand me. Bobby was no theoretician, no dogmatist. He lacked conceptual intelligence. He had to have a visual thing to turn him on. He was a guy who could see an undernourished Indian child and cry—while no one was around to take his picture. He was personal, not ideological. This was the source of his appeal to little people, blacks and whites. But it was foreign to the liberals, to the Murray Kemptons and Jimmy Wechslers and the whole New York *Post* crowd, and that's what so affronted them."

Gore Vidal, the novelist, has a less exalted view of Bobby's alienation from the liberals. Vidal, who boasts a distant kinship by marriage with the Kennedy family, thinks of himself as something of a liberal philosopher. During the Republican convention at Miami Beach in August, he and William Buckley, the conservative, conducted a sustained spat as part of ABC's contribution to enlightened television. But Vidal had long been a Bobby-hater, dating back, it is said, to a day in the early sixties when Bobby called him a name he resented. Vidal was convinced that many other liberals shared his view of Bobby as a political phony.

"Bobby Kennedy was a conventional politician," said Vidal, in his impeccable prep-school accent, "cautious to the point of timidity. At the same time, he was emotionally committed to the rhetoric, if not the substance, of reform. This made for confusion. Lately there were signs he had come to realize that he was living in revolutionary times, but I doubt if he had the means, intellectually or morally, to cope with the new necessities.

"Bobby, like the rest of the Kennedys, was the product of television. This was new. It came along at just the right time for the Kennedys to exploit it, and they knew how to exploit it. You must never rule out the circumstantial side of politics. It was the camera which made the crowds, which in turn generated the charisma.

"With it all, Bobby was touching in many ways. I don't think he himself ever understood what he was all about. He knew he had to rise. That was ingrained in him from the time he was a boy. But he was upset because of these forces he didn't understand. I think he was a continual vacillator, with no sense of how to proceed. If he had become President, he would not have known where to go."

Drew Pearson certainly regarded Bobby as a phony liberal. Like a metronome, Pearson came back again and again to denounce Bobby in the last year of his life. Something of a liberal himself, Pearson condemned Bobby for his loyalty to Joe McCarthy, his role in tapping the telephones of Martin Luther King and others, his effort to embarrass Lyndon Johnson by pressing the Bobby Baker scandal, his dubious judgment in the Bay of Pigs fiasco in 1961. Pearson also maintained that, "As Attorney General, Bobby leaned over backward to protect one of the biggest gas monopolies in the United States. Generally he was more tolerant on antitrust cases than the Eisenhower administration, generally considered to be the friend of big business."

But Pearson, with the tips of his white moustache bristling, went beyond the hard facts he found on the record to reveal the seething anger he felt toward Bobby Kennedy, anger he articulated in his usual pungent fashion.

"Robert F. Kennedy," said Pearson, "was a man with a terrific Senate record, a lot of courage—sometimes bordering on gall— and a strong belief in the divine right of Kennedys. Though the thirteen colonies discarded the divine right of kings a hundred years before Bobby's Irish ancestors migrated to Boston, he still operated on the theory that the nearest relative should inherit the White House throne.

"After the tragedy of Dallas, Bobby Kennedy disappeared for several days. He became distraught, red-eyed and unshaven. No man mourned the death of his brother more than the man who was determined eventually to succeed him.

"On Johnson's biggest day—his inaugural on January 20, 1965, following his landslide triumph over Barry Goldwater— Kennedy made a show of visiting his brother's grave in Arlington. He arrived at the graveside in the morning, but because no photographers were around he came back again in the afternoon. There could be no mistaking the message of the picture, which marred L.B.J.'s inauguration. It was Kennedy's way of reminding the world who should have been President."

This theme of royalty—of the divine right of Kennedys—is one that constantly recurs in discussions of the emotions that Bobby evoked. William V. Shannon, in *The Heir Apparent,* established a comparison between the Kennedys and the Bonapartes, which Murray Kempton embellished in an article in *Esquire.* In large part, this family sentiment was the simple nostalgia that people felt for the brief era of John Kennedy. Bobby, of course, cultivated this feeling by constantly identifying himself with his dead brother. He conveyed it to his staff, which behaved as if it were a royal court. Bobby unquestionably believed that the rules which governed the conduct of other politicians did not apply to him. No one in Washington could mistake that, from his Senate suite, there was exuded the peculiar odor of Camelot, the hypnotizing perfume left behind by his lamented brother Jack.

Victor Lasky, the conservative, explains Bobby's magnetism for the masses as a "desire for heroes, a desire for Camelot, when there never was a Camelot. People kept insisting that when Jack was alive, everyone was happy. In reality, Camelot never existed."

C. Sumner ("Chuck") Stone, a black-power militant, said Bobby had only "derivative charisma," dependent on the impact Jack had already made. Stone, author of *Black Political Power in America,* said that the New Frontier had meant, for the first time, that black men were placed in positions of responsibility. The Great Society, in contrast, was a plantation system. "As for Bobby, he had no style and little ability to inspire men," Stone said, "but blacks had the feeling that everything would be all right if we'd only get back to the Kennedys."

Steve Cohen, a twenty-two-year-old driving force in the Mc-Carthy-for-President campaign, explained that, for his generation, John Kennedy gave "tone and inspiration to our lives." Cohen said that growing to maturity while Kennedy was President gave his generation a special viewpoint. "Naturally we looked to Bobby to carry on the heritage of his brother," said Cohen. "He was glamorous and youthful, with great personal appeal. But in New Hampshire, it became very clear to us that Bobby Kennedy was chicken. We looked to Bobby to fill the emptiness after John Kennedy was shot, and he let us down."

Eleanor Clark French, a prominent liberal Democrat from New York, said she was convinced that Bobby was so popular because "the lower classes would love to have a king and queen." Mrs. French, running for Congress against John Lindsay in 1964, campaigned side by side with Kennedy. "When he climbed up on the hood of a car and grabbed a microphone," she said, "you could see from the faces of the crowd that he brought romance into their lives." Bobby, she said, was embarrassed by all the adulation, but he understood the meaning, in political terms, of the mesmerizing influence he possessed.

Seated in a clubby Princeton restaurant, a psychiatrist attributed Bobby's popular appeal more to his being "a man on a white horse than a movie star or a reigning monarch." But he, too, was saying that Bobby Kennedy fulfilled a mass popular need.

The psychiatrist was Dr. Bryant Wedge, director of the Institute for the Study of National Behavior. For him, Bobby Kennedy had to be understood as the phenomenon of a society in a state of disarray, like the witch hunts of the Middle Ages.

"Our society is obviously going through a great transitional crisis, in which its whole character is changing. The issues are perfectly clear—urbanization, internal migration, mass communication and education, industrialization.

"When big events happen to people, events they don't grasp and that are beyond their control, they need something concrete to grab onto, a person or an idea. Since we're not much on ideology in the United States, we prefer persons.

"Right now, our society is fragmented and incoherent. People are being displaced from their old values. As a result, they're seeking out new focal points, new objects. The deep hostility some feel toward Bobby is the other side of the affection others feel for him. In fact, when Johnson withdrew from the race for President much of the emotion spent on him obviously was transferred to Bobby. In the sense that he was such a positive personality, he solicited these feelings. But it is also true that if Bobby had not existed, society, in its current disorderly state, would have had to invent him. Even now, the search is on for a new Bobby."

Wedge insisted that what made people so emotional about Bobby was the impression that he had a "hidden agenda," that he actually planned to do more than he was saying. This worried businessmen, labor leaders, conservatives generally. On the other hand, it seemed to inspire Negroes and the poor. "Bobby," Wedge said, "had hooded eyes. They showed on every television show, as if he were veiling something.

"Bobby was like de Gaulle, in that he understood the value of mystery in the struggle for power. He was always a little detached and he always seemed to be saying a little more than he did. He was an ideal object for the projection of impulses.

"For an American, Bobby was also a peculiar combination of the ruthless and the idealistic. In the search for power, he was undoubtedly a pragmatist of the Honey Fitz school, the kind of politics played in Boston in the days of his grandfather. Bobby believed the end justified the means—as long as the end was right. He found what was right, I think, in Catholic social thinking. He seemed to have a profound humanist feeling about him. These two concepts—pragmatism and humanism—are not necessarily contradictory, but in America we tend to look on them in that way. Democracy is a system which exalts the means, and Bobby exalted the ends. I don't think Bobby cared so much about democracy but he did care about social justice.

"Once again, this apparent contradiction helps explain why he was loved and hated. Some people were frightened by his ruthlessness, with the inference from the 'hidden agenda' that there was more to come. Some were excited by his idealism, the 'hidden agenda' conveying promises he never made. And all of this must be understood within the disturbing social currents of our times."

Charles Evers, the Negro leader from Mississippi, said he was dedicated to Bobby "because you could trust him; you could see it in his eyes and tell it from the tone of his voice." Evers, who shared with Kennedy the loss of a brother—Medgar, in this case —to an assassin's bullet, said that "most politicians are liars, cheaters and connivers. But Bobby, he was honest. He never let me down. He cared. That's why some people loved him and some people hated him. Medgar and Bobby, they're two men you just can't rustle me up about."

Wes Barthelmes shares Evers' view that Bobby both attracted and offended people by an excessively straightforward, unornamented approach toward life. Barthelmes served for some years as Bobby's press secretary. Too easygoing to meet the demands of Bobby's operation, he has since moved to a less relentless employer. Barthelmes was recently cited as one of the five best aides on Capitol Hill. Even after severing his formal relationship with Bobby, however, he continued to serve him in various informal capacities.

"Bobby had a lot of edges he never bothered to change," Barthelmes said. "The way you saw him publicly is how he actually was. He was incredibly impatient, about planes and speeches, about getting things done. He didn't like being in the Senate, where he couldn't move things around. He didn't like the rituals of politics, playing the game. He just couldn't stand three hours at a stuffy luncheon and he didn't go to them. I remember once scheduling him to speak at a dinner in New York. Naturally, his host expected him to attend a cocktail party at six-thirty, begin dinner at eight, listen to the introductions at eight-thirty and start speaking at nine. I told them the Senator would show up at eight-fifty-five. Needless to say, they were furious. But I had to tell them that it would be eight-fifty-five or not at all. Bobby understood that they were using him, exploiting the prestige of his name, and didn't give a damn about the speech. But he agreed to give the speech and that was it.

"Bobby saw the fraudulency in life and had a sustained feeling about the injustices in the world. He wasn't a hater, but he had a rage inside him that people felt. He thought the world was a crappy place and that you had to try to make it better. He was a tortured guy and he was moved by the torture in others. That unsettled people.

"In the conventional sense, Bobby was bad in politics. The standard labor people, for instance, had little patience with him. The big hacks would come in and he'd question them about racial discrimination in unions. They wouldn't want to talk about anything but minimum wage. Bobby was always asking, always probing. He never played the conventional game. He upset those people by asking those questions. In this sense, I guess he was better as someone's assistant, even as his brother's Attorney General. But he wasn't a politician.

"There were, of course, redeeming qualities about his personality. He had a natural gift of laughter. He unquestionably had a great and beautiful thing going with his wife, and the two of them preferred each other's company to anyone else's. Probably the biggest thing about him was the way he lit up over kids. He loved kids. He much preferred to speak to them than to adults. He could talk to them about baseball and football and Willie Mays and adventure. He conveyed a great physical vigor, which made him one of their own. I've often thought that physical daring, prowess, interested him more than politics. He was, for instance, more intrigued by my having been a paratrooper in World War II than in anything else I ever did. I think he communicated this healthy, vibrant lust for life to kids. Bobby certainly had much of the child left in himself. This, I think, explains his popularity with the young.

"But whether his audience was young or old, Bobby wasn't perfunctory. He didn't lapse into the jargon of the professionals. He conveyed a sense of concern and, in Harlem and Delano, he developed rapport. He seemed to understand blacks and Indians and Jews, mostly, I think, in terms of the British in Ireland. Or maybe it was because he was the runt in a pretty high-powered family. But he felt natural and at ease with these people, and they obviously felt good with him.

"Still, Bobby's powers of communication are not easy to figure out. He was not garrulous. He preferred small groups of people he knew well to unfamiliar people. He communicated, even around the office, more by sense and feeling than by words. Ed Guthman used to say, 'You've got to learn to read the pauses.' Some mastered the technique better than others. I think he and his brother, Jack, had this technique down best and that's how they talked to each other.

"I finally had to leave Bobby. It wasn't so much the demands that he made as the example that he set. You had to run to keep up with him. You had to get up early and stay late. Once you got woven into the operation, there was no privacy left, no life of your own. I had a wife and family and all the rest, and I finally decided it wasn't worth it. But for so many of the others in the operation it was like a religious calling, a vocation, a laying on of hands. Working for Bobby wasn't a job; it was a way of life.

"But say what you will about Bobby, he was a very bright, very positive, very constructive guy. What kept him from turning into an arrogant spoiled child, with a parochial Catholic view of life, running around having a good time, I don't know. He didn't have Jack's worldliness. He was narrowly Irish in many ways. He certainly would never have been a candidate for President if Jack hadn't come before him. But he may have been more sensitive, more reflective, more thoughtful than Jack. And I think that Bobby never stopped trying to keep the rage within him confined to constructive channels."

Perhaps this rage was Bobby's strength and his undoing, the quality that distinguished him from ordinary politicians. But call it rage, even call it magic, whatever it was, it struck the spark of the California crowds, as well as the fanaticism of a California killer. It may have been a product of the demons or a gift of the gods but—as the tragedy of the Savonarolas and the Gracchi and the Saint Joans attest—it exacts a heavy price. Bobby Kennedy possessed a rare capacity to call forth the best in men, and the most wretched. But, before he ever put the best in men to use, the most wretched destroyed him. History may continue to be uncertain about his intentions; it can scarcely be equivocal about his powers.

Walter Washington

BLACK MAYOR, WHITE MIND

I have a special interest in Walter Washington because he is mayor of what has been, for the last fourteen years, my home town. Like a hayseed from Kansas seeing the White House for the first time, I still rejoice in Washington. I am thrilled by the cherry blossoms, find the Lincoln Memorial sublime, yearn for the rehabilitation of Pennsylvania Avenue. I root for the Senators and the Redskins almost as vigorously as for the liberal Democrats on Capitol Hill. I follow the crime statistics with apprehension and feel pain at the sight of the rows of burned-out buildings which have bordered Fourteenth Street since the riots of 1968. I take pleasure in the National Gallery and in Sunday afternoons in Rock Creek Park with my wife and three sons. To me, the city is important.

But it's hard for a Washington home-towner to get a real grip on what's happening here. It's not simply that we can't vote. It's that the forces which control us are so distant, so shadowy, so unreal. A Congressman from Kentucky rules on whether a new bridge spans the Potomac. A Senator from Maryland decides on our civil liberties. J. Edgar Hoover determines our architecture and the Secretary of the Interior lays out our parks. Washington is not so much our city as we are the serfs of a variety of petty barons.

When Walter Washington became mayor in 1967, replacing an amorphous three-man board of commissioners, we began to feel that we had, at least, a symbol of authority in our city. The Mayor was still responsible to the President, not to the people, and he still was forced to bend the knee to the noblemen of the Federal bureaucracy and Capitol Hill. But he was a flesh-and-blood leader, to whom we could look for guidance, maybe even inspiration. Walter Washington was, we hoped, a step toward making this city our own.

When I say "our own," of course, I am referring to those of us who live here. But we are a deeply divided city. We are a wealthy white enclave in the Northwest and a few middle-class pockets, white and black, sprinkled about elsewhere. The rest of our city is outright slum. Walter Washington, like any mayor, must represent us all, while in addition maintaining the favor of the President and the various reigning barons. It's a damned difficult task. Not long ago, the Mayor had the audacity to speak out against President Nixon's crime bill for the District of Columbia—and it almost cost him his job. But recently I noticed also that his picture was displayed on the storefront headquarters of a militant black organization—with the words "Uncle Tom" emblazoned underneath.

This is a profile of Walter Washington as mayor, of the qualities which he as black man brings to the city, of the political pressures he must deal with and of the bitterly riven city which he attempts to keep from blowing apart. It was written after his first year of office, while Lyndon Johnson was still President. I am told it was instrumental in persuading President Nixon, who couldn't find a qualified black Republican anywhere, to reappoint him to his post. Since the profile appeared, Walter Washington's life has become tougher. The country has moved a little closer to racial war. The Republicans have made a mess of racial relations. The

*Southerners are attempting to recapture much of the power they
lost in the final Johnson years. But if Walter Washington is more
uncomfortable than ever before with the agonies of his office, he
is still trying as hard as he can. A lot of us continue to think he's
doing about as well as can be expected.*

WALTER WASHINGTON thinks white. Walter Washington
thinks White. Walter Washington thinks WHITE. WALTER
WASHINGTON THINKS WHITE.

No matter what color you are, you sense it. He goes to cocktail
parties, drinks a martini, and it never occurs to him that his white
hosts wanted a Negro on the guest list. He stands on the street
corner after dark and fully expects the first white cab driver who
comes along to stop. And when the cab goes speeding by, he
thinks the driver must be heading home to care for his sick
mother. He looks Southerners in the eye, and is casual about it.
Perhaps you perceive that this is a man with no visible scars on
his psyche. Walter Washington has none of the paranoia of the
ghetto. You know when you talk to him that he thinks white.

In some parts of town, they take note of it with a sneer, in
others with thanksgiving. But all over town you feel this man with
a black face and a white mind reaching out, desperately trying to
make contact with your world, whatever color it happens to be.

Walter Washington prays that the combination is right, that it
will be digestible both east and west of Rock Creek Park. He
hopes that black faces will smile on his black face, that white
minds will find comfort in his white mind.

But it might work out the other way around. This, after all, is
Washington, D.C. This is the United States of America. This is
three hundred years later. And maybe black faces will blanch with
rage at his white mind, while white minds will darken with hatred
at his black face.

It's no cinch being mayor of Washington.

A honky cop kills a nigger crossing Fourteenth Street and from half the town come angry demands that the cop be strung up, while from the other half can be heard wild applause for upholding *lawanorder*. So the Mayor walks a line between them, sweating to devise a solution that both halves will swallow. If he were Solomon himself, everyone would know that, whatever its terms, the formula is contrived, and both sides get irritated. So he prays for some rainy nights.

And he tries to stop the cops from killing niggers, but it's hard since killing niggers is something of a habit with cops. He yearns for some rest from fighting crises, so he can get something accomplished. He wants to make a *community* out of this fragmented city. He doesn't delude himself about the obstacles. They have broken the spirit of strong men before him. But he resolves to stay reasonable, because he wanted the job and, impossible as it is, there's probably no one in the world, white or black, who could do it any better.

President Johnson got just what he wanted in Walter Washington, but the process of making the choice was circuitous and, apparently, quite difficult. By 1966, home rule was dead. The District's three-commissioner administration was disintegrating under the weak chairmanship of Walter Tobriner. The Byrds and the Broyhills appeared impregnable in their colonial rule. Black people were becoming more sullen and it was freely predicted that the town would soon blow. Johnson decided he had to do something.

He wanted to get Walter Washington into the District Building but he didn't know quite how. Washington, as director of the Housing Authority, was considered the best black administrator in the city government, maybe even better than any white administrator, and though he was no black *leader*, like Walter Fauntroy or Channing Phillips, he was nonetheless well connected in key places. Lady Bird, with whom he had worked on the local beautification program, was particularly fond of him and recommended him warmly.

But Johnson was in a quandary. He was willing enough to replace Tobriner with Washington, but Tobriner, as president of the board, was responsible for the city's police forces—and if there's anything that raises the hackles of a Southerner, especially the kind that gets to Congress, it's the thought of a black man having authority over cops. For a while, Johnson toyed with shifting police supervision out of the board president's hands, but, finally, he decided to leave Tobriner where he was and offer Washington the post of second commissioner.

In June 1966 Washington was invited to the White House, where Joseph Califano, the President's chief assistant, told him of the plan. Washington hesitated. The job Califano offered him was then held by John B. Duncan, the first Negro ever to be a District commissioner. Unfortunately, Duncan exercised his functions timidly, in apparent awe of all the white power that surrounded him. It seemed as if Washington was now being asked to take the "Negro seat" on the commission, a seat designed chiefly to placate the city's blacks, but second-rate, without authority, lacking in dignity. Having lived in Washington during the Jim Crow years, Washington wasn't prepared to go to the back of the bus again.

He asked Califano whether, if he accepted the job, he might expect a promotion to the commission presidency. Califano shrugged and left to check with the President, who surprised Washington by summoning him into the oval office. The President repeated the offer Califano had made, to which Washington replied with the same question. When the President refused to give an answer, Washington politely declined the appointment and went home. Later, the President let it be known that he was damned unhappy at the impertinence and, around the White House and elsewhere, it was assumed that Walter Washington was finished as a contender for any top job in the District of Columbia. A few months thereafter, Washington left the city, in apparent opprobrium, to become housing administrator for Mayor Lindsay's government in New York.

At the end of 1966, with conditions in the District Building getting no better, the President instructed Califano to devise a new and workable governing structure for the District of Columbia and to figure out some way of getting it through Congress. Califano remembers sitting around his second-floor office with some of the boys from the White House and the Budget Bureau, laying out an administrative framework and a legislative strategy. In February 1967, the President announced that he intended to send up to the Hill a plan to reorganize the city government, but he conspicuously left its provisions vague.

In the ensuing months, the White House staff worked furiously on the plan. The President wanted none of the blunders and none of the flaws that led to the unexpected defeat of the home rule bill on the floor of the House in 1965. Staff members consulted with all the important people on the Hill and throughout the city. As the plan approached the final form, the Southerners tried desperately to thwart it. By May the pressure had become so severe that the President let slip publicly that he might forget the whole matter. But a few weeks later, he did submit a plan which, in the House, was channeled through the Government Operations Committee to avoid the District Committee, where Chairman John McMillan of South Carolina and Representative Joel Broyhill of Virginia led the fight to keep the city from controlling its own affairs.

The plan proposed to centralize the administrative functions of the three-man commission in a single commissioner—later to be known as "mayor"—while turning over the legislative functions to a representative nine-man city council. All the new officials, including a "deputy mayor," were to be Presidential appointments. Though the District's statutory powers would remain virtually the same, the city administration would take on the conventional form of a municipal government. McMillan and Broyhill, smelling an unacknowledged step toward home rule, protested bitterly. But on August 11, the House approved the plan by a vote of 244 to 160, while the Senate let it through without objection. It was the first modernization of the District government in eighty-nine years.

The key question now was who the mayor would be. In contention were two totally different concepts, the first providing that he should be a man of national distinction, probably white, while the second held that he should be a proven leader of the District community, probably black. In favor of the first concept was the conservative bloc of Congress, the *Washington Post,* some prominent District Republicans, and the Board of Trade. Arguing for the second was Joe Rauh and the Democratic Central Committee, most of the white liberals, and the recognized spokesmen for the city's blacks.

In the beginning, President Johnson leaned toward the concept of the national dignitary. He sounded out, among others, the celebrated lawyer, Edward Bennett Williams, and the former governor of California, Pat Brown. Finally, he offered the job to Theodore McKeldin, a liberal Republican, who had been governor of Maryland and mayor of Baltimore. The White House says that the President looked upon McKeldin as a transitional figure, who would hold the mayoralty briefly, then turn it over to a local Negro. Califano discloses that the President, at that time, contemplated offering the post of deputy mayor to Walter Washington. But McKeldin, because of age and ill health, declined the appointment, and the President, for reasons that are not clear, shifted his thinking to the alternate concept, which provided that the mayor be a local black.

Califano says the President came up with the choice of Walter Washington on his own. The White House staff assumed that Washington, thanks to the episode the previous June, remained *persona non grata* and did not even suggest his name. Among the candidates suggested to Johnson were Sterling Tucker of the Urban League, Corporation Counsel Charles Duncan, and Roger Wilkins, director of the Community Relations Service at the Justice Department. But Lady Bird, it seems, kept bringing up the name of Walter Washington. Califano says that once the President made the decision to name a local Negro, Washington was the only candidate whom he seriously considered.

On a summer day in 1967, Walter Washington was once again summoned to the White House, to learn that the President of the United States had, in effect, accepted the conditions he, Washington, had set in their previous meeting. In boarding the 7 A.M.

shuttle at LaGuardia Airport that morning, he had run quite coincidentally into his boss, Mayor Lindsay. In reply to Lindsay's queries, he said evasively he was off to see some Federal housing officials about New York problems, but Lindsay was skeptical. That afternoon, Lindsay phoned Califano and demanded, "What the hell's going on here?" Califano told Lindsay that his housing administrator had just agreed to become the District's mayor. Lindsay was furious and decried bitterly Johnson's theft of one of his best men. Califano answered that Lindsay had stolen Walter Washington from Johnson. Finally, Lindsay asked for time to find a replacement and, after a check with the President, Califano agreed.

With the mayoralty appointment settled, Johnson initiated a search for Washington's deputy. It was agreed that he would, naturally, be a white man and that he would, by training, be a city manager of the first rank, qualified to supply the District with efficient administrative direction. As Califano put it, Tom Fletcher's name kept coming up on all the lists that the President received. Fletcher had been city manager of San Diego and, since mid-July, was serving as a deputy assistant secretary at HUD. On September 5, the President decided that his District team would be Washington and Fletcher, and resolved to make the announcement without delay.

Finding Washington in New York was no problem, but Fletcher was en route by car from San Diego to the District with his wife and children. Johnson ordered the FBI to issue an all-points alert for him. While Fletcher was driving through Rapid City, South Dakota, an FBI agent pulled up beside his car and said the White House wanted him immediately. The FBI put up the family in a motel and rushed Fletcher to the nearest Air Force base, where a jet was waiting to take him to Washington. As soon as he reached the White House, he was taken to Califano, who offered him the District's second job. Fletcher accepted, then went in to see the President, with whom he confirmed the deal. Fletcher and the President talked for several hours, then ate a late dinner together. Finally, the President invited Fletcher to spend the night at the White House. A valet supplied a pair of pajamas, and Fletcher went to bed.

The next morning, President Johnson called a press conference, at which Walter Washington and his deputy, Thomas W. Fletcher, were presented to the nation. Immediately afterward, the waiting jet took Fletcher back to Rapid City. He had been gone a total of twenty-two hours. In the interval, the era of white supremacy in the District of Columbia came, at least in an official sense, to a close.

The man who started the new era, the fellow with the black face and white mind, was born on April 15, 1915, in Dawson, Georgia, but while he was still a young child his family migrated northward, to Jamestown in western New York. In those days, Jamestown was a prosperous manufacturing town of fifty thousand people, of whom about a thousand were Negro. Jim Crow was a stranger and black ghettos didn't exist. The boy's father, a factory hand, had steady work and brought home enough money to make life comfortable. When the boy was seven, his mother died, but his father raised him with affection and care. In high school, he was a fair student, and a star in football and track. He remembers there were two Negroes in his graduating class and that most of his friends were white. Walter Washington looks back with fondness on the years when he was growing up, free of reminiscences of discrimination or racial suffering.

Mrs. Marjorie Lawson, formerly a judge of the D.C. Juvenile Court, knew Walter Washington well in those days. Though her home was in Pittsburgh, her favorite aunt lived in Jamestown and she spent all of her summers there. She describes the town, on the shore of Lake Chautauqua, as relaxed and friendly, with amusement parks and skating rinks, beaches and boats. Walter's father, she said, was a wonderful man, admired for the conscientious way he raised his son. For the most part, Negroes made up their own community, she said, but they thought of themselves as neither poor nor disadvantaged and they certainly were not angry at white folks. They were middle-class people living in nice neighborhoods and they had good schools for their children. Black kids like Walter Washington, she said, were brought up with a feeling of self-respect, certain of the prospect of a good education and convinced of their right to be somebody.

Julian Dugas was also part of that summer crowd at James-town. He was a South Carolina boy who came north every summer to work at a lakefront hotel. Mrs. Lawson remembers him as different from the local black kids, but he and Walter Washington became and have remained close friends. "Walter was always at ease with whites," Dugas recalls. "He didn't have the complexes of the Southern agrarian blacks like me. I don't trust any white man, but Walter wasn't so cynical. He wasn't brought up like that." Dugas, who fought his way through college and law school and a hundred fierce battles for Negro causes, is now Walter Washington's right arm in the District Building. Whatever is said about his boss, it's never been said that Julian Dugas thinks white.

After high school, Walter Washington worked for a year in Jamestown, trying to decide what to do with his life. He decided he could surely do better than a Jamestown factory and, in 1934, he came down to Washington to enroll in Howard. He had to work hard to support himself, he said, but in those days you could go to college for fifty dollars a year. He majored in political science and sociology and thought he would become a lawyer. But under the influence of a professor named Ralph Bunche and others, he began getting interested in public administration as a career. Washington ran on the Howard track team and, of all things, played golf. Scholastically, he did little better than a B average, but his fellow students must have recognized other qualities in him because, he remembers, they elected him president both of his class and of the student council.

After Howard, Washington entered American University as a candidate for a Ph.D. in public administration. This was an age of growing professionalization at the top levels of American bureaucracy, but it was audacious, nonetheless, for a Negro to contemplate profiting from the trend. The Federal Government still had few Negroes in major jobs, and the state governments had even fewer. Though more cities were turning to professional managers to run their affairs, there was no indication that any of them were turning to Negroes. It thus required considerable confidence, both in himself and in the country, for a black man to take on the challenge of beating the white man's system.

It was while he was at American University that Walter Washington met Bennetta Bullock, daughter of the Reverend George Bullock, one of the most prominent and respected Negro ministers in town. Miss Bullock was a tall girl, full of ambition and intelligence, radiating that pride that comes from membership in a leading family. Her brothers and sisters were going on to considerable achievement—a psychiatrist, a lawyer, two doctors, a teacher, a school administrator, a social worker. She was herself embarked on a career which would make her the principal of Cardozo High School, then director of the National Women's Job Corps. The Bullocks lived in a spacious house at 408 T Street, N.W., where a generation of Howard students—friends of all of the children—were made welcome. Walter Washington married Bennetta Bullock and moved into the celebrated house—where, in fact, he still lives. The marriage immediately transformed him from an outsider in the city to a member of one of its most respected Negro families.

Shortly before the marriage, Walter Washington went to work as a junior assistant at the local public housing agency, known in those days as the Alley Dwelling Authority. He continued, at the same time, with his studies at American University, getting a master's degree in public administration, then completing the course work for a Ph.D. Lacking the patience, however, to write the required dissertation, he decided to shift his attention back to the law. In 1948, he received his Bachelor of Law degree from Howard. While doing a little moonlighting as a lawyer, he climbed step by step up the bureaucratic ladder at the housing agency, now bearing the more elegant title of National Capital Housing Authority.

People who worked with Walter Washington in those days remember him as an aggressive and hard-working but unflamboyant civil servant, efficient without being officious. Julian Dugas, then a practicing lawyer in the District, described him as "a smooth briefcase operator who had learned the white man's game and was excellent at it." Washington's admirers say he would have made it to the top even if President Kennedy had not ordered the hiring of more Negroes for high positions. Walter Washington seems to have acquired the confidence of the builders, though they had never before dealt with a Negro on matters involving big contracts and lots of money. As for the 50,000 tenants of the public housing projects, he seems to have won their respect, not because he was a great reformer but because—while the fight for equality was intensifying—he knew how to keep up with the times. In Dugas's words, he was "neither a Tom nor a fatmouth." In 1961, Washington was appointed the Authority's executive director, the highest administrative post then held in the District by a black man.

At the same time as he was making his way through the bureaucracy, Walter Washington was extending his influence into the community. At first he became active in Negro organizations —president of the neighborhood civic association and the Southwest Settlement House, member of the board of the Urban League. Gradually he spread his attention to city-wide groups, joining the board of the USO, the Boy Scouts, the Council of Churches, the Visiting Nurses Association. He served as vice-president of the Health and Welfare Council and secretary of the United Givers Fund.

But if Washington was looking for renown as the reward for his efforts, he was not successful. In a poll the *Washington Post* conducted among Negroes in 1966, he received almost no mention for his contributions to the black community. Rated far ahead were the Reverend Walter Fauntroy, now vice chairman of the City Council, Sterling Tucker of the Urban League, District Commissioner John Duncan, Democratic National Committeeman E. Franklin Jackson, and Marion Barry, head of SNCC. But Lyndon Johnson wasn't looking for the winner of a popularity contest in choosing the mayor, and in Walter Washington he found precisely the *combination* of qualities that he wanted.

Walter Washington has been mayor now for more than a year —and it hasn't been an easy year. "There was a mean smell here when I came back," he said. "You couldn't have a meeting without civil disobedience."

He began by working tirelessly to make contact throughout the city, with two lunches and three dinners a day, meetings with various interest groups until midnight. Important as it was, the effort complicated the organization of a new administration, kept him from more urgent business, impaired relations with subordinates. The District Building found it hard keeping up with his unorthodox work habits: poring over papers until the early hours, conferring by telephone at home until late in the morning.

Then, in April, came the riots, making all the desperate moments, the sleepless hours, look so futile. All summer long, there was Resurrection City, creating relentless tension, demanding unyielding vigilance. And with barely a respite between them, clashes between police and groups of young Negroes followed one after another.

Meanwhile, the President of the United States, his boss, became a lame duck. Nationally, a white racist reaction continued to swell.

Yet through it all, Walter Washington consolidated his authority and grew stronger.

He had certain advantages and, unquestionably, an important ally in Lyndon Johnson. The District government as a whole had not acquired significant new power under the Reorganization. But, as the new arrangement unfolded, the Mayor obtained important leverage for a campaign to consolidate and enlarge the role of his office.

First, Johnson did away with his Special Advisor for National Capital Affairs. The position had been set up by President Kennedy, who reasoned that it would help the District to have on his staff someone who could bring its problems to him directly. The flaw in the reasoning was that Charles A. Horsky, who first held the job, was a far stronger personality than Commissioner Tobriner. As the relationship evolved, Tobriner deferred to Horsky for decisions, which caused power to gravitate from the District Building to the White House. Stephen Pollak, Horsky's successor, was less interested in being the city's *éminence grise*. He, in fact, was more than anyone else the architect of the Reorganization Plan. After it was approved by Congress, he recommended that his own office be abolished. Since his return to the Justice Department, the President has left the administration of the District—except during the period of the riots—almost exclusively to Walter Washington.

Walter Washington's power was also increased substantially by the President's effective removal of the Army Corps of Engineers from a policy-making role in the District. The engineer commissioner, although he was normally thought of as the third member of the board, had in fact been the most powerful figure in the local administration. He had exercised control over more than half the District agencies and, by supervising all construction expenditures, actually spent most of the annual appropriation. In the last years of the old government, the District Building rumbled with a power struggle between Schuyler Lowe, the Director of General Administration, and General Robert E. Mathe, the Engineer Commissioner. When the Reorganization Plan was before Congress, the Corps of Engineers lobbied intensively against it. Under the Reorganization statute, the Engineers retain an advisory role, which could conceivably be expanded under some future President into real authority. But Johnson ordered the Corps out of District affairs and the power once exercised by the generals and colonels fell into the hands of Walter Washington.

Perhaps most significant has been the growth of Mayor Washington's power relative to Capitol Hill, particularly since there is no statutory explanation for it. In fact, there is no clear explanation for it at all. It has simply been observed that the four committees of Congress which have direct power over the District have been less inclined to exercise it since Reorganization.

Some theorize that the shift of power away from the Hill was inevitable, that even the Southerners accustomed to dominating District affairs have been influenced by the growing demands of Negroes for a governing role, as well as by the growing complexity of urban problems. They say that the old crowd, perceiving the creeping chaos, was forced to acknowledge that the District could no longer be ruled as a country town and colony of the South.

Chairman McMillan, with a whiff of nostalgia, paid reluctant homage to the change when he testified last year against the Reorganization Plan. "When I became a member of the House District Committee thirty years ago we had a meeting every week, and the three commissioners attended the meeting every week—just automatically came down and attended—without any special invitation. Now, we, of course, extend an open invitation to the commissioners to all our meetings, and possibly they attend once a year, but I realize the commissioners are much busier now than they were thirty years ago." Since Reorganization, McMillan's official contention has been that the District government is more unwieldy than ever, since he has to deal not with a single mayor but with the combination of a mayor and nine councilmen—making a total of ten instead of three. He insists it's harder than ever to get a decision from downtown.

But with no perceptible sign of choking, McMillan and the Southern crowd did swallow the appointment of Washington, though it is no secret that one of the major obstacles to home rule has always been the Southerners' alarm at the prospect of a Negro mayor. When McMillan's office is questioned about his apparent acquiescence to the appointment, the answer is drawled back with a hint of surprise, "Wha, the Chay-man has been wo'kin' with colo'd folks all his laafe." Perhaps he has, as servants and petitioners, but he has scarcely been used to surrendering authority to them.

By carefully cultivating McMillan, Byrd, and the others, Walter Washington has undoubtedly helped to facilitate the transition to the new government. He has attended their prayer breakfasts and called on them in their offices. More important, he has impressed them with his administrative competence and his dedication to his job, qualities they surely didn't expect to find in a black man. He has testified capably on the budget, on legislation, and on the goings-on within the bureaucracy. As Julian Dugas put it, "Whites aren't accustomed to Negroes who are so skilled. When

Walter came on like that, they didn't know what hit them." Certainly, they have been waiting for him to stumble. They seemed stunned, however, as if they haven't figured out how to break Walter Washington, as they broke decades of his predecessors on the Board of Commissioners.

But if the Southern crowd has been prudent, it is not yet beaten, and one would be naïve to assume that they've given up hope for a Dixie restoration. Joel Broyhill has been pushing hard for legislation to take police authority out of the Mayor's hands and give it to an official directly responsible to Congress. Robert Byrd has issued warnings that the Mayor had best not shift any heads of the city departments or make budgetary changes without his approval. The committee staffs, Northern members as well as Southern, complain that the District government does not keep them as well informed as it used to. Probably there are still spies for the Hill in all the departments, waiting for a return of the *ancien régime*. Perhaps the old potentates are marking time, confident that a new man in the White House will give them the opportunity for a counterattack. But, for the moment at least, Walter Washington seems to have them at bay and, to an unprecedented degree, the District is administering its own affairs.

His assumption of authority is most clearly visible in the police department, source of so much of the ill will that has been generated between the races in this city. In the past, the Metropolitan Police functioned as an autonomous agency, indifferent to its responsibilities to the president of the board. Police chiefs maintained a tighter liaison with Capitol Hill than with the District Building. Commissioner Tobriner once asked Chief of Police John Layton to prohibit policemen from addressing Negroes on the street as "boy," but Layton declined in the absence of a direct written order. Washington, recognizing the difficulty of taking over the department himself, invented the post of Public Safety Director. He seized the civil service rating of the retiring Schuyler Lowe to get a top salary for the office; and he hired Patrick V. Murphy, a tough Irish ex-cop from New York with a reputation for sensitivity on the subject of police-Negro relations. Broyhill didn't take well to the appointment at all. He warned Murphy that "crime is our major problem, not the Metropolitan Police Department." Angrily, he declared, "I don't know who is pulling the strings that make him [Murphy] jump, but I think it is a legitimate point of inquiry for the Congress to undertake." Undoubtedly, Walter Washington was pulling the strings, and the atmosphere around police headquarters had been noticeably transformed.

From the beginning, Pat Murphy established who was boss. When Layton failed to notify him of an incident in which some drunken cops went on a shooting spree, he administered a sharp reprimand and, by appointing an assistant chief for daily operations, significantly reduced Layton's authority. While some complained that he should have dismissed Layton, the House District Committee conducted an inquisition to get Murphy to back down. He didn't, but his success did not mean that the Hill's influence in police headquarters has vanished. Recently, Murphy promoted a group of Negro officers to top command positions, but he was politic enough to promote some of the Hill's favorite white officers, too. Murphy said his objective was to create a "reconstructed police department," free of the "simplistic thinking and cop-on-the-beat attitude" which has characterized its operations in the past. His strategy for dealing with the April riots evoked a lot of white criticism, but it saved a lot of Negro lives. Washington leaned heavily on Murphy, whose office was right next to his own, and was not happy when President Johnson sent him off to a major post in the Justice Department. Pat Murphy did not perform miracles, but he modified a long-standing pattern of unhealthy relations between police and the Negro community.

With substantial success, Walter Washington has also moved to assume supervision of the other departments of the District government. He has established his authority over his old agency, the National Capital Housing Authority, as well as over the Recreation Department and the Redevelopment Land Agency, all of which used to function, under the city's antiquated governing structure, as independent units. If the National Capital Planning

Commission eluded him, it was apparently because its chairman at the time of Reorganization was Mrs. James Rowe, wife of the President's crony, who successfully lobbied for her continued autonomy. But restructuring the District government is not simply shifting around the lines of authority on an organizational chart. Washington would like to consolidate his agencies—as New York's Lindsay and other mayors have done—under a handful of highly qualified supervisors, who would then serve as his administrative cabinet. As matters now stand, the District government has some forty departments and one hundred twenty boards of one sort or another. Deputy Mayor Fletcher is responsible for overseeing their day-to-day operations, but obviously the job is stretched beyond the point of adequate control. Fletcher has increased efficiency by delegating most of the commonplace decisions—contracts and promotions, most notably—to the department heads, leaving only the major ones for himself. But he is still bogged down with endless bureaucratic tangles, and has so many petty tasks that he has little time for policy. What stands chiefly in the way of consolidation is the refusal of Congress to authorize the positions needed to hire and pay top supervisors. Thanks only to Lowe's timely retirement did the District have the opening to hire Murphy. But there is more than one way to skin this cat, and Washington has been negotiating with the Civil Service Commission in an effort to get administratively what Congress has withheld legislatively.

In the drive for more efficiency, Walter Washington has been handicapped by an unwillingness to fire longtime employees, however incompetent they may be. It is commonly agreed that he found a lot of deadwood when he arrived in the District Building. In dealing at the lower levels, his hands have been tied by Civil Service regulations. But Washington has all the authority he needs to replace superannuated department heads, and he has chosen not to use it. Some call this weakness. Others consider it generosity. It extends even to his personal staff, where the quality is exceedingly uneven. But whatever the trait, it takes the time of Tom Fletcher and John Staggers, the Mayor's faithful special assistant, to nurse along those who are inadequate. It damages not only efficiency but, perhaps more important, the image of a vigorous, responsive administration that Washington is trying to convey to the people of the city.

He has succeeded best in conveying this image in, of all places, the Department of Licenses and Inspections, long known for its lethargy. He did it by making his most personal appointment, the abrasive Julian Dugas, his old friend from Jamestown. The directorship became vacant on the retirement of Joseph J. Ilgenfritz, quintessence of the old regime—uncommunicative, dedicated to routine, unsympathetic to Negroes. Dugas, in contrast, is outspoken, full of ideas, and determined to pay the black man in this city not only his due but a substantial part of the debt owed him for past abuses. "I told the people in my department that if they don't like Negroes, they better leave," he said. He made clear that he intended "to change the color of this division from rosy-red to brown and then to black." Not only has Dugas hired Negroes at an unprecedented rate but he has lifted the torpor from the department, without being silenced in any way by those who are unaccustomed, even shocked, by his acid candor.

But to Walter Washington, Dugas is perhaps most important as a counselor and confidant. Though Washington works well with Fletcher, Fletcher is an outsider and the Mayor is not completely at ease with him. He prefers talking with Charlie Duncan, his Corporation Counsel, or John Staggers, his special assistant. But, at the end of a long day, he likes most to relax with Dugas and discuss plans and hopes for the District.

Dugas's restless mind ranges freely over schemes for the future, most of them designed to give a better break to the city's Negroes. He wants to bring services out into the neighborhoods by decentralization. He talks of creating more and more jobs to end unemployment among black people and of projects to train them. He foresees bringing industry into Washington—research labs and small factories along New York Avenue beside the tracks, foodprocessing plants to service hotels and restaurants. He contemplates construction of a major convention center to bring more tourist money into the city. He talks of building new marketing facilities to lessen the District's dependence on Baltimore and Richmond. Dugas acknowledges that Walter Washington has only made a start on executing long-range plans for the city, but he has enormous confidence in his friend, and Dugas is sure that Walter Washington will make good.

It is still too early to say whether Walter Washington has made good, though the segment of the city known as the Establishment has been falling all over itself to express its approval. Both the *Post* and *Star* have been passionate in their acclaim, with neither seeing fit to print any significant criticism. Joe Rauh, long identified as the city's leading Democrat, has only praise for Washington, while Carl Shipley and Gilbert Hahn, the top Republicans, have both desisted from partisan carping. Shipley, in fact, announced before the election that he favored Washington's reappointment by a Republican President—though Hahn said that, as a matter of political principle, he preferred Washington's replacement by a Republican.

Nowhere, however, is there more enthusiasm for Walter Washington than down at the Board of Trade, which for years fought home rule and quaked at the prospect of a Negro administration. "I love that man," said William Calomiris, president of the board. His attitude reflects the shift in Establishment thinking, which now holds that only a Negro mayor—provided he thinks white— can maintain the city's stability. Walter Washington has charmed the Establishment and persuaded its members that he both understands and is sympathetic to their concerns. It will lobby to keep him in office, tempted as the new President may be to name his own man. But the Establishment, for all its money and influence, is just a segment of the city, and Walter Washington has yet to establish his credentials with a mass following in the black neighborhoods.

"I haven't seen much difference since Walter took over from the three commissioners," said the Reverend Michael Burton, a black member of the Council on Human Relations. "He's got problems, but I'm not satisfied that he's trying hard enough. I wouldn't call him an Uncle Tom, but very few blacks are appointed to top positions if they don't have personalities that can be controlled by white men. Walter can be controlled."

"Walter's a mild fellow and very conservative," said Julius Hobson, long known for his involvement in black militant causes. "I don't know how a black man can be conservative, but he is. He probably feels he's really part of the power structure, but he's actually an agent of the status quo."

"Mayor Washington's irrelevant to the black community," said Chuck Stone, who speaks for the Black United Front, an organization of Negro militants. "He's a pasteurized Negro."

"Walter's the white people's choice," said another of the recognized black leaders in town, who asked not to be identified. "He represents the Establishment point of view, not the ghetto's. He hasn't made anybody mad since he's been in office. That's bad. He works too hard not to rub people the wrong way."

In a survey of black people, taken for the *Washingtonian* by black pollsters on streets throughout the city, Walter Washington's leadership was by no means overwhelmingly affirmed. Almost all of those questioned could identify the Mayor by name and knew he was Negro. Eighty-six percent said they were proud to have a black mayor. But only 52 percent said they regarded him as an improvement over the former District commissioners, while just 39 percent said they were satisfied with the job he was doing.

It is interesting to note that, in the survey, 48 percent of the respondents answered yes when asked whether Washington had made life better for black people generally. But in breaking down the figures by age, it turns out that 70 percent of those over thirty-five answered affirmatively, compared to only 37 percent of those thirty-five or under. Similarly, 63 percent of those over thirty-five who were polled said that Walter Washington had improved police relations with black people, but this was an opinion shared by only 44 percent of those thirty-five or under.

The conclusion from these figures seems obvious: that there is a serious generation gap in the black community, and that the young demand far more than their elders of the society they share with white people.

Among the young blacks who were surveyed, these were some of the characteristic answers:

"He's a bad influence because he's fooling the black community."—a nineteen-year-old college student, Southeast.

"When people like me can be on the street, he hasn't done his job."—a twenty-year-old unemployed male, Northeast.

"The Mayor doesn't stop people from going to jail. Who cares if the police is smiling when they lock you up?"—an eighteen-year-old unemployed male, Northeast.

"The Mayor has been a mirage. His face is black but he doesn't speak his mind."—a twenty-seven-year-old clerk, Northwest.

What so many of these young people seem to be saying is that Washington, though black, is not really one of them. One of the Mayor's top assistants, a white man, observed that Walter Washington "doesn't think of the Negro people as 'my' people. He is conscious of the black community but sees Negroes as a pressure group. He talks of them as 'they.' He wants to dispel the feeling that City Hall is run by a bunch of white bastards, but he has no intention of conveying the impression that the city is operated for the benefit of blacks."

Recalling the Walter Washington she knew as a young boy, Judge Marjorie Lawson said, "I think the experiences of childhood and of teen-age make you ready for the world. If you're a Negro who doesn't grow up all angry and emotional, you feel different. If you *then* take on the problems of race, you *philosophically* become Negro, maybe *intellectually,* but you're not angry and emotional. That's what's happened to Walter."

"The Mayor is a disciplined man," commented Dugas, "thoroughly disciplined. He trained himself to be a top administrator and that's what he is. He's not insensitive to being a Negro and he wants to prove Negro worth. But, mostly, he's a craftsman in the art of statesmanship."

Walter Washington is a technician, a pragmatist, a practitioner

of the science of government, a twentieth-century civil servant in
the highest white Anglo-Saxon tradition. He is far from indifferent
to the condition of black people in the District of Columbia but
his mission, as he sees it, requires adroitness, not anger.

On the very first day of his term in office, Marion Barry and
Rufus "Catfish" Mayfield, the militant young directors of Pride,
Inc., asked the Mayor to lead a march on the Capitol to demand
restoration of antipoverty funds cut by Congress. Facing five hundred emotional youths in the auditorium of Lincoln Junior High
on Sixteenth Street, Walter Washington declared:

"Let me say to you right now, from the standpoint of my position, I cannot participate in any march on the Capitol. I cannot be
responsible for what ninety-three years have produced. Neither
am I going to jeopardize the process of the government of Washington overnight by any precipitous action. All of you know this is
the first day we've been in office. My heart is with you. My concern is with you. But I've got a budget up on the Hill that reflects
the entire city, not just this room."

The Mayor gets along reasonably well with Barry, Mayfield,
and the other young men of Pride these days. He likes to get out
of the office as often as possible to meet young blacks, to encourage them, to offer them his support. He tries to talk their language, shifting from the crisp, hard accent of the committee
chamber to the soft, slurred speech of the street. The young people seem to like him well enough, but they know he'll never join
them on the barricades.

"Nothing is do or die," Washington commented, in speaking of
his relations with Capitol Hill. "I've got to keep my lines open."
At a recent street demonstration, called to protest one of the re-
current shootings by a white policeman, the Mayor declared, "I
will work to get the Congress to do what the people want."

But the people, at least at this juncture of history, seem less
interested in cool appraisals than in passion, inspiration, intoxica-
tion, and they are impressed but unmoved by the dexterity with
which the Mayor conducts negotiations with a Broyhill or a Byrd.
Walter Washington may be the best man in the world to get things

accomplished as Mayor of the District of Columbia, but his very success may be his undoing with his own black people.

"The times are too late for flamboyant speeches," said Walter Washington. "You can't make it anymore on rhetoric. What Negroes need now is delivery. That's why it's important to make the machinery of government compact enough to respond, in massive fashion, to massive problems. That's why organization and format and programs, colorless as they may sound, are what matter. I like to think of myself as a builder, not a propagandizer. I know that the process is slow. Still, we've got to acquire the capability and the resources before we can make headway."

Walter Washington leans back on the cushions of a leather easy chair. He enjoys his T Street house, where he took up lodging as Bennetta's husband three decades ago. It is solid and reassuring, like the others on the island of gracious living called LeDroit Park, surrounded by a ghetto sea. The downstairs rooms are comfortably but indifferently furnished, not with an eye for style but for the multitude of children they have been called upon over the years to serve. Mrs. George Bullock, the Reverend's widow, remains matriarch of the household, though old now and ill. One son, Dr. William Bullock, a bachelor, has an office in the basement and quarters upstairs. An unmarried daughter also lives in the house. The Mayor and Mrs. Washington have an apartment on the third floor. Between the kitchen and the dining room, servants quietly pad, nodding deferentially to the Mayor and his guests. Walter Washington has been content to remain in the Bullock environment, but he now appears to be the man in the house.

The Mayor, it is generally agreed, works too many hours. He smokes heavily, and compulsively empties his ashtray after every second or third cigarette. But excessive tidiness seems to be one of the few signs of strain. He is conventionally dressed and conservatively groomed. At 200, he is thirty pounds heavier than he was in high school, but he carries the weight nicely. Though he suffers from a chronic sinus condition, he is, overall, in excellent health. His temper is even. If overworked, he smiles easily and relaxes well.

But Walter Washington can't help being businesslike, even when he's being visionary. He is no Pied Piper of Fourteenth and U. He is anxious to give his people what they want—except delusion. He points proudly to achievements of a year in office: neighborhood health centers, Kenilworth landfill, 18,000 summer jobs, Fort Lincoln town development, police reforms, administrative modernization. He has succeeded in getting the authorized Federal payment enlarged from seventy million to ninety million dollars. When the Mayor contemplates the future, it is not in terms of dreams, but of attainable ends.

"We've got to get Government offices programmed into the ghetto, followed by private development. . . . We're not going to build a new economic base until we prepare a labor force—trained or trainable—ready and accessible to new industry and commerce. . . . We've got to create an available land bank of reasonable size—and in this city that's a problem. Maybe we'll have to do more with air rights. . . . I've been talking to the banks about extending more business credit, chiefly into the ghetto. And we've taken some important steps in solving the insurance problem. . . ."

Washington makes no apology for reaching out to the white community as well as to the black. He's not indifferent to the militants' censure, but he exults at having brought many of these militants into steady consultation with the Establishment crowd to lay plans for economic development, as well as reconstruction upon the ashes of the April riots. "There's a lot of nasty talk in those meetings, a lot of jiving," he said, "but they're talking to each other for the first time, they're beginning to learn about each other and they're reaching some understanding." Washington feels that he has made genuine headway in involving black citizens in their own future, through neighborhood councils, advisory bodies, widespread consultation. He even feels he has made an impact as a symbol of hope, not only among the old but also the young.

"But I suppose the feeling will persist," he concedes, "that I'm in the white bag until we have elections for this office."

It is significant that the Negroes surveyed in the *Washingtonian* poll affirmed, by a vote of 96 to 4, their preferences for an elected mayor. Certainly, Walter Washington would be stronger in the black community if he had a popular base. He would, before taking office, have built up an organization, created a following, confronted a challenger, and, with the people's support, been a winner. He would not be a civil servant but a leader and, like Stokes in Cleveland and Hatcher in Gary, not just a politician but a symbol. When he walked the streets, he would be received not simply with courtesy, as he is today, but with cheers. An elected mayor would be the voice of the black people of the city of Washington.

Walter Washington, however, wants to speak not just for the black man but for the *community*. Elections are divisive, polarizing Democrats against Republicans, whites against blacks, rich against poor. The Mayor objected strenuously last spring when the President proposed to "de-Hatch" him, so he could lead a ticket in the Democratic primary. Walter Washington, the trained public administrator, believes the city is best served by his nonpartisanship, by his words on the telephone instead of the platform, by his preference for the unobtrusive resolution of problems over the breeding of public controversy.

For his troubles, Walter Washington has brought the District closer to home rule—on a *de facto* rather than a *de jure* basis—than it has been in ninety years. He has, in a single mad and exhausting year, executed more reforms than any District Commissioner in this century. He has, beyond a doubt, shown the skeptics that black men can run this city. He is what the President had in mind. If he has failed to capture the heart of the black masses—if he has not transformed the ghetto or put all the unemployed to work—he has at least made some progress and he has given the District a better perspective on itself.

McGeorge Bundy

YANKEE ARISTOCRAT IN AN
IMPERFECT WORLD

I guess it was in 1961 when I had my first encounter with Mc-George Bundy. I was starting out as the national affairs correspondent of the New York Post, *having made the jump from the city desk at the* Washington Post. *The Kennedy crowd that had just taken over our city was young and glamorous. People like Mac Bundy, who was as close to the President as anyone, hadn't yet become so jaded that they bothered to unlist their telephones in the directory. I phoned Bundy one night at the dinner hour to pose some question that, to me at least, was quite important. I don't remember what it was. Nor do I precisely remember Bundy's answer. I do, however, recall that, instead of his voice, icicles emerged from the receiver. I apologized profusely for my presumption or my blunder or whatever it was and did not, to the best of my knowledge, ever talk to Bundy again as long as I worked that beat. His victory over me was sharp, clean and effortless, and I never quite recovered from it.*

In the years that followed, Bundy's reputation had its ups and downs. He was invariably acknowledged to be brilliant—but he repeatedly seemed to be a central figure in incredible blunders. I think particularly of the Bay of Pigs, the Vietnam war and the New York school strike. I'm sure he was personally responsible for none of them, but never did he bring to them the judgment or perception that might have rescued them from disaster. Yet, somehow, the Bundy reputation remained immaculate, demonstrating his peculiar capacity to go through life unscathed by his defeats.

Life magazine asked me to do a profile of Bundy early in 1969, a year or so after he left the White House to join the Ford Foundation. I didn't think Life was accustomed to publishing the kind of profile I liked to write, but the circulation, the reputation and the pay were too good to decline.

As president of the Ford Foundation, Bundy was decidedly more accessible to me than he was back in 1961. The foundations, generally, were under fire from Congress and, I presume, he was anxious to have Ford's story told. When I called on Mac, I found him gracious. He put the entire staff of the foundation at my disposal. As far as I could tell, nothing was hidden from me. I did, indeed, come away with the opinion that the Ford Foundation was an eminently useful institution in American society. My opinion of Mac Bundy was a little different.

Mac was certainly as pleasant as he knew how to be. We spent most of a day talking, perhaps four or five hours in all. But, despite his courtesy, I kept being reminded of our initial encounter, because there was always something condescending about Mac—if not toward me personally, then toward the human race generally. However unintentional on his part, he made it difficult for me to forget that he was a Yankee aristocrat and I was brought up in a poor factory town in New Jersey. Perhaps Mac didn't mean it that way but, like the rest of us, he was the victim of his upbringing and, try as he might to be nice, he conveyed the conviction that, to the marrow of his bones, he was someone special.

In any case, my apprehension about Life proved correct and they chose not to publish the piece. I print it here for the first time.

McGEORGE BUNDY drapes his feet casually over a chair, looks through spectacles down his pointed nose and presses a chill smile past clenched teeth.

"I don't mind being a lightning rod for anger," he says nonchalantly, a nasal tone enveloping a prep-school delivery. "Anyone serving that purpose is useful and important."

Bundy has indeed been a lightning rod for anger. Students charge him with promoting the Vietnam war. New Yorkers blame him for stirring up racial discord. Congressmen consider him insouciant about spending money that might belong to the public. It would make other men insecure, but Bundy—whether or not he's useful and important—seems only bemused.

"I don't want to file a defensive brief," he says.

It's one of his favorite expressions, emerging in discussions ranging from Vietnam to grants by the Ford Foundation. It means, presumably, that once he's presented his explanation for a decision, he need say no more. He'll serve up the facts and the reasons, but not the person of McGeorge Bundy. He'll not demean himself with unseemly debate. When reminded that, at one juncture during the teachers' strike, he lost his temper and lashed out vitriolically, he conjures up another of those chill smiles and says, "One has an obligation to remain above it all— but one slips from time to time." Mac Bundy rarely loses his sense of himself by bickering with mortals. He takes great care to remain above it all.

These days, he stays above it all in the president's office at the Ford Foundation, deciding whether a black militant in Cleveland, a rice grower in India, a professor at Harvard or a flute player in Indianapolis will get some of the two hundred million dollars he has to give away every year. His only standard is what's best for the country and the world. But if it seems like an awesome responsibility—to direct the richest and most powerful philanthropic institution in history—Bundy wears it lightly. When a staff member comes to him with a proposal, he makes a decision quickly, without agonizing. It isn't that he's not conscientious. On the contrary, he takes himself very seriously, but he's got a sure touch and he is always certain he's right.

Between decisions, he can gaze down into the courtyard seven floors below, where birds thrive in subtropical foliage. The Ford building is considered, justifiably enough, a masterpiece of contemporary architecture. From the outside, it looks like many others on the east side of Manhattan, but its four interior faces, made entirely of clear glass, encompass a microcosm of African jungle. "It's a hell of a place to invite a community organizer from Harlem," grumbled one of the earthier members of the Bundy staff. But the glass walls seem to convey, translucently, the message that the people at Ford keep no secrets. It's Bundy's boast that the Ford Foundation has nothing to hide.

Bundy spent an entire day last February before a Congressional committee investigating the tax exemptions of foundations, telling all and conceding not a single impropriety to any of Ford's sovereign prerogatives.

The facts were well enough known. In 1936, Henry Ford and his son, Edsel, established a charitable foundation out of ninety percent of the Ford Motor Company's stock—all designated non-voting—to avoid the estate taxes that would deprive their heirs of company control. Over the years, the value of the Ford Foundation's capitalization has grown to more than three billion dollars. While the Ford family continues to run the business, a group of sixteen trustees, two of whom are Fords, take responsibility for the Foundation, the day-to-day operations of which are under Bundy's direction.

Both the capitalization and the income of the Foundation remain tax exempt, but it has not been suggested that Ford—unlike some of the country's twenty thousand other foundations—has turned the exemption into a profit for the benefactors. Ford, in fact, began the practice some years ago of making public a complete report of income and expenditures, which it has urged Congress to require of all foundations.

What the matter before Congress came to, then, is who is better qualified—in terms of service to society—to spend the money? Even Ford's 200-million-dollar income, after all, is barely one-tenth of 1 per cent of the Federal budget. But since this kind of capital accumulation is possible only under Federal tax laws, is it the Ford Foundation, under Bundy and the trustees, or the government, under democratically elected representatives?

For Bundy, the answer is clear. "I think that diversity, plurality, independence, variety, are so important to our life," he told the Congressional committee, "and are getting harder to find because of the pressures of modern life. I think there is the deepest kind of justification, and indeed I would go so far as to say necessity, for the strength of our democratic society to encourage these institutions."

Bundy's approach to the Congressmen could be described, most generously, as professorial. His inquisitors seemed more uncomfortable than he.

"I would not impose a tax burden on them, certainly not at this time," he said, "and I would add, Mr. Chairman, not to do anything which discourages men of means from adding to their resources as the years go by."

Bundy was not saying that the Ford Foundation's objectives were in conflict with the government's but that its role was different. Metaphorically, he has distinguished between "a scout and an infantry division." The scout has a greater flexibility of movement, capacity for audacity and freedom to make mistakes, but he achieves nothing of permanence unless he is followed by the infantry. Traditionally, in the United States, the government has followed—with resources and the power of law—the exploratory work of the foundations in health research, foreign assistance, aid to education, civil rights and, more recently, educational television, population control, Head Start and community action. It is Bundy's position that foundations must continue to act as the scouts of American society and that Ford, because of its preeminent influence, must set a pattern for foundations generally.

"Philanthropy is a very hard business," says Mac Bundy, that same toothy smile spreading, semi-calculatedly, across his angular face. When Bundy is sitting in his office he sips, almost constantly, at a cup of coffee. "It's easy to give away pretty buildings to a nice place. But our social system needs a lot of change, a lot of renewal, which is our problem, too, and that's much harder. "We're concerned about whether our society works. Tearing the whole structure down isn't the best thing to do, but we can't go back, either. Foundations can't take the place of public policies, but we do have a continuing responsibility. It's terribly important for us to sort out what it is."

Though most of Ford's money still flows through conventional channels into the universities, the arts, the underdeveloped countries and traditional research, it is the new, "on-the-streets" projects that have attracted the most attention. Bundy is not necessarily more daring than his predecessors at Ford in supporting these projects, but the Foundation, if it is to discharge its mandate for social renewal, has to do much more in these turbulent days than it did before. Inevitably, the Foundation, in its work with blacks and the poor, clashes with vested political and economic interests, chiefly in the central city, and the judgment of McGeorge Bundy becomes the object of the intensest scrutiny, at levels throughout the society.

It surely came under scrutiny when Ford decided to award travel grants totaling $131,000 to eight members of Senator Robert Kennedy's staff, shortly after the assassination. Bundy personally took responsibility for the decision. He said the recipients were men of unusual talents, which Ford was acting to preserve in the interests of the nation, and that the grants, however unusual, were "fully justified in educational terms." In spite of widespread criticism, he filed no defensive brief.

But if the grants to the Kennedy aides were essentially harmless, Bundy's involvement in the New York school crisis was a factor in a great catastrophe. It is not that Bundy was wrong in supporting school decentralization or responsible for a ten-week teachers' strike. Surely he did not willingly contribute to the animosity that the crisis generated between New York's Jews and Negroes. But it was, as some observed, Vietnam all over again, in that Bundy lacked the sensitivity and perception to see where his early determinations, so casually reached, would lead him. Whether or not he files a defensive brief, Bundy's role in the school crisis inevitably generated serious questions about his judgment.

Bundy, of course, never contends that he doesn't make mistakes. Foundations, he explains, "are, after all, merely human institutions" and he is himself only fallible. But one wonders, after he says it, whether he really believes it.

"We're not going to be frightened out because Ford has been criticized," he says. "Our problem is where do we go from here. One way to avoid attention is to lie low. But we're too big."

Then Mac Bundy adds, with that smile of total self-assurance, "And, besides, it's wrong."

If you're Mac Bundy, perhaps your self-assurance about knowing right from wrong in the big social questions is understandable.

On your mother's side, you trace your ancestors back to the ruling class of colonial New England and from the family tree drop names like James Russell Lowell and Amy Lowell and, not the least of them, Abbott Lawrence Lowell, who for a quarter of a century was president of (what else?) Harvard. And though your father came only from Michigan, he was the traveling companion to Oliver Wendell Holmes, the secretary to Henry L. Stimson and an Assistant Secretary of State under Herbert C. Hoover.

And, naturally, you go to the best schools, like Groton, where the legendary Endicott Peabody used to get little tykes like you and Franklin Roosevelt and Joe Alsop ready to run the country. And from there you go to Yale because, already having links through your mother's family to Harvard, you might as well get tied up with the right people on your father's side. And you do brilliantly at both places, as brilliantly as any student in modern memory, and everybody knows there's a marvelous future for you.

And you feel it too, not just because you're smart and carefully educated, but because you are aware of a mission transmitted to you through the Puritan seed. Those forefathers that all Americans talk about are really *your* forefathers, and from them you've inherited a duty to look out for the country. They've charged you with a responsibility and an obligation and touched you, perhaps, with a notion of destiny. Surely they impart to you the conviction that you know what's best for America.

Mac's sister Hattie—Mrs. G. d'Andelot Belin, wife of a prominent Boston lawyer—says that Mac absorbed his toughness of mind, as well as his strict values, from their mother, the reigning monarch of the clan. In a family with five active and articulate children, Katherine Putnam Bundy was the most active and articulate member of them all. "Mother was the fiercest fighter," says Hattie Belin and, though Harvey Bundy was the wiser of the parents, to this day Mrs. Bundy, no less the matriarch, can scarcely be contained in her aggressive enthusiasm for life.

Mrs. Belin sits ramrod straight on a couch in her handsome living room, a big dog lying at her feet. Her clapboard house, deceptively simple from the outside, is on a narrow street a few blocks from the Harvard Yard. Balancing a coffee cup neatly on her lap, Mrs. Belin speaks with the same self-possession as her brother Mac.

"Mother's sense of righteousness was very deep," she says, "and so's Mac's. Mother always conveyed to us her profound belief in the clear difference between right and wrong. How well I remember our fights over the dining room table. We were a noisy family, and Mother was the noisiest among us. For her, things were black and white. It's an outlook that descends directly from the Puritans and we all have it. But Mac has it more than the rest of us.

"Mother never for a minute forgot that she was a Lowell. She was one of those people who believed that there are three classes in society—upper, middle and lower—and you know which one *she* belonged to. We sometimes kidded her about it, but it was assumed in the family that none of us would want to become bus drivers. Mother took the position that you have this tradition, so why not use it? And I suppose we did."

Hattie Belin was quick to point out, however, that there was nothing solemn in this upbringing. If the winters on Beacon Street were a little somber, the summers brought compensation in the brightness of Manchester, an exclusive beach resort, north of Boston. There the Bundys had a big house, which served as social center for their own children and for vast numbers of relatives and friends. "Those were the days," says Mrs. Belin a bit wistfully, "when the kids didn't think of spending their summers working in the ghettos, but were content to enjoy themselves sailing, playing tennis and going to parties." Even today, it is toward Manchester rather than Boston that the family gravitates. Every summer, Mac goes back with his own children, to reaffirm his loyalty to the Bundy heritage and to the clan.

Inevitably, as Mac Bundy grew to adulthood, he and his brother Bill, just a year and a half older, were constantly being measured up against each other. Though Bill—a year ahead in school—was a head taller and a trifle darker, they looked remarkably alike. They both had high foreheads, thin lips, narrow eyes, rather oversized teeth and sharp noses that seemed designed to look down. And though they loved to compete intensely against each other in games, neither ever seems to have been infected with a serious case of sibling rivalry.

At Groton and Yale, both Bundys were excellent students and fair athletes, but if Bill was acknowledged a slight edge on the playing field, Mac was regarded as a little sharper, deeper and quicker in the mind. Hattie Belin recalls, however, that both were equally rigorous in their dedication to facts and logic, and contemptuous of their sisters' intuitional approach to dinnertime debate. "You haven't done your homework, dear, so please be quiet," she remembers one boy or another saying to her. Bill, even then, was more interested in ideas; Mac was more pragmatic. And of the two, she says, Mac was clearly the more ambitious, taking after Mother rather than after Father. But all through the years of growing up side by side, Bill and Mac remained united as Bundys and, even in their most embattled moments of service to Lyndon Johnson, they never wavered in their loyalty to each other.

But, then, loyalty, integrity, stiff-upper-lip and all that were virtues which were taught the Bundys at home. They showed them during the dark years, when Lyndon Johnson's old Vietnam partisans were abandoning him in droves—and Bob McNamara was saying on the cocktail circuit that he had changed his mind, even if he wasn't yet ready to come out in the open with it. But the Bundys never dropped so much as a hint that they weren't four square behind every bomb that passed the DMZ. Today, Mac is willing to confide that both he and Bill had had reservations but, as he put it, "to curry favor by suggesting your views differ from you boss's is despicable." Hattie Belin says she learned as a girl that undermining your boss is "something you just don't do." The Bundys were used to playing the game hard and rough—his enemies at the White House didn't call him "Mac the Knife" because he liked Brecht—but, as boys, they had absorbed the rules of sportsmanship and it was a matter of honor not to violate them.

At Yale, Mac Bundy majored in mathematics, which his detractors take as further evidence that his tastes have always been coldly analytical, rather than warmly social. (One old friend, actually an admirer, said, "I'd give Bundy the problem any time of building orphanages, but I'd sure as hell never send him an orphan.") Mac, however, resents that easy interpretation. He points out that he was an ardent New Dealer at college and a leader of the liberal forces on campus. His studies, he says, only proved to him that he wasn't cut out for math. After graduation and the traditional year of travel abroad, he enrolled at Harvard with a prestigious scholarship, having decided by now to follow his father's footsteps as a student of government.

In the fall of 1941, at the age of twenty-two, Mac Bundy ran as an antimachine candidate for a seat on the Boston city council. The nomination was Republican, his family's party, but Mac insists his interest was reform, not partisanship. In any case, he ran, by his own admission, an inept campaign and lost overwhelmingly. The experience left him convinced that, whatever he was, he was not fitted for the indelicacies of electoral politics and probably would never hold elected office.

During the war Mac enlisted in the Army—after once being

rejected for poor eyesight—and turned up as military aide to Admiral Kirk, helping to plan the landings in Sicily and Normandy. The late John Mason Brown, the drama critic, shared quarters aboard the flagship *Augusta* with Bundy and recalls his boldness, at one meeting, in correcting General Omar Bradley on some detail in the plan to invade France. Young Bundy, he said, was forever running about the ship, coordinating this or directing that.

Mac returned to his fellowship in government at Harvard after the war and, in the ensuing years, worked at a variety of proper jobs. He did research in New York for the Council on Foreign Relations, an organization of rich and important men anxious to influence diplomatic policy. He helped run the Marshall Plan in Washington under his friend Dick Bissell, later a key figure in the CIA. Most important of all, he accepted the invitation of his father's boss and his own idol, Henry L. Stimson, to collaborate on a book reviewing Stimson's forty years of public service. Mac moved into a house on Stimson's Long Island estate and for eighteen months worked with Stimson and his papers to prepare a manuscript. The book which emerged, *On Active Service in Peace and War,* was received as an excellent work of history.

It's hard to say just how much influence old Stimson had over Mac. Stimson's fine patrician face was certainly familiar to the Bundy boys during the years they were growing up. His conception of civic duty was shared by Harvey Bundy and conveyed to them. Stimson, a Yankee aristocrat, was convinced that public affairs should be conducted by men of proven disinterestedness, distracted neither by venality nor poverty. He was a reformer, with a cold passion for governmental efficiency and an abstract interest in the poor, more out of concern for stability than morality. "Colonel Stimson" is still a frequent subject of Mac's conversation and his autographed picture sits behind Mac's desk at Ford. It would be hard to deny that Stimson had a profound affect on Mac's development, both intellectual and professional.

Mac had only to look back at Stimson, a casual Republican, and observe that he, too, had been soundly thrashed in his one attempt to win elective office. In the decades between President

Taft and President Roosevelt, Stimson was twice Secretary of War, once Secretary of State and, in the intervals, forever off on diplomatic missions. Bill Bundy once commented that "in our house"—where there was a father who followed Stimson on his peregrinations—"the State Department and the Pentagon were interchangeable." Both Bill and Mac, in the course of their own careers, seemed guided by Stimson in regarding diplomacy and military force as interchangeable instruments for the attainment of national objectives. Mac cautions that there are others in his "pantheon"—Walter Lippmann and Learned Hand and James Conant, for instance—but Stimson was certainly the man on whom he most consciously modeled his own life.

Oddly, a second Secretary of State, with a similar outlook on the world, also became an intimate of the Bundys. In 1943, Bill Bundy married Dean Acheson's daughter, Mary, to form a family triumvirate that was to have a powerful influence, many years later, on Vietnam policy. Dean Acheson liked Bill's brother, Mac, and consented to a publisher's proposal that Mac edit a collection of his public statements, which became the book *Pattern of Responsibility*. As an intimate of Acheson following the years with Stimson, Mac acquired both a comfortable familiarity with and a heady taste for State and Defense, the two most important positions in the President's cabinet.

But whatever Mac's long-term goals, he had no intention of going down to Washington to wait around. Bill had finished Harvard Law, worked briefly in Acheson's firm in Washington, then joined the CIA to begin the long climb up the bureaucratic ladder, past Assistant Secretary of Defense to Assistant Secretary of State, the rank once held by his father. Mac went off during the 1948 campaign to write speeches for Tom Dewey and, had his man become President, he would probably have gone with him to the White House. Instead, Mac became a lecturer in government at Harvard, then a professor. By the time he was thirty-two, he was—without ever having bothered to get a Ph.D.—head of Harvard's department of government.

Mac's friends in those days were by no means the Yankee

swells of Boston, but the brilliant young academicians—Irish Catholics and Jews and what-have-you—who were setting off on imposing careers at Harvard. Carl Kaysen, who later succeeded Oppenheimer as director of the Institute for Advanced Studies in Princeton, says Bundy in those days was entertaining and lively, well liked and respected by his peers. He particularly recalls spending New Year's Eve, 1949, at a party with the Bundy family in their house on Commonwealth Avenue, where Mac, he remembers, seemed to be saying to his mother and father: "Here are some of the people I like at Harvard." Shortly afterward, Mac married Mary Lothrop, a pretty girl from a recognized family, who, friends say, added a touch of warmth to his personality. Kaysen acknowledges that many still regarded Mac as arrogant but he points out that, around Harvard, lots of important people took his bearing for high style.

Then, in 1953, Jim Conant stepped down as president of Harvard and an important cluster of support quickly developed to make Mac his successor. Judge Charles Wyzanski, head of the Board of Overseers, was for him and Judge Learned Hand said he would be the authentic successor to Elliott and Lowell. On the faculty and in the university administration, Mac was probably the favorite. He had all the qualifications: intellect, demeanor, articulateness, academic attainment and experience, family connections. Wyzanski says Mac would have made it, except that the Fellows of Harvard had all known him since he was a child and couldn't really think of him, at thirty-four, as grown up. Instead, they found Nathan Pusey, a Harvard man twelve years Mac's senior, and appointed Bundy dean of the faculty, the university's second highest post. There he performed magnificently. Wyzanski, to this day, thinks Bundy would have made a superior president but he says that, because of feelings in the university over Vietnam, Mac will probably never have the opportunity again.*

Though John F. Kennedy was also a Bostonian and a Harvard man, he had never been a friend of Mac Bundy's in those years.

* When Pusey retired in 1970, Bundy was not among the candidates to succeed him. Derek Bok, dean of the law school, became the new president.

But when, in the 1950's, Kennedy organized his brain trust of Harvard intellectuals to help him in his quest for the Presidency, he often heard the name of Bundy and, after his election to the Board of Overseers in 1957, he was able to observe Bundy close up. Occasionally, Kennedy met Bundy socially in those days, but between Irish-Catholic and Yankee aristocrat, relations remained casual. In the 1960 campaign, Kennedy received no help from Bundy, but after the election, Walter Lippmann, himself once a member of the Board of Overseers, proposed Bundy's name for Secretary of State. It's been said in Washington that Kennedy looked elsewhere only because his popular mandate had been so slim. He did, however, decide—to the chagrin of some of his longtime followers—to invite Bundy to join the White House staff. Bundy accepted with alacrity.

Mac became Kennedy's special assistant for national security affairs, a post which gratified exquisitely the Bundy taste for the military-diplomatic blue-plate special. He hired Carl Kaysen as his deputy and proceeded to place his bid for Presidential favor. There's a story around Washington that when Kennedy passed out duties to his aides, Bundy wound up with so many that the President, chuckling, declared that he would retain residual responsibilities for himself. But Mac had no apologies for his appetite. "No one is drafted to come to Washington," he said. "Everyone is a volunteer. They are lured by the possibility of using power and if that's not on your mind when you're there, you don't belong there."

In those early days, Bundy got first-class competition from Dick Goodwin for Latin America, Myer Feldman for the Middle East and Averell Harriman for Southeast Asia. But Bundy's preferences were Europe and military affairs and, though there was much jockeying for position, there was little open discord. Later, however, Kennedy acquired reservations about Dean Rusk, and there gravitated to Bundy responsibilities on foreign policy that extended virtually across the board.

But, curiously, what Mac seemed to enjoy most about power was not its end, but the process by which the end was reached. He was fascinated with procedures and techniques for getting information to the President. He could summarize two conflicting policy recommendations better than either of their proponents. He was relentless in pressing Presidential advisers for more thought and research. One White House colleague remembers how he fed icy, baiting questions to the Chief of Staff, General Lemnitzer, during a debate over Laos, until Lemnitzer, in exasperation, conceded that an invasion would probably mean war.

"The trouble with the way Bundy did his job," said one former Kennedy aide, "was that he tended to look at what worked and forgot to examine what was right. Bobby knew there was more to life than pure logic. But not Mac. He had analysis, not insights to offer the President."

"Mac never understood," said another of Kennedy's favorites, "that the analytical approach leads to error. He has a habit of mind that leans toward math, in which the relevant factors are logical, precise, quantifiable. Intuition always gets left out. Mac was interested in finding the right answer, not asking the right question. That's the kind of thinking that led him astray."

But if Mac was preoccupied with mechanics, he was not, as some have said, indifferent to morality. It was, rather, that to him, morality was indistinguishable from the national interest. What was good for the country was, ipso facto, moral, and vice versa. Diplomacy, then, did not require moral judgment so much as mechanical determination of the right move to make.

During the two great diplomatic crises of the Kennedy years— the Bay of Pigs in 1961 and the missile confrontation in 1962— Mac served up data quickly, efficiently, tirelessly. But he gave no guidance and volunteered no wisdom. Bobby Kennedy, with far less exposure to the facts, showed a much sounder diplomatic instinct. The President was not disappointed in Mac's mastery of his official duties, but he felt let down by Mac's deficiency of perception. If Kennedy planned to appoint a new Secretary of State for his second term—and he almost certainly did—it was unlikely to have been Mac Bundy.

Under Johnson, Mac's role changed significantly. While he had been an outsider among Kennedy's Irish Mafia, he had nonethe--

less found the President intellectually and socially compatible. Johnson's Texas personality, however, was foreign to Mac, and Mac's Harvard ways made the President squirm. Johnson contemplated getting rid of Mac very early, just as Mac contemplated leaving. But Johnson quickly discovered Mac's capacities, as well as the benefits of having a Harvard intellectual around, while Mac quickly discovered the joys of new power, as well as the ability of his ego to withstand Johnson's assaults. "Johnson never understood, the way Kennedy did, the limitations of Mac's usefulness," said a former Irish Mafioso, "because Johnson lacked Kennedy's values." What drew Johnson to Mac, whatever their differences in background, was a common approach to policy and, as the Kennedy people left one by one, Mac stayed in the White House, with more influence than ever.

To Mac, Vietnam was a problem for the American government to resolve, by whatever combination of military and diplomatic force was required. Under Kennedy, he had favored eliminating Diem, "not because Diem was wrong or evil," said one of his own former deputies, "but because he had ceased to be effective." In August of 1964, Mac endorsed the bombing of North Vietnam after the Navy's unconfirmed report of an attack in the Gulf of Tonkin. In February 1965 Mac arrived in Vietnam for the first time, just as the Viet Cong were inflicting a defeat on the American forces at Pleiku. Without waiting, Mac got on the phone to the President and urged that the war be carried directly to the enemy in the North. "Mac thought he was the field commander out there," said a former intimate of the President, "and he really lost his cool." But back in Washington, Mac had supporters not only in Lyndon Johnson but in Bill Bundy at State and the elder statesman, Dean Acheson, and for three years the government relentlessly pursued the objective of bombing North Vietnam into submission.

"Johnson never needed to be convinced about the escalation and the bombing," said one former White House staffer, "but he wanted to have reasons. Mac gave him the reasons. And just as he made the case for bombing, he made the case for intervention in the Dominican Republic. Mac went from crisis to crisis, a skillful driver who never quite knew where he was going. With great loyalty, he provided the rationalization for Lyndon Johnson's prejudices."

But the Vietnam policy—even on Bundy's terms—was turning into a mess: it simply didn't work. One of Mac's assignments was to curb the outrage of the intellectuals and, in June 1965, he lectured them sternly: "There is in many—and especially among those whose concern is for ideas and ideals and those whose hope is primarily for peace and progress—a reluctance to give full weight to the role of power and its necessity in the world's affairs." Yet American intellectuals seemed to be thinking less of power and more of justice. At Harvard, a few weeks later, he was greeted by student and alumni demonstrators, one of whom carried a sign which said, "Bundy, We've Had Enough Lies," while another displayed a placard which asked, "When Will Bundy Pay For His War Crimes?" Wherever he went on college campuses, sentiment against the war was powerful and the Bundy name was anathema.

Meanwhile, up in New York at the Ford Foundation, the board of trustees was feuding with its president of a decade, Henry Heald. Its objection was not so much to his goals or administration as to his unwillingness to share responsibility for major decisions. It was assumed, however, that since his retirement was not far away, Heald would wait to make a graceful exit. Then, suddenly, he announced his resignation and the board had to set out in search of a successor.

It's no surprise that Mac Bundy's name should have figured prominently in the deliberations from the beginning. Ford's standards, after all, were not basically different from Harvard's, and now Mac was twelve years older and substantially more experienced in administration, education and international affairs, all major concerns of the Foundation. And in the philanthropy business, Vietnam was no particular stigma. The only other serious candidate was Robert McNamara, but Bundy seemed to meet the requirements more fully and, in the fall of 1965, he was offered the job.

Bundy took the offer to President Johnson, persuaded that the time had come for him to leave. In 1962, he had ruled himself out of consideration for the Presidency of Yale to stay in the White House. At different times, he had made himself unavailable for other prestigious positions. But Ford presented a real opportunity for public service and it paid seventy-five thousand dollars a year, which was—even with a small inheritance—an important consideration for a man who had four sons to put through school. Perhaps Mac was hopeful, as some have suggested, that the President would hint that a new office—like Secretary of State or Secretary of Defense—might be forthcoming if he stayed. But the President emitted no such hint, so Mac, with a friendly handshake, took off for New York.

So you're Mac Bundy, with a deep sense of social responsibility, and the world is looking to see what you can do at the Ford Foundation. You want to do something big but history decrees that you can't be the first of the great foundation activists. Back in the 1930's, after all, Carnegie had the audacity to commission Gunnar Myrdal to challenge the nation on its treatment of the Negro. And in the late 1950's, Ford itself, aroused by a young staffer named Paul Ylvisaker, undertook, with Heald's blessing, a controversial "gray areas" program that channeled funds into antidelinquency organizations in New York, community action in Boston and New Haven and a campaign to make local courts more responsive to the poor. To be sure, most foundations found over the years that they had enough trouble—from philistines, racists, red-baiters and other foes—just giving away their money to universities, hospitals and the arts. They preferred to limit social experimentation, if they tried it at all, to overseas activities. But now, Mac Bundy, the mood is different and the country is crying out for help. At Ford, the trustees and the staff are fired with zeal to get on with projects for social renewal. Even if you can't be first, the times are made for a man of great endowments and vision.

Hardly have you arrived in New York than Mayor John Lindsay, a fellow Yalie and Yankee aristocrat, spots you and figures that you can be useful to him. He asks you to mediate a dispute between black parents and the Board of Education at I.S. (Intermediate School) 201, where an experiment in community control is underway. You see a trap in acting as the city's agent and you decline, but you agree to put a little of Ford's money into the experiment, as well as your good offices into resolving the differences. Thus you have your baptism of fire in the New York school crisis, and you're quickened by the excitement.

Through 1967, your people at Ford keep a close watch over the uneasy peace at I.S. 201 while catalyzing an agreement between the Board (bureaucracy), the union (Jewish) and the parents (Negro) to establish two more experimental districts, one of them in the Ocean Hill-Brownsville slums of Brooklyn. Perhaps you don't appreciate that the reason the union is going along is to assure widespread backing for its own program to improve public education, based largely on salary increases for teachers. Perhaps you don't recognize the depth of feeling the administrators and the parents bring to the issue of who's to run the schools. But when the state government announces that, under some obscure formula, it can give the city more education funds if the school administration is decentralized, and Mayor Lindsay asks you to draw up a plan, you're delighted at the opportunity and you agree.

So, as a private citizen, you become head of a panel to propose a decentralization program, but inevitably the public will associate any proposal you make with the Ford Foundation. Had Lindsay appointed Board, teacher and parent representatives to your panel, agreement would have been hard enough to reach but, instead, he appointed only outsiders, most of them not even New Yorkers. Later, Lindsay said of the panel members, "their charge was to recommend what had to be done in a perfect world," but he knew New York's world was imperfect and might have foreseen that outsiders would fail to grasp the subtleties of power relationships and group anxieties. Yet you work conscientiously, if a bit naïvely, Mac Bundy, and desperately seek the endorsement of the whole community for your recommendations. If you ever had a chance to succeed, however, it is destroyed when the schools open that fall and the teachers, demanding more wages, are out on strike.

During the two weeks of the 1967 strike, the uncomfortable coalition between parents and teachers that you had helped to create breaks grimly apart. Black parents, along with Puerto Ricans, are outraged at the insensitivity of the teachers to the needs of their children, while the teachers, sanctimonious about the liberalism of their cause, are furious at the betrayal. You are caught in the middle of a three-way struggle, and when your panel makes its recommendations a few weeks later, the Board disassociates itself from them and the union dismisses them. Only the parents appear to approve, and you and the Ford Foundation—having committed a million dollars to the experimental districts—seem irrevocably linked not only to the cause of decentralization but, justifiably or not, to the debacle that ensues.

With Mayor Lindsay, you stand by helplessly while the tragedy plays itself to a climax. The governing board at Ocean Hill-Brownsville runs head-on into the rights claimed by the teachers' union. With the Board of Education too rigid to find a remedy, the dispute—fired by confusion, deception and recrimination—grows more intense. As Ocean Hill becomes more militant and the union more adamant, bitter animosity develops throughout the city between blacks and Jews. When the school year begins in September 1968 the union is again on strike. This time, the strike lasts for the better part of ten weeks. A writer in *The New York Times* calls it "the worst disaster my native city has experienced in my lifetime."

Mac Bundy stretches out his legs and drops them on a coffee table in front of him. At fifty, he still exudes a restless energy, as if impatient with office confinement. He looks as if he might be a military commander, ready to drop his paper work to board a tank or inspect a platoon of men. But he is forever urbane and his talk, though straight and without artifice, is deftly controlled, so he reveals precisely what he wants, and rarely anything more.

"Here at Ford," he says, "we still subscribe to what's in the panel report. I suspect that our role in the events which led to the explosion was at most indirect. For all we know, maybe the troubles that began with I.S. 201 are the start of something better. We don't know if this is the beginning or the end."

Mac Bundy's enthusiasm for promoting social activism at the Foundation does not seem to have diminished in the wake of the teachers' strike. Next year's budget is full of grants in the area of social renewal. Most of them, to be sure, follow the traditional pattern of education and research, and perhaps too few are experiments that genuinely get out "on the streets." But almost all are close to the knife's edge of social instability, the race question, which Mac Bundy regards as the principal threat to our system.

"If we could turn off the psychological color line in America, we'd have one-tenth the problems we have now," he says. "I am really troubled by the white racism that is up and down the line in the American consciousness."

Then, as if to reaffirm the inappropriateness of a moral judgment, he declares: "It is seriously damaging the effectiveness of our society."

Last October, Bundy seemed to reaffirm a disdain for moral speculation when, during Hubert Humphrey's final surge for the Presidency, he made a surprising declaration on Vietnam. Without in any way conceding error in his former position, he said: "We must begin to lift this burden from our lives." He proposed a steady, systematic withdrawal of American forces beginning in 1969, whether or not North Vietnam agreed to a truce.

Cynics—and others—took the statement to be Bundy's bid to become Secretary of State in a Humphrey cabinet. Hattie Belin says she thinks her twenty-one-year-old son Dick, who considers the war so loathsome that he contemplates jail as an alternative, has had a big impact on his uncle. "Mac has said we're in danger of losing a generation," she discloses. If this is a new factor in Mac's equation, he declines to acknowledge it. If there is a logical contradiction in counseling withdrawal without repudiating involvement, he refuses to concede it. In short, Mac Bundy files no defensive brief.*

* Bundy did fundamentally the same thing in March, 1971, in testifying in

"Of course, I knew people would question my motives," he says easily, revealing no qualms. "But it's what I honestly thought and what I'd been saying for some time. President Johnson was unhappy—but I think he got over it.

"Certainly I hoped it would be helpful to Hubert. If not, I don't think I would have made the statement. But you'll have to ask him whether he had any intention of putting me into his cabinet.

"If he had asked me to be Secretary of State, I'd have had a lot to think about. When you're interested in public service, you get into a box if you pick one job and make that a target. But if you're primarily concerned with foreign affairs, then being Secretary of State . . . well, the old green monster of ambition gets us all."

Perhaps Mac Bundy flounders around only when he's questioned about his emotions. He mumbles something about the sentimental appeal of Disraeli and Burke and is clearly uncomfortable dealing in personal terms with abstractions, even commonplace ones like democracy and aristocracy.

"I guess I would have to accept the designation of being pragmatic," he says finally, with some resignation. "But I think you shouldn't exaggerate that. I don't have within me, I suppose, anything as recognizable as Jewish humanism or Bobby Kennedy's Celtic instincts. But that doesn't mean I'm without human feelings."

It is, of course, not an absence but, perhaps, a deficiency of human feelings that has caused resentment of Mac Bundy. Few people believe that, with a couple of decades of public service still before him, he will remain permanently at the Ford Foundation, but his future in government is by no means clear. Though he has cut a wide swath with his capacity, he has left too many ragged edges with his frigidity.

"It's a pity that Mac was never tortured by self-searching," says a close Harvard friend. "He was endowed with so many gifts

---

favor of a treaty to ban the use of tear gas and herbicides in war, without ever acknowledging error in his sanction of tear gas and herbicides in Vietnam.

and such an acute sense of duty, but he was denied the spiritual virtue of humility. This man can be wonderful in ministering to the underdeveloped nation. But he fails in his concern for the underdeveloped heart."

John N. Mitchell

WALL STREET ADMINISTERS JUSTICE

Before Spiro Agnew snatched the title away from him, Attorney General John Mitchell ranked as the number one enfant térrible of the Nixon administration. He seemed determined to irritate liberals, newspapermen, blacks and Democrats. I fell into most, though not all, of those categories. So I must admit that when The New York Times Magazine *suggested I do a profile of Mitchell, I was delighted. It seemed a wonderful opportunity to strike with the cold steel of hard truth against the forces I felt were serving the country badly.*

The trouble was, when I began talking to Mitchell's critics, that I saw the real picture was much more equivocal. A lot of accusations were being made on the basis of signs and signals, but the evidence wasn't there. Much as I'd have liked to, I could not confirm the charges of a policy decision in the Justice Department to sweep away civil rights and repress civil liberties. Neither did I find, of course, that the Attorney General was conducting himself as the guardian of Constitutional virtue, as I personally believed he should. The orientation of the Justice Department under

Mitchell was, indeed, more conservative than it had been under his predecessor, Ramsey Clark. To put it in classical terms, it was much more concerned with social order than social progress. But Mitchell's critics would have liked me to find out that the Justice Department was laying the groundwork for a police state, and I'm afraid I could not.

I spent several hours with John Mitchell himself, who had acquired during the Presidential campaign the reputation of a cold, abrupt and arrogant man. Yet, though I could not call him modest, the man I saw was more shy than cold, more cryptic than abrupt. In fact, if I were to characterize John Mitchell on the basis of one lengthy interview, I would say he had a keen intelligence, a quiet warmth, a soft sense of humor and a mild feeling of astonishment that he had come so far so fast. I was quite prepared to dislike him, then found that I did not.

I'm sorry Mitchell didn't approve of the piece I wrote, but I didn't think he would. It contained much that was genuinely critical of him and the operations of the Justice Department. It indicated that the Attorney General, who had become the President's principal adviser, lacked a clear conception of what public policy should be. It revealed how the Attorney General, despite the esteem in which he was held by Mr. Nixon, had made many mistakes. It raised serious questions about his judgment in choosing subordinates. It also contained some of Mitchell's indiscreet jibes about his colleagues, which I think is what made him angriest. Yet my liberal friends, particularly those who had worked for President Johnson, were convinced that I had pulled my punches.

Let me note in passing that, to me, one of the fascinating aspects of preparing this piece was the tracing of John Mitchell's career through Wall Street. It's amazing how often, during the course of writing these profiles—Javits, Tsien, Rusk, Bundy—I was called down to Wall Street. This says something, I think, about the forces behind American political power but, much as I have tried to determine what those forces are, I have not been successful. Wall Street has a profound influence on American policy, but its means of exercising power are nebulous, its lines to power are diaphanous. John Mitchell is certainly not Wall Street's agent, but he reflects a frame of mind, I think, developed over a lifetime in Wall Street, on which much of our policy decisions depend.

Let me also confess one misjudgment. I blew the chance to interview Martha Mitchell. If I remember correctly, I had a date to have cocktails with her, but we ran into a scheduling problem. Over the telephone, she sounded very pleasant, but giddy and frivolous. Since I was under a deadline, I decided I could safely skip the encounter. What a mistake! Mrs. Mitchell, of course, has since acquired a notoriety that surpasses her husband's. I wonder, if I had met her back then, whether I'd have just scrapped the John profile and written one of Martha. It would probably have been more fun.

AN OLD PROFESSIONAL at the Justice Department, a talented lawyer who has seen administrations come and go, remembers with a certain chagrin his first meeting with his latest chief, Attorney General John N. Mitchell.

"The receptionist met me at the door of the office and, as she always had in the past, offered me a cup of coffee," he said. "With Ramsey [Ramsey Clark, the Attorney General from 1967 to 1969], I'd sometimes finish the coffee just waiting for him. Or, after he called me in, we'd sit across a table sipping coffee together, discussing the case I came to see him about, reviewing its practical and philosophical implications.

"When Mitchell summoned me, my coffee still hadn't cooled. I walked in with my papers in one hand, the cup and saucer in the other. Mitchell lifted his head from the desk and asked me what I wanted. I told him and he answered promptly. Then, with a nod, he dismissed me and returned to the papers on his desk. I was left standing there, the steaming coffee still in my hand, and I wasn't even certain how to escape."

John Mitchell is like that, a man stingy with his time, guarded with his amenities, quick and firm with his decisions.

He's every bit the successful Wall Street lawyer, whose day—whose mind, whose life—is structured to bring the greatest possible yield. He's every bit the puritan, whose mission is his work, whose work is too serious for a frivolous chat or a cup of coffee.

Mitchell is not so much a political partisan as a professional advocate who, finding himself in combat for a client, focuses his skill rather than his passion on preparing the best brief he can.

Until a year or so ago, his advocacy brought him wealth, a plethora of clients and, in a small but select circle, a reputation for excellence. Today, his monetary reward is modest. His clients are reduced to one: the President of the United States. Meanwhile, his reputation has spread spectacularly and he has become increasingly controversial.

It's not surprising, of course, that Mitchell is controversial, given the central theme of Richard Nixon's election campaign. As far back as his acceptance speech in Miami, Nixon declared: "If we are to restore order and respect for law in this country, there's one place we're going to begin. We're going to have a new Attorney General of the United States." The President's decision to give Mitchell the job is a tribute to his confidence in the man, for Nixon obviously has a great deal invested in it.

With characteristic economy of words, Mitchell sums up his conception—and Richard Nixon's—of the Department of Justice. "There's a difference between my philosophy and Ramsey Clark's," he says. "I think this is an institution for law enforcement, not social improvement." It is in translating this conception to practice that Mitchell has been generating debate.

• He has significantly loosened the restrictions under which the FBI and other Federal law-enforcement agencies may tap wires. Although he denies being arbitrary and says he has authorized fewer taps than earlier Attorneys General, he has certainly broken new legal ground by bringing to court the argument that the Government can tap the wires of domestic political organizations if it deems their objectives to be subversive.

• Under his direction, the Justice Department has recommended a court-reform statute for the District of Columbia which contains a provision for the pretrial detention of those considered likely to commit further crime if freed on bond. Though the proposal is more limited than originally anticipated, it has evoked the strenuous opposition of the District of Columbia government and of most civil-liberties organizations. If passed by Congress and held constitutional by the courts, the plan is regarded as certain to become a model for other jurisdictions.

• Against the advice of most of the career lawyers in the department, Mitchell approved the prosecution of eight leaders of the antiwar demonstrations—as well as eight policemen—at the Democratic National Convention in Chicago last summer. In his public statements, he has taken a hard line against student demonstrators, saying in one interview, "When you get nihilists on campus, the thing to do is to get them into court."

• Mitchell has directed the FBI to keep certain militant black organizations, particularly the Panthers, "under surveillance." According to Will Wilson, his assistant for the criminal division, "We put the problem to the FBI, telling them to watch carefully for violations. The FBI takes it from there." As the record has been compiled, the FBI's "surveillance," many say, looks more like a campaign of pure harassment.

It is Mitchell, furthermore, who is considered the architect of the Administration's voting-rights bill, which liberals have denounced for provisions that weaken the protection given black suffrage throughout the South.

But whatever apprehensions some Americans may feel about the trends the Justice Department seems to be setting, President Nixon is clearly impressed with John Mitchell's work. In the power struggle that invariably rages about a President, Mitchell has emerged as a strong man of the Cabinet.

Some interpret the struggle as pitting the liberals against the conservatives in the Nixon entourage—with the liberals steadily losing ground. Mitchell vigorously rejects such an analysis.

"It's tommyrot that we are moving to the right," he says, mentioning as an example the controversy over the decision not to name Dr. John Knowles Assistant Secretary of Health, Education and Welfare and the choice instead of Dr. Roger O. Egeberg. "The Knowles appointment was no move to the right. Look at the guy who was actually appointed. He's more liberal than Knowles, according to his track record. And take the school-desegregation guidelines. These are procedures only to accomplish what wasn't being accomplished. As for the voting-rights bill, I think it is more liberal than the one we are trying to replace, because we are trying to assure the vote for all minorities, North and South.

"And if these people just take the preventive-detention title and run with the ACLU, they'll say it's to the right. But if they read the whole bill, they'll see it's for the community's good.

"Of course, if you think the ABM or the surtax is going to the right, okay. But I don't see it that way."

If Mitchell denies that he's at the right end of the Nixon Cabinet, he is nonetheless hard-pressed to conceal his disdain for Robert Finch, the Secretary of Health, Education and Welfare, who is generally thought to be at the left end. In private conversation, Mitchell's been known to refer to him as "Secretary Fink." He dismisses as pure fantasy the story, published by Theodore H. White in *The Making of the President 1968,* that Nixon invited Finch to be his Vice-Presidential candidate. He considers the Knowles episode a "political abomination," which Finch could have avoided by acting decisively in the early spring. Mitchell is among those in the Administration who speak of "Finch's crowd" at HEW with a hint of a sneer in their voices.

It is John Mitchell's observation that he is the Cabinet member to whom President Nixon pays the most heed—a contention that the men closest to the President rather readily confirm. Over the entire spectrum of foreign and domestic policy, he reveals, the President consults with him often, and he adds, with a sense of self-assurance, that he dispenses his counsel freely.

"Of course, you don't talk about your confidences with the President," he remarks, "any more than you do about your confidences with your wife.

"But I do work closely with the National Security Council, which is not a normal assignment for the Attorney General. And I have been working with the national intelligence apparatus, which extends over the whole lot. And I'm a member of the Urban Affairs Council, which considers most matters of domestic policy. So I think you can come to your own conclusions about the range of advice I give the President.

"I guess I see him once a day or more, when I go over to the White House. And during the course of the day we usually talk on the phone several more times. In the evening, he frequently calls me at home; I have a direct line from the White House switchboard. I think he hears my views on most important questions, and I think he values my judgment."

On the face of it, there is something curious about the esteem in which Richard Nixon holds the word of John Mitchell. Nixon, after all, went through twenty years in politics—during which he came to know every major figure in American public life—before he even met Mitchell. As campaigner he had his pick of Republicans, and as President he can persuade virtually any American to come to his assistance. Yet he has chosen as his chief counselor Mitchell, who, until a year ago, had no experience in partisan politics, no recognized expertise in foreign affairs, a limited exposure to national economic problems and, what's more, not a shred of apparent interest in public questions. As a Wall Street lawyer, Mitchell was not even a member of the bar association in New York City. He belonged to none of the important clubs. He was no well enough known to be included in *Who's Who.* From all appearances, John Newton Mitchell was an insignificant man.

But appearances, of course, can mislead.

Mitchell, born in Detroit in 1913, was raised by moderately wealthy, middle-class parents in suburban Long Island. He attended public schools in Blue Point and Patchogue and was graduated from Jamaica High in 1931, when the Depression was at its worst. Harvard was a possibility, he says, but "I wanted to be a lawyer and I was persuaded by a friend of my father's that it was more *practical* to go to law school in New York—easier to get a clerkship and pass the bar, greater exposure to professors who practiced New York law, easier to establish associations that would be useful later." Though a Protestant, he enrolled in Catholic Fordham, largely because it had an accelerated law program. After two years as an undergraduate he went directly into the law school, choosing the night over the day sessions because, he says, "I could work during the day and use my time better that way." His classmates remember him as a serious young man—but all young men were serious in those difficult days. He was independent-minded, nonpolitical and very intelligent, but not the Number 1 man in the class. He liked to have an occasional beer with his classmates, though they recall no particularly close friendship he made. In 1938, Mitchell received his law degree and shortly afterward was admitted to the New York bar.

The pattern of Mitchell's career was set in his second year at law school, when he obtained a clerk's job at the firm of Caldwell & Raymond on Wall Street. Old "Judge" James H. Caldwell had established a specialty as a bonding attorney, dating back to the railroad issues of the last century. Shortly after Mitchell graduated and became a junior member of the firm, Caldwell asked him to look into Syracuse's proposal to issue bonds for a public housing project, which the Judge designated a "damfool New Deal idea." Mitchell did his research so well that he was called upon for opinions on an increasing number of similar proposals made by other municipalities. "Soon I began getting a percentage of the fees on this specialty," Mitchell said, "and was making more money than the partners. So just before I went into the service, they made me a partner." Before he was thirty, Mitchell's name was added to the title of Judge Caldwell's firm. After three years in the Navy—during which he was commander of the PT squadron in which Lieut. John F. Kennedy served—he returned to the firm and to municipal bonding. Since those days, the profession has grown twentyfold or more, and with it grew not only the demands on Mitchell's legal services but also his prosperity.

Technical though municipal-bond law may be, it is a far less narrow specialty than it may appear at first glance. It required Mitchell to travel widely to meet with politicians who needed his advice to borrow for public purposes. It exposed him to the constitutional peculiarities of almost all the states, as well as to the political problems of his clients. It gave him a familiarity with the ways of city councils and state assemblies, and he learned to find his way through the thickets of bureaucracy. He acquired a facility for sorting out the complexities in dealings between Federal, state and local governments. And he came to know the major figures in the bond market, in financial underwriting and in investment banking. In short, he was a catalyst between major political and financial forces and, if he had no statutory power of his own, his advice was so highly regarded that he became a man of considerable personal authority.

Jerris Leonard, who directed Wisconsin's borrowing agency before becoming Assistant Attorney General for civil rights, calls Mitchell the architect of his state's borrowing program. In the nineteen-fifties, he says, Mitchell drafted the legislation setting up a semiautonomous agency through which the state government could evade its constitutional debt limitation. Later, he said, Mitchell drew up a constitutional amendment which abolished that limitation entirely and put the state on a full-faith-and-credit basis. "Coming from the Midwest, we were awed by New York and Wall Street, where we had to go for our money," says Leonard, "but we had confidence in Mitchell. He analyzed the alternatives carefully and when he gave us his judgment, we accepted it. We borrowed 100 million dollars a year under the program he set up for us—and, of course, he received a percentage of all of that as his fee."

Mitchell's former law partners credit him with devising the scheme called "lease-financing," under which a municipality whose borrowing powers are restricted sets up a quasi-public corporation to build facilities, then leases them back for public use. They also credit him with being the financial wizard behind such New York undertakings as Co-op City, the huge apartment complex in the northeast Bronx; the Transit Authority's purchase of new air-conditioned subway cars, and the establishment of the Educational Construction Fund to reduce the cost of new schools by making them part of apartment buildings.

Mitchell's old associates also maintain that they recall no instance in which he discussed his political convictions. "I could never discern any political leaning from a conversation I had with Mitchell, and I had a thousand of them," says a former partner. "In talking about various bond problems, he never showed a preference for a conservative or a liberal position, for left, right or center." Since Mitchell had to deal with politicians of every kind, it was surely good business for him to reveal no ideological preferences. But his neutrality seemed to go deeper than that. Even John Mitchell II, now twenty-seven and a Wall Street lawyer himself, cannot remember his father's ever having expressed strong political beliefs at home. Says the ex-partner, "I think his bond with Nixon was personal, not political. He seemed to look at Nixon as a client for whom he was compelled to do his best professional work."

Richard Nixon first encountered Mitchell a year or two after migrating to New York from California, where he had been defeated for the governorship. Nixon became the senior partner in the hoary firm known "on the street" as Mudge, Stern (later Nixon, Mudge). Mitchell was the key man in the more specialized firm of Caldwell, Trimble & Mitchell. Their first meetings were as cooperating attorneys, Nixon normally representing the underwriters of bonds, Mitchell the issuers. The two found each other congenial and each respected the other's legal abilities. On a number of occasions, they journeyed to Washington for joint appearances before one Federal regulatory agency or another. Largely out of the relationship between Nixon and Mitchell grew the idea for a merger of the two firms.

In the merger, Nixon, Mudge obtained a group of highly specialized, well-regarded collaboraters who brought with them clients of great potential, while Mitchell got the good name of a rather respected general law firm with the multitude of services it could provide. The partnership took the title of Nixon, Mudge, Rose, Guthrie, Alexander & Mitchell, and on Jan. 1, 1967, John Mitchell moved over to his new office, adjacent to Richard Nixon's, at 20 Broad Street. For all practical purposes, the leadership of the firm had passed into the hands of Nixon and Mitchell.

After the merger, relations between the two men ripened. They met almost daily for business discussions, usually lunched together and frequently shared accommodations on their trips. They played golf together, though Mitchell is of tournament caliber and Nixon just a duffer; they were both avid readers of the sports pages. The Mitchells visited the Nixons at their Fifth Avenue apartment, and the Nixons drove out to see the Mitchells in their roomy frame house in Westchester County. When Nixon began thinking again of running for President, it was natural enough that he should turn for advice to his partner and friend, whatever Mitchell's inexperience in the Presidential stakes.

Mitchell undertook his first real assignment for Nixon by going out to Wisconsin to organize the state. Waiting for him out there was Jerris Leonard, who was planning to run for the Senate, as well as a host of other Republicans he knew. Mitchell was untroubled by the shift from detached professional to committed partisan. "I went out there as a friend, to put together a Nixon team for the national convention," he says. "I knew how to deal with politicians. I had a lot of personal relationships I could count on. I never had a client in my life I didn't call by his first name." Mitchell rounded up his contacts in Wisconsin, put together his organization and left. He repeated the process in about a dozen states, all of which were nailed down—and stayed nailed down— for Nixon by convention time in August.

Meanwhile, Nixon was having trouble with the overall direction of his campaign for the nomination. For various reasons, three chairmen—Gaylord Parkinson of California, Henry Bellmon of Oklahoma and Robert Ellsworth of Kansas—withdrew in quick succession. All the time, Mitchell was there at Nixon's side in New York, clearly not jockeying for position but ready to take on whatever tasks had to be done. Without fanfare, Mitchell seemed to handle any assignment that came his way confidently and skillfully; almost by default, power seemed to flow to him. Gradually, Mitchell was conceded the actual supervision of the campaign, though he was not announced as manager until mid-May. After the smooth success of the Miami operation, Nixon simply kept Mitchell on as manager for the election campaign itself.

But, despite his authority, it is surely not true that Mitchell—as has often been alleged—devised the so-called "Southern strategy" of the Nixon campaign. The strategy was established more by consensus than by any one man's genius. Nixon and his advisers, from top to bottom, analyzed the elements in the race and agreed that victory would lie in a coalition of Southern and Western states. Mitchell's chief contribution, after the polls promised that the strategy would succeed, was to stand firm against any departure, however great the momentary temptation. As one top Nixon aide put it, "Our formula was to hug the ball, fall down and watch the clock." Mitchell was the flawless administrator, not the originator of ideas, in Nixon's victorious campaign.

If Mitchell contributed anything fresh at all, it was the professionalization of the campaign organization. In most campaigns, whether Democratic or Republican, it is considered essential that every major faction of the party have a hand in running the show. As a result, most campaigns wind up overstaffed, with the personnel often distracted by unproductive, sectarian debate. Mitchell, however, declined to pay tribute to factionalism and kept the staff lean and on its toes. Some of Nelson Rockefeller's supporters recall that Mitchell received them one day, listened to their complaints and summarily dismissed them, as if to say, one of them reported, "Boys, we're going to run this election without your help, thanks." Once converted to "the plan," Mitchell became its chief partisan, and what didn't contribute to advancing it didn't interest him at all.

Of course, some Republicans who had never heard of Mitchell did not share the Presidential candidate's confidence in his man. One day, a group of Republican Congressmen invited Mitchell to meet with them on Capitol Hill. As the story has passed into Washington lore, Congressman Clark MacGregor of Minnesota asked Mitchell what qualifications he had to run the campaign. "I'm the only man who can say 'no' to Richard Nixon" was the reply. Mitchell himself tells the story a bit more elaborately. He says he told MacGregor, "I've made more money in the practice of law than Nixon, brought more clients into the firm, can hold my own in argument with him and, as far as I'm concerned, I can deal with him as an equal." Whether or not the answer satisfied the Congressmen, the smooth operation of the Nixon campaign tended to still any criticism of Mitchell's appointment.

One of the insiders at the Nixon headquarters notes that Mitchell's lack of ideology had disadvantages, as well as advantages, in the course of the race. He said Mitchell seemed to think he could buy almost anything—including New York State—and relied too heavily on money. He hired a former network executive as a press aide on the ground that he would know how to intimidate the television correspondents. "I never heard Mitchell say, 'this is right' or 'this is wrong,' " said the former campaigner. "Expressions like that are not part of his vocabulary. What he says is 'it works' or 'it's feasible.' " Whatever guidance Mitchell offered on the issues of the campaign, said the ex-insider, depended on what the polls showed.

"Anyone who's honest," says Mitchell himself, "will admit you never know what you did right or wrong in a campaign. But this one was relatively easy. The factors were clear. We just set a course and stuck by it. And when you win, why then you look good."

Over and over again, during the course of the campaign, Mitchell was asked whether he would accept a high Federal appointment if Nixon were elected. He was invariably emphatic in his answer. The Daily Bond Buyer, the organ of his legal specialty, recorded the following interview shortly after the Miami convention:

Q. "When do you intend to return to your law practice?"

A. "November 6, the day after the election."

Q. "Do you mean to say, sir, that you are totally invulnerable to a bit of Presidential arm-twisting, that you wouldn't be tempted by a strong request to become Attorney General or Secretary of the Navy?"

A. "Absolutely not. I am invulnerable. I will never accept a

Cabinet post. You know, all of our banker friends say I'll accept some plum, and I offer all of them ten to one that I won't. You could do them all a favor by reporting that I mean what I say."

Mitchell is not embarrassed by such early disclaimers. He says he agreed to become Attorney General only because President Nixon insisted on it: "I'd like to return to a quieter life of practicing law and playing golf. I hope they're keeping my seat warm for me at the firm, but I'll stay as long as the President wants me." Meanwhile, he says, he's trying to get the Justice Department "to work."

For Mitchell, getting the department "to work" means arriving at the office at 8 A.M. in a chauffeured limousine, one of the perquisites of Cabinet rank, from his comfortable apartment at the stylish Watergate, where he lives with his wife and eight-year-old daughter, both of whom are named Martha. (Mitchell has a son —the Wall Street lawyer—and a grown daughter by an earlier marriage, which ended in divorce in the nineteen-fifties.)

His day is carefully divided into half-hour segments, of which his subordinates rarely get more than one at a time. Normally, he sees visitors—from both inside and outside the department— from 9 A.M. to 6 P.M. His lunches each week average three at his desk, one with the staff and one on Capitol Hill or at the White House. He usually leaves for home about 7, sometimes a little later.

Mitchell takes personal responsibility for all his speeches. Normally, he outlines them himself in longhand in considerable detail, then turns them over to various divisions of the department for elaboration and checking. Occasionally, he asks Jack Landau, his director of public information, to prepare a first draft. "Make it a big speech," he told Landau, a liberal former newspaperman, when preparations began for his castigation of student radicals last May. When a speech is finished, Mitchell goes over every word of it, "down to the last decimal," Landau says.

The Attorney General is obviously much more comfortable with his job now than he was at first, when word kept filtering out of the department that he was cold, distant and irascible. He is essentially a good-humored man who prefers easy relations to hard discipline, though one would never call him casual in his dealings with people. In company, he is never without his pipe, which he lights and relights. His long-time associates insist it is a device he uses to keep calm, but he maintains that he is not particularly nervous, and if his hands tend to tremble it is the result of a shrapnel wound suffered during the war. Even during the toughest moments of the campaign, Mitchell apparently never lost his self-possession or his temper. As Attorney General, he still does not trust himself to deliver impromptu speeches, but he has developed considerable skill at give-and-take with the press, and even some non-Mitchell men in the Justice Department confess to having acquired a certain fondness for him.

Mitchell himself displays a quiet, ironic humor about his role at Justice. "I get here in the morning," he says, "they wind me up, hand me a schedule and off I go." He obviously is not enthusiastic about the social side of his work, and only reluctantly attends even a minimum of parties at embassies, the White House and the homes of prominent figures in Government or journalism. "I've got long hours and almost no weekends," he says. "I generally get home in time to put on my black tie or an old shirt. Then I start with a Scotch on the rocks and, after dinner, move on to the paper work."

Dealing with the Fortas episode, Mitchell says, was his most painful assignment as Attorney General. As he saw it, the case involved a potential constitutional crisis as well as a confrontation between political parties and top personalities. Mitchell wanted to handle the matter as discreetly as possible, in a manner benefitting colleagues in the legal profession. He chose to pay a quiet call on the Chief Justice to pass along all the information he had on the case. To this day, the Justice Department refuses to disclose what Mitchell told Chief Justice Earl Warren, but a few days after the meeting Justice Abe Fortas resigned from the Supreme Court. After news of his visit to Warren became public, Mitchell was shocked at the criticism leveled at him for somehow abusing the prerogatives of his office.

But the Attorney General's labor is only one ingredient in getting the Justice Department "to work," and there are some who argue that if John Mitchell were sincere he would not have picked a group of frustrated politicians as his principal assistants. Robert Kennedy, these critics say, established the precedent of hiring the best lawyers available to head the divisions of the department. Among Mitchell's appointments, Richard G. Kleindienst, the Deputy Attorney General, was defeated for Governor of Arizona in 1964. Jerris Leonard, head of the civil rights division, was beaten for the Senate last year, as was William D. Ruckelshaus, head of the civil division. Will R. Wilson, head of the criminal division, ran for the Senate against John Tower in Texas in 1961, before changing over to the Republican party. The critics suggest that such appointees create the impression, justified or not, that the department functions with an eye on politics. Such an impression, they argue, drives away the best lawyers. They add that personnel is more important than policy in making sure that the department "works."

John Mitchell becomes impatient at the implication that his assistants are political appointees. "There were no political considerations in the choice of any of these people," he says. "Dick Kleindienst worked with me throughout the campaign, and he was made for the job. I've known Jerry Leonard for ten years, and he's extremely capable. Ruckelshaus couldn't be more qualified. Wilson was the Attorney General and a Supreme Court judge in Texas. They are all my personal selections, and I had a specific reason for picking each one. They all had a certain expertise and I fitted them into the slots where I thought they would go best."

Mitchell has also been said to lack feeling for the current black revolution and to owe political obligations to the South, chiefly in the person of Senator Strom Thurmond of South Carolina, who delivered the bulk of the South's delegates to Richard Nixon at the Republican convention. Mitchell denies both allegations. He cites the reputation he acquired as a bond lawyer in the field of public housing as proof of his liberal credentials. As for a debt to the South, he says, "If the President has an obligation to Thurmond, I don't know of it and I never heard him talk of it. And I've got no political debt to anyone."

Jerris Leonard, who once told a visitor that he spends much of his time dodging arrows fired at him by Senator Thurmond, is a little more illuminating on the attitude the Justice Department brings to the problem of civil rights. "Both John Mitchell and I," he says, "are pragmatic, 1969 conservatives. We face up to the facts of life as they are. We know civil rights are something that the times require." If John Mitchell still uses the word "colored" in his conversation, he nonetheless recognizes the need to press desegregation suits in the courts. If he tried to render homage to the South—whatever the assertions about Senator Thurmond— by modifying one provision of the voting-rights act, he acknowledged that he would have to compensate for it by strengthening another.

"He knows the job has to be done," says Leonard. "He's interested in what works—and I agree that's different from a philosophical commitment to the civil rights movement. We don't get involved in the emotion of it all, but we understand how important it is to get results."

Clearly, however, the results in which Mitchell is most interested lie not in the area of civil rights, but in the area of law and order, for it is here that President Nixon has made his greatest political investment. It is in this area that Mitchell must succeed if the President is to make good on his campaign promises. It is to strengthen the department here that Mitchell has become a partisan of wire taps, preventive detention, the prosecution of peace demonstrators and the "surveillance" of Black Panthers. It is in this area, more than any other, that Mitchell wants the department "to work," and it is law and order with which the department is largely preoccupied.

Even when one talks to Richard McLaren, the Assistant Attorney General for antitrust work, the discussion gradually shifts from the subject of conglomerate mergers, on which he's been rather aggressive, to the use of the antitrust laws for fighting organized crime, to which he is giving increasing attention. "The very basis of organized crime," he says, "is anticompetitive practices, the allocation of territories, unfair concentration. My predecessors began this work, but we're expanding it to see if we can't find criminal violations in these predatory practices."

"The former Attorney General, whom I like and admire," says Deputy Attorney General Kleindienst, once a strong Goldwater supporter, "was not willing to make use of adequate enforcement personnel from the beginning in the case of civil disturbances, for fear of appearing repressive. As a result, the disorders escalated and got out of hand. This Administration is prepared and willing and ready to act immediately. As soon as we're notified of danger, we'll have the National Guard in the armory and the Army on two, four or six-hour alert. . . .

"Our interest is in better-trained, more sensitive police officers. We'd like to encourage the recruitment of more black policemen. But I don't conceive of it to be a function of the Department of Justice to be a policeman of policemen. . . .

"We're going to enforce the law against draft-evaders, against radical students, against deserters, against civil disorders, against organized crime and against street crime. We have several draft-evader cases in the process of being filed. If we find that any of these radical, revolutionary, anarchistic kids violate the law, we'll prosecute. In the last Administration, the Democrats' political debt to Negroes was so great that they were deprived of the capacity to act forcefully. We can't let any segment of society have the privilege of conducting itself lawlessly or the entire fabric of society breaks down."

"I obtained this job," says Will Wilson. Assistant Attorney General for the criminal division, "after I told Senator Tower that I was interested in rackets and organized crime. As a D.A., I was known as an aggressive prosecutor. I don't believe in permissive law enforcement. Tower suggested me to Nixon and Nixon to Mitchell."

Shortly after he was appointed, Wilson instructed Nathaniel E. Kossack, his first assistant, to rout out the "left-wingers" in the department. Kossack, a respected career official who first served under Attorney General William Rogers, promptly announced his resignation. Mitchell got him a post of equivalent rank in another Federal department.

Wilson also proposed reopening the department's case to ban the movie *I Am Curious (Yellow)* but Mitchell overruled him on the ground that the courts would never sustain the action.

"Nixon's interest in crime will make it a public issue," says Wilson. "It will make it an issue at the local level, through the police chiefs and the men on the beat. We're getting substantial increases next year for the FBI and other anticrime personnel. We're getting improved civil-service ratings, which will improve hiring and morale.

"We're also mounting two new strike forces, one in Boston and one in New York. Ramsey Clark had the first conception of the strike force, to put prosecutorial and investigative people on a single team. It's a head-hunting team, and it's worked well against organized crime. We're expanding the concept to include financial analysis and local police.

"Looking for statistics is premature, but there's surely been an upsurge in enthusiasm for fighting crime. I'm sure we're getting results.

"Clark's trouble was that he was philosophically concerned with the rights of the individual. Our concern is more an orderly society through law enforcement. Clark put too many restraints on the law-enforcement agencies. He was like a football coach warning his players not to violate the rules, when he should have been telling them to go in there and win. I'm not opposed to civil liberties, but I think they come from good law enforcement."

Some people, of course, think that good law enforcement comes from attention to civil liberties. One of them, Lawrence Speiser, the Washington representative of the American Civil Liberties Union, says it is customary for an ACLU delegation to pay a courtesy call on a new Attorney General. It took six months, through letters and phone calls, Speiser says, to arrange a meeting with Mitchell. But the Attorney General does not seem concerned about any charges the ACLU or his other critics may level at him.

"I've got a tough enough hide. I love the fact that all the liberals are jumping over me now for wire-tapping, when it was all done by our liberal friends Kennedy, Katzenbach and Ramsey Clark. But I don't much care what the press or anyone else says about me. I didn't ask for this job. I've got no political ambitions, so it doesn't matter. I've never had time to sit around drinking whisky and discussing philosophy. I just try to get things done."

Arthur F. Burns

INTELLECTUAL AS INSIDER

As unsympathetic as I was to the Nixon administration, I recognized early in 1969 that as a political writer I had to develop some lines of communication to the White House, which is—whatever I happened to think of the President—the center of the action in Washington. Under the best of circumstances, it's hard making the transition from one administration, where you know most of the people, to another, where you don't. To make matters worse, as a free lancer, I had never had the opportunity to cover the Nixon campaign, so most of the assistants that the new President brought into the White House after the election were just names to me. I was delighted, then, when The New York Times Magazine *proposed that I do a profile of Arthur Burns, who was Mr. Nixon's chief economic counselor.*

Burns possessed a reputation in those days as the most conservative man in the White House. I'm not sure what I expected when I went to see him, but I found someone who was not only decent and helpful to me but deeply concerned about the economic well-being of those lower levels of society in which conservatives are supposed to have no interest. Over the course of many talks with Burns, as well as with other economists inside and outside the government, I acquired a pretty good education in economics. I learned how much doctrine liberal and conservative economists today hold in common. Within the profession, Burns was, to be sure, a conservative—like a football coach who stresses the fundamentals of blocking and tackling before he's willing to go on to the fancy stuff like draws and fakes. Burns believes the economist's first responsibility is a sound economy, without intolerable inflation or recession, after which he can go on to the fancy stuff like full employment, a higher growth rate, special opportunities for the poor, improved health and educational services. I may still disagree with Burns's sense of economic priorities, but I do not question his good will, even as a conservative within the economics profession.

During the course of the research on the Burns profile, I did talk to enough of the men around the President to acquire a pretty good feel for the White House, though I'll admit I was never completely comfortable there. I preferred the laughing, raucous, semi-uncouth Irishmen, Italians and Jews who worked there under the Democrats to the punctilious, well-mannered fellows in the Brooks Brothers suits who surrounded Mr. Nixon. I am not being in any way critical of their treatment of me. In fact, I was particularly grateful to Herb Klein, the President's communications director, who tipped me off several weeks in advance that Arthur Burns would be named chairman of the Federal Reserve Board, so that I would not be left with outdated information because of the time lag between preparation of my manuscript and its publication. As a result, the piece, appearing on the heels of the appointment, had an extra measure of timeliness. I mention this to acknowledge that if I am generally uncomfortable with Nixon's people, it is as much my personality that is responsible as theirs.

As for Burns, he was unusually pleased with the profile and phoned to say it contained more about himself than he, perhaps, had known. I was quite pleased for, despite my unconcealed aversion to conservatives as a class, I had developed a genuine fond-

*ness for this wise and gentle man. As long as Burns remained in
the White House, I saw him from time to time, but at the Federal
Reserve, whose works are normally enshrouded in secrecy, I have
seen him less. It's interesting that, at the Fed, he's not considered
so much of a conservative. He may not yet be a "radical"—as he
predicts he might become in this profile—but he's proven far more
audacious than some of his former colleagues in the White House.
His words, in fact, are rather prophetic, as I read over them again.
They show how much he is, indeed, his own man.*

AT A MEETING some weeks ago with his White House advisers, Richard Nixon went out of his way to cite with approval
the "conservatism" of Dr. Arthur F. Burns, the sixty-five-year-old
professional economist who bears the unique title of Counselor to
the President. Nixon extolled Burns's rigorous stand, taken both
publicly and privately, in behalf of major cuts in the Federal
budget as the means to help stop inflation. This stand has given
Burns the reputation of being, perhaps, the most conservative
member of the Nixon entourage.

Burns listened with evident satisfaction to Nixon's praise, then
spoke up in his quiet yet forthright manner. "But Mr. President,"
he said, "in the event of a recession, I'll be a dangerous radical."

What Burns was saying was that in this, the era of Keynes, the
professional economist must be judged differently from other men
who make their names in politics. Long gone are the days, among
professional economists at least, when "conservatives" were distinguished from "liberals" by their exhortations on the virtues of
the balanced budget. In the Keynesian era, economics is not
nearly that simple.

Now Burns, the ranking member of the President's staff and
the only member accorded Cabinet status, has been promoted
from his position as *primus inter pares* at the White House. On
October 17, the President disclosed that Burns, his mentor in economics, would soon assume chief responsibility for the nation's

credit and currency policies as Chairman of the Federal Reserve Board. Suddenly, Burns's "conservatism" has become an object of interest both at home and abroad, wherever men think about economics or worry about American economic policy.

Personally, Burns has no objection to being called a conservative. He rather promotes the designation, in fact. It is, first of all, congenial to his temperament.

A former Columbia University professor, he dresses in bland blues and grays, with nondescript neckties, and parts his hair carefully down the middle, as if to do otherwise would somehow appear rakish. He speaks ponderously, stopping often to seek out the correct word. "I doubt," says an old friend, "if I have ever heard Arthur express himself impetuously." He is invariably courteous, with an old-world flair. He smokes a pipe, and seldom makes jokes.

It has also been politically useful for Arthur Burns to be known as a conservative. It has made Republicans comfortable with him. For a staff member at the White House, it is a solid credential. It is expected to be an indispensable attribute to his work with the banking world at the Fed. For practical reasons, then, Burns would never disclaim being a conservative.

Yet Arthur Burns has been heard speaking passionately against the war in Vietnam. He has made clear that he opposes the Justice Department's indifferent enforcement of the civil rights laws. He has acquired a reputation among his colleagues as a strong supporter of civil liberties.

Back in the mid-1950's, Burns was considered the liberal of the Eisenhower Administration as Chairman of the President's Council of Economic Advisers. His chief antagonist was Secretary of the Treasury George Humphrey, who espoused a kind of classical conservatism, which held that the chief responsibility of government was the preservation of private wealth. In those days, Burns was looked up to, mainly by liberals, as the "conscience of the Government." His economic thinking has not changed appreciably since that time.

Even a "liberal" economist like Walter Heller, who was President Kennedy's chairman of the Council of Economic Advisers, acknowledges that he and Arthur Burns do not disagree on their general approach to maintaining economic stability.

Indeed, professional economists, who would comfortably label Heller "liberal" and Burns "conservative," would never use the term "left-wing" for one or "right-wing" for the other. Such designations are normally reserved for outright socialists on the one hand, or for the old-fashioned champions of laissez-faire on the other. Whatever their differences, Heller and Burns are much nearer the center in their perception of the imperatives of economic policy.

Heller points out that liberal and conservative economists no longer argue the necessity of using the Government's fiscal and monetary powers to prevent serious fluctuations in the economy. Indeed, while Burns was at the council, he defied the purveyors of the traditional Republican dogma which holds that morality equals a balanced budget. When the economy showed signs of decline in mid-1953, Burns urged Eisenhower to spend more and tax less, with the result that the recession was relatively brief and mild.

"The essential difference," Heller says, "is that he put much more emphasis on the ups and downs of the business cycle. We put emphasis on attaining full employment and a high growth rate in the economy. But it was a matter of emphasis, not of goal. Certainly, I would never deny, even if I disagreed with his methods, that Arthur Burns has a highly developed sense of humanitarianism."

One of Burns's former students, himself now a respected economist, explains Burns's professional outlook this way:

"He is a creature of the Great Depression. That was the period when he was growing to professional maturity, and he saw the whole economic system disintegrate before him. The lesson he learned was that the avoidance of catastrophic change is the first objective of economic policy. He acquired the conviction that the economist's chief responsibility is to keep the economic machinery working.

"We younger people, not having experienced the Depression in a personal way, tend to take the machinery for granted. Right or wrong, we assume it will keep working in satisfactory fashion, so we move on elsewhere, to the problems of economic expansion, or to the problems of poverty, housing, health, leisure. I suppose that's why we're considered liberal and he's not. He has the stamp of his generation—and he may be right in his long-run concerns."

Burns concedes that he is a man preoccupied with keeping the system functioning without serious mishap. All his life, he has been a student of business cycles, those alternating swells and shrinkages of business activity which have historically characterized capitalist economies—and he feels that economists still do not know enough of the phenomenon to justify complacency about their ability to master it.

He explains his reputation for conservatism among economists in these terms:

"I suspect that some of my colleagues are unduly fascinated by economic instruments and have given insufficient attention to the workings of the business mind of America. I weigh that heavily in questions of policy, and I'm not always sure that I have the answer.

"Specifically, before I judge whether some proposal is good or bad, I ask how the businessman is going to react. I've studied the businessman of America. He has his strengths and he has his weaknesses, but it is within the framework of his psychology that the economist in America must operate. It's the way those fellows respond to the world that determines whether you and I have stable jobs."

In his professorial way, Arthur Burns goes on to explain that high business income in the United States goes into building up productive capital, unlike Latin America or the Middle East, where accumulated assets are normally hoarded or spent on luxuries. He says that whatever the ethical justification, equality of income for all would be a disaster for the masses, for there would be no available funds for investment and the standard of living would inevitably erode. Investment, he says, must be looked upon as a social asset in our culture.

"The well-being of the country, therefore, depends on the favorable expectations of the investing class," says Burns. "As I see it, the role of Government must be to shape policy to improve these expectations."

Burns sternly dismisses the suggestion that his perception of economic policy, "conservative" as it might be, implies an indifference to the poor. He points out that employment depends heavily on investment, and that unemployment does more injury to the poor than to the rich. He notes with pride that he strongly endorsed the elimination of all taxes on most family incomes below $3,500: "Since we talk of $3,500 as the poverty line, why tax it? Why drive people deeper into poverty? We're only talking about $700-million in taxes, out of a budget of $200-billion. That's not inflationary. It's simple justice." Whatever its technical attributes, Burns says, economics must still be treated as a moral science.

But it is inflation, Arthur Burns says, which over the years has worried him most, because it poses the greatest threat to the operation of the economic system.

Insofar as his appeal for anti-inflation economies has limited liberal social programs, Burns has had his reputation as a conservative enhanced. In the recent battle within the White House over welfare reforms, for instance, Burns was popularly depicted as the Administration skinflint, pitted against the warm-hearted Daniel P. Moynihan, another Presidential assistant. But Burns is not loath to disclose that he took the "liberal" position against major expenditures for the supersonic transport (SST) and in favor of the restoration of funds to the National Science Foundation. "In a way, I think the ABM fight did some good," he adds. "Military budgets are not sacrosanct and must be examined in the same way as every other budget."

Burns says that part of his objection to inflation is that it falls more heavily on the poor than on the rich. But more important, it generates undue exuberance about the economy, creating the threat of a bust, if not a bust itself, which ultimately discourages investment. And without investment, Burns says, we are—rich and poor alike—all lost.

He makes much of the significance of the economic "atmosphere," as a factor quite apart from any action which Government might take. He reaches back thirty-five years to criticize Roosevelt, not for his reforms but for "scaring" business during the process of reform. He criticizes President Kennedy for making the business community "despondent" with the attack on the steel industry in 1962. He commends the current chairman of the Fed, William McChesney Martin Jr., for the contribution he has made to the economic atmosphere by his anti-inflationary posture, though he has reservations about the way Martin's monetary decisions have affected the economy itself. And it is Burns's concern about the economic atmosphere that explains his relative indifference to proposed tax reforms; the haggling over them, he feels, tends to confuse and upset the business community. In Burns's view, it is important that the Government convey the impression that it is certain of its course—and that the course is sympathetic to business investment.

Because Burns feels that government must appear consistent to the business community, he has been a firm opponent of "fine tuning" the economy. "Fine tuning" is the name that economists have given to a variety of monetary and fiscal devices by which government can theoretically neutralize slight tendencies toward recession or inflation. Short-term changes in the tax rate or intermittent tendering of investment credits to industry, neither of which he favors, would constitute "fine tuning." It differs from conventional Keynesian countercyclical action chiefly in its transience. Burns praises, for example, President Kennedy's announcement in 1962 that he would propose an across-the-board cut in taxes to stimulate long-term business expansion. That gave businessmen new confidence in the system, he says. But he is exceedingly dubious whether "fine tuning" works. More important, he believes that, as a practical matter, it can so thoroughly muddle the economic atmosphere that business investment suffers.

For the most part, President Nixon has followed the thinking of Arthur Burns in his conduct of the American economy. Burns acknowledges that Nixon has at times weighed political factors more heavily than the economist would have liked. But Burns has been around Government long enough to recognize that an economy cannot be run in a vacuum, without the President's taking into account the manifold other demands that are made upon him. Now, the President will be without the benefit of Burns's advice at the White House, but he will have one less economic worry at the Fed. Though Nixon has not appointed a "yes man" in Arthur Burns, he can be confident of having a man who will not go off on a course independent of the Administration. In all, he could surely have found no one for the job more highly regarded by his professional colleagues and more personally congenial to himself.

Arthur Frank Burns was born of Jewish parents in Stanislau, Austria, in 1904, and came to the United States at the age of ten. His family settled across the harbor from New York in the city of Bayonne, New Jersey, where his father earned a meager living as a house painter. "Arthur's basic philosophy was undoubtedly formed by the poverty of those years," says a very old friend. As a young man, Burns helped his father in his menial work; but at home, the Jewish tradition of scholarship burned strong. When Burns finished high school in 1921, he enrolled at Columbia and, four years later, graduated as a Phi Beta Kappa in economics.

In 1930, while working for his Ph.D. at Columbia and teaching economics at Rutgers, Burns came to the attention of Wesley Clair Mitchell, perhaps the most eminent American economist of his day. Mitchell was the principal luminary of the National Bureau of Economic Research, an organization he had founded a decade earlier out of the recognition that economics, as an intellectual discipline, was severely handicapped by a deficiency of facts. The National Bureau had taken for its mandate the development of new tools to refine economic study, while desisting meticulously from abstract theorizing and, above all, political partisanship. Indeed, since Mitchell began, the projects undertaken in the offices of the National Bureau in midtown Manhattan have imparted a whole new dimension to the science of economic analysis. Mitchell first made Burns a fellow at the National Bureau, then appointed him to its professional staff. While still pursuing his career in teaching, Arthur Burns began his lifelong study of business cycles at the bureau and, step by step, became Wesley Clair Mitchell's protégé and heir apparent.

His work at the National Bureau of Economic Research intensified Burns's natural penchant for skepticism and caution. The bureau published Burns's doctoral dissertation on production trends in 1934. A decade later, he and Mitchell completed what has become a classic study of business cycles. Burns, meanwhile, climbed to the top of the academic hierarchy at Rutgers, then accepted a prestigious full professorship at Columbia. Within the economic community, Burns was already considered something of a conservative, chiefly because he kept pointing to flaws in Keynesian theorizing, but he was by no means labeled a doctrinaire. By the mid-nineteen-forties, in fact, he was widely acknowledged to be one of the most thoughtful, solid and erudite— if not terribly original—economic scholars in the United States.

When Mitchell went into virtual retirement in 1945, Burns, by the natural order of things, assumed the title of director of research, which made him the operating head of the National Bureau. As director, Burns wrought little change in the bureau, but rather abruptly the bureau changed him. For the first time he was thrust into close contact with the business tycoons, the labor leaders and the foundation chairmen who served on the bureau's board of directors and were largely responsible for its financing. Suddenly, the college professor, meekly pursuing his sedentary research, was called upon to become a man of the world, casually making his way back and forth among people of money and power. Burns made the transition with remarkable adeptness and, by his own testimony, much enjoyed his new milieu. He was now not only an eminent scholar, but a friend of people who had access to high places.

It was no great surprise, then, when Dwight Eisenhower selected Burns as the Chairman of the Council of Economic Advisers after the election of 1952. Under Leon Keyserling, Truman's last chairman, the council had fallen into rather low esteem—a focus of partisanship rather than scholarship—and Eisenhower was known to be seeking someone to restore its good name. During the confirmation hearings, Burns appalled some Republican Senators by confessing that he was a registered Democrat who supported Eisenhower but had voted for Roosevelt throughout the New Deal years. Apart from a handful of such disgruntled Republicans, however, the nomination was greeted as ideal, both inside the economics community and out, and it was widely agreed that, by his mere presence, Burns gave the Council of Economic Advisers new dignity.

In his memoir of the Eisenhower Administration, Presidential Assistant Sherman Adams gives a colorful account of the relationship which developed between Burns and the President:

"When I took my first look at Burns . . . I had a sinking sensation. If someone had asked me to describe the mental image I had of the type of New Deal official we were in the process of moving out of Washington, this was it—a glassy stare through thick lenses, peering out from under a canopy of unruly hair parted in the middle, a large pipe with a curved stem: the very incarnation of all the externals that were such anathema to Republican businessmen and politicians. I wondered if we would both be thrown out of Eisenhower's office. But I swallowed hard and invited the professor to follow me in.

"If Eisenhower had any misgivings, he kept them to himself. To me, Arthur Burns turned out to be a pleasant surprise. He and Eisenhower got along fine. They shared the same outlook and philosophy. Far from being the abstract and impractical professor, Burns had his feet planted solidly on the ground and had no difficulty in more than holding his own in arguments at the Cabinet table with such hard-headed protagonists as [Secretary of the Treasury George] Humphrey. . . . One morning, after Burns finished a detailed outline of contributions that various government departments could make toward strengthening the economy, Eisenhower said to him admiringly, 'Arthur, my boy, you would have made a fine chief of staff overseas during the war.' "

Between Burns and Eisenhower there gradually grew a warm bond of mutual admiration and respect. Between Burns and Richard Nixon, during these years, there developed a different relationship, one that was highly intellectual and intensely practical. Burns liked the analytical qualities of Dick Nixon's mind. He quickly learned that, whatever Nixon's political prejudices, he was one of the few at Eisenhower's Cabinet meetings who could be persuaded by well-reasoned arguments, carefully built upon factual evidence. Burns and Nixon never developed a deep human relationship, but each was attracted to the other's capacity to reduce a complex position to a lucid, well-organized argument and, early on, they formed an alliance which was to last over the years.

"Of course, I knew of the mistrust that intellectuals felt for Dick Nixon," says Burns. "I brought a certain wariness myself to my first encounters with him. I had heard of his election campaign against Helen Gahagan Douglas and the other incidents that made up his reputation. But what I encountered, to my surprise, was a fellow intellectual. Dick Nixon leads a solitary life of the mind. He's not gregarious, and he doesn't spend his time with large numbers of people. I remember the first time I met Hubert Humphrey. He slapped me on the back and said, 'Hello, Arthur,' and I never saw the man before in my life. Nixon's nothing like that. It's extraordinary that he's been so unpopular over the years with intellectuals. He's really one of us—and I seem to be one of the few who have been willing to take him for what he is."

Burns found the experience of working with Nixon and his powerful colleagues in the Eisenhower Administration both gratifying and stimulating—maybe even excessively so. He says that by this time he had made the leap into the world of the business people, "perhaps not ideologically but surely politically." In a way, the change disturbed him, because he was not yet ready to forgo his identity as a college professor. Burns says he could feel himself coming down with "Potomac fever," becoming attached to the bustle of government crisis, being infected with a sense of his own importance. With great anguish, he finally resolved to leave the Administration, and at the end of Eisenhower's first term, Burns resigned from the Council of Economic Advisers to return to Columbia and the National Bureau of Economic Research. Some of the cynics in the economics community have suggested that Burns, the master analyst of business cycles, saw from the signs that another recession was impending and wanted to get out before he could be saddled with the blame. To be sure, there was a recession in 1957, but Burns dismisses the contention as nonsense.

As it turned out, Burns was now neither fish nor fowl. His colleagues at Columbia detected a declining interest in the university's affairs, while at the National Bureau it was felt that he could no longer apply himself to the strenuous, often tedious, demands of economic scholarship. To be sure, Burns remained a favorite among students at Columbia and a competent administrator at the bureau, but he seemed to take greater delight in serving on committees or advisory boards to which he had been invited by various officials of government. He had also, since leaving the Administration, been elected to the boards of directors of several corporations, and now spent more time than ever in the company of businessmen. To his academic associates, it was clear that Burns missed the pleasures that had come from direct involvement in the affairs of the world.

In March 1960 Burns called on his friend Nixon in the Vice President's office in the Capitol and told him that, unless the Government acted decisively, there would surely be a recession in the fall which might very well destroy his chances for becoming President of the United States. Nixon took this information back to the Eisenhower Cabinet, where the men closest to the President greeted it with an indifference that Nixon found annoying. Equally irritating to him was the view of William McChesney Martin, who discerned nothing in the economy to upset the Federal Reserve Board. Both the Cabinet and the Fed declined to take the action, fiscal or monetary, which Burns regarded as essential to head off the slump. A few months later, the decline which Burns predicted got under way and reached its bottom in November, just as the voters were marching to the polls. Nixon was, indeed, defeated for the Presidency—by the narrowest of margins—but at least, his faith in Burns had been reaffirmed.

Burns remained in close contact with Nixon during those years in the cold, when the other party occupied the White House. The Democrats regarded him as the best of the "opposition" economists and seemed to call on him whenever they wanted to give a bipartisan flavor to some pronouncement. Burns could, however, be very political when he chose, and on several occasions issued stinging gibes at Democratic economic policies. At the University of Chicago early in the Kennedy years, he characterized the President's economic advisers as "gay stagnationists" for failing to see the momentum which Eisenhower's policies had given to the economy. The President's advisers, feeling that Burns had failed utterly to understand the economy's growth potential, were decidedly not amused by this partisan attack. Surely, during these years, Burns's reputation also grew more conservative. In an economic study in which he participated for Governor Rockefeller, for instance, he criticized the concept of the minimum wage—not out of disdain for the poor, he said, but because it needlessly deprives teen-age, unskilled and elderly workers of jobs. Burns, in these years, thus became more identified with Republican positions, though retaining his reputation as the most sensible and convincing of the conservative economists.

In the mid-60's, about the time that Nixon began thinking once again of running for the Presidency, Burns began breaking his ties with both the National Bureau of Economic Research and with Columbia University. Some of the foundations that supported the bureau had started to hint that it was, perhaps, time to initiate the search for a younger man. Burns did not take well to the suggestion but recognized that he had to accept it. Acknowledging that he could not install his own protégé, as Wesley Mitchell had installed him, he set out in search of a successor and, at his recommendation, the bureau in 1967 elected John R. Meyer, a forty-year-old Harvard professor, as its new head. Meanwhile, at Columbia, Burns became increasingly estranged from his colleagues, not so much personally as professionally. In fact, the science of economics had, in recent years, taken on new dimensions. The new generation of economists leaned more heavily on mathematics, even on computers, and dedicated its time to such problems as how to bring medical services to the poor. At both the National Bureau, where he remained in an honorific position, and at Columbia, Burns, as the country's foremost expert on business cycles, seemed almost old hat. Burns finally left the bureau altogether, though his departure was not without acrimony. As for Columbia, he was welcome to stay on; but, tempted by the California sun, he took leave for a year to teach at Stanford, then decided to stay there. As the academic year drew to a close, however, Nixon had begun his campaign for the Presidency and needed Burns back in New York.

As much as anyone, Burns was Nixon's intellectual adviser as he stumped the country—but, admittedly, there was little room for the intellect in the Republican campaign strategy. Nixon promised to stop inflation, which even the Democrats conceded was getting out of hand, but there was, on the whole, very little debate over issues, especially economic issues.

After the election, Nixon summoned Burns for a talk on what role he might play in the new Administration. It was certain that Burns would not become Secretary of the Treasury, for Nixon had always maintained that he wanted to have an international banker in the post. Burns, in turn, made clear that he could not resume his old job as chairman of the Council of Economic Advisers, because that would be too much like going backward to an earlier era of his life. The third alternative was the chairmanship of the Federal Reserve Board, and Nixon did tell Burns that, if he wanted it, he could have the appointment. The only problem was that Bill Martin's term did not expire until January 31, 1970. Burns told the President-elect that he would, indeed, like to become chairman of the Fed and offered to go back to Stanford and wait. For a time, it appeared that he actually would. Then, during the week of the Inauguration, Nixon received Burns again and asked him to remain in the White House with the unprecedented title of Counselor to the President and the rank of a Cabinet officer. Burns felt that he could not refuse.

Burns was not sorry he stayed, if only because he found that he still enjoyed the heady atmosphere of government's center stage. He and his wife, Helen, liked going to White House dinners and embassy parties. They took pleasure in evenings with other high government officials, but, if an old friend from academic life happened into town, Burns was rarely too busy to spend a few intimate hours with him. Burns had always been known as a gracious guest and a generous host. Though he was slow to give up his Manhattan co-op overlooking the East River, he had no trouble adjusting once again to the pace of life in the capital.

At the White House, Burns was, by far, the oldest and most experienced of the President's general assistants. Most of the men Nixon brought with him from the campaign were in their thirties and forties. At the beginning, Burns was able to show them around, for few of them had ever worked in government before. As the months passed, he was frequently able to share with them the knowledge which the years had imparted to him and, quite often, to save them from their own impetuousness. The other members of the staff tended to defer to him but testified that, in the inevitable White House squabbles, he never tried to pull the rank associated with either his age or his closeness to the President. Burns, then, got along well with his colleagues but, obviously, was not completely happy as a staff man. In retrospect, it is clear he was impatient to take on his impending responsibilities at the Fed.

In his toils for the President, Burns performed a variety of assignments, many of them in no way related to economics. He drew up the President's recommendations, for example, on the constitutional amendment to abolish the Electoral College. He fought hard to include work incentives in the program for welfare reform. In addition, Burns acted as a conduit to the President for an older generation of Republicans and the business élite.

To be sure, his economic thinking, having shaped the President's own economic philosophy, dominated the Administration's formulation of economic policy. But Burns now exercised little influence on the President in the reaching of day-to-day decisions. At best, he shared the President's ear on economic matters with

Secretary of the Treasury David Kennedy, Chairman of the Council of Economic Advisers Paul McCracken and Budget Director Robert Mayo. Burns himself freely admits, when questioned, that he was far from indispensable in the White House hierarchy.

"I look forward today to going to the Fed," Burns said after his appointment was announced. "But it's not going to be easy. Martin's been there a long time and it will be hard to make any changes. He's done a fine job over the years, though I confess I don't agree with some of his actions."

In private talk, Burns says he believes there's been too much public argument within the Fed over policy. He questions Martin's judgment in releasing a large supply of currency into the economy last year, when the Administration's policy was to tighten up against inflation. He says that in general there must be more coordination between the Fed and the other agencies of government on overall economic policy.

"I don't anticipate any trouble in my new job, however," Burns says, "though I already see allusions in the press to my friendship with Nixon, as if that would determine the Fed's policies. But, as well as anyone, Nixon understands that the Fed is legally autonomous, and it would not occur to him to try to dictate to me.

"If I can say anything at all about what I will do at the Fed, it is that I will continue to use its powers over credit and currency to fight against inflation. That's the Government's policy, and it will be mine."

Thus Burns's view of the Federal Reserve System corresponds to his conviction that the Government should speak with a single strong voice to encourage the confidence of business investors. But Burns also appears to have a more limited conception of his responsibilities than his predecessor.

"The responsibility of the Fed is to supervise monetary policy —that is, the supply of credit and currency. I don't think it is the chairman's job to lecture the other branches of government on taxation and spending policies. The Federal Reserve Board's autonomy was conceived for the purpose of maintaining the integrity of the currency. I think it's quite proper, then, that the money authority be independent of the political authority.

"I guess that means my days as a Nixon adviser are over. I don't expect I'll be seeing the President any more, except in certain formal meetings. Of course, being Dick Nixon's associate doesn't mean that I've ever been his crony. I haven't. But I don't think he'll invite me to the White House for any private chats—and if he did, I'm not sure that I'd be entirely comfortable.

"But remember, the President's thinking and mine on economic policy are very similar. We both have the same goals for the economy—full employment and continued prosperity, without any inflation, though, of course, that's a combination which represents an ideal and is very difficult to achieve. But the President and I do see eye-to-eye on rather conservative methods for reaching this goal. I'm sure there'll be times when our opinions diverge. I might have to make a decision with which he will, for important reasons of his own, disagree. But I do think that if the chairman were consistently at odds with the executive, a prudent man, one interested in good government, would resign. However, I can't presently conceive of any situation in which that is likely to occur."

Milton Friedman

INTELLECTUAL AS OUTSIDER

Milton Friedman was just coming into vogue as an economist when The New York Times Magazine *asked me to do a profile of him and his work. His unconventional ideas, in theoretical as well as in political economics, were beginning to move beyond his small coterie of followers, both into the academic community and into the general world. For me, a Friedman profile was an opportunity to encounter a fresh set of provocative notions. If my piece on Arthur Burns gave me a layman's guide to the discipline of economics, my brush with Milton Friedman gave me my graduate degree.*

I should confess, however, that I was influenced during the course of an interview with Friedman while I was doing the Burns portrait by the fact that Milton was a skier, and that he had a house in Vermont where he spent most of the winter. Being a ski nut myself, I calculated that if I scheduled my interviews of Friedman correctly, I'd probably get in a few extra days on the slopes. I told Friedman of my designs by telephone, and he liked them just fine.

I then proceeded to talk to more damned economists than I can remember. I saw them from the Brookings Institution and the Council of Economic Advisers in Washington, from the economics department at the University of Chicago, the National Bureau of Economic Research in New York and M.I.T. in Cambridge. My objective in doing the Friedman piece, after all, was a little different from what it had been in the earlier profiles; I was seeking not only to understand a man but, more important, a set of connected ideas. Intellectually, it was exciting as any work I had ever done.

I reached the Friedman house in Ely, Vermont, on a cold night a week or so before Christmas, 1969. Milton was surprised to see me drive up to the door, for most cars—even those rented at the airport from Hertz—can't make it through the snow to the Friedman mountaintop. Milton, all five feet three of him, greeted me in his checkered lumberjack shirt and snowproof boots. He led me into the house, introduced me to his wife, mixed me a drink and invited me to sit down for supper. Without very much delay, we began to talk—and I think we talked about politics and economics for four consecutive days, interrupted only by our descents down the slopes of Mount Killington.

My mind was profoundly jogged by the hours of talk with Milton Friedman. I found that he really made me re-think many of my liberal preconceptions, which was not an easy thing for me to do. But Milton was willing to challenge any intellectual convention, liberal or conservative. Here, in my view, was a genuine radical, equally contemptuous of the dogmas of left and right. In some of his ideas, I continued to think that he was dead wrong. Occasionally, it seemed to me, his line of reasoning led him off into the backwaters of the absurd, but even then he was provocative. I won't say that those lovely days in Vermont made me into a Friedmanite, but I acknowledge that they did, to use Paul Mc-Cracken's word, make me Friedmanesque.

Milton Friedman is, in my mind, the quintessence of the intellectual as a political power. He holds no office and his hands are on none of the levers of influence in Washington. He conquers by the force of his ideas, which is why he was so pleased to have The New York Times Magazine, *which everyone in Washington reads, give his ideas its attention. For my part, it was a hell of an experience.*

HALF-JOCULARLY, Milton Friedman says that his favorite country in the world is Japan, because he's such a tall man there. Friedman admits unhappily to being just five feet three, but adds that when he was an undergraduate he measured at least five feet four and a half. He's been squashed down since then, he says.

But if Milton Friedman has been squashed down in height, that's surely about all. In economics, he is certainly the most irrepressible, outspoken, audacious, provocative and inventive thinker in the United States—and even at five feet three, he may stand taller than all his colleagues in the profession. When the Nobel Prize is next awarded for economics, it is regarded as even money that Milton Friedman will win it.*

Nonetheless, it's hard to get responsible people, whether in academia or in government, to acknowledge that they've been influenced by Friedman. He is disturbing, if only because of his contempt for the conventional economic wisdom. He is too aggressive in challenging the premises themselves of long-standing economic policy. He's just too damned radical. And, in many circles, the fact that he was tied up with Barry Goldwater during the 1964 campaign doesn't recommend him either.

Still, there is no doubt that at Harvard and M.I.T., where he is considered a heretic, to say nothing of the University of Chicago, where he is the chief luminary of the "Chicago school" of economics, his ideas have had an enormous impact. Meanwhile, down in Washington, the people who make policy have begun to realize that there might be a lot of good sense in what Milton Friedman's been saying.

Currently, the doctrines known as Friedmanism are engaged in

* He didn't. Paul Samuelson did.

a major assault upon the Federal Reserve System, the high church of economic orthodoxy. The Fed is the issuing authority for the nation's money. It is empowered to regulate the supply of money in circulation—usually defined as actual currency, plus checking-account balances—through such devices as the sale and purchase of Government bonds, the setting of reserve requirements for banks, or even the actual printing of bills. It also exercises certain leverage over the use of this money by influencing the interest rate at which most credit flows.

The Fed's goal is to contribute to economic stability, normally by "leaning against the wind," a wind which may be inflationary in some cases and deflationary in others. Friedmanism shares this goal but contends that the Fed has been going after it backwards.

Friedman argues that the Fed has blundered by tinkering with interest rates to stabilize the economy. Instead, the Fed should concentrate on regulating the quantity of money itself and let interest rates fall where they may. Friedman says the Fed's preoccupation with interest rates is not merely useless; it is positively harmful. In fact, he goes a step further by arguing that not only interest rates but Federal fiscal policy itself—that is, Federal spending and taxation—have a negligible impact on economic stability.

This rather extreme view—which holds that taxes, spending and interest rates do not compare in importance with the size of the money supply—has been designated, chiefly by its disgruntled opponents, as Friedman's "Only money matters" doctrine.

Friedman seized upon this doctrine in the course of preparing, with Dr. Anna Schwartz, the book called *A Monetary History of the United States,* now recognized as a classic in the literature of economics. From the data he accumulated, he made the observation that economic instability over the past century has been the consequence principally of abrupt fluctuations in the money supply. During the Great Depression of the 1930's, for example, the Federal Reserve Board allowed the quantity of money in circulation to shrink by more than a third, with disastrous results. From these observations, Friedman concluded that the Fed should aim to keep the money supply stable—or have it increase (via a fixed rule laid down by Congress) at a steady percentage to keep up with economic growth.

Milton Friedman's reputation as a provocateur waxes by the moment as this doctrine makes headway in the corridors of power, particularly in the Fed, which changes chairmen this week. But because Friedman, at fifty-seven, is the reigning "monetarist" in the United States, it should by no means be assumed that his disruptive ideas stop there. His mind ranges across the entire field of economics and spills over into politics itself. To him, virtually no concept, no institution, no personality is sacrosanct.

When he was a twenty-one-year-old graduate student at the University of Chicago, he emerged from a couple of days in a sickbed with a corrective of the work of Professor Arthur C. Pigou of Cambridge, one of the leading economists of the day, which was published in the eminent Quarterly Journal of Economics. Ever since, he's been a gadfly, but because his capacity to nettle is matched by an indisputable scholarly brilliance, he could never quite be ignored.

Some say his most significant work is not on monetarism at all, nor on political economics, but in an abstruse book meant only for the experts called *A Theory of the Consumption Function,* which showed that consumption, in the short run, tends to remain constant despite sharp fluctuations in income. Though it may be true that Friedman is at his best in technical economics, he has not become a major public figure because of his esoteric economic theories. Rather, it is because he is willing to leave his ivory tower and, in behalf of ideas that are dear to him, come out scrapping.

He was born in Brooklyn of Jewish immigrant parents and raised in Rahway, New Jersey, where his father did sweatshop work that provided a marginal income for the family. When he reached college age, he won a scholarship to nearby Rutgers and came to the attention of a young economics professor named Arthur Burns, who recognized in him a superior mind. Friedman also came under the influence of a young professor named Homer

Jones, who had brought with him from the University of Chicago certain ideas about how to rescue the country from the Depression through a selective return to laissez-faire economics.

Friedman, who at first specialized in math, acknowledges that it was Burns who steered him into economics, while it was Jones who had the greatest impact on his early intellectual development. Jones, he says, steered him to the graduate school at the University of Chicago.

But much as his brilliance was recognized, Friedman was far from an immediate success in the intellectual world. Leaving Chicago, he had difficulty getting a university position. Some academic mandarins maintained that he was more interested in being daring than thorough, and there was some truth to the charge. Others considered him excessively aggressive, a compensation, friends observed, for his small stature and uncomely visage. In at least one instance, and probably more, he was a victim of academic anti-Semitism.

So, from the mid-1930's to the end of World War II, Friedman held a variety of Government jobs, and for a time it appeared he would end up a government statistician. Thanks to Arthur Burns, he was given a staff appointment at the National Bureau of Economic Research, where he also worked part time at scholarship.

Apart from one year on a campus, during which he was the subject of a bitter intrafaculty fight, it was not until 1945 that he got his first teaching post, at the University of Minnesota; and only the following year that he was invited to return, with faculty status, to the University of Chicago. Except for various visiting professorships, it is there that he has remained since.

Because he has championed economic freedom in an age when the left has put its faith in Government intercession—whether of the Marxian or the Keynesian variety—Milton Friedman has inevitably been considered a "right-wing" economist, an impression seemingly confirmed by his association with Goldwater in 1964.

But if the term "right-wing" implies an inordinate sympathy for the vested interests of society, along with a high degree of indulgence for existing social institutions, then nothing could be further from the truth. Friedman is no Chamber of Commerce economist, and surely no Bircher. Whatever the classical foundations of his thinking, he professes ideas that are warmly social and espouses programs that are, within the framework of our time, genuinely radical. Friedman may not be a pure egalitarian, but he has no tolerance for a system of government that proclaims programs to help the poor but winds up with a structure that enriches the rich.

It's been said there is something anomalous in Friedman's denial of the responsibility of government for establishing social and economic justice—a responsibility rather commonly acknowledged by today's Jewish intellectuals. Friedman does not conceal the influence of Jewish social thought, as well as his own impoverished upbringing, on his intellectual development.

He rejects the contention that he lacks the concern common to so many Jews for humanitarian ends. But he says that Jewish intellectuals often forget that a Jewish community survived for two thousand years in the Western world because it was able to carve out for itself a niche in the free market. So he believes that the underprivileged and the poor in our own day have far better opportunities to improve their status in a fluid, competitive system than under a paternalistic bureaucracy that preserves the status quo in the name of justice.

At the heart of the Friedman principles, then, is a deep cynicism about the processes of government, founded largely on the judgment that men are essentially incompetent or venal, if not both. In a way, the feeling goes back to Montesquieu and Jefferson during the Enlightenment, and to Lord Acton in the last century.

But if Montesquieu, Jefferson and Acton feared political tyranny, Friedman's preoccupation is chiefly with economic tyranny. He simply does not believe that a governmental system can be devised which will not be taken over by vested economic interests and exploited for the preservation and enhancement of their own wealth. He concludes, then, that individual opportunity is best served when the power of government is least.

Despite the favor he has found among many conservatives and

right-wingers, Friedman has sometimes contemplated characterizing himself as a "philosophical anarchist." The term, however, is probably too strong. It is enough to say that he would organize his society on the basis of individual economic freedom, curbed by government only to the degree necessary to keep markets free, competition open and innocent bystanders unharmed.

This essentially anti-Government approach appealed strongly to Goldwater in 1964 and in the course of several meetings together he borrowed heavily from Friedman without ever accepting the Friedmanite cosmology *in toto*. Four years later Richard Nixon, though more conventional in his economic thinking, also turned occasionally to Friedman for ideas. If the press has tended to exaggerate Friedman's personal influence on both men, neither of whom he saw very often, Friedman himself makes no apologies for voting Republican and giving advice to one or the other. However different his social objectives may be from theirs, he reasons that they are more likely than liberal Democrats to build a system that approximates his ideals.

Most of Friedman's formulations on the political economy were laid out earlier in this decade in a book called *Capitalism and Freedom* (known by the wags as "Capitalism and Friedman"). Many members of the economics community regard it as a shameless political tract, unworthy of a scholar. But Friedman, while acknowledging it as a popular and not an academic work, is extremely proud of it. He has named his summer home "Capitaf" in its honor. He is pleased that it is collateral reading in economics at many colleges and that, in paperback, it sells tens of thousands of copies every year.

Many of the ideas Friedman conveys in platform talks and in the column he now writes every third week for *Newsweek* first appeared in *Capitalism and Freedom*. Taken as a whole, it unfurls the Friedmanite cosmology. Examined in parts, it provides interesting and useful hypotheses for solving some of the country's most puzzling politico-economic problems.

Friedman's prescription for maintaining the economy vigorously competitive, thereby striking at privilege and serving the consumer, is an odd mélange of ideas previously heard from both left and right. He would abolish protective tariffs (left), oil subsidies and quotas (left), and farm-price supports (right). He would abolish corporate income taxes (right), but he would require corporations to attribute all their earnings to stockholders, who would be taxed on them at the regular rather than the capital-gains rate (left), and he would discourage amassing of great reserves as a temptation to gobbling up other companies.

He would deprive the regulatory agencies of their rate-setting powers (right), without impairing safety regulations (left), in order to encourage more price competition within such industries as securities, airlines and railroads, and he would open radio and television licenses to public bidding (left). He would repeal such codes as would require auto manufacturers to install seat belts, on the ground that individual purchasers can make that decision (right), but he would retain such requirements as the installation of antipollution devices, on the ground that these devices protect the rights of third parties (left).

Friedman acknowledges that in the case of natural monopolies, such as the telephone system, there is no ideal means of maintaining competition. But so great is his distrust of bureaucrats that he concludes that, in preference to a public corporation or a regulated industry, it is better to take a chance with private monopoly.

His formula for dealing with poverty is, perhaps, even more daring—though it is the one that the Government, under President Nixon, has come closest to adopting. Friedman, once asked what he thought was the best way to help the poor, replied, "Give them money." To implement this simple idea, he devised the now celebrated plan for a negative income tax, which would put money into the hands of the poor without their having to pass through a labyrinthine welfare apparatus.

But as Friedman sees it, the negative income tax would change little, unless accompanied by other basic reforms. What he proposes is to do away with the bureaucracy not only of welfare but of the war on poverty, urban renewal, Medicare, minimum wage and even Social Security itself. The Social Security system, cornerstone of the New Deal's program for social justice, particularly irritates him. Financed by a "regressive" system of taxation, it takes from the poor at a much more onerous rate than from the rich, yet rewards the rich more generously than the poor.

Similarly, Friedman says that Federal housing programs—which bulldoze away the homes of the poor while subsidizing mortgages on the homes of the rich—are basically discriminatory and unjust. As for the minimum wage, Friedman figures that it rigs the market place in favor of the upper echelons of the labor force, and drives the old and the young, whose market value is below the legal minimum, completely out of work.

Friedman is frank to admit that he does not, in principle, approve of a system that takes money from some citizens to give it to others, whether the beneficiaries are rich or poor. He feels it is an impingement on freedom and, if he had his way, the poor would be supported by private volunteer charity.

But he acknowledges that reliance on charity would be impractical, if not inhumane, and, as he sees it, the negative income tax is the best alternative. As long as it provides the poor with a livable income, while presenting them with built-in incentives to work, their buying power would assure them an adequate diet, decent medical care and suitable housing. Furthermore, he says, freed of oppressive bureaucracies, they could make their own spending decisions and, having an impact on the law of supply and demand, influence the market place to meet their needs.

Education, too, Friedman would open to the competition of the market. Like most Americans, he observes that the quality of the public schools has declined diastrously in our time, even though billions in new funds have been spent upon them.

The chief victim of this inferiority in educational opportunity, he points out, is not the rich but the poor. "Let a poor family in a slum have a gifted child," he says, "and let it set a high value on his schooling. . . . The 'good' public schools are in the high-income neighborhoods. The family might be willing to spend something in addition to what it pays in taxes to get better schooling for its child. But it can hardly afford simultaneously to move to the expensive neighborhood. . . . Our present school system, far from equalizing opportunity, very likely does just the opposite."

What Friedman wants to do is to break the virtual monopoly of the educational bureaucracy over mass schooling in the United States. To achieve this end, Friedman would grant for each school-age child a "voucher" good for a certain sum of money, preferably equal to the average per capita cost of public education. A family would then be empowered to present this voucher either at the nearest public school or at the private school of its choice, where it would serve as full or partial tuition payment. Such a system, he says, would at once encourage competent educators to build a network of private schools, which would then compete for students against the public schools—giving both a positive incentive to maintain a high level of quality.

The Government's role in this plan would be to enforce certain minimum standards, perhaps including a prohibition of racial discrimination. Otherwise, it would leave the private schools free to cater (be "responsive") to the needs and peculiarities of their student bodies.

It goes without saying that the Keynes-oriented economists of our day—and that probably includes a substantial majority—do not share Milton Friedman's faith in the competitive market, or his distrust of the processes of government. Many see even his advocacy of a fixed rule for governing the money supply, leaving to fallible men a bare minimum of discretion, as proceeding directly from ideology rather than from scholarly analysis.

"Sure, Milton has forced us to tighten up and see things in a more balanced way," said Arthur Okun, a Keynesian and former chairman of the President's Council of Economic Advisers. "But he doesn't see things in a balanced way himself. You can't buy and sell everything on the market, like honesty and racial equality. Under Milton's system, why not wives? Why not votes? Milton talks as if it's a perfect—or perfectible—marketplace, where everyone has perfect information and perfect understanding when he makes his marketplace decisions. But I think Milton's world is only a caricature."

Paul Samuelson of M.I.T. says that Friedman mixes up sequence with causation and that in his desire to be a "big swinger" on the economic stage he engages in "intellectual tightrope walking." Nonetheless, there is more than enough hard logic in Friedman's arguments to keep the Keynesians from dismissing them as hokum. And there is even some factual evidence—as in the recent successful readjustment of European exchange rates on the open market—that at least a few of his positions on economic freedom are correct.

As for Friedman's money doctrine, what the generation of economists nurtured on the teachings of Lord Keynes seemed to have forgotten is that Keynes himself had recognized a major function in the money supply. This was obscured by the lessons Keynes taught about the role of government fiscal policy in maintaining economic stability.

Friedman never claimed that he invented the money doctrine, but he did reintroduce it to the general body of economic thought, in a fashion so scholarly and persuasive that it could scarcely be ignored. Samuelson has injected more and more of Friedmanesque monetary theory into successive editions of his basic economics textbook—in use in most colleges—while denying vigorously that Friedman has had anything to do with it. Samuelson, often looked upon as Friedman's principal rival for America's first Nobel prize for economics, now readily admits that "money matters," but in common with other Keynesians he dismisses as nonsense the Friedman doctrine that *"only* money matters."

Now two of the seven members of the Fed's board of governors have aligned themselves publicly with the principles, if not with the details, of Friedman's teachings, and there is indication that perhaps one or two more have become private converts. In Congress, the prestigious Joint Economic Committee has recommended that the Fed shift to essentially Friedmanite policies, and within the President's Council of Economic Advisers, Chairman Paul McCracken has confessed to being "Friedmanesque," if not a full-fledged Friedmanite. It is now being said that opinion at the Fed is so closely divided that future policies will be determined by the incoming chairman, Arthur Burns—who was Milton Friedman's first teacher of economics at Rutgers and is now one of his most intimate friends.

Already, the Fed has conceded the existence of Friedman, if only by beginning to publish periodic figures on the nation's money supply. One of the Federal Reserve System's twelve semi-autonomous regional banks, the St. Louis branch, has been virtually captured by Friedmanism, and researchers there have done much to substantiate the essence of Friedmanite doctrine. (The research director in St. Louis is none other than Friedman's other Rutgers mentor, Homer Jones.)

But William McChesney Martin Jr., the Fed's chairman since 1951, is an ex-stockbroker, not a professional economist, and, according to most careful observers of the Fed, he barely perceived what Friedman was trying to convey. Besides, the members of the Fed, taken as a whole, could scarcely help but react negatively to a message that was so clearly directed against them. In *A Monetary History,* published in 1963, Friedman designates the Federal Reserve System as the villain bungling the nation into economic disruptions. If Friedmanism has quietly infiltrated the Fed, Friedman himself has found no reason to change that judgment on the basis of Federal Reserve policy since.

In bringing this judgment up to date, Friedman cites the Fed's much-disputed decision to stuff a large quantity of money into the economy just after Congress, as an anti-inflationary fiscal move, passed the surtax in 1968. What followed was a vast new surge of inflation, which even many non-Friedmanites blame on the Fed.

Then, in the middle of last year, the Fed decided to reduce the rate of increase in the money supply to zero. Again and again, Friedman has argued that this policy is so drastic that it will lead directly to an economic recession. The full impact of this policy, he said, would take about six months to be felt—which makes him believe that a recession is now imminent. Friedman acknowledges a rather remote chance that he is mistaken, since economics is a science based on probability rather than mathematical certainty. But he is prepared, as are his antagonists, to consider the recession which he predicts as a fundamental test of Friedmanite doctrines.

So persuaded is Friedman of the institutional incompetence of the Fed that if he *really* had his way, he says, he would abolish it altogether. In its place, he would have Congress legislate a fixed annual rate of increase in the money supply, somewhere around four per cent. At the moment, he says, economists still do not know enough about the processes of the economic system to justify constant intercession, and a fixed rule could hardly be worse, and would probably be better, than the Fed's tinkering.

Arthur Burns, in testifying before the Senate Banking Committee prior to his confirmation last December, gave the first public clue on the position he takes on Friedmanism. To no one's surprise, Burns revealed himself to be far more conventional in his views than Friedman himself. He regards a reduction in Federal spending and a balanced budget as fundamental to halting inflation. He considers it important to have the Government's anti-inflationary posture appear "credible" to the business community. He does not dismiss interest rates as a significant factor in economic stability.

But Burns conceded that he saw more than a little truth in Friedman's recession forecast, and he said his "impulse" was to follow Friedman—though not with the rigid Friedmanite formula —in maintaining a relatively constant but gradually increasing supply of money in circulation. Thus it became quite clear that, after William McChesney Martin goes at the end of this week, Milton Friedman will have won a victory (though hardly an unconditional surrender), and the Fed will never again be quite so casual about whether or not "money matters."

What makes Friedman such a formidable antagonist of the Keynesians, apart from the strength of his ideas, is his skill as a debater and polemicist. Samuelson says that Friedman's style surpasses his integrity and that Friedman simply ignores arguments and evidence that are not useful to him. He maintains that Friedman's personal powers of persuasion are so great that, if he died tomorrow, most of his ideas would vanish with him. Whether or not this is wishful thinking, it is true that Friedman can be devastating on the speaker's platform. A year ago, in a celebrated debate on "Monetary vs. Fiscal Policy," Walter Heller, President

Kennedy's chairman of the Council of Economic Advisers, was torn to shreds by Friedman's arguments.

Yet Friedman, if he was once considered a pushy Jewish kid from New Jersey, is now acknowledged to be unfailingly thoughtful and courteous. Desisting from the technique of withering insult, he couches his arguments, both on the platform and on paper, in the most sweetly reasonable terms, though without ever sacrificing a cutting edge. If he resorts to one tricky semantic ploy, it is in charging his opponents with failing to "prove" some contention. But since it is virtually impossible to prove anything in economics, his opponents often turn it around and use the same ploy on him.

With all of this heated back-and-forth, much of it spilling outside the boundaries of the economics community, Friedman has become something of a public figure. Though he has many distinguished followers in the Chicago School, it is he who is constantly in demand at other universities, both to lecture and to make extended visits. As a general rule, he accepts as many of these invitations as possible, for he considers them part of his responsibility. He is also called upon at far higher fees to speak before business groups, but he turns most of these down on the ground that they are a form of self-indulgence, without discernible results.

Friedman rarely refuses an invitation to testify before Congressional committees, however, and he gave a prodigious number of hours to the President's Commission on an All-Volunteer Armed Force, since he feels very deeply that young men should not be compelled to serve as draftees and that the military services should improve salaries and other benefits to the point where they become competitive in the job market.

He has also been telephoned by President Nixon, who has solicited his advice on the prospect of a recession. All of this attention unquestionably flatters him. He enjoys the feeling of being an influential person. But he recognizes that, for reasons of temperament and conviction, he will probably never hold a Federal policymaking position. There is no reason to doubt, however, that he enjoys being an outsider, challenging, provoking and irritating the conventional minded and forcing them to ponder the possibility that their most strongly held beliefs might require a bit of change.

But then, why should Friedman contemplate having it otherwise? At the University of Chicago, he has influenced a generation of the country's finest young economists, and students continue to vie to become his disciples. His colleagues admire him and freely admit his preeminence among them. They are the focus of his social life and his partners in Socratic discourse, his favorite pastime. He has a charming wife, Rose, herself a University of Chicago economist by training, who cooks his dinners and edits his writing. His twenty-four-year-old son David, a University of Chicago graduate student, idolizes him and faithfully plays back his ideas, albeit in a much fiercer version. He has a light teaching schedule, which enables him to hop to Japan or London or Miami for professional meetings and, most important, to spend almost half the year in the spot he loves the most on earth, his summer home in Vermont.

Just after the war, Friedman started spending his summers in Vermont, near the cottage of his good friend, Burns. Ultimately, he and Rose bought several hundred acres on top of a mountain, a mile or so from the Connecticut River on one side and the Burns house on the other. A few years ago, they bulldozed a road to a point just beneath the summit and there built a comfortable, modern house, hexagonal in shape and with huge panes of glass that overlook the Connecticut River valley and some of New England's grandest mountains.

Here Milton Friedman and Rose normally remain from midsummer to Christmas, occasionally leaving for a trip of a few days, now and then receiving visitors, but most often isolated from the world. It is here, at a small desk between a huge stone fireplace and the panorama outside, that Friedman, in an old wool shirt and baggy pants, sits down to work. Depending on his mood, he spins new theories or prepares new polemics.

Only at the first snowfall does the routine change. Then he throws a pair of skis into a four-wheel-drive Land Rover and makes his way to a nearby chairlift. Friedman isn't as adroit a skier as he is an economist, but he plays both games the same way. He takes on the toughest mountain, then audaciously, irrepressibly, relentlessly, scrappily, fights his way through the trees and across the ice from the top to the bottom. More often than not, he arrives a bit bruised but still on his feet. Yet, with barely a moment to catch his breath, he's ready to take on the next adversary, mountain as well as man, that dares challenge him.

Not bad for a guy who's five feet three.

William O. Douglas

FRONTIERSMAN ON THE COURT

When Harvey Shapiro of The New York Times Magazine *asked me to do a rush profile of Justice William O. Douglas, I replied that I thought he was already one of the best-known men in public life and that there didn't seem to be very much left to say about him. Harvey—justifiably, as it turned out—dismissed my evaluation. As I had learned in writing the Dirksen profile some years before, a lot of publicity in the newspaper doesn't necessarily add up to the understanding of a man. Harvey rightly insisted that Douglas was an enigma waiting to be unraveled and, because he was once again in the news, the profile had to be done at once. I was persuaded. It isn't every day, after all, that a Supreme Court justice—especially one whom many Americans consider among our great moral philosophers—has impeachment proceedings brought against him. I suddenly saw that this had the potential of a great story, and I dropped everything to start on it.*

There were, of course, many people in Washington who knew Douglas well—old New Dealers, former law clerks, other judges, fellow outdoorsmen, legal scholars, ex-wives. None of them, as I found out, knew him in all his complexity. Each of them, it seemed, had encountered only a facet of him. I gave up very early trying to find a single person who could tell me what Bill Douglas was all about, and went to work trying to put together a mosaic that I hoped would add up to approximately a whole man.

Not surprisingly, the ex-wives were the most knowledgeable and I was delighted that they agreed to talk to me. Several former law clerks also conveyed important perceptions to me. The legal scholars provided me with information on Douglas's social and judicial philosophy. The former New Dealers filled me in on the history, the other judges talked of Douglas in his capacity as a professional. I made a fortuitous trip to the Yale Law School, where Douglas had once taught, and by accident ran into two professors who shared more insights with me than the men I had expressly gone up there to see. Between them all—plus a rather extended study of some law books—I put together what I thought was a rather plausible picture of a complex man.

Douglas himself was harder to deal with. Normally, I think, he would have been glad to talk to me. In the past, he had granted interviews freely to journalists and biographers. But, after first treating the impeachment effort as inconsequential, he was persuaded to take it seriously, so he retained a lawyer who advised him to discuss the case with no one. After much negotiation conducted by phone through the intermediary of a secretary, I finally reached a compromise with Douglas: he was taking a Saturday hike along the C. & O. Canal and if I wanted, he said, I could tag along. I don't take sixteen-mile hikes every day, but I wouldn't be intimidated. So at dawn I was up and, shortly afterward, out in the sunshine with Douglas and his pretty young wife, Cathy. We didn't talk about the impeachment, because I had promised that we would not. We didn't, in fact, talk about much of anything besides the birds and the bees in the woods. But I did, at least, have the opportunity to spend a few hours with him and acquire some impressions of my own about the personality of Bill Douglas. I think of him now as more difficult than lovable, which is probably not surprising. But I hesitate to contemplate what the Supreme Court some day will be like without him.

Y OU CAN tell the hikers from the tourists by looking at their feet.

The tourists come to the C. & O. Canal as a rite of spring, to pay homage to conservation, to see Justice Douglas in the flesh, to be a little stylish. They wear sneakers, sometimes even sandals, and before they are far along on the sixteen-mile trek, many of them begin to limp. But the hikers wear sturdy boots, laced high over the ankle, and they march with a fierce step.

William O. Douglas is a hiker. The finish of his boots is rubbed away by encounter with wood, rock, mud and brambles. The uppers are stretched from use, the thongs frayed.

Bill Douglas, however, doesn't walk as fiercely as he once did. Sixteen years ago, when he led the first hike down the canal, he strode at almost five miles an hour, with rarely a stop to catch his breath. "That was nearly a trot," he says without emotion. Douglas hardly ever betrays emotion. "There weren't many who could keep up with me in those days." Since then, he's saved the C. & O. Canal from the roadbuilders who wanted to pave it over, but he keeps up the annual hikes as a public warning that natural beauty, in an industrial society, is never completely out of danger.

Now seventy-one years old, Bill Douglas has slowed to three miles an hour, and he wears a pacemaker inside his body to regulate the rate of his heartbeat. He stays no longer at the head of the pack and, now and then, even some of the tourists pass him by. He often removes his floppy Western hat to fan his brow and he takes frequent breaks to rest. It's at those moments that he sits on a log or a small knoll and, while his strength returns in the shade, entertains his admirers with lectures on wildlife or anecdotes about the New Deal or public morality.

"One day in 1939," he reminisces, "I was out on the golf course when a caddy ran up to me and said that the President wanted to talk to me on the phone. I knew there was a vacancy on the FCC and I really thought F.D.R. was going to offer it to me. But he didn't. That's when he told me he was going to put me on the Court. . . ."

One of the circle of listeners hands Douglas a copy of his controversial new book, *Points of Rebellion,* and asks him to dedicate it to a friend. The man says his friend often quotes Douglas's statements. The Justice signs the book and quips dryly, "Your friend had better stop quoting me, or he'll soon be cited for some kind of criminal violation."

Douglas looks at a small cottage, surrounded by brilliantly colored spring flowers, bordering the canal. "I guess there are a lot of public officials who'd like to live out here where it's quiet and relaxing," he says, "but it's far away and you'd have to keep your black tie in town. And your wife would wonder what you're doing out every night. Then pretty soon, she'd find out. . . ."

The joke seemed particularly pointed from a man whose morals have been denounced publicly all over Washington. Surely Douglas's willingness to flout convention—not only by taking wives much younger and more frequently than justices are supposed to, but by making provocative political statements and by writing disturbing judicial opinions more often than justices are accustomed to—lies near the source of the impeachment proceedings currently under way against him in Congress.

Yet in Washington, where appearances are often far removed from reality, it is probable that the proceedings will barely touch on Justice Douglas's nonconformism. Minority Leader Gerald Ford of Michigan, chief of the impeachment movement, took pains to declare in his opening foray on the House floor: "I have no personal feeling toward Mr. Justice Douglas. His private life, to the degree that it does not bring the Supreme Court into disrepute, is his own business. One does not need to be an ardent admirer of any judge or justice, or an advocate of his life-style, to acknowledge his right to be elevated or to remain on the bench. . . . Mr. Justice Douglas has been criticized for his liberal opinions. . . . Probably I would disagree, were I on the bench, with most of Mr. Justice Douglas's views. . . . But a judge's right to his legal views, assuming they are not improperly influenced or corrupted, is fundamental to our system of justice." In giving his reasons for pressing to impeach Douglas [i.e., to accuse him of misconduct in office], Ford cited no less an authority than the highly respected Justice Benjamin Cardozo. As Ford put it, what is required of judges is, in Cardozo's words, "not honesty alone, but the punctilio of an honor the most sensitive."

Ford's staff has drawn up a bill of particulars against Douglas which was introduced in the House by Congressman Louis Wyman of New Hampshire and co-sponsored by one hundred ten of his colleagues. The bill says nothing of Douglas's marriages and divorces. It touches on his political opinions rather lightly, quoting only such an extravagant statement as "the powers-that-be faintly echo Adolf Hitler" from *Points of Rebellion*.

It puts its chief emphasis on a potpourri of charges of violations of the law and judicial ethics—association with one foundation (Parvin) that was getting money from gamblers, and with another (Center for the Study of Democratic Institutions) that organized an international conference to improve relations with the Soviet Union, the reprinting of an excerpt from *Points of Rebellion* in a magazine containing photos of sexual intercourse (*Evergreen*) and the appearance of one of his articles in a magazine published by a litigant (Ralph Ginzburg) before the Supreme Court. Indeed, some of Douglas's most vigorous supporters acknowledge that he has been prone to indiscretion—but indiscretion has not in the past been recognized as grounds for impeachment.

What is perhaps more worthy of note is that the one hundred ten sponsors of the anti-Douglas resolution are all conservative Republicans and Dixiecrats. This seems to be persuasive evidence in support of the hypothesis which virtually everyone in Washington accepts: that the undertaking seeks not simply to impeach William O. Douglas but to discredit the liberalism for which he has long stood, the liberalism inherent in the domestic programs of Democratic Administrations since the New Deal and, perhaps more important, in almost two decades of bold judicial opinions by the Earl Warren Court.

Unquestionably in these stormy moments of accusation and counteraccusation, Douglas finds comfort in the presence at his side of Cathy, his fourth wife. Douglas met Cathleen Heffernan, daughter of a railway clerk, while he was visiting some friends in Portland, Oregon about five years ago. She was blond and blue-eyed, with a trim figure and a soft, fresh face. And she was only twenty-two. Cathy was then dividing her time between studying sociology at Marylhurst, the local Catholic college, and working as a waitress in a downtown restaurant.

Douglas's two-year-old marriage to Joan Martin, herself only twenty-five, was going poorly and he was attracted to Cathy at once. The two saw each other from time to time over the ensuing months and in July 1966, shortly after Douglas's divorce, he and Cathy were married. They spent their honeymoon at Douglas's mountain retreat, Goose Hunt, in the Cascades.

In hiking along the C. & O. Canal, Cathy, in a tailored green pants suit, chooses style over comfort, in sharp contrast to her husband's tattered attire. Yet her attitude toward him, without being clucking, is warmly solicitous. It is she who notifies him when he has earned a break in the march—or, indeed, when he is so obviously tired that he must take one that is unscheduled. And it is she who scouts the trail ahead for a shady spot. "He keeps us going," she says playfully, "by telling us there's lunch around the bend. Except there always seems to be another bend." But it is Douglas, not Cathy, who appears most anxious to get around the bend, to get that much closer to home and an end to the long walk.

When Douglas married Cathy, official Washington was scandalized—or, more accurately, rescandalized—for it had been scandalized when he took twenty-three-year-old Joan as his third wife. Douglas's first marriage, to Mildred Riddle, mother of his two children, had ended in 1954 after thirty years; friends said he simply outgrew her. His second marriage, to Mercedes Hester, ended after nine years of intense personality conflict. Joan, said his friends, was a "rebound"—and their interlude was terminated by mutual agreement because she simply couldn't stand the Douglas pace.

But Cathy, according to their friends, has been perfect for Douglas. Strong but not aggressive, good for his ego but far from a sycophant, she has imparted new zest to his old age. Some say she gives Douglas a feeling of immortality. Though he is unmistakably paternal toward her, he responds with obvious joy to her sparkling youth. Occasionally, Douglas puts his arm around Cathy's shoulder as they walk side by side. It is virtually the only sign of tenderness he allows himself.

The display of emotion has always been a major problem for Bill Douglas. At one point during the hike, a group of Negro children from a local school met him with signs thanking him for his Supreme Court decisions. Douglas was clearly touched, but equally embarrassed, and he greeted them clumsily, as if they were middle-aged lawyers from the bar association in Dubuque. He was also pleased by the young people who, at intervals on the route, held up signs which read, "A Peach, Justice Douglas," a retort to his detractor's slogan. Yet he was unable to give more than a timid nod to these young people.

At the Supreme Court, two generations of law clerks have consistently found Douglas distant and detached, presumably indifferent to their well-being if not oblivious of their presence. While Justices like Holmes and Frankfurter made dedicated apostles of the law graduates who served them, Douglas brushed by his clerks, often winning their respect but rarely their affection.

One former clerk tells of how Douglas brusquely placed a bottle of Scotch on his desk one day with the laconic observation, "They tell me it's your birthday," then stalked off to his office. The young man, nonetheless, was touched by the gesture. Another, who became close enough to Douglas to go mountaineering with him from time to time, said, "You knew he was really trying to tell you something important when he helped you roll up your sleeping bag. That was the only way he could communicate affection. But I understood how hard it was for him, and I appreciated it."

Few of the law clerks, however, got that close to Douglas. Most did their jobs without recognition, even without significant intellectual contact. Now and then, usually on a holiday, they might be invited for dinner to the Douglas home, where they found unaccustomed conviviality. If they brought along a pretty wife, the chances for a relaxed and genial evening improved, for Douglas responded unmistakably to attractive women. But, on the whole, the clerks left after their year at the Court with the feeling that they scarcely knew Douglas, and that he didn't know them at all. As one put it, "I kept thinking that Douglas was another of those liberals who loved humanity in the abstract, but couldn't stand people in particular."

One result of this aloofness is that Douglas has been deprived of the sustained influence in the legal community that many of his colleagues on the Court have enjoyed. Without a dedicated cult of apostles to spread his judicial message, he radiates less authority, exercises less power than he otherwise would.

Yet, despite Douglas's disabilities in personal relations, his energetic mind and undeviating liberalism consistently generated talk in earlier years about his possible candidacy for elective office. In 1944, Roosevelt actually proposed his name to the party bosses as one of two acceptable choices for the Vice-Presidential nomination. The bosses opted for the other choice, Senator Harry Truman of Missouri, and Douglas remained on the Court. On occasion, Douglas has indicated that if he had become President, the history of the past quarter-century would have been different. He has said he would never have dropped the bomb on Hiroshima and would have averted the confrontation with Russia that produced the cold war. But when the anti-Truman forces within the Democratic party proposed to draft him in 1948, he turned them down decisively, as if he really didn't want to become President after all.

Indeed, it is hard to envisage Bill Douglas as a President. Though he is the quintessence of both intellectual and man of action, he is the antithesis of the back-slapper, the perpetual smiler, the sufferer of fools, the skillful arbitrator and ready compromiser, the dealer in pleasant rhetoric. Surprisingly, Douglas shows up rather often at Washington parties, even predictably boring ones; friends say that, like most public officials, he enjoys the adulation he inevitably receives in crowded salons and ballrooms. But it is not easy to see the successful elective official in this man who is basically shy, fundamentally introverted and more than a little difficult to get along with.

For those interested in psychoanalytical speculation, clues to the Douglas character are plentiful. William Orville Douglas was the son of an impoverished Presbyterian minister who rode the circuit from Minnesota to the Pacific preaching the gospel in the frame churches of simple frontier communities. His mother, a Midwesterner, was conscientious and devout, and she saw to it that her son had a stern Protestant upbringing.

When Douglas was six, his father died. "As I stood by the edge of the grave, a wave of lonesomeness swept over me," he has written. "My throat choked up, and I started to cry. I remembered the words of the minister who had said to me, 'You must now be a man, sonny.' I tried to steel myself and control my emotions."

Indeed, in true Presbyterian fashion, Bill Douglas learned to keep a tight rein on his emotions. And, if he has been harshly criticized by the conformists for departures from rigorous Protestant morality, it is also true that his Presbyterian upbringing imparted to him a kind of missionary spirit that makes him believe whatever he believes with deep, self-righteous zeal.

After the death of Douglas's father, the family moved to Yakima, Wash., where shortly thereafter he came down with a case of infantile paralysis that was nearly fatal. A country doctor saved his life, and his mother, by administering constant salt-water baths and unremitting massage, restored the use of his legs. The illness, however, left Douglas weak and spindly, subject to fainting spells, headaches and nausea. Douglas recalls how neighborhood boys mocked his infirmities. He also remembers being gradually enfolded by an overprotective mother who was determined to spare him from the realities of the outside world.

"This solicitousness set up a severe reaction," Douglas has written. "It seemed to me I was being publicly recognized as a puny person—a weakling. Thus there began to grow in me a great rebellion."

To prove he was not inferior, Douglas threw all his energy into the schoolroom. His natural brilliance, combined with his diligence, earned him an almost perfect academic record.

"But my scholastic achievements did not solve my difficulties," he wrote. "There was the haunting thought that infantile paralysis had left me a weakling, that I was indeed a cripple, unable to compete with other boys in the physical world. And the physical world loomed large in my mind. I read what happened to cripples in the wilds. They were the weak strains that nature did not protect. They were cast aside, discarded for hardier types. . . . Only strong men can do the work of the world—operating trains, felling trees, digging ditches, managing farms. . . . By boyhood standards, I was a failure. If I were to have happiness and success, I must get strong."

So Bill Douglas took to the outdoors, inspired by Mount Adams, the great peak of the Cascades which he could see from the back porch of his mother's house. "Adams subtly became a force for me to tie to," he wrote, "a symbol of stability and strength." He began to climb, higher and higher, faster and faster, always pushing himself to his limits. "Following these hikes, the muscles of my knees would twitch and make it difficult for me to sleep at night. But I felt an increasing flow of health in my legs, and a growing sense of contentment in my heart."

Yet, whatever gratification Douglas has found during a lifetime in the outdoors, it is important to note that he has never dealt with the rigors of the outdoors very comfortably. Whether or not as the result of his childhood infirmities, his body never adjusted to the wind and cold, the nights of sleeping on hard ground, the frequent encounters with hunger and thirst. Douglas has been injured many times, and feels pain acutely. Yet he drives himself onward, as if he must continue to prove his robustness to the bullies back in Yakima. In 1949, he was almost killed when he and his horse skidded off a steep mountain trail in Oregon. The horse rolled over on him and broke all but one of his ribs. The accident would

never have happened, an old friend said, had he not been riding
on terrain that was too difficult for his abilities. As soon as he was
mended, however, Douglas went back to the outdoors, anxious to
take on increasingly menacing physical challenges.

There was another, perhaps more important, challenge that
gave direction to Douglas's life, but one of which he writes much
less directly and forthrightly. "Bill used to tell me," one of his
closest old friends reveals, "what it was like living on the wrong
side of the tracks in Yakima. The kids didn't make fun of him just
because he was weak. They also taunted him because he was
poor, and Bill never forgot it. I've had many conversations with
him about the 'establishment' in Yakima and how contemptu-
ously it treated him.

"Bill has never forgotten that he was once poor. Maybe the
memory keeps him a little frightened. But unlike so many men
who make it big, he has never ceased to identify with the poor.
Bill hated the Yakima 'establishment' and, when he left town to
go to law school, he vowed he would cut those people down to
size. He's worked ever since—with a widening horizon—to keep
that vow."

Deciding against a career in conservation, Douglas resolved to
become a lawyer and to model himself after the great Western
progressives of his era, Hiram Johnson of California and William
Borah of Idaho. After graduating from Whitman College in
Washington, he spent a few years soldiering during World War I
and a few more teaching school to earn some money. Then he
hopped a freight east, stopping at hobo jungles along the way,
until he reached New York, where he enrolled in Columbia Law
School.

Douglas finished second in his class in 1925, with a specialty of
business law. He then worked for two years in a major law firm
on Wall Street, and spent another year practicing general law
back in Yakima, before returning to Columbia to join the law-
school faculty. He soon fell out with Columbia's autocratic president, Nicholas Murray Butler, and moved to Yale. There a young
dean named Robert Hutchins was bringing some important innovative ideas to the law school.

Back in those days, the Yale and Harvard law faculties were locked in debate over how the Constitution should be interpreted in the courts. Under Hutchins's guidance, Yale argued that unless the judicial interpretation of the Constitution took into account the changing times, the Constitution would actually lose it traditional meaning. At Harvard, Felix Frankfurter pressed the belief that the legislative and executive branches should meet the demands of change and that the courts should keep constitutional interpretation relatively strict and literal. The Yales contended that new areas of knowledge—psychiatry and sociology, for instance—should have an influence on legal decisions. The Harvards stayed faithful to the more conventional limits of the law.

At Yale, Douglas joined forces with Hutchins, who became one of his closest friends. When he was named to the Supreme Court some years later, Douglas became the symbol of the Yale theories. Symbol of the Harvard school was Felix Frankfurter himself. Whatever their personality differences—which were considerable —the intellectual rift between the two men ran so deep that they became and remained bitter enemies.

In 1934, Douglas left Yale to go to work for the Securities and Exchange Commission, the agency set up under the New Deal to watch over the stock market. There Douglas could make great sport of slaying "establishment" dragons, already held in disesteem for the chicanery disclosed after the 1929 crash. Douglas's work caught the attention of Joseph P. Kennedy, the commission chairman, who began to groom him as his own successor. (The friendship the two men formed was such that, two decades later, Douglas took Kennedy's son Robert on a world tour. It is said that Douglas's influence during this trip changed Bobby from a right-wing McCarthyite to a humanitarian and a liberal.)

In 1936, Roosevelt did appoint Douglas to the S.E.C. chairmanship. Indeed, some say the years which followed were Douglas's happiest, as he shared an easy intimacy with men joined together in the New Deal's holy mission of reducing the power and influence of the "establishment."

Still, when Brandeis retired from the Supreme Court in 1939, Douglas encouraged his friends to lobby Roosevelt in his behalf.

The President vacillated, while searching for an appointee more closely identified with the West than a former Yale professor. Then Senator Borah, Douglas's boyhood idol, held a press conference to claim Douglas as one of the West's own sons. The clinching factor, ironically, seemed to be that Roosevelt considered Douglas's chief rival for the appointment, Senator Lewis Schwellenbach of Washington, too radical for the court. In fact, four votes were cast in the Senate against Douglas's confirmation, on the ground that, having worked on Wall Street, he must be a reactionary. But Douglas was indeed confirmed and became, at the age of forty-one, the youngest Justice since Joseph Story in 1811.

In thirty years on the Supreme Court, Douglas has, of course, not been known as a reactionary. But those who regard him as the Court's extreme left pillar overlook the fact that he has written significant decisions in such undramatic areas as bankruptcy, rate-making, mergers and securities law, drawing heavily on the *expertise* he acquired long before he became a judge. His detractors also often ignore the fact that he has perhaps the quickest mind on the bench, capable of rapidly discerning the issues of a case, and the most facile hand, capable of producing decisions in perhaps a third the time of his nearest judicial rival. Douglas writes significantly more opinions than any other member of the Court.

His speed and flexibility are not without compensating faults: Douglas irritates his colleagues by his obvious boredom with extended argument. Still, his fellow judges acknowledge that he does his homework and, in the privacy of the Court's chambers, he argues his points well.

What chiefly makes Douglas controversial among professionals is that he appears to make up his mind first, devising later the intellectual content to justify his conclusions. To those lawyers who consider jurisprudence a deductive science, more or less on a level with math, this process is anathema. They are offended that Douglas often reasons with his guts, that he knows full well which party he favors before he sits down to listen to the arguments or study the precedents. Such critics—usually law professors, though as often liberals as conservatives—find that he lacks the quality of detachment which judges are supposed to possess. They find Douglas's mental processes untidy. These critics, while frequently in sympathy with his point of view, call Douglas's methods pure judicial cynicism.

Douglas's defenders, acknowledging that their man doesn't go by the legal textbooks, reply that all judges sense beforehand what conclusion they will reach on a case, though they may not be candid enough to admit it. Douglas, they say, simply abjures the elaborate steps other judges take to conceal their prejudices. The current debate over "strict construction" is pure bunk, they say. Douglas is as "strict" on the First Amendment as another judge may be on, say, the states' rights. One man's strict construction, they add, is another's tortuous reasoning. What matters fundamentally on the Supreme Court is political viewpoint. Conservative judges, they say, almost always come out with conservative opinions, while Bill Douglas consistently comes out on the side of the Bill of Rights against repression and on the side of the underdog against the "establishment."

If Douglas, then, is to go down in history as an important judge, it will be because his opinions have shown how the law can be applied to conditions in a dynamic society. He is too impatient to be a fine craftsman and, as the years have passed, his opinions are acknowledged to be less and less the models of clarity one hopes for from a justice of the Supreme Court. When one searches for his "landmark" decisions, one finds that they are relatively few. Indeed, like many great judges of history, much of his outstanding work has been in dissent. To be sure, Douglas was an anchor in the Warren Court's liberal majority, but in the famous decisions of that era—Watkins, Brown, Miranda, Escobedo, for example—Douglas wrote very few of the majority opinions. Instead, he explored new ground in the area of constitutional liberties, and worked to make the Constitution a more reliable guide for the free society he idealizes.

Douglas's goals, it is probably fair to say, have changed little since he came to the Court in 1939. Intellectually, he has nonetheless grown—in part from his travels among foreign peoples and in part from extensive reading outside the field of law. Some would say he has brought increasingly wider perceptions to his interpretations. Others would contend that he now distinguishes more vividly what he values from what he despises in American society. Some would say simply that he has become more radical. Obviously, Douglas long ago determined that he didn't care about becoming a great legal technician. Instead, he is willing to let his rank among judges be established on the basis of the impact his presence has had on the conditions of American life.

Take his dissent on a conviction of student demonstrators for engaging in a mass protest. Notice how the opinion brushes away the mythology of American democracy and applies the law directly to the way the political process actually works:

> The right to petition for the redress of grievances . . . is not limited to writing a letter or sending a telegram to a Congressman; it is not confined to appearing before the local city council, or writing letters to the President or Governor or Mayor . . . Legislators may turn deaf ears; formal complaints may be routed endlessly through a bureaucratic maze; courts may let the wheels of justice grind very slowly. Those who cannot afford to advertise in newspapers or circulate elaborate pamphlets may have only a more limited type of access to public officials. Their methods should not be condemned as tactics of obstruction and harassment as long as the assembly and petition are peaceable. . . .

Notice again how Douglas, in writing of a juvenile's right to counsel, deals not with a legal abstraction but conveys the understanding of how a young boy feels when faced with the police in a precinct house after dark:

> Age fifteen is a tender and difficult age for a boy of any race. He cannot be judged by the more exacting standards of maturity. That which would leave a man cold and unimpressed can overwhelm a lad in his early teens. This is a period of great

instability which the crisis of adolescence produces. Mature men might possibly stand the ordeal from midnight to 5 A.M. But we cannot believe that a lad of tender years is a match for the police in such a contest. He needs counsel and support if he is not to become the victim first of fear, then of panic.

Note also how Douglas can be a "strict constructionist" of the guarantee of equal protection under the law when he writes of the poor man's right to counsel:

> Certainly he who has a long purse will always have a lawyer, while the indigent will be without one. I know of no more invidious discrimination based on poverty.

Douglas is also "strict" in his opinions on obscenity—opinions for which he has been so widely criticized. But in his "judicial restraint," he could almost be taking a leaf from Frankfurter's textbook. He declares:

> We are judges, not literary experts or historians or philosophers. We are not competent to render an independent judgment as to the worth of this or any other book, except in our capacity as private citizens.

In his ruling against the ban in Boston of the film *I Am Curious (Yellow),* Douglas struck back at some of his critics. "I have consistently dissented," in obscenity cases, he wrote, "not because, as frequently charged, I relish obscenity. I have dissented before and now because I think the First Amendment bars all kinds of censorship. What can be done to literature under the banner of obscenity can be done to other parts of the spectrum of ideas when party or majoritarian demands mount and propagandists start declaiming the law."

Surely, whatever one may think of Douglas's position on obscenity, one must affirm that he is no opportunist but remains faithful to his conception of the rights granted to Americans under the Constitution. Even some of his friends, however, wonder whether his conception of his marital prerogatives is simply "the public be damned," or whether it's more complicated than that.

In searching for an answer, one notes that many years ago Douglas wrote: "The right to privacy [is] no less important than any other right carefully and particularly reserved to the people." The statement suggests Douglas holds, as a matter of personal conviction, that his marriages are his own business, and no one else's.

Douglas has never made a public response to the criticism of his proclivity to divorce and remarry. For whatever enlightenment it sheds, his two living ex-wives—Mercedes Hester Eichholz and Joan Martin Nicholson, both themselves remarried and residing in Washington—now speak glowingly of Douglas, occasionally see him and acknowledge, in retrospect, that they were temperamentally unsuited to him. Douglas himself has conveyed something of his philosophy of marriage in an opinion he wrote for the Court in 1965. It suggests that he attaches to it a rather high degree of importance.

"Marriage is a coming together for better or for worse, hopefully enduring and intimate to the degree of being sacred. It is an association that promotes a way of life, not causes; a harmony in living, not political faiths; a bilateral loyalty, not commercial or social projects. Yet it is an association for as noble a purpose as any involved in our prior decisions."

It is hard to tell how troubled Douglas has been over the criticism of his marriages. One can imagine that he was bemused at being dropped from the Washington Social Register, but he surely cannot have been indifferent to the displeasure of his colleagues on the Court. Much has been written about the falling out between Douglas and Justice Hugo Black, who stood together for a quarter-century on almost every dispute to come before the Court. Ostensibly, their differences have revolved around Black's recent embrace of more conservative legal positions. The two men have said cruel things about each other's jurisprudence in recent years from the bench. But hardly anyone who knows the two doubts that the real source of discord between them is Black's disapproval of Douglas's frequent change of wives.

But though Douglas's marriages have made him controversial, it is also true that they represent only part of the circumstances that have made him vulnerable to a concerted political attack. Surely the impeachment fuse would never have ignited had not a series of events, quite apart from Douglas's own activities, conjoined in the past year or so. Douglas, of course, has always been denounced by partisans on the right and has shrugged off many threats of impeachment before. But circumstances have made this challenge to him appear particularly serious.

• Had Justice Abe Fortas not been forced to resign from the Court for receiving a stipend from a foundation supported by the financier Louis Wolfson, attention would probably never have focused on Douglas's annual salary of $12,000 from a foundation supported by the financier Albert Parvin. The differences between the two relationships, however, are significant. Parvin, though indirectly related to gambling interests in Las Vegas, was not the object of any legal proceedings by the Government. There has been no evidence that Parvin's money was illegally obtained. Furthermore, Douglas personally ran the Parvin Foundation's program to bring foreign students to Washington to learn about American Government, a program highly regarded.

• Had the nomination of Judges Clement Haynsworth and G. Harrold Carswell to fill Fortas's seat not been rejected by the Senate, Republican politicians would not have been likely to seek retribution by going after Douglas. In a thinly veiled threat during the Haynsworth debate last November, Ford announced that he was looking into the possibility of Douglas's impeachment. After Carswell's defeat, he moved to carry out the threat.

• Had Douglas timed the publication of his most recent book, *Points of Rebellion,* a little differently, he might not have fanned the outrage of the establishment to quite such a heat. To be sure, Douglas had for years been assailing such establishment institutions as the CIA, the Pentagon, the military-industrial complex, Congressional investigating committees and the FBI. But this book, while not particularly good, was particularly provocative and it came out during a crisis in public order in the nation. It predictably gave offense to many with statements like this:

The modern-day dissenters and protesters are functioning as the loyal opposition functions in England. They are the mounting voice of political opposition to the status quo, calling for revolutionary changes in our institutions. . . . Today's establishment is the new George III. Whether it will continue to adhere to his tactics, we do not know. If it does, the redress, honored in tradition, is also revolution.

Douglas's friends say it is insane to read passages such as this as incitements to revolution. Precisely the opposite is intended, say these friends. They repeat the same warning that Douglas has been issuing for years—that if the society does not reform itself, if it does not provide the freedom and equality which its Constitution promises, then indeed revolution will inevitably follow. These friends point to admonitions like this one of some time ago, in which Douglas quotes Chief Justice Charles Evans Hughes:

> The greater the importance of safeguarding the community from incitements to the overthrow of our institutions by force and violence, the more imperative is the need to preserve inviolate the constitutional rights of free speech, free press and free assembly in order to maintain the opportunity for free political discussion, to the end that government may be responsive to the will of the people and that changes, if desired, may be obtained by peaceful means. Therein lies the security of the Republic, the very foundation of constitutional government.

This April, Douglas wrote a concurring opinion in which he indicated clearly his distaste for violence. He said:

> Radicals on the left historically have used [provocative] tactics to incite the extreme right with the calculated design of fostering a regime of repression from which the radicals on the left hope to emerge as the ultimate victor. The left in that role is the *provocateur*. The Constitution was not designed as an instrument for that form of rough-and-tumble contest. The social compact has room for tolerance, patience and restraint, but not for sabotage and violence.

But Vice President Agnew, for one, chose to interpret Douglas's words as an attack. Agnew replied that Douglas's record would have to be "thoroughly examined. . . . It seems rather unusual for a man on the bench to advocate rebellion and revolution, and possibly we should take a good look at what the Justice is saying and what he thinks, particularly in view of the fact that two fine judges have been denied seats on the bench for statements that are much less reprehensible, in my opinion, than those made by Justice Douglas."

It was four days after the remark by Agnew that Ford formally proposed Douglas's impeachment on the floor of the House and saw to the introduction of the impeachment resolution signed by one hundred ten Republican and Southern Democratic Congressmen.

Douglas at first refused to take the matter seriously—he had dismissed a hundred threats before. But some of his old friends— Clark Clifford, former Secretary of Defense; Ben Cohen, one of the original New Deal Brain Trusters; David Ginsburg, an important Washington lawyer and Douglas's first law clerk—went to him with the warning that the move was serious. As they saw it, the impeachment proceeding was nothing less than an effort by the Nixon Administration to stifle dissent and build a campaign issue for the fall election. After analyzing Ford's statement and the impeachment resolution, they concluded—over Ford's strong denial—that the Administration was deeply involved in it all. Finally Douglas agreed to fight, and appointed as his official counsel Simon Rifkind of New York, a former judge and an old classmate at Columbia Law School.

The matter is now before Congressman Emanuel Celler's Judiciary Committee of the House—Ford having failed to get a special committee appointed that would be less favorably disposed to Douglas. Celler, conceivably, could quash the entire proceeding if he chose, but he has promised a thorough investigation of all the allegations—the Parvin relationship, statements in *Points of Rebellion,* additional declarations by Douglas of a political nature, a variety of other business dealings. For his part, Douglas has agreed to turn over to the committee all of his nonjudicial records and, presumably, to testify personally if he is asked. President Nixon has announced that the Administration, too, would cooperate officially in the inquiry.

In a legal sense, the case turns on a fine constitutional point. Rifkind and his associates maintain that a Justice, according to the Constitution, can be impeached only for "high crimes and misdemeanors." Ford argues that, since the Constitution says a judge can sit only during "good behavior," the grounds for impeachment are much wider. As Ford put it with astonishing candor on the floor of Congress, "an impeachable offense is whatever a majority of the House of Representatives considers [it] to be at a given moment in history."

Such a doctrine seems to suggest that a majority can impeach a judge for any cause at all, including membership in the wrong political party. Rifkind's team says Congress will not stoop to pure partisanship and insists that the precedents all lean in the other direction. Though it is generally agreed that the House will not find that Douglas committed "high crimes and misdemeanors," hardly anyone will bet against the possibility that a majority in Congress will vote—if it comes to a vote—for impeachment anyway.

Still it is generally agreed that the outcome will ultimately be decided by the politics of the matter. If the House impeaches, the Senate must convict by a two-thirds vote before Douglas can be removed.

But even if the Republican-Dixiecrat coalition can get a majority in the House, there is little chance that it can get the necessary two-thirds of the votes in the Senate. Yet a close vote would be a victory of sorts—a conservative show of strength, a triumph for Administration morality, an exhibition of power by the "silent majority."

Of all the possibilities, what appears least likely is that Douglas will resign under pressure, as Fortas did. Deep down, Bill Douglas is probably a little tired of the Court and wouldn't mind retiring to his mountain home in the West. But he'd never give the establishment the satisfaction. In all these many years, he's never flinched in his resolve not to retreat before the bully-boys of Yakima.*

* Editor's Note: The Celler Committee voted not to impeach Douglas, thus ending the proceedings in the ninety-first Congress.

James Farmer

BLACK OVERSEER ON THE
PRESIDENTIAL PLANTATION

This is more than a profile of James Farmer. For lack of a better description it is a composite of the blacks working for Richard Nixon. It's the piece I dropped to do the portrait of Justice Douglas and, by the time I got back to it, the 1970 summer slump had intervened, some of the people I wanted to see had vanished on vacation and I had taken on some new writing commitments. Finally, at the end of July, I went off with Jim Farmer to Gary, Indiana, where I covered a speech he delivered to an anti-poverty group and where I met the city's embattled black mayor, Richard Hatcher. I finished a last draft of the article for The New York Times Magazine *sitting on the porch of a house we had rented for the month of August at Rehoboth Beach, Delaware, listening to the waves pound against the shore. Actually, I don't think the delay did the piece any harm—for the blacks with whom I kept in touch seemed to feel about tthe Nixon administration at the end of the summer exactly as they felt at the beginning of the spring.*

To my surprise, the piece was not very difficult to do. I had an-

ticipated a communications problem across the color barrier. In other days, I had tried to do articles on the Blackstone Rangers in Chicago and the Black Panthers, and I had found suspicion of a white writer so great that I could not do either job successfully. When I wrote the profile of Walter Washington, I hired two young black men to conduct street interviews for me and I am sure that without a day of experience at the craft they were better at it than I would have been. The blacks who hold assistant secretaryships in the Federal government are, of course, extremely sophisticated. But they were both black and bureaucrats, a combination which I thought might be deadly for an inquisitive white writer.

It wasn't deadly at all. I might be deluding myself, but I have the impression that I got pretty level answers from almost everyone I talked to—or at least as level as their political predispositions permitted. If they were lying, after all, why would they poor-mouth their own boss? What I found for the most part were intensely decent men—not the "Uncle Toms" that President Johnson's blacks told me I would find—who agonized constantly about the Nixon administration and the role they personally played in contributing to it.

But because I have congratulated myself on the ease with which I carried on candid conversations with black men does not mean I've concluded that there is no barrier between us. As one black official said to me, "Let's not kid ourselves. We're working in whitey's world, not our own. And if we want some power, we have to exercise it on whitey's terms and in whitey's structure. I hate having to interpret everything I see through whitey's eyes and translate everything I say into whitey's words. But it's not our world—and I'm not sure that it ever will be." Such a commentary on our society is sad to me, but I think it's accurate. With few exceptions, the black men working in positions of some responsibility for the Nixon administration feel themselves in a dilemma. I resent having their integrity impugned by those who feel righteous in staying out. I think they are, for the most part, doing what they believe is right. And it's very hard for them.

IT was one of those hot summer mornings in Washington and a hundred or so young black and white students fidgeted uncomfortably, despite the air-conditioning, in the fifth-floor conference room of the Department of Health, Education and Welfare. These were HEW's summer interns, bright kids still in college, willing to give the system more of a chance, if one could judge by their comments, than the system was willing to give them. It was one of the periodic "bitch" sessions that HEW accorded them, and the personnel officer who stood before them, himself black and under thirty, fidgeted far more than they under the rat-tat-tat of their questions.

There were only a few scattered straights in the crowded room. Most of the black boys wore dashikis, the girls Afros; the white boys had hair spilling over their collars, the white girls' hair often brushed their waists. They all seemed impatient, as if stimulated by some undercurrent of intellectual electricity. Sex and color notwithstanding, their questions conveyed a community of outlook, a unaninimity of concern—for their own personal relevance, for the programs to which they had contributed, for the bureaucratic methods they had found so discouraging, for the goals of the American Government in race, education, poverty, health.

A group of young black men, remarkably assured and articulate, were particularly persistent. Exceptionally well-informed, they asked questions about why the Secretary had said such-and-such about segregation in the schools, why the job-training programs had recruited so few blacks, why a major contract had gone to a white contractor who had not submitted the lowest bid, why a grant had been made to a professor to perform a "racist" study. Occasionally, a voice from the rear, white or black, would murmur, "Right on," but mostly the audience just listened carefully. The personnel officer, the straightest arrow in the room, apologized for one thing, promised to do his best to change another and gave his assurance that he would surely look into a third. It was obvious from the students' growing restlessness that they were dissatisfied with the answers.

Meanwhile, a big black man, conspicuous if only because he was fifty, slipped puffing and perspiring into the conference room. He smiled and waved as he made his way to the rostrum through the tightly packed rows, jostling chairs as he went. When he sat down, he took off his wrinkled coat, and he mopped his wide brow and thinning gray hair with a handkerchief. He lit up a cigarette, lustily, almost as if he would swallow it, and he exhaled the smoke expansively. As he sat there, his shirt still damp and his tie askew, waves of excitement pulsated through the room. The personnel officer, his timidity accentuated by contrast with the newcomer, tried his best to ignore him, but the crowd listened no longer. Finally he gave up and introduced the late arrival. The man's title was Assistant Secretary for Administration of the Department of Health, Education and Welfare. His name was James Farmer.

Jim Farmer stood up and, in the booming voice that had stilled angry crowds for a decade or more throughout the tumultuous South, declared:

"Brothers and sisters," and he waited a moment for the effect to sink in. It did.

"I've done my time in jails throughout the South. I've had to get out of town on many an occasion at a fast march. The dues in the movement were high in those days.

"We did accomplish something, however. We improved conditions of life for the black middle class. But in retrospect, we see that we didn't do anything for the poor. I'm here now to change that. I'm here because I have some power and this is where the action is.

"My views haven't changed since my days on the picket line. I'm not telling you to reduce the pressure on the Government or on me. We need people out there to keep the heat on us.

"Without some of us on the inside, however, all the picket lines in the world won't help. Sure there's good reason to criticize the

Administration. But I think that makes it all the more necessary, brothers and sisters, to have someone working for you from within."

Looking at the faces brought together in the conference room, it seemed fair to conclude that there wasn't a doubter in sight. Some of those young people may have come wondering whether Jim Farmer had sold out to Dick Nixon in going to work for HEW, but Farmer has a peculiar power before a crowd. Without a script, with barely a plan, with only a casual study of his audience, he can make people respond however he wants—with laughter or tears, sympathy or anger, love or indignation. Even Farmer admits that his calling is oratory, not bureaucracy. Neither the young men in dashikis nor the young girls with hair streaming down their backs gave the slightest sign that they regarded Jim Farmer with anything but esteem.

Farmer had been a great find for the Nixon Administration. Founder of the Congress of Racial Equality back in 1942, he had been a stalwart of the civil rights movement through its most difficult years. He had been jailed for forty days in Mississippi, teargassed and electric-prodded in Louisiana. He had left as CORE's national director in 1966 to lead a national literacy program, only to be embittered by President Johnson's disavowal of the undertaking. In 1968, he ran unsuccessfully for Congress in Brooklyn as a Liberal with Republican endorsement. After the election Richard Nixon, in search of a few blacks to embellish his Administration, found Farmer available. He offered him a prestigious job, and Farmer accepted.

As the Administration's most prominent black man, Farmer has been in the spotlight relentlessly since he joined HEW. He has been attacked by the left, both black and white, as well as by the red-necked right. *Life* magazine recently called him "a disappointment to blacks and the Administration," without citing any evidence to sustain the assertion. The press generally, and most recently the Afro-American chain of papers, has never stopped predicting his imminent resignation. But, having already outlasted one HEW Secretary, Farmer stays on, arguing to whoever will listen that he's doing more good for the cause on the inside than he would on the out.*

In answering the questions of the college interns, Farmer larded his talk with words like "goodies" and "clout" and "muscle" to illustrate how important his job can be to the well-being of the black poor. He never claims, whether his audience is white or black, an evenhandedness of concern; Farmer admits that his constituency is black and maintains that his role is to serve it. He tells the interns that the "unconscionable effort to destroy the Black Panthers" must stop. He denounces "the new *Herrenvolk* theory" of Dr. Arthur Jensen, which hold that, in important ways, blacks are genetically inferior to whites. He promises to seek to eliminate the practice of disallowing the display of Huey Newton and Malcolm X posters in HEW offices. Perhaps most important, he echoes none of the propaganda emanating periodically from the White House that the Nixon Administration, despite its reputation, is really good for blacks. Indeed, if there is a theme at all to Farmer's words, it is that a black man need not like working for President Nixon but can justify it on the purely pragmatic grounds that, without him, some unsympathetic white man would be doing his job.

Blacks in the Nixon Administration are few in number and, from an over-all perspective, their collective power is not great. Yet, the President's spokesmen boast of Richard Nixon's black appointments. Some months ago, a Republican campaign brochure appeared, entitled "Black Leadership in the Republican Administration." It contained the pictures of no fewer than one hundred fifty federally employed Negroes, along with the extravagant claim that "the Nixon Administration has in one year surpassed all other Administrations in the participation of black leadership in high positions." It also quoted President Nixon as saying: "When I finish office . . . I would rather be measured by my deeds than all of the fancy speeches I may have made. I

* Editor's Note: Farmer finally did resign just before Christmas, 1970, shortly after this profile appeared.

think then that black people may approve what we did. I don't think I'm going to win them with words."

But the brochure reflected fewer deeds than it pretended. When one deducts from the one hundred fifty photographs those hold-overs from the Johnson years, the career civil servants, the Foreign Service officers who obtained their posts by examination, the private secretaries and lower-court judges and part-time consultants, there remain perhaps nine or ten blacks at the assistant secretary level, and only a few of them hold policy-making positions. In the previous two Administrations, a black was named to the Cabinet (Robert Weaver at HUD), the Federal Reserve Board (Andrew Brimmer), the National Labor Relations Board (Howard Jenkins), the directorship of the United States Information Agency (Carl Rowan) and the Supreme Court (Thurgood Marshall). The current nine or ten assistant secretaries hardly compare in aggregate political power, and only two or three of them generally identify with or actively defend the Nixon Administration.

The brochure, as it turned out, had problems even more severe than its credibility, however. On the one hand, blacks in Government were outraged that they were being exploited by the Republican party to convey a false impression. On the other hand, the proponents of a "Southern strategy" were appalled at the possible repercussions the brochure might have among their favored voters. The net result was that "Black Leadership in the Nixon Administration" died a quiet and unmourned death.

The last election provided ample evidence to both the blacks in Government and the Southern-strategy crowd that, politically, the Republican party was making little headway among the country's Negro population. Of the twelve blacks elected to Congress in 1970, all were Democrats. Of the thirty-six Negroes who ran for the Senate and the House of Representatives, or for governorships, only seven were Republicans, and six of these ran against black Democrats. In one of the most dramatic upsets of the year, Wilson Riles, a black Democrat, beat incumbent Max Rafferty, a conservative Republican, for State Superintendent of Public Instruction in California.

According to statistics published in the authoritative Congressional Quarterly, 90 per cent of the black voters in the nation cast their ballots in 1970 for Democrats. Indeed, whatever the blacks in Government may be doing, it is clear they are not building up popular black loyalty to the Republican party.

The small band of black officials who say they are trying to exercise some influence inside the Government includes, besides Jim Farmer, two Assistant Secretaries of HUD, Samuel Jackson and Samuel Simmons; the Director of the Community Relations Service, Benjamin Holman; the Assistant Postmaster in charge of Planning and Marketing, Ronald B. Lee; the Chairman of the Equal Employment Opportunity Commission, William Brown 3d, and an Assistant Secretary of Labor, Arthur Fletcher, who is in charge of enforcing the "Philadelphia Plan," the Administration's innovative, if not very successful, program for obtaining jobs for blacks in the construction industry.

Ostensibly, their conduit to the President runs through Robert J. Brown, a thirty-five-year-old Presidential assistant and the only black man on Mr. Nixon's immediate staff. Brown, a Democrat, was running a successful public-relation's business in North Carolina when, in 1968, he decided to work in the campaign of Robert Kennedy. After Kennedy's death, Clarence Townes, a black staff man on the Republican National Committee, recruited him for a job in the Nixon campaign. Later, Brown was invited to remain, presumably to serve as Mr. Nixon's black man in the White House. Predictably, Brown has little power, and virtually his only public exposure has been within the nation's black community. Brown, however, has chosen to be a booster for the Nixon Administration.

"Sure I get my bumps for being here in the Administration," said Brown, in the round, slurred, melodic tones of the black South, "but I'm here by choice. Hell, I don't have to grow my hair down to my knees to prove I'm standing up for what I'm supposed to. I've got no hang-up for that. I've been in demonstrations and marches. I know what it is to be black, have no shoes and eat cold beans for breakfast. I don't care if someone calls me Uncle Tom. If they do, they don't know who got hit on the head at white lunch counters. We kicked down the doors for the kids calling us Uncle Toms now. I can do my thing in my way as well as they can do theirs. Who are they to say that my way is wrong and theirs is right?"

Brown, while professing great admiration for Hubert Humphrey, the Democratic Presidential candidate in 1968, said he chose to work for Richard Nixon in the conviction that Nixon could accomplish more for black people. He maintains it is unfair that Nixon's achievements in the fields of minority enterprise, hunger and welfare reform have been unappreciated and unrecognized by blacks.

"We just don't get the support of the black community," Brown said. "There are too many Negroes getting hung up on symbolic issues, rather than paying attention to what's going to help the folk now. We've had too much symbolism. In this Administration we're trying to make substantial improvement in the lives of the poor."

Some would say that Brown, because he is so powerless, serves only a symbolic purpose himself in the Nixon Administration. In fact, as other blacks in the Government have put it, he is not even President Nixon's "house nigger." That distinction belongs to Leonard Garment, the chief White House adviser on racial matters, who is white.

Many noticed that when Attorney General Mitchell went to Mississippi after the killing of the black students at Jackson State, he was accompanied not by any of the Administration's Negroes but by Garment. Similarly, when Bishop Stephen Spottswood, board chairman of the NAACP, recently charged the Nixon Government with being "anti-Negro," it was Garment who sent a long telegram in the Administration's defense.

Unquestionably blacks—both inside the Government and outside—resent Garment's preeminence in racial matters. It is not that Garment is disliked or distrusted. He is actually held in considerable esteem. He is one of the few real liberals among Nixon's advisers. But in these days, with blacks reaching out for the political power long denied them, the feeling is widespread that they should, at least, dominate the affairs which directly affect them. Bob Brown, as everyone knows, is not a dominating man, but he is not to blame if there is not strong black influence in the White House. It is no secret that if President Nixon wanted a powerful black man around him, it would be up to him alone to say the word, and he would have one immediately.

One might also question the President's judgment in selecting James Johnson for the responsibility of recruiting more blacks for jobs throughout the entire Federal bureaucracy. A tall, gangling, dark-skinned Negro, Johnson is Vice Chairman of the Civil Service Commission. He came to his position by a curious route— curious, at least, for a black man. After twenty-one years in the Marines, he retired as a chief warrant officer, the highest rank ever earned by a retiring black marine. He then settled in California, where he went into insurance and real estate, developed conservative political views and established some tenuous ties with the John Birch Society. With these credentials, he was appointed by Governor Ronald Reagan as the state's Director of Veterans' Affairs. Desisting conspicuously from any identification with the civil rights movement, Johnson became an outspoken Reagan booster. When asked at his confirmation hearing why he never enrolled in a civil rights organization, he answered: "I can serve my race and my country better by being an individual, good American."

At forty-four, Johnson still carries himself like a marine and answers questions with a military directness. His sentences have a patriotic flavor that seems peculiarly anachronistic. Like Bob Brown at the White House, he dismisses the charge of "Uncle Tom" as being totally unfounded. He has known discrimination since his boyhood in Chicago, he said, and in the Marines he beat it down by high performance and sheer determination. At the Civil Service Commission, he said, he will work to eliminate racial bias and recruit more Negroes into responsible Federal positions.

Unfortunately, the Civil Service Commission—chief recruiter of talent for the Government and the agency principally respon-

sible, under law, for the enforcement of equal-opportunity practices—has itself one of the poorest records in the Federal service
in the area of racial equality. As of a year ago, the top ranks of
the commission—meaning the forty-three officials in the three
highest civil service grades—contained no Negroes. Dropping
down a grade, of the next 118 officials on the ladder, only four
were Negroes. Although current figures are not available, the
commission itself acknowledges that the picture has not changed
appreciably in the past year.

Last February, Robert E. Hampton, Chairman of the Civil
Service Commission, told a group of reporters that, as a matter of
policy, the Government was dropping whatever special efforts it
was making to hire blacks. He said the Administration believed
such pressures amounted to discrimination in reverse. The following day he issued a statement saying that his remarks had been
misunderstood, explaining that his real concern was the tendency
on the part of some agencies to take on unqualified people without
potential for career advancement. Yet, despite this explanation,
the suspicion remained that the commission had indeed lost its
zeal for equal-employment programs, though a black man named
Jim Johnson remained Hampton's Vice Chairman.

"I believe I can't be just the Negro Commissioner. I've got to
be Commissioner of all the people," said Johnson, whose position
contrasted sharply with Jim Farmer's open commitment to his
"constituency" of blacks. "If I'm in charge of discrimination, it
must be not only discrimination against blacks but women, Jews,
the aged, failures, everyone. We've got to bring all groups into the
mainstream of America—and I include the white South in that.
We can't leave any groups out.

"Nonetheless, I do go out to speak in many Negro colleges, to
encourage these young people and let them know of the jobs that
exist. Yet, in the final analysis, the Negro must learn for himself
the importance of education and the way the economy and the
political structure function. We've got enough teachers, ministers
and social workers. We've got to put our people into the hard
competitive fields. Science, for example, is where it is. So I don't

want Negroes just shoved into jobs for the sake of jobs, at the lowest levels. I want them in the training and internship programs. If you can't make your way within the Government structure, you're in bad shape. That's what minorities have to correct."

Sam Simmons, Assistant Secretary for Equal Opportunity in HUD, would agree with those last remarks. He admits he has become discouraged over President Nixon's leadership in civil rights but, he says, "Government policy is one thing. Islands of progress are another. In my day-to-day work, I'm not getting sabotaged." He thinks, however, that blacks have a long way to go before they will exercise real power within the Government, no matter who is President or what party rules.

Simmons contrasts those blacks holding "traditional" positions focusing on the social problems of the Negro with those holding "power" positions concerned with decisions and policy-making. He points out that most blacks, including himself, are still in "traditional" jobs. Only a few, like Ron Lee at the Post Office, hold "power" jobs where they influence not only racial matters but money, personnel, planning, American society as a whole.

The problem of getting Negroes into power jobs is not just discrimination, Simmons points out, although that's a large enough part of it.

"The process is more subtle than just discrimination," Simmons explained. "People pick their own kind for the big jobs. The cats from the Eastern schools have the advantage of familiarity. They understand the system. People know them. They're easy to check on. We're just not part of the process. We're from the wrong schools, the wrong parts of town, go to the wrong clubs and the wrong banks."

Part of the process also, Simmons says, is the built-in defeatist attitude of young blacks contemplating Government service. It leads them to take the "traditional" jobs, assuming they will never get ahead in the "power" positions.

"When some intelligent Negro kid comes to me for advice these days, and he tells me he's got a good job offer in, say, relocation or social services, I tell him he's out of his mind. I tell him to go into budget, finance, personnel. I don't want to see young black college graduates going into teaching, social work, corrections. That's easiest, of course, and it's where they can find jobs. But they've got to deal with money and policy and enforcement if they're going to make a dent. Those are the decisions that matter. That's where the power is."

Assistant Postmaster General Ronald Lee, a West Point graduate, was on active duty as a major when he received a White House fellowship in 1965 to serve on President Johnson's staff. There he impressed Lawrence O'Brien, who, on becoming Postmaster General, asked Lee to become his head of Planning and Analysis. Resigning his commission, Lee held this job until the Democrats were defeated in 1968. When Winton Blount was named Postmaster General, he invited Lee back—with sub-Cabinet rank, five hundred employes under his supervision and the power to design the structure of a new postal corporation, as well as immediate improvements in the operation of the nation's postal service.

"I'm a Democrat and I'm black," said Lee with casual detachment and obvious self-confidence. "I'm not involved in making policy for the Administration, as I would be if I were in the State or Defense Departments. My job is to keep the postal system running and I'm tested—the department is tested—every day in the real world. But because I'm black, I keep this little reminder in front of me. It says: 'Do something for equality every day.'

"On the inside, I do what I could never do on the outside. I recommend blacks for key jobs. I've helped black businessmen to get Government contracts. I've influenced the deposit of postal funds into black banks. I receive calls for help not only from black postmen but from black farmers and students, too. Sometimes I receive a letter addressed to the 'Black Assistant Postmaster,' and I know that it'll be a plea from a Negro for some kind of help.

"But don't misunderstand me: I'm not completely comfortable here. I receive demands from my Negro friends every day that I defend my relevancy. I am constantly castigated and often told that I ought to resign. I am told that the very fact that I am here is contrary to the central needs of black people. But I didn't take this job just to help blacks. It was a good opportunity for me personally, and it puts a black man in position of considerable responsibility."

Lee speaks nostalgically of the "Black Mafia" he knew when he worked in the White House under President Johnson. It was composed of a half dozen or so Administration blacks who met regularly with Vice-President Humphrey and with whom the President would himself consult over a particular racial problem or complaint. Its principal figures were Roger Wilkins, head of the Community Relations Service, and Clifford Alexander Jr., first a Presidential counsel and then Chairman of the Equal Employment Opportunity Commission. These men recognized that they represented a major force—the black vote—within Lyndon Johnson's coalition of supporters. As a result, the "Black Mafia" did make an impact, and its members felt that they had a significant role to play in bringing the Negro viewpoint into the Administration's decisions.

Under Nixon, Lee said, there is a band of black officials in regular communication with one another, professionally and socially, who try to exercise a certain influence. During the wildcat postal strike last spring, for example, they worked throughout an entire weekend to keep racial tensions out of an already explosive situation. They are frequently on the phone with one another, discussing this problem or that, the meaning of a statement made at the White House or the Justice Department, the implications of an event in Birmingham or Chicago. Characteristically, they meet at one another's homes on a Saturday night and, over Scotch-on-the-rocks and potato chips, agonize over the Administration's relations with the black Americans, and collectively search their souls to justify their own participation in it.

But, as much self-examination and discussion as they give to the situation, Lee acknowledges that the group has had little influence within the Administration, rarely meets with the President or even the men in intimate contact with him, and possesses only a shadow of the power of Johnson's "Black Mafia."

"The people who elected Richard Nixon to the Presidency do

not represent my best interests as a black man," said Lee. "I know that. As long as I'm here in this job, I'll do the best I can and be totally loyal to 'Red' Blount, my boss. But I don't stop being black while I'm here and my reaction to many of the policies and statements that come out of the Administration would be the same, whether I were in the Government or not. I don't have to support everything that comes out of the White House.

"The Administration knows what we blacks are doing for our cause. I suppose there are even a few of us who are laying our jobs on the line. But I suppose we'll just continue to lobby for what we believe is important. I suppose I've got to continue asking myself every day whether I can do more for my people inside the Government or outside. And as long as I think that 'inside' is the answer, I'll remain."

Working within the President's party poses some of the same dilemmas for a natty blackman with a modified Afro named Clarence Townes, a special assistant to the chairman of the Republican National Committee. He's been with the committee since shortly after the Goldwater debacle in 1964. He used to have "for Minorities Division" attached to his title, but that was dropped when Richard Nixon became President. As he himself puts it, engaging in a burlesque that is common to blacks, he is the committee's "house nigger."

"Ray Bliss, who was chairman when I was hired, was very conservative on racial matters," Townes explained, "and I knew it. But he encouraged me to get involved with [Martin Luther] King and [Roy] Wilkins and to bring some of their aspirations into the Republican party. Since Bliss left, we've abandoned all black programs in the committee. We don't want the black vote. We had a big conference of national Republican leaders recently and one of the seminars was 'The Black Vote.' Almost nobody showed up— except maybe a handful of black Republicans, all over forty-five, all of them hand-picked by white folks, and they were all whiter than the whites that picked them.

"As I see the black vote now, there's a total fear of what's called the Southern strategy. Blacks understand that their well-being is being sacrificed to political gain. There has to be some moral leadership from the President on the race question—and there just hasn't been any. To the blacks the President has placed the name of the Republican party in greater darkness than it was in under Goldwater.

"Why do I stay at the committee? I don't know. Maybe I'm afraid of catching hell when I go back to black country where I came from. It's a kind of pride, I guess. Maybe I can't admit to my kids and my friends that I've been wrong. Sure there are some blacks with nice titles working for the Administration. Some of them are doing a lot for their people. But they've got no power. Politically, they ain't scratching nothing."

Jim Farmer, of course, does believe he's "scratching" something. As the most visible black in the Nixon Government, he sees importance not only in the substance of power but in its appearance. He's sensitive to the charge that he's "window dressing" for President Nixon. He knows he must show his "constituents" that he can really make things happen. Farmer stoutly points out that he has under his direct supervision the expenditure of several hundred million dollars and a dozen programs that affect the lives of hundreds of thousands of Americans. He is using that power, he argues, to help poor blacks.

Unfortunately, there is no litmus test to ascertain whether it is objectively true or a convenient rationalization. Decision-making in a vast bureaucracy is too complicated to permit a determination of whether a black man here and there makes a difference on the major policy issues. Farmer unquestionably has influenced the direction of funds into individual social programs. He has, perhaps, modified hiring and training policies within HEW and he has helped some blacks get contracts which they would otherwise have missed. In a tense confrontation with Mississippi, he persuaded the White House to save an ambitious Head Start program for black children by overriding the veto of Governor John Bell Williams. But it is equally clear that he has had no impact on, say, school desegregation policies, even at HEW, and he carried no weight last spring when the President sent the education appropriation back to Congress on the grounds that it was too high.

Sometimes, when he is not before an audience, Jim Farmer likes to take off a minute to think it all over. It is hard to say, when he emerges from a deep sleep on an airplane or sinks into an overstuffed chair in his office, what memories are piercing the obvious fatigue. Farmer has proud recollections of staring down Mississippi cops, of firing up young civil rights workers, of persuading black field hands to cast their first vote. He has made an important personal impact on American society. Surely he himself recognizes how incongruous it appears, even in his middle age, that he spends much of his day shuffling papers behind a desk for Richard Nixon's Administration.

"Make no mistake," Farmer said, "this is no love feast. The President is a politician, as he ought to be, and I don't care what he thinks of me. I couldn't care less what he feels in his heart of hearts when he goes into his closet and prays to his God. I don't care how much political progress his party makes in the black community. What I care about is how much leeway he gives me, Jim Farmer, to work for my fellow blacks. If I can help make some progress, that's what matters.

"Of course, I have to keep weighing the pros and cons of this job. I can take the criticism. I knew when I agreed to come here that I was painting a bullseye on my chest, and that I'd be in a crossfire between right and left. But I've learned a few things about how to move through the bureaucracy, and that's essential for a black man to do.

"When I shave in the morning, I look in the mirror to find out what looks back at me. If I feel good, I know I'm all right. When the time comes that I don't feel so good, I know I'll have to make a change. For now, I think it's useful that I'm on the inside. But I'll have to take the moments as they come."